Environmental Policy in the EU

The European Union (EU) has a hugely important effect on the way in which environmental policies are framed and implemented in many different parts of the world, but especially Europe. The new and comprehensively revised edition of this well-known textbook provides a state-of-the-art analysis of the EU's environmental policies.

Comprising five parts, it covers the rapidly changing context in which EU environmental policies are made, the key actors who interact to co-produce policy and the most salient dynamics of policy making, ranging from decision making through to implementation and evaluation.

Written by leading experts in the field, individual chapters examine how the EU is responding to a multitude of different problems including biodiversity loss, climate change, energy insecurity, and water and air pollution. They tease out the many important ways in which the EU's policies on these topics co-evolve with national and international environmental policies. In this third edition a mixture of learning features are employed to ensure that undergraduate and postgraduate students fully understand how EU policies in this vital area developed in the past and how they are now adapting to the rapidly evolving challenges of the twenty-first century.

Andrew Jordan is Professor of Environmental Politics in the Tyndall Centre for Climate Change Research at the University of East Anglia, UK.

Camilla Adelle is Senior Research Associate in the School of Environmental Sciences at the University of East Anglia, UK.

Environmental Policy in the EU

Actors, institutions and processes

Third edition

**Edited by Andrew Jordan
and Camilla Adelle**

LONDON AND NEW YORK

First edition published 2002 by Earthscan
Second edition published 2005

This edition published 2013
by Routledge
2 Park Square, Milton Park, Abingdon, Oxon OX14 4RN

Simultaneously published in the USA and Canada
by Routledge
711 Third Avenue, New York, NY 10017

Routledge is an imprint of the Taylor & Francis Group, an informa business

British Library Cataloguing in Publication Data
A catalogue record for this book is available from the British Library

Library of Congress Cataloging-in-Publication Data
Environmental policy in the EU : actors, institutions and processes / edited by
Andrew Jordan and Camilla Adelle. — 3rd ed.
    p. cm.
  Includes bibliographical references and index.
  1. Environmental policy—European Union—Case studies.
  2. Environmental policy—International cooperation—Case studies.
  I. Jordan, Andrew, 1968– II. Adelle, Camilla.
  GE190.E85E575 2012
  363.7'0561094—dc23   2012004401

ISBN13: 978–1–84971–468–6 (hbk)
ISBN13: 978–1–84971–469–3 (pbk)
ISBN13: 978–0–203–10982–3 (ebk)

Typeset in Times New Roman by
Keystroke, Station Road, Codsall, Wolverhampton

Contents

Boxes

Tables

Contributors

Camilla Adelle is Senior Research Associate in the School of Environmental Sciences, University of East Anglia, UK. She is interested in environmental policy and governance within the European Union (EU) and beyond.

Jason Anderson is Head of European climate change and energy policy at the Worldwide Fund for Nature's (WWF) European Policy Office. This office leads advocacy on European policy and legislation in support of WWF's conservation objectives.

David Benson is Lecturer in Environmental Politics, Policy and Governance at the School of Environmental Sciences, University of East Anglia, UK. His research interests include EU integration and environmental policy, multi-level environmental governance, environmental budgeting and public participation in environmental management.

Charlotte Burns is Lecturer in the School of Politics and International Studies at the University of Leeds, UK. She is interested in environmental policy and politics, the European Parliament and decision-making processes in Europe and beyond.

Tom Delreux is Associate Professor of Political Science at the Institut de Sciences Politiques Louvain-Europe and the Institut d'Etudes Européennes at the UC Louvain (Louvain-la-Neuve). His research interests include European environmental policy and policy making, the external dimension of the EU's internal policies, and inter- and intra-institutional relations in the EU.

Wyn Grant is Professor of Politics at the University of Warwick, UK. He is interested in agricultural impacts on the environment, having most recently worked on biological alternatives to chemical pesticides.

Andrew Jordan is Professor of Environmental Politics in the Tyndall Centre for Climate Change Research, School of Environmental Sciences, University of East Anglia, UK. He is interested in the policy and governance of environmental problems in different contexts, especially the EU.

Christoph Knill is Professor of Comparative Public Policy and Public Administration, Department of Politics and Public Administration, University of Konstanz, Germany. His main research focus is the comparative analysis of policy and institutional change, including, in particular, environmental, social and morality policies.

Ludwig Krämer was, for more than 30 years, a judge in Germany and an official in the environmental department of the European Commission. He now works as an environmental legal consultant.

Andrea Lenschow is Professor of European Integration and Policy in the Department of Social Science at the University of Osnabruck, Germany. She has published on comparative and EU environmental policy, theories of institutional and policy change, Europeanization, policy implementation and policy convergence.

Duncan Liefferink is Lecturer in Political Science of the Environment (Environmental Policy in Europe) at the Radboud University Nijmegen in the Netherlands. His main research fields are European and comparative environmental politics, with a particular interest in the inter-relationship between national and EU environmental policy making.

Per Mickwitz is Research Professor of Environmental Policy at the Finnish Environment Institute. He is interested in the theory and practices of environmental policy evaluation for reflexive governance, and in the stability of and change in different socio-technical systems, especially energy systems.

Marc Pallemaerts is Professor of European Environmental Law at the University of Amsterdam and Professor of International and European Environmental Law at the Université Libre de Bruxelles. He also heads the Global Issues and External Action Programme at the Institute for European Environmental Policy, with offices in London and Brussels.

Sebastiaan Princen is Associate Professor in Utrecht University's School of Governance. He is interested in policy making in the European Union and other international organizations, with a focus on agenda-setting processes.

Emmanuelle Schön-Quinlivan is Lecturer in Politics in the Department of Government, University College Cork, the Republic of Ireland. She specializes in European politics, public management and institutional change and has published extensively on the impact of the Kinnock reforms on the European Commission.

Adriaan Schout is Head of the European Studies programme at the Netherlands Institute for International Relations ('Clingendael'), which is based in The Hague, the Netherlands. For many years he has combined research and consultancy on European governance questions for national and European institutions.

Irina Tanasescu is a member of the Political Science Department at the Free University Brussels, Belgium. Her main research interests include stakeholder involvement in EU policy making, deliberative democracy and EU decision making.

Jale Tosun is Assistant Professor of Comparative Policy Analysis and Public Administration at the University of Konstanz, Germany. Her research interests comprise environmental and energy policy making in different contexts.

John Turnpenny is Senior Research Associate in the Tyndall Centre for Climate Change Research, School of Environmental Sciences, University of East Anglia, UK. His research focuses on the relationship between science, evidence and public policy making.

Martin Unfried is an Expert at the European Institute of Public Administration, Maastricht, the Netherlands. His specialisms include environmental policy, climate change and the integration of environmental policies into other sectors.

Rüdiger K. W. Wurzel is Reader and Jean Monnet Chair in European Union Studies at the University of Hull where he is Director of the Centre for European Union Studies. He has published widely on issues to do with European environmental policy, EU and German politics, and new modes of governance.

Anthony Zito is Reader in Politics and Joint Director of the Jean Monnet Centre for Excellence at Newcastle University. He studies public policy making in the EU and its member states, with a particular emphasis on environmental policy.

Foreword

These are 'interesting times' for environment policy. When I started my mandate as European Commissioner for Environment over two years ago, we were still on the crest of a green wave, although it was beginning to curl under along with the dipping economy. In the years prior to that, against a background of what seemed like permanent growth and prosperity, the environment had enjoyed something of a vogue. We saw politicians and businesses trying to out-green each other. World leaders said grand words about climate change and protecting biodiversity and every car advert showed a low-consumption vehicle alone in a pristine environment, perhaps surrounded by cute furry animals.

But in the current economic climate, there is a real danger that environmental progress is seen as a luxury we can no longer afford. Environment is thought to bring costs rather than economic benefits. This could not be further from the truth, and this message needs to be spread worldwide. With the growing world population and increasing shortages, we have to start using resources more efficiently. And 'resources' means not just wood, minerals and metals but also water, fertile soil and clean air. Not only are these essential components of the environment but they are also vital inputs that keep our economy functioning. If we use them more efficiently, our production and business costs will go down, making us more competitive and creating more jobs. Of course we will need to make processes more efficient – and invent new processes – but these innovative eco-industries are another area of economic growth where Europe can then lead the world. And there are opportunities for 'greening' all economic sectors. So there is no conflict between managing resources to protect the environment and economic prosperity.

What is needed are some fundamental changes in behaviour, not just on environmental matters but in all policy areas. In fact, it could be argued that 'environment' is not a separate sector in the same way as agriculture or transport but is a part of every aspect of life. Where we live, and the houses we live in; how much we travel, and the modes of transport we use; how much we buy, and where it comes from – and this applies not just to food but all the products we consume. There are so many small choices that can make a world of difference – or a different world. It is up to political leaders to explain the reasoning behind different choices and their economic and environmental benefits.

In terms of environment policy, the EU still tends to set global standards – and continues to enjoy the support of the vast majority of its citizens. Since the last edition of this book in 2005, we have been learning to live together as a Union of 27. The ten new countries which joined in 2004 added vast areas of land – much of it virgin countryside – which has considerably enriched our natural heritage. Much of this is now part of our Natura 2000 network of protected areas which covers almost 20 per cent of the EU.

Another significant EU achievement has been REACH, our scheme to promote substitution of dangerous chemicals and to foster innovation of new and safer substances. We have been working to improve the quality of our inland waters and our seas. And we have made real improvements in our waste collection and treatment; in some countries rates of landfill – the worst solution to the waste problem – are now virtually zero.

It could be argued that we now have all the environment legislation we need – although new challenges keep coming up, such as ship dismantling, nanotechnology, shale gas, phosphorus and so on. But laws alone are not enough. We need to make more effort to ensure that they are properly applied throughout the EU. Full implementation of our laws is a matter not just for European and national authorities, but also for local authorities, businesses and citizens. Which is why this book is so valuable. By teaching what EU environment policy is and why and how it is made, this book should ensure that later generations understand it and respect it as vital for our survival and prosperity.

Janez Potočnik
European Commissioner for Environment
Brussels

Preface

If 'a week is', to use former UK Prime Minister Harold Wilson's well-known phrase, 'a long time in politics', then the seven years which have elapsed since the publication of the second edition of this book, in 2005, seem like an eternity. A huge amount has changed in the European Union (EU). Two more states (Romania and Bulgaria) have joined as members and there are several more in the long queue to join, including Croatia, Iceland and Turkey. The Lisbon Treaty was adopted after a long and tortuous ratification process, creating new EU-level actors including, for the first time, the equivalent of a foreign ministry – the European External Agency Service – and a President of the European Council.

What about the EU's environmental policy? Does it exhibit the same sense of change? On the face of it, no. In many ways, it is no longer the energetic and slightly unpredictable policy sector that it once was. In fact, many chapters in this new edition show how it has settled into a more predictable pattern of development, underpinned by norms, procedures and, of course, lots and lots of detailed rules. Mature and more settled, yes, but certainly not static; it has continued to produce new policies and new politics sometimes in unforeseen and unexpected ways. A whole raft of new climate and energy policies emerged in the late 2000s, for example; new sources of energy such as biofuels and oil from tar sands have been intensively debated in Brussels; and the Parliament has significantly re-strengthened its influence over more aspects of national policy development.

But what has really changed since 2005 is the wider political and economic context in which the EU processes all its policies, including those addressing the environment. Politically, the EU as a whole has moved decisively to the right since 2005. By the end of 2011, only three of the 27 states were led by centre-left parties – Austria, Denmark and Slovenia. Crucially, in none of the six largest, most populous states, including Germany, was the left in overall control. One has to go right back to the early 1980s to find the last time that the parties of the right were so strongly in the ascendant. This is important because environmental policy has tended to advance further and faster when parties of the centre and the centre left are in control. The public too is more sceptical of the EU and more willing to challenge its existence. Turn-outs in European elections have continued to fall, Eurosceptical parties are on the rise in many states, and the public seems far less inclined to vote through new treaties in national referenda, limiting the ability to make further quantum leaps in European integration. And, most crucially of all, the economic situation in Europe has worsened appreciably, especially following the onset of the sovereign debt crisis in 2008. First of all in Greece and then later in Spain and Italy, politicians have struggled to secure political backing for austerity measures sought by the EU.

Together, these changes in the wider context have rudely confirmed some basic facts about the EU that had hitherto been hidden – that it is, *au fond*, an elite project, introduced without a political vote; that its popularity is ultimately sustained not by strong environmental policies, but by continuing economic growth and prosperity; and that there may be hard political limits to an 'ever closer Union'. In 2012, the EU found itself in the eye of an intense storm, trying desperately to mediate between catastrophically indebted member state economies and international financial markets. For the very first time, the existence of the Euro – and with it the EU itself – began to be openly questioned. Until then, this whole issue was strictly taboo. Can the EU improvise its way out of what the Commission President, José Manuel Barroso, described in his 2011 state of the union address as the 'the biggest challenge in the history of our Union'? That is very much the question of the moment and the foreseeable future.

On the face of it, these are very hard times indeed for those pushing for stronger environmental measures. Many of the chapters in this new edition reveal that some of the hard-won policy gains of the past are under unprecedented pressure as economic issues become more and more pressing. However, they also identify some unexpected opportunities for those who are willing and able to exploit them. For example, the economic crisis has given the EU a right to intervene in national budgetary and macro-economic affairs that was firmly refused by the Maastricht Treaty in the early 1990s. These are matters of the very highest politics which have traditionally been 'off limits' to European environmental policy makers. And those who can show that environmental protection has an immediate economic payoff may also prosper. Witness, for example, the debates about ecosystem services and the financial costs of not complying with environmental rules.

One way or another, these are very interesting times for those pursuing, and/or wishing to understand, EU environmental policy. Putting together the third edition of this book has proved to be both hugely stimulating and challenging. The first and second editions have sold well and we wanted to build on them. But they were originally conceived as handbooks not textbooks; ten years after the publication of the first edition, we felt that a more systematic re-write was warranted to meet the more refined learning needs of students. Therefore, 17 of the 20 chapters in this edition are completely new; only three contain re-published material. And all 20 employ pedagogical devices such as summary guides, lists of key learning points, guides to further reading and specimen exam questions. Together, we think they offer a uniquely systematic treatment of the most relevant contexts (Part 1), actors (Part 2) and policy dynamics (Part 3) of EU environmental policy. Some of the topics (e.g. the Commission – Chapter 6, policy evaluation – Chapter 15, and the role of appraisal in policy making – Chapter 12) are barely covered at all in the existing literature.

Acknowledgements

We have incurred a number of debts in producing this textbook. Jonathan Sinclair-Wilson at Earthscan originally encouraged us to have a third go at distilling the essence of EU environmental policy into one book. Nick Bellorini at Earthscan, and then Louisa Earls and Charlotte Russell at Routledge, greatly assisted us in the production process, and Janez Potočnik, the European Commissioner for Environment, very kindly agreed to write the Foreword. Sarah Clarke at UEA re-keyed the three re-published chapters, and David Benson and Tim Rayner commented on several chapters.

Routledge and the editors would like to thank the following authors and copyright holders for their permission to reprint them:

- Chapter 2: from C. Knill and D. Liefferink (2007) *Environmental Politics in the EU,* Manchester University Press, Manchester (pp. 1–26).
- Chapter 4: from 'Environmental Policy in the EU: Bridging, Policy, Politics and Polity Dimensions', in K-E. Jorgensen (eds) *et al.* (2006) *Handbook of EU Politics,* Sage, London (pp. 413–431).
- Chapter 13: from 'The European Union', in A. Jordan and A. Lenschow (eds) (2008) *Innovation in Environmental Policy?* Edward Elgar, Cheltenham (pp. 159–179).

We would also like to state that certain sections of these Chapters were written by the editors and not the contributors, i.e. the Summary Guide, the Summary Points and the Key Questions.

We would also like to acknowledge the support of the Leverhulme Trust for funding Andrew's Major Research Fellowship (F00204AR) and the European Commission project LIAISE for funding Camilla's involvement.

Last but certainly not least, we would like to thank the contributors who responded promptly and cheerfully to our numerous and extensive comments and requests. We hope you learn as much from reading what they have written as we have. Without them, this new edition would simply never have happened.

Andrew Jordan
Camilla Adelle
Norwich
January 2012

Abbreviations

ALDE	Group of the Alliance of Liberals and Democrats for Europe
BP	British Petroleum
BRIC	Brazil, Russia, India and China
BSE	Bovine Spongiform Encephalopathy
CAN-Europe	Climate Action Network Europe
CAP	Common Agricultural Policy
CBD	Convention on Biological Diversity
CEFIC	European Chemical Industry Council
CEN	European Committee for Standardization
CENELEC	European Committee for Electrotechnical Standardization
CFP	Common Fisheries Policy
CLIM	Temporary Committee on Climate Change
CO_2	carbon dioxide
COP	Conference of the Parties
COREPER	*Comité des représentants permanents* (Committee of Permanent Representatives)
CSD	Commission on Sustainable Development
DG	Directorate General
DG XI	Directorate General for the Environment (now 'DG Environment')
DG Environment	Directorate General for the Environment (formerly 'DG XI')
DG CLIMA	Directorate General Climate Action
DG ENTR	Directorate General Enterprise
DG ENV	Directorate General for the Environment
EAP	Environmental Action Programme
EC	European Community
ECA	European Chemicals Agency
ECI	European Citizens' Initiative
ECJ	European Court of Justice
ECOFIN	Council of Finance Ministers
ECR	European Conservatives and Reformists Group
EEA	European Environment Agency
EEB	European Environmental Bureau

EEC	European Economic Community
EEE	Electrical and Electronic Equipment draft Directive
EENF	Environmental Evaluators Networking Forum
EER	Energy Efficiency Requirement for End-use Equipment draft Directive
EFD	Europe of Freedom and Democracy Group
EIA	Environmental Impact Assessment
EMAS	Environmental Management System
EMU	European Monetary Union
ENDS	Environmental Data Services
ENVI	Committee of Environment, Public Health and Food Safety
EP	European Parliament
EPI	Environmental Policy Integration
EPP	European Peoples' Party
ETS	Emissions Trading System
EU	European Union
EUL/NGL	Confederal Group of European United Left/Nordic Green Left
Euratom	European Atomic Energy Community
FoEE	Friends of the Earth Europe
G10	the Green Ten (environmental lobby groups)
G20	Group of 20 (major industrialized states)
GAERC	General Affairs and External Relations Council
GDP	gross domestic product
GM	genetically modified
GMO	genetically modified organism
Greens/EFA	Group of the Greens and European Free Alliance
HEAL	Health and Environmental Alliance
IA	Impact Assessment
IBMA	International Biocontrol Manufacturers' Association
IFN	Friends of Nature International
ILUC	Indirect Land Use Change
IMPEL	Network for the Implementation and Enforcement of Environmental Law
IPCC	Intergovernmental Panel on Climate Change
ISO	International Standard Organization
LCD	lowest common denominator
MEA	multilateral environmental agreement
MEP	Member of European Parliament
MOP	Meeting of the Parties
NEPI	new environmental policy instrument
NGO	non-governmental organization
OECD	Organization for Economic Co-operation and Development
OLP	ordinary legislative procedure
OMC	open method of coordination
QMV	qualified majority voting

REACH	Registration, Evaluation, Authorization and restriction of Chemicals
REIO	Regional Economic Integration Organization
RIA	Regulatory Impact Assessment
RPA	Risk and Policy Analysts
S&D	Group of the Progressive Alliance of Socialists and Democrats
SDS	Sustainable Development Strategy
SEA	Single European Act
SEA	Strategic Environmental Assessment
SUV	sports utility vehicle
T&E	Transport and Environment
TEN-T	Trans-European Network
TEU	Treaty on European Union
TFEU	Treaty on the Functioning of the European Union
UK	United Kingdom
UN	United Nations
UNCED	UN Conference on Environment and Development
UNEP	United Nations Environment Programme
UNFCCC	United Nations Framework Convention on Climate Change
US	United States
WPE	Working Party on the Environment
WPIEI	Working Party on International Environmental Issues
WSSD	World Summit on Sustainable Development
WTO	World Trade Organization
WWF	World Wide Fund for Nature

1 EU environmental policy

Contexts, actors and policy dynamics

Andrew Jordan and Camilla Adelle

Introduction

At its founding in 1957, the European Union (EU) had no environmental policy, no environmental administration and no environmental laws. The European Economic Community (EEC), as it then was, was primarily an intergovernmental agreement between six like-minded states to boost economic prosperity and restore political relations in a Europe ravaged by two world wars. Most of the environmental policies of the EU have emerged only in the past 40 years or so. Today, the EU has some of the most progressive environmental policies of any state in the world, although, curiously, it does not possess many of the formal attributes of a state such as an army, a common system of taxation or a constitution.

The central aim of this book is to provide an introduction to the history and constituent institutions of EU environmental policy, to explain how the EU makes and implements different environmental policies, and to introduce some of the most salient academic debates about the past, present and future role of environmental policy in Europe and the wider world. It is very important to know about these things because EU environmental policy heavily shapes, and is significantly shaped by, international and national environmental policies. Not only is the EU an active disseminator of high environmental standards globally, but it also heavily affects – or Europeanizes – those in its own member states. This book aims to help you to better understand and appreciate its role: first, by examining the wider *context* in which it makes policy (the historical background, the formal rules and legal procedures, etc.); second, by summarizing the main *actors* that interact with one another to shape and implement it; and third, by examining the *policy dynamics* through which different ideas and political interests are translated first into concrete policies and then, perhaps eventually, tangible changes in environmental quality.

The chapters of this book view these issues from a range of different perspectives. Thus, Part 1 ('Contexts') describes the emergence of this particular policy area over the past 40 years and the underlying institutional structures and rules governing its operation, as elaborated in the founding treaties (see Box 1.1). A myriad of different actors (some state, some non-state), work within these rules and procedures to secure their policy objectives. These different actors are summarized in Part 2 ('Actors'). They are shown to have different goals (or interests), different resources and to operate at different levels of governance. The manner in which they interact on a day-by-day basis to shape specific items of EU policy is summarized in Part 3 ('Policy dynamics'). Part 4 ('Future challenges') explores a number of problems (some relatively new, others that have emerged slowly) that are likely to challenge the EU as it moves forward. Finally, Part 5 ('Conclusions') reflects on what has been learnt about the functioning of EU environmental policy in the past 40 years, and looks forward to the next phase in its development.

Box 1.1 The founding treaties

'The founding treaties' is a term often heard in discussions relating to the EU. They are the legal agreements that created the EU and which, crucially, establish its powers and procedures. There is not one single treaty but a series of treaties which build upon one another. The founding treaties include the Treaty of Paris (establishing the Economic and Steel Community) and the two Treaties of Rome: one establishing the European Atomic Energy Community (Euratom) and the European Economic Community (EEC). Reading the titles (or parts) of these treaties powerfully illustrates the concerns that contributed to the establishment of the EU – those relating to economic growth and energy security. It is for this reason that the EU is often termed a system of economic governance.

The Treaty of Rome that established the EEC has been revised several times by, *inter alia*, the Single European Act, the Maastricht Treaty and the Amsterdam Treaty (signed in 1986, 1992 and 1997, respectively). These treaties are not easy or, it has to be said, that exciting to read, but they establish, in very broad terms, the roles of the various actors in the EU. This is extremely important because the EU is only allowed to discharge powers that have been expressly allocated to it by the treaties. The text of directives and regulations will, for example, note which article of the treaties permits the EU to act. The whole question of the EU's competences is deeply political. Many of the cases that are brought before the European Court of Justice turn on the precise legal base (or power) of the EU to act in a given area. That said, it is important to remember that these powers are not set in stone; they change subtly over time in the period between treaty amendments, as different actors jockey for influence. In many ways, environmental policy provides a perfect case study of how policy powers can initially develop outside the formal framework of the treaties, and then are gradually drawn into them. Chapter 3 explains how the most recent treaty – the Treaty of Lisbon in 2009 – tried to draw together the provisions of all previous treaties into one consolidated text. It thus amended the Maastricht Treaty and the Treaty of Rome, and in the process renamed the latter the Treaty on the Functioning of the EU (TFEU).

This book assumes no prior knowledge of the EU, but those who are entirely new to the subject or who require a more detailed review of its history, law and institutions, may wish to consult some of the items listed in the Guide to Further Reading section at the end of this chapter. Before moving on, however, it is very important to pause and reflect on what the term 'EU' actually denotes, as it can cause confusion. This is the subject of Box 1.2. The rest of this chapter introduces the remaining chapters of the book and begins to identify some analytical questions and puzzles that resonate throughout the text; ones that we shall return to in the concluding chapter.

Box 1.2 What is 'the EU'?

The EU has been variously described as a system of multi-level governance, a political system and a federal state in the making. 'What is the EU' is therefore a somewhat existential question. But what does the term 'the EU' refer to? Until the ratification of the Single European Act (SEA), signed in 1986, the European Union was officially known as the European Economic Community (EEC). The SEA officially re-christened this entity the European Community (EC), a term which remained in popular use until 1992 when the Maastricht Treaty created the European Union with a new, three-pillar structure: one comprising the EC; another covering foreign and security matters; and a third dealing with justice and home affairs. Strictly speaking, the term 'EU' only really applies to events *after* 1992. However, most people now use the acronym 'EU' to describe its entire history and all its policy responsibilities. For the sake of convenience, this term is used to cover all the activities before and after 1992, unless otherwise specified. In general, and unless otherwise specified, the text of this book also refers to the articles of the most recent Treaty of the EU, the 2009 Lisbon Treaty, which is explored in more detail in Chapter 3.

Part 1 Contexts

Chapter 2, by Christoph Knill and Duncan Liefferink, seeks underlying explanations for the startling transformation of this policy area from what have been termed a series of 'incidental measures' (Hildebrand, 2005) to a sophisticated, multi-level governance system in which policy-making powers are shared between supranational, national and subnational actors. One of the questions that Christoph Knill and Duncan Liefferink dwell on is how such a transformation occurred, given the unfavourable legal and institutional pre-conditions which existed in the late 1960s. It does seem remarkable today, but the word 'environment' was not even mentioned in the Treaty of Rome. Their analysis shows that policy makers, acting without any legislative authority, cleverly defined environmental policy as an element of trade policy. In time, EU environmental policy did not simply emancipate itself from its status as a by-product of economic and market integration, but in turn began to affect the functioning of the internal market (Weale, 2005).

In effect, they show why the formal wording of the EU's founding treaties offers an important but incomplete perspective on EU action in any given area. Since 1957, there have been numerous treaty changes which have substantially strengthened the EU's environmental powers (see Table 1.1). In Chapter 3, David Benson and Camilla Adelle bring this story right up to date with an analysis of the

Table 1.1 Significant treaty changes affecting EU environmental policy

Year signed	*Year in force*	*Treaty*	*Changes affecting environmental policy*
1957	1958	Rome	No mention of environment
1986	1987	Single European Act	Environmental Title added Article on environmental policy integration added Qualified Majority Voting (QMV) for the internal market
1992	1993	Maastricht	'Sustainable growth respecting the Environment' becomes one of the tasks of the Community (Article 2) Environment Title strengthened to include mention of 'precautionary principle' Integration Article (Article 130r) was reinforced The number of policy areas where the Council could adopt environmental legislation using QMV was extended Co-decision strengthened the role of the European Parliament in developing environment policy
1997	1999	Amsterdam	Article 2 strengthened so that 'Sustainable development of economic activities' made an explicit objective of the EU Integration Article given more prominence (Article 6) Co-decision becomes the normal process for agreeing environment policy
2001	2003	Nice	QMV changed to establish a double majority of member states and votes cast
2007	2009	Lisbon	Environment Title (174–176, TEC) substantively unchanged but numbering changed (now Articles 191–193, TFEU) Integration Article now Article 11 Article 2 strengthened so that the EU shall work for the 'sustainable development of Europe' and the 'sustainable development of the Earth' (now Article 3, TEU)

Source: Based on Farmer (2011).

amendments introduced by the 2009 Lisbon Treaty. One of the puzzles that they address is why the EU felt it necessary to adopt another round of changes so soon after the adoption of the Amsterdam and Nice Treaties. They also investigate the emerging impact of the changes it made. They conclude that some innovations are yet to become fully operational, some are already having significant impacts, and some have arguably failed to have any effect thus far; or as they suggest – *comme ci, comme ça*.

Chapter 4, Andrea Lenschow completes this contextual overview by exploring the way in which the puzzling emergence and evolution of EU environmental policy have been studied by academics. This proves to be a highly illuminating exercise. She shows how academics have addressed a number of very salient questions: how and why this sector developed as a policy area; why it selects certain kinds of governing instruments but not others; and why we only know so much about the overall performance of its policies in ameliorating policy problems.

Part 2 Actors

Throughout the 1970s and early 1980s, items of EU environmental policy were agreed by the Council of Environment Ministers on the basis of proposals submitted by the Commission (see Chapters 5 and 6). In the 1980s, this bilateral arrangement gradually gave way to a more diffuse web of activities centred on a set of trilateral links between the Council, the Commission, and the European Parliament. Matters which had been successfully contained in discrete inter-governmental committees of national bureaucrats and state-sponsored scientists began to leak out, energizing national and international pressure groups, disrupting national practices and exciting public interest. What had been a relatively short cast list of actors over time became steadily longer and longer; the impact and importance of 'Brussels' began to grow.

The chapters in Part 3 focus on some of the most important actors who, together, 'make' EU policy. These include, first and foremost, the member states, which of course originally established the EU. In Chapter 5, Rüdiger Wurzel describes the central role they perform in the various councils in which they meet to determine policies. He shows that, in the past, EU environmental policy was heavily shaped by greener (or 'leader') states such as Germany, the Netherlands and Denmark, pushing the EU to adopt standards that were as high if not higher than their own, national standards. Having already adopted high standards in their own territories for domestic reasons, these states had an obvious incentive to share the political and economic pain (as well as reap 'first mover' advantages) by 'exporting' them to other, less environmentally ambitious (or 'laggard' states). But he questions whether the division between 'leaders' and 'laggards' is as stark as it used to be, given, for example, the tendency for states to adapt their preferences and bargaining tactics as a result of their membership of the EU. The next three chapters then focus on the other main institutions of the EU, namely: the European Commission (Chapter 6, by Emmanuelle Schön-Quinlivan); the European Court of Justice (Chapter 7, by Ludwig Krämer); and the European Parliament (Chapter 8, by Charlotte Burns). The final two chapters extend the focus to the most important civil society actors, namely lobby groups (Chapter 9, by Camilla Adelle and Jason Anderson) and business (Chapter 10, by Wyn Grant).

Part 3 Policy dynamics

Putting these different actors alongside the rules and institutions described in Part 1 produces an extremely complicated picture, which does not neatly correspond to any commonly accepted plan of national policy systems. The aim of Part 3 is to try to make greater sense of the whole by looking at each stage of the policy process in turn, running from agenda setting through to policy evaluation. In Chapter 11, Sebastiaan Princen begins by investigating the first of these stages – the one in which problems 'out there' are perceived and made sense of, and political agendas are thus 'set'. After discussing the different types of agenda that can be discerned at EU level, he presents a framework for understanding agenda-setting processes. One of the many puzzles he tries to unpick is why issues come onto the EU agenda at the time they do, and what kinds of challenges and opportunities actors face when they try to bring an issue to the EU agenda.

Chapter 12 by Camilla Adelle, Andrew Jordan and John Turnpenny then explores the stage at which policies are formally discussed and eventually adopted. The existing literature suggests that this process is too densely populated with veto players (i.e. actors whose views have to be taken into account) for any single actor or group of actors (including, it should be said, member states) to consistently dictate the direction of policy making. More often than not, EU policies are 'the aggregated and transformed standards of their original champions modified under the need to secure political accommodation from the powerful veto players' (Weale, 2005: 136), i.e. the resulting picture resembles less a grand master plan imposed from the top down, and more a blend of many different elements – in short, a complicated 'policy patchwork' (Héritier, 2002). The mismatch between this patchwork and the pre-existing policies of the 27 member states creates the ideal conditions for *Europeanization* – the process through which EU-level policies affect domestic systems. The picture that is emerging from academic studies (summarized in Chapter 4) is one of *differential* Europeanization. In other words, every state appears to have been affected by EU membership, even those so-called leader states (see Chapter 5) that worked the hardest to construct EU policy in the first place. In spite of what we may sometimes read about in the press, more multi-levelled forms of environmental governance in the EU have not created more *uniform* environmental governance (Jordan and Liefferink, 2004; Weale *et al.*, 2000: 468). A greater role for 'Brussels' has not yet produced a single model of policy at the national level.

Camilla Adelle, Andrew Jordan and John Turnpenny examine how far policy level Impact Assessment (IA) has provided the kind of 'standard operating procedure' which EU policy processes have traditionally lacked. With IA, the EU – and principally the Commission – has sought to establish a more structured, step-by-step framework to guide policy development. However, they are less certain about whether IA has really changed decision making in practice: raw politics often trumps the need to follow administrative procedures.

One perennial challenge that typically emerges at this particular stage of the policy process is how to ensure that policies in different sectors do not undermine one another. In Chapter 13, Andrew Jordan, Adriaan Schout and Martin Unfried show that the EU has made significant efforts to engage in policy coordination, that is, to integrate environmental thinking into the operation of all policy sectors. The puzzle that they try to understand is why the EU has adopted such an ambitious position in relation to environmental policy integration, when its implementing capacities are so very limited. In doing so, they highlight another paradoxical feature of the EU – that its fragmented institutional and political structure, on the one hand, facilitates the adoption of visionary policy objectives, but, on the other, actively undermines their implementation. In a sense this paradox re-appears in the next policy stage – implementation. In Chapter 14, Andrew Jordan and Jale Tosun explain how and why the full implementation of policy in the EU remains not just problematic, but perhaps impossible to achieve. A whole host of solutions have been offered at one time or another, some of which could, if deployed, end up compounding the problem. But in many respects, the causes of poor (or at least imperfect) implementation reside in the very structure of the EU. Consequently, there are, they conclude, likely to be no panaceas. This takes us to the hoary debate about policy evaluation. The importance of subjecting all policies to a full post-adoption ('*ex post*') evaluation is an intuitively simple and appealing one. But in practice, Chapter 15 by Per Mickwitz reveals that this ideal proves to be a lot more complicated to live up to when policy powers are divided vertically and horizontally. There are a whole host of technical reasons why attributing impacts to specific policies is challenging; there are also many political reasons why the EU lacks a well-established culture of policy evaluation: states, for example, do not take kindly to having their failings aired in public.

The discussion thus far may have given the false impression that EU policy has been mostly unaffected by external events. In fact, a far larger proportion of EU policy derives from international-level discussions than is commonly thought. What does this entail? First and foremost, it involves EU-level actors (chiefly the Commission and the Presidency of the Council) working alongside the member states in international discussions. Chapter 16 by Tom Delreux gives an overview of the EU's status as a partner in international environmental negotiations. Looking at how the EU functions internally when it acts externally in international environmental negotiations, Tom Delreux discusses the internal division of competences, and the external representation and internal coordination processes in the EU. He also notes that the drive to give the EU an international environmental face has, in turn, boomeranged and affected its internal policies via a process which is rather analogous to the internal process of Europeanization. This 'outside–inside' dynamic adds another dimension of complexity to the dynamic, patchwork nature of EU environmental policy.

Part 4 Future challenges

The chapters in Part 4 examine some of the most salient policy challenges that are likely to arise in the future. The first relates to the main instruments of policy. The EU's role in shaping the overall goals of national environmental policy in Europe should by now be obvious. In contrast, its role in determining the choice of implementing instruments used at the European level – be that regulation or taxation – is not nearly as well understood; an omission which Andrew Jordan and his colleagues consider in Chapter 17. Then there is the equally daunting challenge of ensuring that the EU remains democratically legitimate. No system of governance – let alone a young, multi-levelled one such as the EU – can possibly hope to endure unless it is seen as legitimate by its citizens. In Chapter 18, Irina Tanasescu takes up some of these highly pertinent themes. She examines how the main institutions of the EU are actively seeking to enhance their legitimacy by structuring their consultation interactions with the public and other key stakeholders. Another challenge relates to the underlying purpose and direction of the EU. In the past, the end purpose of the EU has been left tantalizingly ill defined – 'an ever closer Union amongst the people of Europe'. What kind of union that should be has never been specified (hence the continuing political debate about whether it is or may eventually evolve into a federal state), nor has the type of human development been fully decided upon. In Chapter 19, Marc Pallemaerts investigates how far the EU has fulfilled its commitment to implement the principle of *sustainable* development – that is, economic development that is socially inclusive *and* within environmental limits – both internally and in its interactions with other parts of the world.

Part 5 Conclusion

Finally, Chapter 20 draws together the main themes of the book and explores the next phase in the very dynamic and important development of EU environmental policy.

Guide to further reading

- There are many textbooks on the history and inner workings of the EU. Of these, Wallace *et al.* (2010), Bache *et al.* (2011) and Cini and Pérez-Solórzano Borragán (2010) are notable in that they include chapters devoted to environmental policy.
- Bomberg *et al.* (2008) and Bache *et al.* (2011) are notable in that they focus on the policies of the EU.
- The third edition of Hix and Høyland (2011) offers a novel attempt to understand the EU as a 'normal', as opposed to a special, political system; an approach which is also adopted in this book.
- Every single item of EU environmental policy is summarized in Farmer (ed.) (2011), an online manual published by Taylor & Francis.

References

Bache, I., George, S. and Bulmer, S. (2011) *Politics in the EU*, 2nd edition, Oxford University Press, Oxford.

Bomberg, E., Peterson, J. and Stubb, A. (2008) *The European Union: How Does It Work?*, 2nd edition, Oxford University Press, Oxford.

Cini, M. and Pérez-Solórzano Borragán, N. (2010) *EU Politics*, 3rd edition, Oxford University Press, Oxford.

Farmer, A. (ed.) (2011) *Manual of EU Environmental Policy*, Taylor & Francis, London, available at: http://www.europeanenvironmentalpolicy.eu/ (accessed 19 August 2011).

Héritier, A. (2002) 'The accommodation of diversity in European policy-making and its outcomes: regulatory policy as a patchwork', in A. Jordan (ed.) *Environmental Policy in the European Union*, Earthscan, London, pp. 180–197.

Hildebrand, P. (2005) 'The EC's environmental policy, 1957–1992', in A. Jordan (ed.) *Environmental Policy in the European Union*, 2nd edition, Earthscan, London, pp. 19–41.

Hix, S. and Høyland, B. (2011) *The Political System of the European Union*, 3rd edition, Palgrave, Basingstoke.

Jordan, A. and Liefferink, D. (eds) (2004) *Environmental Policy in Europe: The Europeanization of National Environmental Policy*, Routledge, London.

Wallace, H., Pollack, M. and Young, A. (eds) (2010) *Policy Making in the EU*, Oxford University Press, Oxford.

Weale, A. (2005) 'Environmental rules and rule making in the EU', in A. Jordan (ed.) *Environmental Policy in the European Union*, 2nd edition, Earthscan, London, pp. 125–140.

Weale, A., Pridham, G., Cini, M., Konstadakopulos, D., Porter, M. and Flynn, B. (2000) *Environmental Governance in Europe*, Oxford University Press, Oxford.

Part 1
Contexts

2 The establishment of EU environmental policy

Christoph Knill and Duncan Liefferink

Summary guide

The environmental policy of the EU has developed in a remarkable fashion in the past four decades. An increasingly dense network of legislation has emerged, which now extends to all areas of environmental protection. This holds not only for air pollution control, water protection and waste policy, but also for nature conservation and the control of chemicals, biotechnology and other industrial risks. Environmental policy has thus become a core area of European politics. Such dynamic developments could hardly be expected in light of the legal and institutional conditions which existed in the late 1960s. This chapter describes the establishment of EU policy in three phases. It illustrates how policy makers, acting without any legislative authority, initially made a clever move to increase the EU's capacity to act by defining environmental policy as a trade problem. In the course of time, EU environmental policy emerged as a formal policy area, with its own policy actors, policy principles and procedures.

The beginnings: environmental policy as trade policy

The Paris Summit meeting of heads of state and government of the European Economic Community (EEC) in October 1972 can be viewed as the beginning of an independent EU environmental policy. Just a few weeks before the enlargement of the Community to Denmark, the United Kingdom and Ireland (on 1 January 1973), a declaration on environmental and consumer policy was adopted at this summit. The declaration granted the European Commission the task of drawing up an action programme for environmental protection. To this end, a task force was created in the Commission, from which today's Directorate General (DG) for the Environment has emerged.

This very First Environmental Action Programme was adopted by national government representatives in July 1973 at the first meeting of the Council of

Environmental Ministers and formally enacted a few months later. Thus, for the first time, the governments of the member states had granted the Union an environmental policy mandate (Hildebrand, 1993; Liefferink *et al.*, 1993: 2ff.).

Reasons for environmental policy action at the European level

The most important reason for the introduction of a common environmental policy was the fear that trade barriers and competitive distortions in the Common Market could emerge due to the different environmental standards (Johnson and Corcelle, 1989). Diverse national standards for certain products, such as limitations on automobile emissions for the lead content of petrol, posed formidable obstacles to the free trade of these products within the Economic Community (EC).

In establishing the EEC, the member states had in fact agreed on a general ban on so-called non-tariff trade barriers (Articles 29 and 30).[1] In Article 30, however, exceptions to this general ban were specified. Thus, among other things, such trade restrictions which are justified for the 'protection of the health and life of humans, animals, or plants' are exempted. Although Article 30 stipulates that such trade restrictions may not constitute random discrimination, this allowed the member states to a large extent to design their own environmental policy after all, even if this led to trade obstacles (Rehbinder and Stewart, 1985: 29ff; Holzinger, 1994: 68).

Against this background, EU environmental policy was primarily a policy flanking the Common Market. This is also evidenced by the fact that even before the formal beginning of EU environmental policy, individual environmentally relevant measures were passed in the area of chemicals control and the regulation of automobile emissions. However, these measures were not part of a coordinated and goal-oriented European environmental policy (Jordan, 1999: 3). They were motivated instead by competition policy, or to be more precise, the realization of the Common Market by harmonizing national legal and administrative regulations.

Besides competition policy motives, an additional factor in the establishment of the EU environmental policy is the fact that since the middle of the 1960s numerous environmental catastrophes have not only led to the increased international politicization of environmental problems, but also underlined the cross-border nature of certain forms of environmental pollution (Liefferink *et al.*, 1993: 1). The growing international perception of environmental problems was brought to light at the United Nations Conference on the Human Environment, which took place in Stockholm in 1972. Within the framework of this conference, the member states of the EU increasingly began to deal with the environmental policy consequences of the European integration process (Jordan, 1999: 3).

The main focus was placed here on the problem of cross-border air pollution. Cross-border pollution became an international issue for the first time when the acidification of Scandinavian lakes came to light. It had become evident that the cause of the acidification and the resulting decline in the fish stock could not be attributed to Swedish emissions. The cause of the acid rain was instead the air pollution in other countries – in particular, the UK as well as the industrial areas of Central and Eastern Europe (Boehmer Christiansen and Skea, 1991). Thus, from the beginning of the 1970s, the problem of acid rain increasingly led to the realization that environmental pollution did not stop at national borders, but had to be addressed by cross-border measures. The relevance of this notion for the development of EU policy is also expressed in the related documents from the EU Commission (European Commission, 1984: 11).

Along with the economic and ecological motives just described, the existing literature also frequently makes reference to an additional factor which has facilitated the creation and development of the EU environmental policy: the goal of improving the living conditions in the EU. This objective results from the Preamble and Article 2. The goals of a 'continual improvement of living and employment conditions' and a 'rapid increase in the standard of living' mentioned here were interpreted by the Community institutions in terms of not only a quantitative, but also a qualitative rise in the standard of living. This interpretation implies that the improvement of the state of the environment is also one of the goals of the EU (Rehbinder and Stewart, 1985: 20ff; Holzinger, 1994: 67; Krämer, 2000).

The explicit orientation to these objectives is not only evident in the Introduction to the First Environmental Action Programme. In justifying its environmental policy activities, the Commission also retrospectively points out that this aspect – along with economic and environment policy motives – was of great significance: 'In 1972 it has become clear that we had to act because ... [t]he development of completely different living conditions in the member states would not be politically justifiable' (European Commission, 1984: 11).

Environmental policy without an explicit legal basis

In political and legal terms, the environmental policy of the EU particularly distinguishes itself from other policy areas such as trade, agricultural, or transportation policy in that it was not mentioned in the Treaty of Rome establishing the EEC. In other words, there was no explicit treaty basis which could have underpinned EU environmental policy.

Due to these circumstances, the request made by the heads of state and government at the Paris Summit in 1972 to push forward with the development of a European environmental policy entailed an interesting question, for legal experts in particular. As there was no treaty basis, it was totally uncertain at that point in time what could serve as the legal foundation for the fulfilment of the EU's political objectives.

The first discovery in conjunction with this was that if the treaty text were to be interpreted dynamically, environmental policy would be regarded as an essential goal of the Community, even though it was not explicitly mentioned. Otherwise, it would hardly be possible to fulfil the resolution reinforced in the treaty's Preamble that living and working conditions must be improved under the changing circumstances of increasing environmental awareness. In the treaty text itself, the catalogue of measures formulated in Article 2 in particular offered indications of a dynamic interpretation. This kind of dynamic interpretation was not only generally accepted by legal experts (Rehbinder and Stewart, 1985: 20ff), but also by the European Court of Justice which recognized this development as a legitimate further interpretation of the law and designated environmental protection as an essential goal of the Community in various decisions. Through this, the pursuit of environmental policy goals was legally supported by the Community for the first time. However, this did not solve the problem that a concrete treaty article still had to be found on which environmental measures could be based. It eventually turned out that the stipulations in Article 94 and 308, which were usually drawn on together as a basis of authority, resulted in new opportunities for environmental policy action.

Along these lines, Article 94 contains a general authorization for the Community to harmonize legal and administrative regulation in the member states which have direct ramifications for the establishment or the functioning of the Common Market. Accordingly, the adoption of environmental policy regulations could be substantiated by the fact that different environmental requirements in the member states constitute trade barriers in economic terms (Johnson and Corcelle, 1989: 4).

Above all, product-related environmental regulations (product standards) – i.e. the regulation of the environmentally relevant features of goods – were affected by this provision. For example, the definitions of limits for car exhaust emissions or the specification of standards with regard to the lead content of petrol fell under this. Here it was evident that deviant national product norms could become technical trade barriers which upset the functioning of the Common Market. However, supported by the case law of the European Court of Justice, Article 94 was additionally used as a legal basis for the harmonization of production-related environmental regulations (production or process standards). These entail technical specifications, which must be taken into account when designing production sites and the production process, such as the definition of dioxin limits for waste incineration facilities (Rehbinder and Stewart, 1985: 25).

However, several restrictions were associated with the use of Article 94 as a basis for environmental policy action. First, these resulted from its economic policy objectives, according to which only those measures are subject to the Community's harmonization authority which serve the purpose of completing the Common Market. Hence, Article 94 did not serve as a legal basis for environmental activities without a concrete reference to economic matters. A second restriction resulted from the fact that this article required the existence of legal or administrative provisions in at least one member state. European harmonization is not necessary or possible until at least one member state has proceeded to act (Holzinger, 1994: 68).

Third, from the standpoint of environmental protection, it was ultimately problematic as the authority for harmonization in Article 94 did not refer to the level of the environmental standards. Nothing about the targeted level of protection could be inferred from this article. The approximation of national environmental provisions for reasons of competition does not necessarily always have to lead to desirable results with respect to environmental policy. Thus, European harmonization at a weak level can serve to block more stringent national measures. A related problem is the fact that harmonized environmental standards frequently do not do justice to the ecological conditions which might vary from country to country.

In the areas in which Article 94 was not applicable, Article 308 could not be used as a subsidiary legal basis for EU environmental policy. Article 308 enabled the Community to pass suitable measures in such cases in which action on behalf of the EU appears necessary to achieve its objectives, even if the treaty does not explicitly include the authority necessary for doing so. As the objectives mentioned in Article 308 have to be achieved 'within the framework of the Common Market', however, it was generally assumed that the legal acts based on Article 308 must in some way be related to the economic objectives of the Community (Rehbinder and Stewart, 1985: 26). Thus, Article 308 only covers economically related environmental problems at best.

We have seen that the two decisive foundations for European environmental policy activity were to a great extent pegged to the realization of economic objectives. The prevalence of economic objectives results from the original design and function of the ECC as a purely economic community. Along these lines, the creation of a European environmental policy, which was taking shape 15 years after the signing of the Treaty of Rome, was not founded exclusively, but for the most part, on economic objectives.

To be sure, besides the economic objectives, other motives also played a role: the awareness of the increasing significance of environmental problems; the view that a healthy environment is the basis for the prosperity which the Community strives for; and a conviction that the EU might be the suitable institution to solve various problems of cross-boundary and global environmental pollution. However, between these ecological objectives and the foremost goal of creating a Common Market, there was a disparity in favour of market integration, which resulted in a kind of 'economic bias' in European environmental policy (Holzinger, 1994: 70). It was not until the middle of the 1980s and the signing of the Single European Act (SEA) in 1986 that economic and ecological objectives were put on a more equal footing within the Community.

Growing policy output despite unfavourable legal conditions

In light of this constellation, there was no reason to be particularly optimistic with regard to the expected output of environmental measures by the EU. Acting on the legal foundations for trade policy, how was the Community supposed to be able to achieve the bold environmental objectives formulated in the First Environmental Action Programme of 1973?

An additional complicating factor was the fact that both Articles 94 and 308 required a unanimous vote by all the member states of the Council of Ministers. As a consequence, member states who believed themselves to be at a disadvantage due to the proposed measures (for example, because they feared economic harm for their industries), were generally able to block decisions in the Council of Ministers.

Considering these relatively unfavourable starting conditions, the result of this first phase of European environmental policy can by all measures be regarded as a success. Within about a decade, a very substantial set of European environmental laws had emerged, with many important areas of environmental policy being regulated at the European level (see Haigh, 2000). By the middle of the 1980s, not only had three additional environmental action programmes, characterized by a constant broadening of environmental objectives and activities, been passed, but also around 200 binding legal acts, primarily in the form of directives and regulations (Liefferink *et al.*, 1993: 2ff; Weale, 1996: 597; Zito, 1999). There existed at least a basic consensus between the member states on the necessity of a common environmental policy.

A comprehensive programme for European environmental policy has emerged from an initial series of more or less coincidental and non-coordinated activities. In legal terms, this programme still relied on its trade policy foundations, but with regard to its political aims, it had increasingly freed itself from purely economic motives. Even if environmental policy formally could only be substantiated as trade policy, on the informal level, environmental policy goals had increasingly come to the fore as the motivation for joint environmental measures. European environmental policy has gradually developed into an independent policy domain of the Community, even without having a relevant legal basis (Knill, 1995: 132–3; Sbragia, 2000: 294–5).

For instance, in the 1970s, relatively strict limits with regard to water pollution control were passed, which went far beyond what would have been necessary for mere market harmonization. These entailed minimum requirements for the quality of surface water, bathing water, fishing water, shellfish water and drinking water. Some very far-reaching measures were also passed by the EU in the areas of waste law and chemical control. The same holds for air pollution control, for which important quality thresholds on individual pollutants were passed. From the beginning of the 1980s, these were supplemented by various and sometimes very extensive directives to combat air pollution by industrial plants (Jordan, 1999: 10).

Many of these measures entailed great costs for the member states and their industries. For instance, complying with the strict quality thresholds for drinking water required the installation of expensive filter and purification technology by the national water supply companies. These policies also led to additional costs for the administrative and institutional adaptation of the member states in order to ensure the compatibility of national regulations with the European specifications (Héritier *et al.*, 1996; Knill and Lenschow, 1998; Knill, 2001).

There is an array of reasons for the formidable development of the European environmental policy despite the difficult legal and institutional preconditions. Some observers point out that the member states were confronted with growing domestic pressure due to environmental issues, which strengthened their willingness to cooperate at the European level. In particular, at the beginning of the 1980s, environmental problems were increasingly politicized in several member states. One might note here forest dieback (*Waldsterben*) due to acid rain (see above), which triggered extensive environmental policy activities in Germany, above all.

The transnational character of the problem of acidification, but also the feared damage to the competitiveness of industries, which were now confronted with strict national environmental regulations, facilitated a very active role for Germany at the European level. Together with other member states such as the Netherlands and Denmark, the Germans attempted to enhance the level of protection and the regulatory requirements for European environmental policies. Despite the reservations of other member states, they triggered certain dynamics at the European level, leading to the adoption of European standards which in part went significantly beyond the existing provisions in the individual member states (Héritier *et al.*, 1996; Sbragia, 2000).

Furthermore, there are also indications that during the negotiations at the European level the representatives of the member states were frequently not able to properly assess the economic and administrative implications of the measures decided on, in particular, during the initial phase of European environmental policy. Or to put it more bluntly: some of the member states were not totally aware of what they had got into during the European negotiations. Thus, the member states accepted extremely strict quality standards for drinking water proposed by the Commission, whose implementation at the national level turned out to be highly problematic and only feasible at great cost. Individual member states also had false notions about the binding legal character of European directives. For example, the UK had accepted European directives, assuming that the specified limits were to be interpreted merely as non-binding recommendations instead of legally binding requirements (Sbragia, 2000: 296).

In individual cases, these factors certainly may have played a role. However, they on their own do not suffice to adequately capture and explain the dynamics of European environmental policy making. As we will demonstrate, there are several structural aspects as well, which influence the interest constellations and patterns of the interaction of the central actors in European environmental policy. Yet before we ultimately explain the puzzle of the relatively comprehensive environmental policy activities, despite the unfavourable preconditions, we will first round off this overview. As already indicated, the adoption of the SEA in 1986 brought about a few lasting changes.

The Single European Act: an environmental policy as an official task of the Community

With the SEA, environmental policy was explicitly declared to be a task of the EC. The uncertainty with regard to the legal basis of EU environmental policy was thus eliminated. The necessary legitimation for environmental policy activities, which had previously been based on economic integration, was replaced by legitimation on the basis of environmental policy goals. The background and concrete ramifications of this development will be examined more closely in the following sections.

The political background

The decisive motivation for the adoption of the SEA was rooted less in environmental than economic policy motives. The foremost goal of the SEA was to accelerate economic integration within the Community in order to complete the Common Market. The explicit establishment of environmental policy as an official domain of the EU occurred to a certain extent as a by-product of economically motivated reforms. In the middle of the 1980s the Community was still far from the goal of the Common Market as formulated in the Treaty of Rome, despite certain advances. It appeared that the harmonization of national legal and administrative provisions necessary for the realization of economic goals was often very sluggish. Above all, it was feared that the process of economic integration might also stagnate after the accession of Spain and Portugal in 1986. As it was difficult enough to bring about unanimous resolutions in the Council of Ministers with ten states (Greece had joined the EU in 1981), the situation was anticipated to further deteriorate with the accession of additional member states. These concerns were additionally compounded by economic developments. Stagnating growth, high unemployment rates, as well as fears that the EU could lose ground economically against the USA and Japan, increased the willingness of the member states to endorse the institutional reforms aimed at completing the Common Market more quickly (Young and Wallace, 2000).

With this constellation in mind, it seemed surprising at first glance that the SEA also strengthened the EU's basis for action in environmental affairs. Nevertheless, at the conference of heads of state and government which led to the SEA, there was soon a consensus that environmental policy should be made an explicitly legitimate area of Community action (Sbragia, 2000). This development can be explained on the basis of three factors.

First, the previous policy development had made it clear that a Common Market could not be achieved by the member states merely by transferring economic authority to the EU. The development had illustrated that market and trade obstacles result not exclusively from different customs and tax regulations, but also, among other things, from different environmental policies in a more general sense.

Second, the explicit mention of EU environmental policy in the treaty ultimately only confirmed in legal terms what had already been accomplished *de facto* in the preceding years. The basic legitimacy of the joint environmental policy had already been acknowledged. In light of the considerable number of existing legal acts and action programmes, it seemed only reasonable to use the opportunity of the SEA to anchor this policy area in the treaty (Holzinger and Knill, 2002).

Finally, it should not be overlooked that, regardless of the necessity of environmental regulation as an aspect of the Common Market, the Commission and the European Parliament in particular played a very active role in promoting the establishment of environmental policy authority in the treaty. Here it suffices to mention that vital institutional interests on behalf of the Commission and Parliament geared at gaining new capacity for action vis-à-vis the member states were crucial. In other words, both the Commission and the Parliament hoped for new methods of political influence by enhancing their environmental policy authority.

This overall constellation of diverse interests and motives facilitated the emergence of relatively far-reaching legal and institutional reforms. Although these developments were primarily geared to complete the Common Market, they went hand in hand with significant changes in the common environmental policy.

An explicit basis for EU environmental policy

With the adoption of the SEA, the goals and principles of EU environmental policy were defined for the first time in the treaty. Moreover, this resulted in important changes in the decision rules for environmental policy. The concrete changes here were twofold: first, a new title – 'environment' – was added to the treaty, comprised of Articles 174–6. Second, the introduction of new rules to accelerate economic integration had ramifications for the design of the European environmental policy. These legal changes were based, in particular, on Articles 18 and 95.

Basic principles of the common environmental policy

Articles 174–6 are to be regarded as the actual environmental articles of the treaty. They include not only provisions on the general significance and the goals of the EU environmental policy, but also define the basic principles and decision-making procedures by which these goals are to be achieved. Furthermore, general conditions with regard to the allocation of European and national environmental policy responsibilities and possibilities for action are specified.

Article 174 (1) offers a relatively detailed definition of the objectives of EU environmental policy, including the following aspects:

- preserving, protecting and improving the quality of the environment;
- protecting human health;
- prudent and rational utilization of natural resources.

Article 174 (2) codifies several main guidelines which serve as the basis for achieving environmental policy aims. Interestingly, these principles for the most part had already been formulated in the First Environmental Action Programme. Their implementation up to then had only been successful to a certain extent. They entail the following principles:

- *The precautionary principle*: environmental policy action should not be taken only when concrete damage has been demonstrated, but instead should be directed at preventing dangers and risks.
- *The principle of action at the source*: environmental damage should be combated at the source where it originates.

- *The polluter-pays principle*: he or she who pollutes the environment or creates a risk to it shall bear the costs for the prevention, removal of and compensations for any environmental damage.
- *The principle of integration*: the demands of environmental protection should be taken into account during the formulation and implementation of measures in other policy areas of the Community (such as transport, regional or agricultural policy).

Article 174 (3) specifies criteria and restrictions which are to be considered during the development of environmental action programmes and individual measure. Hence the common environmental policy is supposed to consider the current state of science and technology as well as the economic and social development of the Community and the regions. At the same time, the foundations are laid for the introduction of regionally differentiated environmental standards by establishing that the respective environmental conditions in the individual regions of the Community must be taken into account. Previously, the Community was under a certain pressure to set uniform standards, because environmental protection measures usually had to be based on the harmonization stipulation of Article 94.

Moreover, the 'subsidiarity principle for environmental policy', which had already essentially been formulated in the First Environmental Action Programme, was formally added to the treaty (Jordan, 1999). According to this principle, the Community is only allowed to become active in the area of the environment, when the 'objectives can be better reached at the Community level than at the level of the individual member states' (Article 174 [4]).

Article 176 authorizes the member states to maintain or introduce stricter environmental rules than those of the Community. However, the member states are only granted this possibility to the extent that national specifications exceeding those of the European provisions are in accordance with the goals of the treaty. The result of this change is that unilateral national policies are not allowed when they stand in the way of the goal of completing the European Common Market. This kind of Common Market relevance comes into play, in particular, when tradable products are affected by demands for environmental protection.

Legal arrangements and decision rules

The SEA served not only to explicitly anchor the basic features of EU environmental policy. It also offered a concrete basis for action at the Community level. In this regard, two articles should be particularly emphasized: the general basis of Article 175 and the special authorization for action for trade-related environmental measure of Article 95 of the treaty. These two articles differ above all in terms of their stipulations with regard to the decision-making procedure in the Council of Ministers.

The general authorization for the Community to decide on the necessary measures to fulfil the environmental policy objectives specified in the treaty can be found in Article 175. As for the decision-making rule, the article stipulated that as a rule, the decisions in the Council of Ministers must be reached unanimously. Thus, as far as this section of the treaty is involved, the SEA did not bring about any change with respect to the decision-making procedure for environmental policy matters. As had been the case with the environmental measure on the basis of Articles 94 and 308, each member retained a power of veto and could block political decisions, if necessary. However, Article 175 is only significant in cases where there is no other treaty basis for action. Such a basis exists, in particular, for environmental regulations which have an impact on the realization of the Common Market, i.e. all rules which previously had to be based on the harmonization provision of Article 94. The SEA introduced a new legal basis for such measures.

Article 95 facilitates the harmonization of national legal and administrative regulations in the course of the completion of the Common Market, which are defined more precisely in Article 18 (i.e. creation of an area without internal borders, free movement of goods, services, people and capital). Like Article 94, Article 95 is therefore motivated purely by trade policy (Holzinger, 1994: 73). Accordingly, Article 95 is always taken into consideration as a special legal basis for environmental protection measures by the EU, if they are relevant to the completion of the Common Market.

The question of whether European environmental regulations are of relevance for the Common Market – and thus must be decided on according to Article 95 – had significant implications for the decision-making process in the Council of Ministers. While under Article 175 the principle of unanimity applied, Article 95 provided for a new decision-making procedure, the so-called cooperation procedure, for all decisions on regulations concerning the completion of the Common Market. To accelerate the process of European market integration, decisions were to be taken by qualified majority voting (QMV), implying that individual member states could no longer rely on a veto position in order to block environmental policy proposals.

At the same time, the cooperation procedure enhanced the European Parliament's right to participate in the legislative process. This was a significant change because the Parliament has always been a progressive driving force for environmental protection (see Chapter 8) since it hoped to receive a positive response from the public and from voters. Under the new procedure it became directly involved in legislative decisions of the Council and received a right to suspensory veto.

The political effects: new opportunities for action

What were the concrete effects of the SEA for the structure and development of the European environmental policy? On the one hand, the changes initiated by the SEA

> helped to entrench and formalize the EU's involvement by placing environmental protection on a firm legal footing and enunciating a set of guiding

principles. In some respect, they merely formalized ideas and rules that were already an integral feature of day-to-day policy-making in the EU.

(Jordan, 1999: 11)

On the other hand, the SEA opened new possibilities for environmental policy action at the European level. Particularly noteworthy in this regard were the new articles on the environment which generally authorize the EU to act on environmental policy matters independently of trade policy motives. This way, the Commission was no longer required to link its proposals for environmental measures to the completion of the Common Market. This enabled the Commission to intrude into new areas of environmental policy and develop measures which hardly would have been justified on the basis of earlier legal foundations (Articles 94 and 308). An important example of this is the directive passed in 1990 on the free access to environmental information. This measure, which entails extensive access rights for the public to environmentally relevant data from national authorities, could hardly have been legitimized by trade policy goals (Haigh and Baldock, 1989: 21).

A second aspect which is significant with regard to the expansion of environmental policy authority concerns the introduction of majority decision making on environmental measures relevant to the Common Market, it was generally expected that decisions by a qualified majority would enable more innovative environmental policy making which goes beyond the lowest common denominator. It is frequently pointed out in this regard that in majority decision the states with the least interest in environmental protection can be outvoted and, consequently, the environmentally slowest state no longer determines the pace and the stringency of European environmental policies (Jordan, 1999: 11; Sbragia, 2000). From the standpoint of the individual member states, searching for coalition partners to enforce national interests now turned out to be more promising than blocking negotiations (Knill and Héritier, 1996: 228).

However, in the academic debate there is little agreement on whether and the extent to which the change in the decision-making procedure at the European level increased environmental policy dynamics. While, on the one hand, observers accepted the intuitively plausible hypotheses that a higher level of environmental standards could be expected with qualified majority decisions, Holzinger (1994) points out that such a scenario cannot be taken for granted. Rather, this depends on the majority conditions and coalition possibilities in the Council of Ministers. With this in mind, it is plausible that more environmentally ambitious states in the Council of Ministers will not produce a sufficient majority to enforce stricter environmental norms. There is even the potential danger of these countries being outvoted by the countries which are interested in less strict standards. Under the cooperation procedure, ambitious states no longer have a veto right either. Thus they are no longer in a position to block the introduction of weak standards on the basis of Article 95.

From this theoretical standpoint, there are many reasons to assess the impact of majority decisions on European environmental policy in a more differentiated fashion. The effects vary with the concrete constellation of national interests in the Council of Ministers. In this regard, moreover, significant shifts in the balance of power have taken place after the EU enlargements. For example, in 1995, the accession of environmentally ambitious states such as Sweden, Finland and Austria made the environmental policy 'forerunners' more influential (Holzinger, 1997). The accession of ten Central and Eastern European countries in 2004, by contrast, might imply a reversal of this trend, given the fact that the new members might place a stronger interest on economic rather than ecological development.

However, it is difficult to test these theoretical considerations on the basis of empirical developments in EU environmental policy (see Chapter 4). There are no systematic findings, only investigations into individual areas. Nevertheless, these do include studies offering evidence of high standards in EU environmental policy exceeding those of the most progressive member states. However, these investigations also show that the often extremely complicated environmental policy measures by the EU cannot simply be reduced to the concepts of high and low standards or lowest common denominator. Thus, it is not possible to draw firm conclusions on the impact of different decision-making rules in the Council of Ministers on EU environmental policy.

An additional complicating factor in this regard is that we have been witness to a fundamental transformation in the patterns of environmental policy regulations since the beginning of the 1990s. This change was triggered in particular by the Fifth Environmental Action Programme, published in 1993. It manifests itself in the declining trend for the EU to specify strict and extensive limits. Instead emphasis is increasingly being placed on new instruments, which prioritize economic incentives and the self-regulation of industry as well as greater participation rights for the public (see Chapter 17). This new designation was particularly aimed at the increasing significance of policy areas other than economic integration (European Communities, 1992: 8). These divergent regulatory concepts cannot easily be compared and contrasted with regard to their concrete ramifications for the level of European environmental protection. Regardless of that, we must keep in mind that the SEA laid out crucial foundations for the establishment and expansion of the EU's capacity for action in environmental policy. This triggered a development which was subsequently enhanced by further legal and institutional reforms.

Institutional and political changes since the 1990s: gradual shifts

Compared to the reforms initiated by the SEA, which created a comprehensive legal basis for a joint environmental policy, more recent legal and institutional reform developments have resulted in relatively small changes for EU environmental policy (see Chapter 1). However, while the legal and institutional development thus offers evidence of a gradual, but constant increase in the significance of EU environmental policy, a certain weakening and stagnation of the environmental policy dynamics have become apparent in terms of the political activities. We are confronted with the paradoxical situation that the increasing legal and institutional anchoring of EU environmental policy coincides with the stagnation of its political dynamics. This scenario is in stark contrast with the initial phase of EU environmental policy in which a respectable environmental policy programme was drawn up despite the weak legal and institutional basis.

Legal and institutional changes

As for the increased institutional and legal underpinnings of European environmental policy, one should in particular emphasize the developments resulting from the Treaties of Maastricht and Amsterdam. The creation of the European Environmental Agency (EEA) marks the further institutionalization and strengthening of the EU environmental policy.

The Maastricht TEU, which has been in effect since 1993, was a continuation of the developments introduced by the SEA. The centrepiece of this treaty is the creation of the EU, which since then has provided the overall institutional framework for the entire European integration process. It is based on three pillars: as a companion to the Common Foreign and Security Policy (Pillar III) and cooperation in the areas of Justice and Home Affairs (Pillar II), the so-called first pillar is most relevant here. It consists of the European Atomic Agency (Euratom), the European Coal and Steel Community and the EEC. In the SEA, the EEC was renamed the European Community, the core of the newly founded EU. Besides the introduction of European economic and monetary union and the concretization of European civil rights, the treaty provides new and expanded authority and individual policy areas. These entail not only consumer protection, health, research, technology, education and culture, but also environmental protection.

While the Treaty of Maastricht defined the basic parameters for further integration, the Treaty of Amsterdam (ratified in 1999) introduced relatively few new innovations. Most importantly, the heads of state and government at the intergovernmental conference in Amsterdam could not agree on the necessary institutional reforms to facilitate the 2004 accession of new member states. Nevertheless as a whole, the Treaties of Maastricht and Amsterdam provide a series of new legal and institutional specifications for the common environmental policy, which essentially concern decision-making procedures, goals and principles.

The increased significance of environmental policy became apparent in the changes in the decision-making procedure which the Maastricht Treaty provided. Environmental policy measures on the basis of Article 175 were henceforth to be decided by QMV, as was already the case for measures relevant to the Common Market on the basis of Article 95. These changes in decision-making procedure were followed by a further strengthening of the Parliament in the Amsterdam Treaty (Judge *et al.*, 1994). However, the development of new regulatory concepts cannot be viewed exclusively against the background of the stagnating environmental policy dynamics at the European level. They were also a reaction to the often ineffective implementation of harmonization measures at the national level (see Knill and Lenschow, 2000). Moreover, the Treaty of Maastricht expanded the tasks of the Community, emphasizing that the task of the Community was to promote environmentally sustainable growth. This wording was once again modified in the Amsterdam Treaty to 'achieve a balanced and sustainable development' (see Chapter 19). It thus is applicable as a guideline for policy making in all policy areas of the EU (Jordan, 1999).

The Treaty of Amsterdam additionally served to reinforce the further integration of environmental policy goals into other policy areas as a principle of common environmental policy (see Chapter 17). This was primarily achieved by no longer hiding the transversal character of environmental protection in the environmental articles, and linking it directly to the description of the spectrum of tasks of the Community at the beginning of the treaty (Article 3) (Lenschow, 1999). This promise to strengthen environmental policy concerns vis-à-vis other policy areas of the Community. This held in particular for the position of the DG Environment as compared to other DGs within the Commission (Haigh and Lanigan, 1995) (see also Chapter 13).

The creation of the EEA, which began its work in 1994, implies an additional reinforcement and institutionalization of EU environmental policy. An essential task of the agency is the formation of an overarching Environmental Information and Observation Network. On the basis of the information gathered through the existing environmental information systems of the member states, an improved inter-community exchange of environmental data was supposed to be achieved by examining, collecting and evaluating them in a centralized manner. At the same time, this should ensure a better foundation for the formulation and implementation of European environmental policies (Dilling, 2000). Following the Treaties of Maastricht and Amsterdam, a further revision was adopted in Nice in 2000. The consequences of this revision for the environmental field were very limited, however. Since Nice, an attempt was made to replace the existing treaties by a new, comprehensive Constitution. However, in the end, the existing treaties were simply amended once again in the Lisbon Treaty, which was signed in 2008 and entered into force in 2009 (see Chapter 3).

The political development: reduced dynamics

If we look back at the dynamics of EU environmental policy since the beginning of the 1990s, we find two opposing trends. While we can ascertain, on the one hand, a continual legal and institutional expansion and reinforcement of the basis for environmental policy action, we observe to a certain extent a cooling off of the environmental policy boom at the European level. This holds, in particular, when compared to the rate of environmental policy activities during the 1980s. The increasing legal and institutional anchoring of the European environmental policy thus paradoxically goes hand in hand with stagnating political dynamics (Zito, 1999: 31).

This conclusion is based on two observations. First, there appears to have been a certain decline in political significance both at the national and the European levels despite all the legal and institutional enhancements. Problems associated with environmental protection no longer have the same priority on the political agenda of the EU and most member states as in the 1980s.

There are various reasons for this development. Besides the general slow-down in economic growth from the beginning of the 1990s and the persistent problem of high unemployment, we should also mention increased competition in the wake of international market liberalization. All these factors reduced the willingness of the member states to pass stricter environmental regulations which might have negative effects on the position of their industries in the midst of international competition. '[T]he political commitment to impose stringent and intrusive regulations through command and control processes has diminished very significantly' (Sbragia, 2000: 294–5), a trend which has continued into the 2000s.

Second, as a consequence of this general political development, we can observe a certain reorientation of environmental regulation at EU level. In contrast to developments in the 1980s, the definition of uniform legally binding limits is no longer the main focus of EU environmental policy. Instead, the Commission increasingly is focusing on more flexible and less harmonization-oriented regulatory concepts, which allow the member states greater room to manoeuvre with regard to the implementation of policies. These new instruments are marked in particular by the fact that they are legally less demanding for the member states than previous measures. They concentrate less on specifying detailed standards, which all member states must equally comply with, and more on stimulating and enhancing national environmental policy reforms (see Knill and Lenschow, 2000).

As a whole, the consequence of these developments is that European environmental policy has partially lost its function as a driving force behind the constant increase in the level of environmental protection in the EU. This is the case despite the continually high number of environmental policy measures passed at the European level, of which a significant part is in fact still aimed at harmonizing national environmental standards (Jordan, 1999: 15). However, our assessment should not ignore the fact that the slow-down in environmental policy dynamics since the 1990s is not an exclusively EU phenomenon. It can be observed at the member state level as well.

Summary: three phases of EU environmental policy

If we sum up the developments in EU environmental policy, we can distinguish three phases. In the first phase (1972–87), the European environmental measures were legally justified primarily by trade policy motives. The main focus was initially the goal of harmonizing different national environmental regulations, which might stand in the way of the completion of the Common Market. As a consequence of increasing cross-border environmental problems and the pioneering role of individual member states (Anderson and Liefferink, 1997), a respectable programme of often very ambitious measures and activities emerged despite a weak legal and institutional basis. This was accompanied by the gradual emancipation of environmental policy as an independent policy domain detached from the area of economic integration, even though the corresponding legal foundations did not yet exist.

The second phase (1987–92) is primarily characterized by the legal and institutional consolidation and further development of the common environmental policy. The SEA formally codified what informally was already a reality. Environmental policy was subsequently anchored in the treaty as an official field of activity of the Community. A new treaty title in the SEA also served to lay down the aims, principles and decision-making procedures for environmental policy. This resulted in a considerable expansion of the EU's environmental policy authority. On the one hand, environmental measures no longer necessarily had to be substantiated by trade policy goals. On the other hand, a new decision-making procedure was introduced for environmental measures relevant to the Common Market, which allowed for qualified majority decisions in the Council of Ministers. Thus, it was generally expected (although only partly confirmed in practice) that stricter environmental standards would be passed that went beyond the lowest common denominator of the member states.

The third phase (post 1992) has been characterized by two opposing trends: from an institutional and legal standpoint, the developments triggered by the SEA were gradually revised and updated, in particular, in the Treaties of Maastricht and Amsterdam and through the creation of the EEA. Contrary to this trend, however, we have witnessed how environmental policy dynamic has weakened to a certain extent. EU environmental policy lost momentum on the European agenda as opposed to other policy areas. This was associated with at least a partial decline of the EU's environmental policy as a motor for stricter and more far-reaching environmental regulations in the Community. It remains to be seen how this development will proceed in the future.

Key questions

1   Why did EU environmental policy develop in the late 1960s?
2   How did actors supportive of deeper integration establish a greater role for the EU?
3   Why did EU environmental policy suddenly expand?
4   Describe the main principles of EU environmental policy. To what extent do these differ from the principles of national environmental policy?
5   Describe the main phases of policy development since the 1960s. What kind of phase is EU environmental policy currently in?
6   Did environmental policy emerge in a similar fashion to other EU policy areas or did it follow its own unique trajectory?

Guide to further reading

- For other accounts, see Benson and Jordan (2010) and Jordan (1999).
- McCormick (2001) explores the successes and failures of EU environmental policy in a very readable text.
- For the first attempt to explain the genesis of policy area in this area, see Rehbinder and Stewart (1985).
- For a much more detailed analysis, see Weale *et al.* (2000) or various chapters in Jordan (2005). Liefferink *et al.* (1993) offer a very comprehensive but now somewhat dated account.

Note

1   Throughout this chapter we use the current numbering of treaty articles as introduced by the Amsterdam Treaty, in force since 1999.

References

Andersen, M.S. and Liefferink, D.J. (1997) *European Environmental Policy: The Pioneers*, Manchester University Press, Manchester.

Benson, D. and Jordan, A.J. (2010) 'Environmental policy', in M. Cini, and N. Pérez-Solórzano Borragán (eds) *European Union Politics*, 3rd edition, Oxford University Press, Oxford, pp. 358–74.

Boehmer Christiansen, S. and Skea, J. (1991) *Acid Politics*, Belhaven Press, London.

Dilling, R. (2000) 'Improving implementation by networking', in C. Knill and A. Lenschow (eds) *Implementing EU Environmental Policies*, Manchester University Press, Manchester, pp. 62–86.

European Commission (1984) *10 Jahre Umweltpolitik*, European Commission, Brussels.

European Communities (1992) *Die Europäische Union*, Office for Official Publications of the European Union, Brussels.

Haigh, N. (2000) *Manual of Environmental Policy*, Maney Publishing, Leeds.

Haigh, N. and Baldock, D. (1989) *Environmental Policy and 1992*, Institute for European Environmental Policy, London.

Haigh, N. and Lanigan, C. (1995) 'Impact of the EU on UK policy making', in T. Gray (ed.) *UK Environmental Policy in the 1990s*, Macmillan, Houndmills, pp. 18–37.

Héritier, A., Knill, C. and Mingers, S. (1996) *Ringing the Changes in Europe*, De Gruyter, Berlin.

Hildebrand, P.M. (1993) 'The European Community's environmental policy, 1957 to "1992"', in D. Judge (ed.) *A Green Dimension for the European Community*, Frank Cass, London, pp. 13–44.

Holzinger, K. (1994) *Politik des kleinsten Gemeinsamen Nenners?* Edition Sigma, Berlin.

Holzinger, K. (1997) 'The influence of the new member states on EU environmental policy making', in M.S. Andersen and D. Liefferink (eds) *The Innovation of European Environmental Policy*, Scandinavian University Press, Copenhagen.

Holzinger, K. and Knill, C. (2002) 'Path dependencies in European integration', *Public Administration*, vol. 80, no. 1, pp. 125–152.

Johnson, S.P. and Corcelle, G. (1989) *The Environmental Policy of the European Communities*, Graham & Trotman, London.

Jordan, A.J. (1999) 'The construction of a multi-level environmental governance system', *Environment and Planning C*, vol. 17, no. 1, pp. 1–17.

Jordan, A.J. (ed.) (2005) *Environmental Policy in the European Union: Actors, Institutions and Processes*, 2nd edition, Earthscan, London.

Judge, D., Earnshaw, D. and Cowan, N. (1994) 'Ripples or waves: the European Parliament in the European Community policy process', *Journal of European Public Policy*, vol. 1, no. 1, pp. 27–52.

Knill, C. (1995) *Staatlichkeit im Wandel*, Deutscher Universitätsverlag, Opladen.

Knill, C. (2001) *The Europeanization of National Administrations*, Cambridge University Press, Cambridge.

Knill, C. and Héritier, A. (1996) 'Neue instrumente in der europäischen Umweltpolitik: Strategien für eine effektivere Implementation', in G. Lubbe-Wolff (ed.) *Der Vollzug des europäischen Umweltrechts*, Erich Schmidt Verlag, Berlin, pp. 209–234.

Knill, C. and Lenschow, A. (1998) 'Coping with Europe', *Journal of European Public Policy*, vol. 5, no. 4, pp. 595–614.

Knill, C. and Lenschow, A. (eds) (2000) *Implementing EU Environmental Policies*, Manchester University Press, Manchester.

Krämer, W. (2000) *EC Environmental Law*, 4th edition, Sweet & Maxwell, London.

Lenschow, A. (1999) 'Transformation in European environmental governance', in B. Kohler-Koch and R. Eising (eds) *The Transformation of Governance in the European Union*, Routledge, London, pp. 39–61.

Liefferink, D., Lowe, P. and Mol, A. (eds) (1993) *European Integration and Environmental Policy*, Belhaven, London.

McCormick, J. (2001) *Environmental Policy in the European Union*, Palgrave Macmillan, Basingstoke, pp. 75–86.

Rehbinder, E. and Stewart, R. (1985) *Environmental Protection Policy: Vol. 2*, De Gruyer, Berlin.

Sbragia, A. (2000) 'Environmental policy', in H. Wallace and W. Wallace (eds) *Policy-making in the European Union*, Oxford University Press, Oxford, pp. 293–316.

Weale, A. (1996) 'Environmental rules and rule-making in the European Union', *Journal of European Public Policy*, vol. 3, no. 4, pp. 594–611.

Weale, A., Pridham, G. and Cini, M. *et al.* (2000) *Environmental Governance in Europe*, Oxford University Press, Oxford.

Young, A. and Wallace, H. (2000) 'The single market', in H. Wallace and W. Wallace (eds), *Policy-making in the European Union*, Oxford University Press, Oxford, pp. 85–114.

Zito, A. (1999) 'Task expansion: a theoretical overview', *Environment and Planning C*, vol. 17, no. 1, pp. 19–35.

3 EU environmental policy after the Lisbon Treaty

David Benson and Camilla Adelle

Summary guide

The protracted development and ratification of the Lisbon Treaty were characterized by significant speculation, and indeed heated controversy, over its alleged impacts on EU politics, policy and governance. Several years on from its formal signing into EU law, precisely what changes did it introduce and what have been their consequences for the everyday practices of environmental policy? In this respect, this chapter focuses on the Lisbon Treaty measures that directly affected certain specific aspects of EU policy making, namely, the legal principles and objectives of EU policy; the allocation of competences between the EU and its member states; the EU institutions; more general policy-making procedures; and hopes for more participatory forms of democracy. Many of these changes are yet to become fully operational, but some have already strengthened the EU's environmental powers, whereas others have weakened them. In summary, *comme ci, comme ça* – neither good nor bad.

Introduction

After several years of controversy, all 27 EU member states finally ratified the Lisbon (Reform) Treaty in 2009 (see Box 3.1), thereby marking another important milestone in the institutional evolution of the Union. Throughout this period, public and political debate on the treaty, mirroring the development of its ill-fated predecessor the EU Constitution, tended to centre on the degree to which further national powers would be ceded to Brussels. Politicians and the populist press in member states such as the UK decried the treaty as an example *par excellence* of the ongoing federalization of the EU, citing its potentially negative consequences for national sovereignty. Far less attention at the time was paid to understanding its actual implications for key policy sectors such as the environment; crucially few analyses have sought to assess how the treaty has subsequently influenced them in practice.

Box 3.1 The Lisbon Treaty

The Lisbon Treaty is in fact a set of amendments to the two main existing treaties governing the EU: the Treaty on European Union (TEU) and the Treaty establishing the European Community (TEC). The latter was given a new name in the Lisbon Treaty: the Treaty on the Functioning of the EU (TFEU). The text of both these treaties can be found in one 'consolidated' document (Council of the European Union, 2008).

(Farmer, 2011)

'Lisbon', as the agreement is now commonly known, followed the pattern of previous treaty revisions by inserting legal amendments into existing texts. As ostensibly a state-based international organization, the EU's primary legal and institutional framework is determined by its founding agreements; the 1957 Treaty of Rome, which created the European Economic Community (EEC), and the 1992 (Maastricht) Treaty on European Union which founded its successor, the EU. Changing this framework requires the assent of national governments in a mutually agreed amending treaty. Several significant changes to EU environmental policy and governance had already been made by previous amending treaties (see Chapter 2), most notably the Single European Act (see Hildebrand, 2005), although Lisbon did introduce some innovations in terms of the environmental 'rules of the game'. As we go on to discuss, although relatively minor compared to earlier amendments they could nonetheless have long-term repercussions for the environment, both within the EU and further afield.

In discussing the significance of these developments, this chapter adopts the following structure. First, it provides a contextual overview of the development of the Lisbon Treaty development, explaining how it evolved out of political demands for wider EU reform. Second, implications for the environmental sector are then outlined by focusing on Lisbon's amendments to: the EU's core operating principles and policy objectives; the division of powers or 'competences' with member states; key institutions; policy-making procedures; and democratic processes. Third, the chapter then examines the practical impacts of these changes on EU environmental policy making. Finally, it reflects on the prospects for future policy making in this area. Our reflections are guided by one leading theoretical model of EU institutional change. For liberal intergovernmentalists, state-bargained treaty changes are the principal determinants of European integration. As such, they are the 'grand bargains' through which the key actors – member states – surrender sovereignty to collective EU decision making, while retaining overall control (Moravcsik, 1998: 1–2). Integration thereby proceeds via a 'sequence of irregular big bangs' (ibid.), each defining the space for subsequent political action. If these theories are correct, the (albeit limited) changes introduced by Lisbon should influence subsequent environmental politics, policy and governance in rather predictable ways.

Summary points

- The ratification of the Lisbon Treaty in 2009 marked an important milestone in the evolution of the EU.
- While the new treaty created a great deal of animated debate about its impacts on national sovereignty, little attention has since been paid to understanding its impacts on the day-to-day operation of particular policy sectors such as the environment.
- This chapter examines the background to Lisbon, and examines its impact on environmental politics, policy and governance.

To Lisbon and beyond: scandal, crisis and then a Greek tragedy?

The origins of the Lisbon Treaty are quite complex. First, as discussed above, the EU's primary legal and institutional framework is contained in its founding treaties. Unlike a conventional federal state, the EU lacks a formal constitution delineating its powers vis-à-vis its constituent member states. Tensions have consistently emerged with national governments over the EU's incremental incursions into their powers: what Pollack (2000) calls 'competence creep'. Second, this dynamic has been shaped by the form of integration historically promoted by EU elites, known as the Monnet Method. Also referred to as 'integration by stealth' (Weale, 1999), through this strategy the EU gradually assumed powers over areas of low political salience such as agriculture and the environment. Although the Monnet Method was hugely successful in expanding EU political integration, it created a unique system of governance characterized by many pathologies, not least its democratically sub-optimal decision making. Some commentators consequently refer to a resultant 'democratic deficit' (Follesdal and Hix, 2006), with many European citizens feeling disconnected from the often opaque, technocratic and insular world of Brussels. Finally, the EU has sought to constantly expand geopolitically as well as institutionally. Each successive round of enlargement has generated tensions over the subsequent direction of European integration and the institutional capacity of the EU to cope with the new entrants.

These dynamics led to a crisis point in the late 1990s. First, continued enlargement threatened the EU with institutional paralysis. The EU was engaged in an accession process with former Eastern Bloc countries which would dramatically expand its membership, but was still reliant on intergovernmental decision-making procedures designed in the 1960s. Second, and more significantly, the Commission was rocked by successive scandals (see Chapter 6). After allegations of financial mismanagement and nepotism, the entire Commission was forced to resign in response to a subsequent Parliamentary investigation. With the Commission heavily weakened, public faith in EU institutions and the European project plummeted, leading to widespread demands for reform.

The failure of another treaty amendment – the Treaty of Nice in 2001 – to adequately address these 'pathologies' precipitated a chain of events that ultimately led to Lisbon. While maintaining EU commitments to eastern enlargement, the negotiations at Nice side-stepped any agreement for reforming EU institutions and decision making. Neither did they adequately tackle the EU's perceived democratic deficit and its ever-expanding powers. However, the Nice inter-governmental conference did call for these issues to be aired at another meeting. These included: how competences should be allocated in the future; how existing treaties could be streamlined; how citizens' interests could be codified into a charter of fundamental rights; and how the role of national parliaments in EU decision making could be redefined.

In an attempt to revive the EU's flagging credibility, European Commissioner Romano Prodi had by this point already initiated a debate on EU governance (Prodi, 2000). In the wake of the Nice Treaty, the Commission published a White Paper on Governance in 2001 calling for institutional change which was debated by national leaders at the European Council in Laeken, Belgium. As a result, the 2001 Laeken Declaration adopted at that meeting advocated a federal-style 'constitution' written anew to replace the sprawling mass of founding treaties (see Chapter 1), in order to improve the EU's accountability, efficiency and democratic legitimacy. A consultative Convention was then established by EU elites to discuss the drafting of a constitution. The first draft of a constitution was duly completed in 2003. Heads of government gave their approval to the resulting Treaty Establishing a Constitution for Europe, formally signing the agreement in Rome in 2004 amid much fanfare. Yet ratification proved to be anything but trouble-free.

Each EU treaty requires the consent of national parliaments before it can become law; a factor that fundamentally influenced subsequent events. Ratification of the constitution was dealt a fatal blow by successive public referenda in two founding members – France and the Netherlands. When voters did this in 2005, it plunged the EU into further turmoil. Although domestic issues were a contributory factor, they undoubtedly reflected deeper anxieties among European citizens over the pace and scale of integration, and the elitist nature of the European project. Thus, by trying to address its perceived 'democratic deficit', the EU had ironically succeeded in further alienating its citizens. A two-year 'period of reflection' then ensued as political leaders sought to resolve the situation.

This period of political limbo ended when the German Presidency of the EU brokered another agreement. The Berlin Declaration, issued by the EU Council in March 2007, contained a pledge to adopt a new amending treaty (i.e. pointedly *not* a constitution) by 2009. A panel of elite politicians and bureaucrats (dubbed the Amato Group) drafted a new treaty, christened the Reform Treaty, which formed the basis of the Lisbon Treaty, formally signed by governments in December 2007. Almost all the innovations contained in the constitution were retained and some new features were added, but more controversial proposals for an EU flag and anthem were quietly dropped. However, following the trend established by the earlier constitutional process, this new Lisbon Treaty was rejected in another national referendum, this time in Ireland. Irish voters were subsequently 'invited' to vote again after being given reassurances regarding Lisbon's impacts on their national sovereignty. This time the text was voted through. Despite further obstructionism by the Polish and Czech governments, Lisbon was finally ratified, becoming legally binding in late 2009, almost eight years after the Nice conference.

By this point in time, however, the controversies that had swirled around the treaty process had been subsumed by far more powerful currents of concern. Near systemic collapse of global financial markets in 2008 hit several EU states hard, with the more open economies of the UK, Hungary, Latvia and Ireland being particularly badly hit. As the EU has since been preoccupied with shoring up monetary union and the eurozone, primarily by supporting an ailing Greek economy with extensive financial bailouts, debates over the implementation of Lisbon and its alleged negative implications for national sovereignty no longer make front page news. Nonetheless, it is very important to reflect on its impacts on everyday practice, particularly regarding environmental policy.

Summary points

- European integration has arguably produced a complex, multi-levelled form of governance, lacking democratic accountability.
- In attempting to improve its transparency, efficiency and democratic accountability, the EU first introduced an ill-fated constitution, but this failed to secure political support and was dropped.
- A new Lisbon Treaty was drafted and adopted by the EU in 2009 after a convoluted ratification process.

The Lisbon Treaty: improving the environment?

Having endured this rather tortuous and painful process of treaty reform, what innovations did the EU actually introduce with the new treaty? In more general terms, while not nearly as ground-breaking as previous treaties, Lisbon did contain several important general features. Most notably the cumbersome 'pillar' structure of the EU introduced by the Maastricht Treaty (see Chapter 2) was replaced by a simpler delineation of its competences. So, instead of separate pillars for security and foreign affairs, and justice and home affairs, all EU competences were split into three categories: 'exclusive', 'shared' and 'supporting' categories. Henceforth, the EU enjoys 'exclusive' powers over certain limited issues; it must 'share' others with national governments, and only plays a 'supporting' role in governing some specific areas controlled by states. Meanwhile, new institutional innovations included the introduction of a High Representative for Foreign Affairs and Security Policy; a rather grand title effectively for the EU's foreign minister. In addition, the EU created a semi-permanent President of the European Council to partly replace the old six-monthly rotating Presidency (see also Chapter 5).

Changes aimed at streamlining voting procedures in the Council of Ministers were also introduced. Lisbon also significantly increased the European Parliament's powers by expanding the policy issues subject to co-decision (i.e. joint decision making) with the Council, and further enlarged the list of issues subject to qualified majority voting in the Council. The Parliament therefore received a more significant role in decision making (see Chapter 8), while the scope for individual states to block initiatives under unanimity voting declined.

Aside from these general measures, Lisbon introduced a set of more sector-specific changes. New shared competences (discussed below) were added to the burgeoning list of EU powers, while the Union also acquired a supporting role in diverse sectors such as tourism, intellectual property rights and sport. Lisbon also contained several new innovations that have a bearing on the environmental policy sector. We categorize the main ones in relation to their core legal, power-sharing, institutional, procedural and democratic features (Benson and Jordan, 2010).

General principles and objectives

The development of the EU is underpinned by core legal principles and objectives contained in the opening articles of its founding treaties. These include a commitment to sustainable development. Introduced by the 1997 Amsterdam Treaty, sustainable development is (in theory at least) a central objective of all EU policy making (but see Chapter 19). Changes to the precise wording of this commitment were made by Article 3(3) of the Lisbon Treaty, broadening the scope of the Amsterdam conception, while redefining sustainable development in terms of meeting goals inherent in the internal market. Article 3(5) also extended this principle beyond the borders of the EU, stating that the Union shall 'contribute to peace, security, [and] the sustainable development of the Earth' (Council of the European Union, 2008: 21). Sustainable development was also made an objective of EU external relations.

Lisbon also enhanced the principle of environmental policy integration (EPI) and legal commitments to animal welfare. A means of integrating environmental concerns into cognate policy sectors such as energy (Jordan and Lenschow, 2008), EPI was first introduced into EU policy making by the Single European Act and then made a core principle by the Treaty of Amsterdam (see Chapter 13). In revising this commitment, Article 11 of Lisbon stated that '[e]nvironmental protection requirements must be integrated into the definition and implementation of the Union policies and activities, in particular with a view to promoting sustainable development' (Council of the European Union, 2008: 68). A new article was also introduced in the treaty governing animal welfare.

The allocation of competences

Treaty changes can have a strong influence on the balance of powers or competences between the EU and its member states. A formal EU legal competence for the environment, for example, was first introduced by the Single European Act, leading to an expansion in environmental policy making. Lisbon further reallocated powers upwards to the EU in environmentally related areas, primarily by creating new competences for civil protection and energy production and consumption. Pre-existing environmental powers (under Article 191) remained unchanged in the Lisbon Treaty, apart from an obligation on EU institutions to promote 'measures at international level to deal with regional or worldwide environmental problems, and in particular combating climate change' (Council of the European Union, 2008: 173). While this did not in itself constitute a new legal power – the EU had already participated in international climate change negotiations for some time – the wording appears to be aimed at providing the EU with a stronger negotiating role alongside member states where responsibilities are often not clear-cut (see below and Chapter 16).

Changes were also made to the principle of subsidiarity. First introduced by the Single European Act for environmental policy and then extended to all EU policy making by the Maastricht Treaty, subsidiarity dictates that decisions should be taken at the lowest effective or efficient level. The principle was designed to diffuse tensions over the allocation of competences. Lisbon enhanced the capacity of national parliaments to invoke subsidiarity by allowing them to challenge legislative proposals produced by the Commission if they are perceived to violate the principle. A system known as the 'yellow card' and 'orange card' approach was introduced, whereby national parliaments can initially object to a proposal through submitting a reasoned opinion to the Commission (the 'yellow card'). If a revised proposal does not satisfy the majority of governments, the Commission must then refer its reasoned opinion to the Council and European Parliament, who will jointly decide the fate of the proposal (by issuing an 'orange card').

However, a more significant change in terms of competences was the new competence (Title XXI) for energy. Despite the Treaty of Rome not providing an explicit competence for energy, the Commission was subsequently able to incrementally develop a *de facto* energy policy, by introducing measures for *inter alia* energy security, renewables, research and development, and the deregulation of energy supply markets (Màtlary, 1997). This policy expansion was achieved through reliance on pre-existing treaty legal articles, principally market harmonization powers. Several factors precipitated the need for a legally based common policy, most notably: threats to EU energy security from increasing import dependency; the Commission's ongoing programme to deregulate energy markets; and, climate change (see Jordan *et al.*, 2010). Following on from the Council's decision to adopt a common EU energy policy in 2007, an energy title was included in Lisbon, with specific powers outlined in Article 194. Related powers were also introduced for promoting trans-European energy supply networks such as oil pipelines.

Finally, new competences were introduced in related articles covering solidarity and civil protection. Just as in energy policy, the EU had already developed *de facto* powers over civil protection on the basis of its existing powers, introducing a Mechanism for Civil Protection, a civil protection financial instrument and an Action Programme. Lisbon, however, added a new Title (XXIII) on Civil

Protection, providing EU supporting powers to encourage greater cooperation between member states in preventing, and protecting against, man-made or natural disasters, including those exacerbated by climate change. This power could be exploited by the EU to further communitize climate change adaptation policy – an area to date largely untouched by Brussels. Related measures that could aid adaptation to climate change were introduced by a new article set within the 'Solidarity Clause' (Title VII). It obliges member states, in the event of terrorist attack and natural and man-made disasters, to help each other under the co-ordination of the EU Council. Some cross-over therefore exists with the require-ment for civil protection, particularly regarding climate change-related events such as floods, droughts and storms.

Institutional developments

Uncertainty surrounds how the major institutional changes outlined at the start of this section could impact on environmental policy. For example, the new semi-permanent Council Presidency created by Lisbon could reduce opportunities for greener states to upload their preferences to the EU policy process. After Lisbon, sectoral councils, such as the environment, were also chaired by a combination of ministers from three member states for a fixed period, reducing the scope for environmental 'entrepreneurs' to shape the policy process. Alternatively, in the past when a less committed member state was at the helm, the pace of change tended to drop, so the new system could also make policy making less episodic.

The prospects for stronger environmental policy could also be enhanced by the changes made to external relations and climate change policy making. Prior to Lisbon, responsibilities for foreign affairs were somewhat confusingly divided between the Council and a Commissioner for External Relations. Under the treaty, foreign issues are supposed to be coordinated by a single person – the High Representative of the Union for Foreign Affairs and Security Policy – although member states are still free to conduct their own foreign policies in parallel. The post-holder, appointed by the European Council, chairs the Foreign Affairs Council and is Vice President of the Commission. According to van Schaik and Egenhofer (2005), such a move could significantly boost the EU's ability to negotiate new international environmental agreements in areas such as climate change. A High Representative with a dedicated joint diplomatic corps (known as the European External Action Service) should, the thinking goes, be better equipped to coordinate member state interests with the Commission and thereby present a more united front.

Procedural innovations

Lisbon also expanded the European Parliament's powers within the EU policy process through increasing the scope of co-decision. This decision-making rule determines that the Council and the European Parliament co-decide measures equally. Introduced originally by the Treaty of Amsterdam, co-decision was officially renamed the 'ordinary legislative procedure' and expanded to many more policy areas by Lisbon. Almost all environmental issues became subject to co-decision along with related aspects of transport, energy, fisheries, external trade, and regional and agricultural policy, providing an opportunity to further 'green' these areas.

Meanwhile, Lisbon introduced changes to unanimity voting in the Council. It will, from 2014 onwards, mean that qualified majority voting (QMV) will become the dominant decision rule for intergovernmental decision making, with states then being unable to unilaterally block measures. This change is unlikely to influence environmental policy that greatly since almost all issues were already decided by QMV apart from fiscal affairs (i.e. green taxation), land-use planning, aspects of water management, and the determination of national energy mixes. However, a so-called *passarelle* clause was also introduced that allows the Council (acting unanimously) to decide to apply QMV to issues which would otherwise be adopted unanimously.

Participatory democracy

As mentioned above, the EU is perceived by some to exhibit a 'democratic deficit'. Acting on these concerns, the constitution was intended to facilitate the greater engagement of citizens, although as discussed earlier in the chapter it was, somewhat ironically, rejected in public referenda. Yet one significant mechanism for citizen participation developed in the old Constitutional Treaty was retained in Lisbon, namely the so-called 'right of citizens initiative'. Here, the Commission can be 'invited' to introduce a legislative proposal in areas of EU competence on receipt of support of '[n]ot less than one million citizens' (Council of the European Union, 2008: 26). This new commitment appears significant for environmental and civil society groups since it offers them new opportunities to mobilize support for their campaigning and directly access the policy process. Attempts were also made to increase EU transparency by enhancing public access to information. In this respect, Lisbon stated that '[a]ny citizen of the Union . . . shall have a right of access to documents of the Union institutions, bodies, offices and agencies' (Council of the European Union, 2008: 70). Although there are some exceptions to this rule, particularly regarding European Court of Justice procedures, the EU policy-making system is, in theory at least, one of the most openly accessible globally.

Summary points

* Several changes were introduced by Lisbon. These include *inter alia*: a new EU commitment to sustainable development and animal welfare; more EU powers to address climate change, energy policy and civil protection; and changes to enhance the ability of the EU to negotiate international treaties.

> • At the same time Lisbon reduced the ability of national governments to veto environmental decision making, but it also introduced a new mechanism to allow NGOs to shape policy agendas by soliciting citizen support.

Looking back

From a liberal intergovernmentalist point of view, Lisbon in environmental terms represents something of a 'bargain', if not essentially a 'grand' one. We could on the basis of the above summary conclude that these changes have resulted in visible and concrete alterations to EU environmental politics, policy and governance. But, in reality, the picture is less clear. This section therefore revisits the above categories to assess progress since the adoption of the treaty.

General principles and objectives

Assessing the influence of the new commitments to sustainable development and EPI suggests that their impacts have been variable. Sustainable development has dropped down the EU's policy agenda in recent years (Benson and Jordan, 2012; see also Chapter 19 in this volume). Commitments to the principle made in the Sixth Environmental Action Programme (2000–12) belie a variable implementation record with some economic and social trends improving but many environmental indicators following a downward curve (Benson and Jordan, 2012). Moreover, as the economic situation has worsened post 2008, the discourse of sustainable development has been effectively downgraded by more market-friendly language within policy circles, exemplified in the revised Lisbon Agenda for jobs and growth (European Commission, 2010a). Sustainable development is perceived here more in terms of competitiveness and notions of 'green growth' and tackling climate change, suggesting that the prioritization of the principle contained in the Lisbon Treaty was, in retrospect, largely rhetorical.

EPI has enjoyed similarly mixed success. While environmental concerns continue to be slowly integrated into parallel sectors, mostly notably energy under the climate change agenda (discussed below), they still have yet to fully permeate other policy areas such as agriculture, transport, international trade and fisheries. The latter sector is particularly concerning from an environmental perspective. The Common Fisheries Policy is currently undergoing a reform process in an attempt to fix a quota system which has been described by the UK environment ministry as fundamentally 'broken' (Defra, 2011).

The allocation of competences

The reallocation of some competences from member states to the EU institutions has not (yet) led to any significant implications for EU environmental policy.

Korhonen (2011) asserts that in the first year of the Lisbon Treaty neither the 'yellow' nor 'orange' card had been used. However, an increasing number of parliamentary opinions being sent from national parliaments indicate that this system may be used in future. It is also unclear what implications the Solidarity Clause will have in practice (for example, if and how it could be triggered by natural disasters related to climate change). This is because it is still not known how this loosely formulated article will be implemented (Myrdal and Rhinard, 2010; van Ondarza and Parkes, 2010). In addition, it has been argued that the impact of the new 'Energy Title' is somewhat dampened by the wording of Article 194 which preserves the energy sovereignty of member states to choose between their energy sources (Pallemaerts, 2011). Since these new provisions are 'without prejudice to Article 192(2)(c)' (which sets out the legal basis for EU environmental policy), this leads to the somewhat paradoxical result that further encroachment upon the member states' energy policies is in principle more possible under EU environmental policy than under the newly recognized EU energy policy (Pallemaerts, 2011).

Institutional developments

Despite the supposedly clearer delineation of institutional responsibilities for foreign affairs introduced by Lisbon, subsequent events have demonstrated that confusion often still reigns. The European Commission has used the treaty on several occasions to argue that it, rather than the Council, should represent the EU in international environmental negotiations. For example, in 2010, the Commission refused to participate in formal negotiations on a global mercury treaty because the Council would not allow it to be the sole negotiator (ENDS *Europe Daily*, 7 June 2010; see also Chapter 16 in this volume). A similar dispute took place in May 2011 when agricultural ministers could not agree on whether the European Commission should participate in talks on a legally binding forestry agreement (ENDS *Europe Daily*, 18 May 2011). Such disagreements have occurred before (e.g. over discussions on the trade in endangered species) but Lisbon has provided the Commission with additional ammunition to expand its policy powers.

Additionally, the appointment of Catherine Ashton as the EU High Representative for Foreign Affairs and Security Policy does not yet appear to have made a significant difference to how the EU coordinates or presents its position in international environmental agreements. Catherine Ashton's performance has been criticized and she arguably still retains a relatively low profile in world affairs (e.g. *The Telegraph*, 22 November 2009). This is especially the case in EU climate diplomacy. At the Cancun Conference of the Parties of the United Nations Framework Convention on Climate Change in December 2010, it was the European Commission (specifically Connie Hedegaard, the Climate Action Commissioner), and the Belgian Presidency of the EU, which maintained the highest visibility in both presenting and forming the EU's position (European Commission, 2010b). The establishment of the European External Action Service and the reorganization of the EU delegations into true diplomatic missions have also failed to make significant impacts on international environmental governance. However, the EU can now use these new institutional arrangements to pursue a more direct approach to climate change diplomacy through bilateral agreements, which may yet prove effective in the post Copenhagen period (van Schaik, 2010).

Procedural innovations

The European Parliament has not yet begun to fully exert influence through its newly expanded powers. However, ongoing reforms of three major EU policies in areas in which the European Parliament has gained increased decision-making powers (i.e. the EU budget, the Common Agricultural Policy, and the Common Fisheries Policies) nonetheless offer significant opportunities. The Commission published its proposals for a new EU budget at the end of June 2011, setting out the overall spending amount and general categories for the period 2014–20. Under new, post-Lisbon, arrangements, the European Parliament can either reject or approve the budget when it has been amended by the Council. It could use this new power, for example, to insist that the Regional Development Fund and the Cohesion Fund are 'climate-proofed' (i.e. do not undermine climate change objectives) and that the Natura 2000 network of protected areas throughout Europe receives sufficient funding. Although the European Parliament has had a reputation for being the EU's greenest institution (see Chapter 8), this has not been evident in early discussions on the post-2004 EU budget. A report published by the European Parliament's Policy Challenges Committee, and adopted by the plenary in June 2011, was heavily criticized by environmental groups for failing to move the debate beyond the lowest common denominator (Birdlife, 2011; Mathews, 2011).

The Commission was due to publish its legislative proposals for the reform of the Common Agricultural Policy (CAP) in July 2011 but in the event these were delayed. These proposals will open the door for the European Parliament to push for a greener CAP in delivering environmental public goods. However, the European Parliament's Committee on Agriculture and Rural Development has been reported to be 'overwhelmingly in the hands of members [of the European Parliament] close to farm interests' (Zahrnt, 2011: 13). In addition, members of other Parliamentary committees also interested in the CAP (for example, the committees on budget, the environment, development and industry) have not (yet) challenged their colleagues on the agricultural committee (ibid.). A similar picture of the European Parliament favouring sectoral interests is also appearing with regard to the Common Fisheries Policy, which is due to be reformed in 2012. However, this could potentially change as both Green Party members and a new cross-party group 'Fish for the Future' have recently become more active (fishnewseu.com, 2011).

Participatory democracy

Finally, the much-vaunted European Citizens' Initiative (ECI) has taken time to get off the ground. The Commission published a draft regulation, setting out the rules and procedures for implementing this in March 2010 (European Commission, 2010c). However, it was not formally adopted until February 2011 (Regulation EU No. 211/2011), and then took a year until it could be applied. Therefore, the Commission only accepted petitions from 1 April 2012. Thus, it is still early days for the ECI, and it is difficult to say whether it will result in any new legislation with implications for the environment. That said, initial interest in the mechanism (including the first ever, unofficial, petition, see Box 3.2) indicates that it may yet become a useful tool for environmental lobby groups with extensive grassroots membership.

Box 3.2 A European Citizens' Initiative petition on GMOs

The first petition to collect the necessary one million signatures from citizens in at least seven member states was organized by Greenpeace, one of the largest campaigning environmental lobby groups in Brussels. The petition called for a moratorium on genetically modified crops until the 'health and environmental risk assessment is improved'. It was launched in March 2010 after the Commission had decided to authorize the cultivation of the genetically modified 'Amflora' potato. Although the petition was presented in December 2010 to the Health Commissioner John Dalli in the full glare of the media, it was never officially registered by the Commission because it was prior to the entry into force of the ECI Regulation. Whether the Commission eventually translates this demand (or any others) into legislation depends on whether the EU deems it has the competence to act and that the request is not contrary to 'EU values'. The Commission has already proposed a system where national bans against genetically modified crops authorized by the EU could be enacted, but this has been rejected by member states. If the Commission declines to act on it, it will have to explain why it has ignored one million signatures.

(European Commission, 2011); ENDS *Europe Daily*,
10 December 2010; Greenpeace, 2010)

Summary points

- Thus far, the impacts of the environmental innovations contained in Lisbon have been mixed.
- Few of the new treaty's innovations have radically strengthened EU policy in this area.
- Lisbon confirmed the maturity of the environmental sector. There was, for example, little radical expansion in the EU's powers. For example, the EU lacks coherence in international environmental negotiations

despite the presence of the new High Representative for Foreign Affairs and a new joint diplomatic service.
- However, there are already signs that the new European Citizens' Initiative is being employed to push policy agendas in a more environmental direction.

Lisbon: current and future perspectives

In our opening section we observed that the process to develop, agree and ratify the Lisbon Treaty was dominated by debates over its alleged negative implications for national sovereignty – fears that have largely subsided in the intervening period as more pressing concerns related to the very survival of European integration have emerged. We also argued that, in contrast, few analyses had been conducted on the treaty's implications for day-to-day activities in significant areas of EU policy such as the environment. So which innovations did Lisbon introduce and what have been their consequences for environmental politics, policy and governance?

Responding to these questions, the chapter identified several critical treaty changes related to the environment and explored their impacts since the ratification of Lisbon. When viewed through a liberal intergovernmentalist lens, treaty changes should represent 'grand bargains' made between national governments that then determine subsequent phases of integration in a rather straightforward and predictable fashion. In the case of Lisbon and the environment, this perspective can already be challenged. Few innovations introduced have had an immediately significant influence, although some, such as the ECI, have only just been formally agreed.

There are, however, two reasons to doubt that intergovernmentalists are completely right on this point (i.e. that treaty changes should represent 'grand bargains'). First, past treaty amendments have strongly influenced environmental politics, policy and governance over the long term (Weale, 1996). First impressions can, in other words, be deceiving. Measures such as the subsidiarity mechanism, the new Foreign Minister, the Parliament's increased powers and the ECI are yet to fully bed in. For the moment, therefore, we should reserve judgement. Lisbon does in theory enhance the Union's ability to address complex cross-scale problems such as unsustainable development and climate change; whether EU actors choose to utilize these new powers remains to be seen. Second, many of the most significant environmental policy innovations were introduced by earlier treaty amendments (see Chapter 1), most notably the Single European Act. As EU environmental policy has matured, treaty changes have undergone a temporal decay curve, with progressively less innovations being made. Lisbon may consequently have had less impact simply because there is less scope for radical change than there was ten or 20 years ago.

Summary points

- This chapter has identified several critical treaty changes related to the environment and explored their policy impact since 2009.
- These changes relate *inter alia* to EU legal principles, competences, institutions, procedures and the overall democratic legitimacy of the EU.
- While few innovations have yet to exert a significant and immediate influence, they may eventually have a lasting impact on EU environmental policy.

Key questions

1   Why was EU reform initiated so soon after the Nice Treaty?
2   Why did the proposed constitution prove so controversial in some member states?
3   What are the major implications of the Lisbon Treaty for EU environmental policy?
4   To what extent have changes introduced by Lisbon influenced environmental policy, politics and governance in practice?

Guide to further reading

- Piris (2010) provides one of the few easily accessible, non-legal texts available on the Lisbon Treaty, while Jordan and Fairbrass (2005) give an account of the Nice Treaty from an environmental point of view.
- For more legal accounts of the environmental dimensions of Lisbon and the doomed constitution, see Beyer *et al.* (2004) and Vedder (2010).
- Integration by stealth and the Monnet Method are tackled by leading political scientists such as Albert Weale (1999) and Giandomenico Majone (2009).

References

Benson, D. and Jordan A. (2010) 'European Union environmental policy after the Lisbon Treaty: plus ça change, plus c'est la même chose?' *Environmental Politics*, vol. 19, no. 3, pp. 468–474.

Benson, D. and Jordan, A. (2012) 'Sustaining the development of the European Union? Taking stock and looking forwards', in T. Coutto (ed.) *Environmental Politics and Policy*, Getulio Vargas Foundation (FGV), Rio de Janeiro.

Beyer, P., Coffey, C., Klasing, A. and von Homeyer, I. (2004) 'The Draft Constitution for Europe and the Environment', *European Environmental Law Review*, vol. 13, no. 7, pp. 218–224.

Birdlife (2011) *The SURE report on the Multi-Annual Financial Framework*, Birdlife International, Brussels, available at: www.birdlife.org/community/2011/05/the-sure-report-on-the-multi-annual-financial-framework-%E2%80%93-will-this-become-a-report-of-the-least-common-denominator/ (accessed 29 June 2011).

Council of the European Union (2008) *Consolidated Versions of the Treaty on European Union and the Treaty on the Functioning of the European Union*, Council of the European Union, Brussels.

Defra (Department of Environment, Food and Rural Affairs) (2011) *The Common Fisheries Policy*, Defra, London, available at: www.defra.gov.uk/environment/marine/cfp/ (accessed 29 June 2011).

ENDS, *Europe Daily*, available at: http://www.endseurope.com/.

European Commission (2010a) *What is the Difference between Europe 2020 and its Predecessor the Lisbon Strategy?* European Commission, Brussels, available at: http://ec.europa.eu/europe2020/services/faqs/index_en.htm (accessed 19 January 2011).

European Commission (2010b) 'Climate change: Cancún conference must mark significant step towards legally binding global climate framework', European Commission press release, 29 November 2010 (IP/10/1620), available at: http://europa.eu/rapid/press ReleasesAction.do?reference=IP/10/1620 (accessed 18 July 2011).

European Commission (2010c) *A Proposal for a Regulation on the European Citizens' Initiative* (COM (2010) 119), European Commission, Brussels.

European Commission (2011) *How Will the European Citizens' Initiative Work?* European Commission, Brussels, available at: http://ec.europa.eu/dgs/secretariat_general/citizens_ initiative/docs/eci_work_en.pdf (accessed 29 June 2011).

Farmer, A. (2011) *Manual of European Environmental Policy*, Taylor & Francis, London, available at: http://www.europeanenvironmentalpolicy.eu/ (accessed 10 October 2011).

fishnewseu.com (2011) 'Euro MPs warned of grim future for European fish stocks', available at: http://www.fishnewseu.com/latest-news/world/6052-euro-mps-warned-of-grim-future-for-european-fish-stocks.html (accessed 29 June 2011).

Follesdal, A. and Hix, S. (2006) 'Why there is a democratic deficit in the EU: a response to Majone and Moravcsik', *Journal of Common Market Studies*, vol. 44, no. 3, pp. 533–562.

Greenpeace (2010) 'ECI rules agreed. Now it's time to address first ever citizens' initiative on GMOs', press release, 15 December 2010, available at: www.greenpeace.org/eu-unit/en/News/2010/eci-rules-agreed-now-it-s-tim/ (accessed 29 June 2011).

Hildebrand, P.M. (2005) 'The European Community's environmental policy, 1957 to 1992: from incidental measures to an international regime?', in A.J. Jordan (ed.) *Environmental Policy in the European Union: Actors, Institutions and Processes*, 2nd edition, Earthscan, London, pp. 19–41.

Jordan, A.J. and Fairbrass, J. (2005) 'European Union environmental policy after the Nice Summit', in A.J. Jordan (ed.) *Environmental Policy in the European Union: Actors, Institutions and Processes*, 2nd edition, Earthscan, London.

Jordan, A.J. and Lenschow, A. (eds) (2008) *Innovation in Environmental Policy? Integrating the Environment for Sustainability,* Edward Elgar, Cheltenham.

Jordan, A.J., van Asselt, H., Berkhout, F., Huitema, D. and Rayner, T. (eds) (2010) *Climate Change Policy in the European Union*, Cambridge University Press, Cambridge.

Korhonen, K. (2011) 'Guardians of subsidiarity: national parliaments strive to control EU decision making', *FIIA Briefing Paper 84*, May 2011, The Finnish Institute of International Affairs, Helsinki.

Majone, G. (2009) *Europe as the Would-be World Power*, Cambridge University Press, Cambridge.

Mathews, A. (2011) 'European Parliament displays little courage in its report on the future EU budget', available at: http://capreform.eu/european-parliament-displays-little-courage-in-its-report-on-the-future-eu-budget/ (accessed 29 June 2011).

Màtlary, J.H. (1997) *Energy Policy in the European Union*, Macmillan, Basingstoke.

Moravcsik, A. (1998) *The Choice for Europe: Social Purpose and State Power from Messina to Maastricht*, UCL Press, London.

Myrdal, S. and Rhinard, M. (2010) 'The European Union's solidarity clause: empty letter or effective tool?' *UI Occasional Papers*, No. 2, Swedish Institute of International Affairs, Stockholm.

Pallemaerts, M. (2011) 'Climate change, natural gas and the rebirth of EU energy policy', in P. Winand (ed.) *Securing Sustainable Energy Supplies in Europe and Australia: Policy-Makers, Business, Scientists, NGOs on Energy and the Environmental Challenge*, PIE Peter Lang, Brussels.

Piris, J.C. (2010) *The Lisbon Treaty: A Legal and Political Analysis*, Cambridge University Press, Cambridge.

Pollack, M.A. (2000) 'The end of creeping competence? EU policy-making since Maastricht', *Journal of Common Market Studies*, vol. 38, no. 3, pp. 519–538.

Prodi, R. (2000) 'The State of the Union in 2000', speech delivered at the European Parliament, 13 February, European Parliament, Brussels.

van Ondarza, N. and Parkes, R. (2010) 'The EU in the face of disaster: implementing the Lisbon Treaty's solidarity clause', *SWP Comments* 9, German Institute for International and Security Affairs, Berlin, available at: www.swp-berlin.org/fileadmin/contents/products/comments/2010C09_orz_pks_ks.pdf (accessed 29 June 2011).

van Schaik, L. (2010) *The Dutch and European Contribution to International Climate Policy: Building Blocks for a Viable Strategy*, Climate, Energy, Environment and Water Department of the Netherlands Ministry of Foreign Affairs, The Hague, available at: www.clingendael.nl/publications/2010/20101100_CESP_paper_vanschaik.pdf (accessed 29 June 2011).

van Schaik, L. and Egenhofer, C. (2005) 'Improving the climate: will the new Constitution strengthen the EU's performance in international climate negotiations?' *CEPS Policy Brief*, No. 63, February, Centre for European Policy Studies, Brussels.

Vedder, H. (2010) 'The Treaty of Lisbon and European environmental law and policy', *Journal of Environmental Law*, vol. 22, no. 2, pp. 285–299.

Weale, A. (1996) 'Environmental rules and rule-making in the European Union', *Journal of European Public Policy*, vol. 3, no. 4, pp. 594–611.

Weale, A. (1999) 'European environmental policy by stealth: the dysfunctionality of functionalism?' *Environment and Planning C*, vol. 17, no. 1, pp. 37–51.

Zahrnt, V. (2011) 'A guide to CAP reform politics: issues, positions and dynamics', *ECIPE Working Paper* No. 03/2011, European Centre for International Political Economy, Brussels.

4 Studying EU environmental policy

Andrea Lenschow

Summary guide

Environmental policy has received tremendous attention from scholars, considering the relatively late appearance of this policy at EU level. Environmental policy analysis speaks to several much larger debates on the dynamics in EU policy making and the nature of the EU polity. These include understanding how and why this sector has developed as a policy area, the kind of instruments used to govern policy problems and their performance in ameliorating policy problems. The literature is divided into three analytical phases: the first deriving from an International Relations perspective; the second drawing on public policy approaches; and the third focusing on the 'bigger picture' of European governance. This chapter concludes that scholarship on EU environmental policy has not only contributed to general discussions in EU policy analysis, but on occasions has driven them.

Introduction

Environmental policy has received tremendous attention from EU scholars. Considering the relatively late appearance of this policy in the list of competences of the EU and its comparatively marginal status in the economy-dominated policy repertoire, this is notable. Numerous environmental crises and accidents exciting citizens and scholars alike since the 1970s, and the emergence of an environmental social movement in several European countries, may all be part of the explanation. Yet, even after green politics in Europe quietened and environmental policy gained a 'normal' status in the *acquis communautaire*, this attention never subsided. This chapter will argue that the study of environmental policy lends itself to contribute to several larger debates on the dynamics in EU policy making and the nature of the EU polity.

For policy analysts, three questions are of particular interest: (1) how did the policy emerge and develop as a policy area?; (2) what kind of decisions are being made?; and (3) how does the policy perform? Political scientists with a stronger interest in the political system of the EU, in turn, will wonder about the structures of governance that can be found in this policy area, and hence the relations between the different levels of the polity as well as patterns of public–private interactions.

With regard to EU environmental policy *per se*, we note: (1) its rapid expansion and step-wise institutionalization; (2) the agreement of regulatory standards often exceeding the so-called lowest common denominator (LCD) among the decision makers; and (3) nevertheless increasing concern about the effectiveness of the policy. In tackling these questions and searching for explanations, the literature on EU environmental policy may be divided into three analytical phases. First, research on environmental policy began from an international relations perspective, as was true for most EU-related analyses. The grand debate between inter-governmental and neo-functional approaches to explain integration processes framed initial investigations of the emergence and spread of the policy. However, the institutional and legal set-up of the EU, the single market as the main reference point for policy makers in all fields and the open constellation of actors joining together in policy making were soon identified as clearly distinct from international organizations or regimes, and analysts began to look for the characteristics of the domestic politics of the EU. In this second phase, authors borrowed conceptual vocabulary from especially institutional, ideational and policy network approaches (for the general analytical turn, see Peterson, 2001: 300ff).

Methodologically, EU environmental policy research during these first two phases was dominated by individual or comparative case studies. Those interested in the big picture of EU politics and polity development – in particular, scholars outside the public policy community – may have been disenchanted by the bias towards piecemeal and rather microscopic investigations of single policy items or limited instances of environmental pollution. But arguably, in recent years we have entered a third phase in researching EU environmental policy, which shifts attention towards the bigger picture of European governance. EU governance, understood as a particular rule-making structure consisting of multiple layers, is characterized by policy fragmentation, and sits on shaky democratic grounds. Triggered by the performance question, the analysis of EU environmental policy pinpointed the close connection between policy reforms, and polity features and dynamics. The process of policy making and the choices of policy instruments in the environmental field indicate novel features in the EU polity, namely, the rise of less hierarchical relations in governing the Union and shifts in the balance between public and private actors. Notably, these governance implications are not limited to Brussels, but reach upward to the international level as well as downward to the national and regional levels. The influential book-length study of EU environ-mental policy making and the emergence of diverse policy styles in the policy repertoire by Héritier and her colleagues (1994; 1996) first signified this change of perspective.

This chapter is structured into three parts. Part one will review the literature on the emergence of the policy and highlight the turn from integration to domestic theories. Part two will turn to the question of environmental policy performance, identifying three different perspectives that have been adopted in the literature – investigating the level of regulation, implementation and effectiveness. Finally, this chapter establishes the link between environmental policy making and the more general process of a European polity making. It is my intention to show that scholarship on EU environmental policy has not only picked up general discussions on EU policy making and integration, but it has also been a driver for entering new debates.

Emergence and expansion of the policy: moving from niches to centre stage

Environmental policy initially was not among the range of competences that the Treaty of Rome originally attributed to the European Communities (see Chapters 1 and 2). Nevertheless, European environmental policy was arguably already founded in the 1960s when directives were adopted to deal with dangerous substances, noise and exhaust emissions of motor vehicles. In fact, the literature identifies several periods in the process of environmental policy expansion and institutionalization. During the 'founding period' from 1957 to 1972 (Zito, 1999: 24) a few 'incidental measures' were passed (Hildebrand, 1993: 17). The second period began with the adoption of the first (non-obligatory) environmental action programme in 1972; until 1987, 118 major new pieces of environmental legislation were adopted (Jordan *et al.*, 1999: 382) amounting to the early institutionalization of the policy field. EU environmental policy spread to cover all environmental media (air, water, soil) and major problem areas (such as waste, dangerous substances/chemicals, nature protection, etc.). The year 1987 was a watershed in the evolution of European environmental policy in the sense that the Single European Act (SEA) formally included environmental policy in the range of Community competencies, ending ambiguities as to the judicial status of environmental measures (see also Chapter 2). Subsequently, until the early 1990s, the number of newly adopted pieces of legislation sky-rocketed and the annual rate of major innovations rose to around 10 (Jordan *et al.*, 1999: 383). The notion of the EU as a regulatory state reflects this growth of regulatory policy competency (Majone, 1996). Also, thereafter the total number of new adoptions continued to be high (Haigh, 2004), but the 'high-water mark' (Zito, 1999: 28) for the passage of truly new and major items has now passed. Arguably, since the formulation of the Fifth Environmental Action Programme of the EU in 1992, the focus has begun to shift to selected priority areas (such as climate change or biodiversity), to attempts at streamlining or improving existing policies (e.g. in the field of water protection) and to mainstreaming environmental objectives in EU policy making (see Chapter 13).

In tracing the analytical accounts for this process of expansion and institutionalization of European environmental policy, I shall argue that we can see a shift from integration to domestic politics theories; the latter, in turn, may be roughly divided into actor-oriented and institutionally oriented approaches.

Integration theories

While early scholarship on EU environmental policy in the 1980s was mostly devoted to the description of the emerging policy field and its ambiguous legal basis (Rehbinder and Stewart, 1985; Johnson and Corcelle, 1989), the history of quantitative and qualitative expansion of EU environmental policy constituted the first big theoretical puzzle for scholars in this field. It was first approached from an integration theory perspective, following either (liberal) intergovernmentalist or neofunctionalist lines of argument. Jonathan Golub most strongly took the inter-governmentalist position. Analysing the process of adopting the packaging waste directive (Golub, 1996a), he found that attempts by supranational and societal actors to influence the policy-making process did not translate into real power, capable of moving member states to change policy positions. Hence, intergovern-mental bargaining in the Council resulted in a directive reflecting the lowest common denominator (see also Huelshoff and Pfeiffer, 1991, for a similar assess-ment). In his work on the UK's role in EU environmental policy making, Golub maintains that concerns for the protection of national interests and state sover-eignty have determined British behaviour in EU policy negotiations (Golub, 1996b), and presumably the behaviour of other member states as well.

The intergovernmentalist paradigm did not gain any dominance in explaining environmental policy making in the EU, however, not least because the rather remarkable expansion of the field did not usually come at the price of LCD decisions. State-centred analyses more generally did seek to resolve this puzzle, however. Such studies pointed to the interesting pattern of green member states (Liefferink and Andersen, 1998), that is 'pioneers' (Andersen and Liefferink, 1997) or 'leaders' (Héritier, 1996; Sbragia, 1996), successfully pushing for the adoption of strict regulation. The influential study by Héritier and her associates (1996) on the adoption process of several environmental directives and regulations identified first moving member states as being able to set the European policy agenda and to strongly influence regulatory style and standards in the legislation to be decided. Duncan Liefferink and Mikael Skou Andersen later refined the first mover terminology by distinguishing: (1) between direct pushing of environmental policy and indirect strategies, typically via the internal market policies, as well as (2) purposeful approaches which are clearly directed at the EU level and incremental action rooted in domestic politics (1998: 256ff).

Neofunctional theory was the second large point of reference in the earlier accounts of the development of EU environmental policy. But rarely was neo-functionalism treated as a coherent explanatory framework. In light of the peak of environmental policy adoptions following the single market programme, some authors identified the functional link between market integration and the harmon-ization of national environmental (or other regulatory) policy as one important explanatory factor, in the sense that European regulation served to level the playing field for national producers (e.g. Weale, 1999). Most scholars writing in the tradition of neofunctionalism took functional pressure as a given, however, and concentrated on actor-centred push factors. A case in point were the contributions of an activist European Court of Justice (ECJ) (see Chapter 7), which had interpreted the treaty framework in an expansionist fashion and allowed environmental policy to enter the Community *acquis* by way of reference to functional linkages with already established competences of the Community (Koppen, 1993). Similarly, the Environmental Directorate General of the European Commission had been building a role for itself by searching for new policy niches, exploiting political windows of opportunity for policy expansion and forming green alliances within the institutional framework of the EU (e.g. Weale and Williams, 1993: 61; Sbragia, 2000) (see also Chapter 6). Also the second entrepreneurial organ, the European Parliament, received much attention (Judge, 1993; Judge *et al.*, 1994; Bomberg and Burns, 1999) (see also Chapter 8), insisting both on progressive environmental regulation (and implementation) as well as on being given the institutional powers to intervene. These studies shared the theoretical interest in establishing some link between functional expansion and the more general European integration project.

The well-known criticism of the neofunctionalist paradigm as exaggerating the linear progression for task expansion has been voiced with regard to environmental policy analyses as well. Furthermore, the interest in such progression began to fade after environmental policy was firmly established as a policy field in the EU and the institutional co-evolution – in the form of extending the rule of qualified majority voting (QMV) to most aspects of environmental policy and expanding parliamentary powers first to cooperation (Maastricht), then to co-decision powers (Amsterdam) – slowly came to a close. Analytical attention shifted from macroscopic views of the development of the policy area as a whole to more detailed studies of the policy-making process within EU institutions and between the EU level, member states and societal actors.

Organized interests, policy networks and epistemic communities

While green political parties are widely ignored in the investigation of EU environmental policy making (see below), environmental interest groups are not (Hull, 1993; Mazey and Richardson, 1993; Hey and Brendle, 1994; Webster, 1998) (see also Chapter 9). In part, the literature on lobbying and the influence of interest groups is framed as a critique of state-centric accounts. Environmental groups were shown to shape the policy agenda in Brussels and influence the decision-making process, using a mix of strategies, ranging from political pressure and campaigns to the provision of policy advice and information. Case studies, for instance, on the formulation of car emission policy, the greening of the structural funds or the Union's marine policy (cf. Arp, 1993; Long, 1995; Lenschow, 1997; Heard and Richards, 2005), highlight how environmental groups managed to mobilize member states sympathetic to their concerns, raise awareness of environmental problems inside the Commission and even shift the balance of interests inside the Parliament. The emergence of Eurogroups in Brussels, typically organizing as a network of nationally organized NGOs, and their close interaction with the supranational organs of the Community, have been read as supporting neofunctionalist theory and suggesting that interest groups would form in response to functional spillover and play a central role in European political integration.

Increasingly, attention shifted towards the structure of interest intermediation in the EU, however, and with it to the literature of comparative politics. The study of environmental policy raised the issue of the relative influence of diffuse interests, vis-à-vis the presumably privileged and better organized business interests (see Chapter 10). Mollifying normative concerns about biased representation, scholars were pointed to the existence of multiple access points in the EU system (Pollack, 1997), sympathetic EU institutional actors (Marks and McAdam, 1996) and the ample opportunities to make use of and even change often instable interest constellations inside Community organs or even within the business community. It is in this context that the analysis of interest intermediation in the EU is frequently mixed with reflections on the role of ideas and discourses. It was shown that common interests between previously adversarial business and environmental groups emerged due to novel discourses on 'ecological modernization' (Weale, 1992; Hajer, 1995), sustainable development (Lenschow, 1999) (see also Chapter 19) or policy specific frame shifts leading to a reinterpretation of policy positions among core actors (cf. Jachtenfuchs, 1996; Lenschow and Zito, 1998). Such frame shifts relied on the power of ideas at least as much as political networking and pressure.

Organizationally, environmental groups have adapted to the framework of interest intermediation in the EU by forming a grand coalition and coordinating their activities in order to handle the workload and appear as cohesive as possible (Hey and Brendle, 1994; Webster, 1998). Indeed, Sonja Mazey and Jeremy Richardson argue that 'groups lobbying in this [i.e., the environment] sector face the same range of opportunities as other groups' in the EC and that, apart from the need to deal with more dispersed and more informal policy-making processes in the EU, the same 'fundamental rules of the game' apply as do in national political systems (Mazey and Richardson, 1993: 109–110).

Taking a broader perspective on green politics, however, and inquiring into the capacities or intentions of European groups and political parties to mobilize a larger public for environmental objectives, the differences between the EU and national systems are striking. Looking at parliamentary structures first, it is notable that the activities of the Environment Committee received more attention than the contributions of the green party group within the Parliament (but see Bomberg, 1998a). The strong representation of the Green Party (or Parties) in the Parliament and its influence in policy making have been reflected surprisingly little – in part, of course, because this representation indeed may have little to do with an EU-wide green mobilization but rather with the nature of European elections as largely second-order national contests (see also Chapter 8).

Furthermore, there is no evidence of a (green) social movement emerging transnationally (Imig and Tarrow, 2000; Rucht, 2001). Rather, the multi-level system seems characterized by a division of labour, with environmental groups in Brussels following the more technocratic traits of policy making, whereas national groups are more strongly grounded in society. This structure, of course, mirrors the elitist and technocratic bias in the neofunctionalist vision of integration: green voters or environmental movements do not push environmental policy forward in the EU; networks of self-declared policy advocates do. These networks are formed either on the basis of exchange relations with actors interacting strategically, or they reflect ties that are based on shared core beliefs (Sabatier, 1998) and may even result in the formation of epistemic communities (Zito, 2001).

Institutional perspectives

In light of the dramatic expansion of EU policy, the emphasis on the functional pull–push for environmental policy is not surprising. But there have been both empirical and analytical reasons to investigate the impact of institutional structures as well. Empirically, authors wondered about the real impact of institutional reforms on environmental policy making. The environmental policy field has been an interesting test case, given the gradual institutional co-evolution already mentioned. Did it make a difference to establish a *de jure* status for a *de facto* policy? Did QMV ease negotiations in the Council, contributing to more and faster decision making? What has been the impact of the expanded legislative competencies of the Parliament? The impact of the institutional framework on actors' strategies has been quite evident. Hence, in the period between the introduction of the environment title into the treaty in 1987 and the extension of QMV to environmental policy, treaty games became a feature of policy making, with the Commission avoiding the procedurally less favourable environmental Articles (ex) 130 r–t and continuing the market route to environmental policy (via ex Article 100a) (Hildebrand, 1993; Hovden, 2002). This institutional mess was resolved in subsequent treaty reforms (Wilkinson, 1992; Jordan 1998), assisted by Court rulings supporting the pro-integrationist strategies of the Commission and the Parliament (Koppen, 1993). Most authors reflecting on the increasing embeddedness of environmental policy imply institutional lock-in effects.

A more complex picture emerges with regard to the impact of institutional changes on the efficiency of decision making and the empowerment of the Parliament (Andersen and Rasmussen, 1998; Jordan et al., 1999; Kasack, 2004). Reflecting on post-Maastricht expectations that decision making in environmental policy would ease, due to the spread of QMV and the introduction of co-decision making, Jordan and Liefferink (2004) detect no uniform pattern or trend in the efficiency of decision making across policy sub-areas. Mikael Skou Andersen and Lise Nordwig Rasmussen (1998) show that co-decision making counteracts the efficiency gains of QMV. Christiane Kasack (2004) finds that the simplification of the co-decision procedure in the Amsterdam Treaty did not increase adoption rates either; nor did it further empower the Parliament. The impact of the Nice Treaty – placing the large member states in a more powerful position and lowering the threshold for reaching decisions – still needs to be researched, although arguably it will be the increased membership of the EU and not the reformed procedures that will produce the most notable impact (Homeyer et al., 2000;

Jordan and Fairbrass, 2001) (see also Chapter 3 for an analysis of the impact of the Nice and Lisbon Treaties).

Besides these links between the institutional and procedural treaty reforms and changes in policy making as well as output, the more stable system characteristics of the EU have also been shown to impact on policy making. This literature is more strongly embedded in a meta-debate on the distinct nature of the political system of the EU and its effects on actors' identities, interests and values, and hence both political strategies and policy choices. Here, environmental policy studies serve as illustrations for broader arguments. Hence, we learn about the peculiar institution of the EU presidency with its implications for European policy agendas (Andersen and Rasmussen, 1998) (see also Chapter 11) and as triggers of European thinking in the governments holding the chair (Wurzel, 1996). Albert Weale more pessimistically reflects on the EU 'system of concurrent majorities' (1996: 594) where agreement is needed by a high proportion of participants extending from Commission, Council and Parliament to functional constituencies. Accordingly, he suggests that system characteristics lead important decisions to fail or to be reached at suboptimal levels. This is especially evident with regard to coordination with other policy sectors such as transport, industry and agriculture. My studies and those of others (Lenschow, 1999; 2002a) highlight similar structural constraints, although showing a slightly less gloomy picture. While both the institutional (that is, fragmented) and the normatively market-biased structure of the EU pose severe constraints on policy coordination, there are limits to a complete policy lock-in at the sectoral level (see Chapter 13). Héritier (1997) attributes these limits most pointedly to 'strategies of subterfuge' in a fluid polity, giving rise to informal politics.

All in all, the puzzle of task expansion in the environmental policy field has been tackled using a range of theoretical approaches, both from the European integration school and the canon of comparative politics and policy making more generally. Given the dynamic and sometimes unexpected evolution of the policy, these studies helped advance theoretical debate more generally. Nevertheless, I shall argue below that truly novel and innovative perspectives were developed with respect to other empirical questions and puzzles.

The performance of the policy: high standards, but poor implementation?

Public policy derives much of its legitimacy from solving problems, although the assessment of problem-solving capacity and effectiveness may be a complex matter. The effectiveness of EU environmental policy has been analysed from three perspectives: (1) investigating the level of environmental standards defined by EU decision makers; (2) analysing policy compliance and implementation; and (3) questioning the merits of traditional regulatory instruments. This succession of perspectives implies an increasing reflection on the nature of the multi-level system of the EU. At the same time, it is evident that the analysis of environmental outcomes is largely neglected by political scientists and instead left to other disciplines.

Regulatory standards and regulatory competition

Task expansion in the field of European environmental policy can only be meaningful from a problem-solving perspective if the agreements that have been reached in Brussels change the status quo, are capable of protecting the environment and reduce existing pollution levels and harmful practices. The literature on the forms and strictness of EU environmental regulation can be divided into two strands, elaborating on different competitive dynamics among member states.

One point of departure is the economic theory of regulatory competition (e.g. Oates and Schwab, 1988; van Long and Siebert, 1991), which is applied to regulatory policy generally and predicts a race to the bottom in cases where national barriers to trade are removed. National producers encounter international competitors who may benefit from less rigid – and hence less costly – regulatory conditions at home. In the name of international competitiveness, high regulating states are expected to reduce the regulatory burden on their national industry. EU environmental policy serves to lower such competitive pressure and corresponding transaction costs among member states. Assuming that the competitive logic nevertheless still applies to the process of setting EU standards, the theory expects LCD decisions.

Neither internationally (Vogel, 1995; Jänicke, 1998; Drezner, 2001) nor in the EU (Holzinger, 1994; Eichener, 1997; Scharpf, 1997) does the literature find much empirical support for races to the bottom, however. Staying within the rationalist and state-centric paradigm, Fritz Scharpf (1997) advanced the theory of regulatory competition by systematically modelling negotiation situations with respect to the distinction between product and production (or process) standards. The theory now predicts high(er) environmental product standards in the EU because previously low regulating states face the credible threat of trade barriers if they insist on their low standards. The option of declining market entry does not exist in the EU with respect to non-product standards and hence the theory predicts either fairly low minimum standards or the failure to reach any agreement. The empirical test ends inconclusively, however. On the one hand, we see a clear dominance of product over production standards in EU environmental policy; also, EU product standards typically exceed the LCD level. Running counter to these expectations are the fair number of non-product directives on matters such as environmental impact assessments, public access to information, ecological auditing or the protection of flora, fauna and natural habitats that have been passed in the EU at demanding levels for member states (Héritier *et al.*, 1996; Knill and Lenschow, 1998). Hence, there is still reason to puzzle.

Surveying the literature, we find general and EU-specific attempts to explain these patterns. Holzinger (2002) and Thomas Bernauer with Ladina Caduff (2004) alert us to the need to investigate the real cost of regulation and the social context in which it may be imposed. The assumption that the preferences of cost-bearing producers determine the negotiation position of governments certainly ignores that environmental regulation creates benefits as well as costs for a society. The business community may be too heterogeneous and interest group politics too influential to generalize state positions simply on the basis of the regulatory status quo and the competitive situation of the country. Also, the EU is not easily comparable to other international cooperative settings such as the World Trade Organization (WTO). During the pre-decision-making phase the central role of bureaucratic working groups and of independent advisory committees frames decision making along technocratic and scientific as opposed to competitive lines (Eichener, 1997; for a different assessment, see Andersen and Rasmussen, 1998). Not least, the option of QMV and the greater legislative role of the Parliament tend to operate against LCD dynamics.

Novel in the analysis of EU policy making has been the observation of environmental policy scholars that member states may not only compete over standards but also over regulatory styles and approaches. Hence, the traditional dominance of a legalistic policy style and technology-based policy solutions in the EU has been attributed to Germany winning the (implicit) competition over setting the environmental policy agenda in Brussels, whereas the emergence of procedural standards in the EU repertoire has been credited to the UK's waking up to EU policy making (Knill, 1995; Héritier *et al.*, 1996; Jordan, 2002). In short, besides acting in the interest of economic competitiveness, member states follow a second logic of regulatory competition, namely to keep legal and administrative adaptation costs related to implementing EU regulation at a minimum. They may therefore pursue a first mover strategy and attempt to shuttle national policy makers into influential positions inside the Commission, in order to push national models onto the EU agenda. Consequently, we find types of regulatory policy (such as production and process standards) and levels of standards in the EU repertoire that would not have been expected from a narrow, economic regulatory competition perspective.

Policy compliance and implementation

There may be yet another reason for high and wide-ranging regulatory standards in the EU. Patterns of lax implementation could explain member states' acceptance of potentially costly regulation (Macrory, 1992; Eichener, 1997; Jordan, 1999) (see also Chapter 14). Implementation deficits, in turn, are linked to weak enforcement mechanisms in the EU. Underscoring this point, some authors have compared the EU to international regimes in policy implementation (Skjærseth and Wettestad, 2002). Although the EU clearly differs from regimes in adopting legally binding directives and regulations, it lacks the capacity to control practical implementation, as well as effective sanctioning mechanisms. Hence, similar to regimes, it relies on softer social practices. These, however, may be particularly effective given the close and iterative decision-making context in the EU (cf. Young and Levy, 1999). Regime scholars therefore tend to view the EU as a model structure featuring institutional characteristics to which regimes might aspire or as a test case for regime-theoretic propositions.

Such social practices fail if either the problem structure or the interest constellation prohibits good policy that may be implemented effectively. The environmental problem at hand may be too complex, involving too many uncertainties or invoking too many contrasting opinions for decision makers to produce consistent and potentially effective negotiation results. Regime theorists would acknowledge the Council of Ministers to be vulnerable to such constellations like any other intergovernmental settings. They would expect the social capacity to overcome disagreement to be larger in the Council than in international regimes, however. Critical 'insider' observers of EU policy making, by contrast, have gone so far as to argue that implementation failure tends to be encoded in the decision-making practices in the EU (Weale *et al.*, 2000: 296ff). Commission activism, symbolic politics in the Council and missing enforcement capacities have resulted in a long-lasting neglect of this part of the policy cycle (Jordan, 1999: 74; similarly Collins and Earnshaw, 1993; Snyder, 1993; Tallberg, 1999). Arguably, this neglect is mirrored in the presentation of the data on (non-)compliance which have been claimed to produce statistical artefacts (Börzel, 2001). But, these records are likely to underestimate the real extent of implementation failures as the problems coming to the attention of the Commission or the Court are strongly biased towards non-reporting or the incorrect transposition of EU directives into national law. They take too lightly the problems of practical implementation on the ground.

Recent implementation research has begun to focus on the issue of deficient practical implementation and identified the preference for top-down steering as a possible cause. Arguably, the dominant hierarchical and non-discretionary policy style at the EU level is not only the result of first mover successes of countries with legalistic regulatory preferences like Germany, but is more systemic in nature. As long as the market rationale of levelling the (regulatory) playing field for producers acts as a main motive for EU environmental policy, there will be some tendency to harmonize national standards. Second, non-discretionary measures may replace high levels of trust, especially in times of rising and increasingly heterogeneous membership, and help the Commission to compensate for weak enforcement structures (cf. Kelemen, 2000). Such top-down regulatory style, however, necessarily causes problems of implementation in a heterogeneous setting like the EU. Obligations formulated on the EU level may not fit into national legal and administrative systems and may overtax local capacities or willingness to adapt (Knill and Lenschow, 1998; 2000; Börzel, 2000). We may face a real dilemma in EU environmental governance! This issue was further pursued in two directions. First, it was deemed worthwhile investigating the pro-claimed shift towards new, softer and more flexible policy instruments. Second, the notion of fit (or misfit) between EU and national structures became influential in 'Europeanization' research more generally.

Choice of policy instruments and modes of governance

The discussion of soft modes of governance is very much *en vogue* in EU politics and academic reflection, generally. Often this discussion focuses on the intro-duction of the open method of coordination (OMC) in social policy. However, soft modes have spread widely and environmental policy has been an early field for experimentation. Here, the term 'new instruments' signifies the move to a more cooperative, less hierarchical governance approach and may be divided in two classes. Economic instruments cover eco-taxes, emission fees, emission certificates, state subsidies, tradable permits and the like. Context-oriented regulation subsumes procedural law (i.e. information and participation rights) as well as cooperative or non-binding agreements between private and state actors or among private actors (see also Chapter 17). Both forms emphasize the responsiveness to local conditions. Flexibility (not uniformity), participation (not top-down command) and learning (not sanctioning) are some keywords characterizing this new philosophy. Implementation gaps and evidence of deficient effectiveness of EU policy had raised concerns about the dominant hierarchical and legalistic style. Post-Maastricht debates about subsidiarity (Collier *et al.*, 1993; Golub, 1996c), and the emergence of a global deregulatory trend, contributed to the reform agenda. Yet, national policy innovations including environmental incentive systems (e.g. eco-taxes and charges), information tools (e.g. eco-labels, eco-management) and greater involvement of private actors (by way of participation, co-regulation or self-regulation) provided the models for EU-level proposals (Golub, 1998; Mol *et al.*, 2000; De Clercq, 2002; Jordan *et al.*, 2003). In quantitative terms, few so-called new policy instruments have been adopted so far (Héritier, 2002; Holzinger *et al.*, 2003). Nevertheless, quantitative data do not capture the varied scope of old and new policy instruments, with old-style instruments typically being much more specific than new incentive or information tools which aim at broader behavioural change (see Chapter 17).

A more critical question concerns the effectiveness of these new instruments, which returns us to the implementation literature. This literature hinted that the widely assumed superiority of bottom-up or new approaches rests on very demanding assumptions. The fact that new instruments allow for more discretion and flexibility does not mean that they are easier to handle. The contrary may be the case – particularly in countries with hierarchical legal and administrative cultures (Knill and Lenschow, 2000). Furthermore, information and voluntary instruments strongly rely on the responsiveness of societal actors and some level of environmental mobilization; they are incapable of building such societal structures from scratch (Börzel, 2000). Moreover, national experience with softer modes of governance suggests the need for some shadow of the hierarchy in order to keep actors committed to the policy objectives (Mayntz and Scharpf, 1995; De Clercq, 2002). For the future of EU environmental governance, this points to the need for complementary instruments, mixing top-down and bottom-up elements (Hey *et al.*, 2005). It also calls on the Commission to supervise new instruments, and hence develop new managerial capacities in Brussels. Will centralization be the consequence of new, softer regulation? This rather paradoxical prospect – if true – may take us out of the dilemma identified above and poses an interesting avenue for future research. It also leads us to wider considerations of the system – as opposed to merely tools – of (environmental) governance in the EU.

Policy making as polity-in-the-making

We saw that the initial concern with European policies grew from a much wider interest in European integration. The rise of policy competences in Brussels and the strengthening of supranational elements were taken as evidence of a European polity in the making. Recent scholarship on European environmental policy making returns to the polity issue from a policy-up perspective. In a more open-ended way it asks how policy making interacts with the development of the political system of the EU. There are three dimensions to this development. First, policy making not only reflects but also shapes governance structures in the EU. Second, EU policy making and policies impact on the member states, both as actors involved in policy formulation and implementation and as political systems. Third, the EU has appeared as a new actor in international environmental politics and is potentially changing international governance. This final part will consider these polity dynamics in turn.

The Brussels perspective

When we speak of an EU polity, we have not yet specified what kind of polity is emerging in Europe. The term 'governance structure', which is often used to characterize the EU system, conveys that we are not faced with a state, but with a less formal and less hierarchical political structure. Such structures require new forms of coordination to bridge potential gaps between vertical levels and across horizontal fields of governance, as well as between public and private actors (see Chapter 13). Earlier I referred to the network concept as highlighting the range of actors and their interactions in EU policy making. Increasingly – and especially in the continental European literature – networks are looked at as elements of such a governance structure. This concept is used to capture the fluid forms connecting a multitude of actors in the EU generally (Peterson, 2004) and with respect to environmental policy making in particular (Héritier *et al.*, 1996; Bomberg, 1998b). Nevertheless, the network terminology is too encompassing to account for the very different constellations that have emerged in the environmental policy field. It also sidelines the one hierarchical structure that does prevail in EU environmental policy, namely, the law. Below I will characterize the constellation of networks as it emerges from the literature on environmental policy.

We first observe informal and open networks particularly in the early policy formulation phase, when a wide range of interested parties might form (temporary) alliances to shape the problem perception among policy makers in Brussels and propose suitable solutions. This network formation is helped by the open structure of especially the Commission, allowing easy access to policy advocates (see Chapter 9). The small size of the Commission and its dependence on external information, on the one hand, and the Commission's power of policy initiative on the other hand, create the resource interdependence that has been argued to be the logical core to policy network building.

Second, we see more narrow, technocratic and stable forms of elite networks and policy communities, which become involved in the actual policy setting and implementation. These tend to be orchestrated top-down, serving the interests of the member states and the Commission. We find policy-specific networks including Commission officials and national administrators bridging the gap between EU law making and its local application. They have the double function of advising policy makers on what is feasible on the ground and in raising the level of acceptance among the policy receivers. For instance, the implementation network of Commission officials and representatives of relevant national (or local) authorities (IMPEL) has become an important forum for considering the technical, administrative and cultural feasibility of EU environmental proposals early in the game as well as for improving the capacity and willingness of local implementers through the exchange of experiences (cf. Dehousse, 1992: 391). Especially the comitology committees, which are composed of member states and Commission representatives and assist the Commission in the development of implementation regulation, must be understood as bridges between the levels of political authority (Töller, 2002).

Third, increasingly we see private stakeholder involvement taking new forms. It was already hinted in the previous part that new modes of governance are emerging as alternatives to legally binding environmental law, introducing elements of private and corporatist-style governance operating in a shadow of hierarchy. In the area of technical standards and norms the EU has firmly institutionalized a new approach of regulated self-regulation (Voelzkow, 1996; Egan, 2001) by delegating responsibilities to European standards bodies. We also observe increasing experiments with self- and co-regulatory environmental agreements of corporate actors. While some of these voluntary agreements merely serve as a bridge 'to initiate European policy making in areas previously entirely reserved to member states' (Héritier 2002: 195), the development of public–private partnerships and their implications for traditional governance in the EU will be important to watch. These forms most closely correspond to the network governance as described by Beate Kohler-Koch (1999: 25f), with the state acting as mediator or activator and actors negotiating as equal partners. Notions of equal, non-hierarchical partnerships must not blind anyone to the fact that these are rather exclusive public (in the case of comitology) or public–private networks. While they may be capable of closing the gap between the administrative and private (typically industry) addressees of European environmental policy, such networks raise democratic concerns. In the environmental field the Parliament, as well as the non-business European NGO community, has started to mobilize against such governance structures privileging technocratic elites and corporate actors, insisting on either parliamentary control or more inclusive network structures (see Chapter 18).

When environmental policy is analysed as an area involving horizontal interdependencies, network governance assumes yet other characteristics. In this perspective, environmental policy depends on sectoral decision makers – for instance, in transport or energy policy – integrating environmental objectives into their respective policies. Environmental policy can thus only be effective if it is successfully mainstreamed. But such environmental policy integration (EPI) faces the same cognitive and institutional constraints as other forms of mainstreaming. Comparing the EPI process in the reforms of the regional development fund, the cohesion funds and the common agricultural policy (CAP), I have argued that deeply embedded policy-specific norms – e.g. associating environmental problems with smokestack industries or (regional) development with large investment projects – have prevented sectoral policy makers from perceiving environmental destruction as their problem. Sectoral perceptions were reinforced by segmented legal and institutional structures (e.g., the Cohesion Fund being formally linked to the Economic and Monetary Union convergence criteria) and closed policy communities (Lenschow, 1997). In recent years there have been attempts at macro-planning EPI within the European Council which have called on many Directorates General in the Commission to develop sectoral integration strategies, targets and timetables and to identify best practice examples. These macro strategies mirror soft governance like the OMC within EU institutions (Lenschow, 2002b). However, these initiatives rely too naïvely on the sectors to self-organize cross-sectoral networks (Schout and Jordan, 2005: 218) and develop the skill of horizontal coordination. Policy actors have little intrinsic motivation and perceive neither real pressure nor incentives to build bridges connecting formerly separate policy sectors. The analysis of EPI hints that in the absence of hierarchical pressure, soft governance at the macrolevel needs to be accompanied by management at the meso- and micro-levels in order to produce the intended learning and reform processes.

In sum, the network metaphor has facilitated understanding various dynamics between policy making and building a governance system. While networks are built in light of the opportunities and constraints created by the institutional framework as well as the interests of central actors in the EU governance structure, they also become characteristic elements of the polity in the making. While networks responding to the vertical interdependencies in the EU come with a strong elitist and technocratic accent, networks to overcome horizontal fragmentation are still in their infancy, inhibited by strong institutional and cognitive barriers.

The member state perspective

Recent years have seen intense discussions about Europeanization, broadly defined as the impact of EU policies and polity structures on domestic structures. Research on environmental policy has been a main contributor to this literature, arguably it has even been a front runner. There have been two sides to environmental Europeanization research: on the one hand, authors investigate the processes of member states – mostly governments and executives – learning to play the European policy game (see also Chapter 5). National adaptation processes are observed in order to better understand the policy patterns emerging in Brussels. The 1996 study by Héritier and her associates falls into this category; it explains the patchwork of European environmental policy with member states adjusting strategies and membership identities to the challenges of policy making and implementation. Historically the most interesting case has been the UK, which moved from a passive to a pro-active role implying far-reaching learning processes inside the executive (Jordan, 2002). Germany, by contrast, had understood the first mover advantage early, yet may have failed to consolidate this position by, for instance, developing a European personnel policy. Petr Jehlička and Andrew Tickle (2004) raise the interesting question of how the new Eastern European members of the EU will play the game and what consequences this might have for future EU environmental policy. On the basis of expert interviews, they identify two slightly contradictory patterns, namely, passivity and reactivity, on the one hand, and support for new policy instruments and more effective policy integration, on the other hand (see also Schreurs, 2004). The first pattern is expected by many, given that environmental policy does not rank high on the priority list of national policy makers in Eastern Europe. The consequence would be a slow-down and potential renationalization of EU environmental policy making (cf. Homeyer *et al.*, 2000). The second pattern can be understood as aspects of the process of emancipation from an authoritarian past and a spreading liberal ideology. Whether it will be sustained depends on the capacity of these states to implement these soft and discretionary instruments, which – as outlined above – assume a certain level of societal responsiveness and organizational flexibility.

Most recent literature takes Europeanization as the dependent variable; hence it adopts the second image-reversed perspective to understand transformations of national governance or policy. Generally, this literature is dominated by institutional perspectives emphasizing the constraints to national adaptations. It comes in several distinct variants: the keywords are (mis)fit, veto points and capacities. EU environmental policy typically takes the form of a directive that needs to be transposed by national legislatures, and regardless of the type of instrument, it usually requires public administrations to implement it on the ground. The extent and timing of implementation, but also the exact shape that is given to the policy, therefore depend on the performance of legislative and administrative actors. The analysis of veto points gives us a good idea of the procedural hurdles a directive needs to take and the potential that it is blocked, delayed or implemented in a minimalist fashion (cf. Haverland, 2000). The concepts of fit and misfit alert us to the fact that EU directives may not pose the same legislative and administrative adaptation challenge to all member states. The argument is that legislators and administrators tend to resist high adaptation requirements and hence extensive Europeanization especially if the core of pre-existing and potentially affected policies and administrative procedures is institutionally deeply embedded and stable (Knill and Lenschow, 1998, 2000; Knill, 2001).

The analysis of institutional (mis-)fit and of the impact of administrative capacities – which has become particularly topical since the 2004 expansion of the EU (cf. Carmin and Vandeveer, 2004; Homeyer, 2004) – makes explicit the close relationship between the Europeanization of policy and that of governance structures such as legal traditions, administrative structures, procedures and interest intermediation. This goes beyond the more narrow concern of implementation studies. Andrew Jordan and Duncan Liefferink (2004) have edited the most comprehensive study to date, which compares patterns of Europeanization in environmental policy and political structures across member states. While all countries have witnessed a pattern of Europeanization – more deeply with regard to policy content than concerning structures and policy styles – the group of 'strongly Europeanized' states is small, consisting of the UK, Ireland and Spain (Jordan and Liefferink, 2004: 237). It will be interesting to see whether Eastern European states follow the example of the cohesion countries. Importantly, Europeanization has not resulted in the convergence of policy or governance structures across member states, confirming the institutional notion of path-dependency.

The international perspective

Finally, the multi-level governance structure should be extended to cover the EU's role in international environmental politics. As international conventions are usually formal agreements between sovereign states, and as the EU obviously is not a state, this process has involved the establishment of new procedures and routines both internationally and within the EU, challenging traditional multilateral practices (Sbragia and Damro, 1999; see also Chapter 16). International environmental policy making is as much about procedures as about content – this is also reflected in the literature. The question of whether to accept the EU as a party to an international convention is controversial for non-EU partners and within the EU itself. Over the years, 'mixed agreement' with the Community and the member states as signatories have emerged as the normal pattern in international environmental agreements (see Chapter 16). Despite some persistent ambiguities, EU member governments have become increasingly willing to coordinate their positions and act collectively, while international partners have come to expect 'the Union' in some form to appear at the negotiation table.

This evolution is mirrored in the analytical approaches taken to study the EU in international agreements. Initially, the main puzzle was to explain how the member states reached agreement on a common position to be presented to other negotiating partners. We were alerted to preference constellations and rules – like the reciprocity rule or burden sharing arrangements – to facilitate agreement (Skjærseth, 1994). In addition, institutional constellations, like the Commission mediating or the Presidency seeking a profile, can play a role (cf. Jachtenfuchs, 1990). While such constellations are not specific to international environmental policy making, Chad Damro and Pilar Luaces Méndez (2003) suggest that exactly the mixed or dual representation, which seemed a compromise solution at first, gave the Community an intergovernmental as well as 'federal' external personality. Member states submitted to it as national interests seemed protected and were given added weight in the Union. In the next – empirical and analytical – phase, EU leadership became an issue. Alberta Sbragia and Chad Damro argue that during the process of institutionalization, the EU evolved from a 'Vienna laggard to a Kyoto leader' in global environmental negotiations (1999: 53). EU member states had developed a collective spirit in the sense that they had become used to accepting national restrictions and even to agree on differential treatments among themselves. In the case of the Kyoto Protocol, the intra-EU burden-sharing agreement, which allocates different greenhouse gas reduction commitments to the member states, strengthened the EU's negotiation position as it was able to commit itself to the toughest (collective) target of an 8 per cent reduction. Joseph Jupille (1999) is less convinced about the collective maturity of the EU and argues that such leadership is dependent on favourable decision rules internally. Only if the EU decides on its international negotiation position through QMV will we see a tendency for the EU to push for international outcomes and succeed due to its bargaining weight. In either case, however, it is notable that the EU was willing and capable of developing international leadership in the soft area of environmental policy, forcing international regimes to accommodate procedurally and substantively.

In the longer run, such a leadership role depends on credibility, namely the EU's capacity to comply with its international commitments, like the Kyoto targets or the sustainable development agenda, effectively (cf. Lightfoot and Burchell, 2005). Here, international expansion of EU environmental policy ends up on familiar terrain – a potential implementation deficit which could undermine the project.

Conclusion

This chapter set out to review the contributions of EU environmental policy research to the general understanding of EU policy making and governance. The reader will have noted that environmental policy scholars have danced at many parties. In the early years, they analysed policy through the lenses of the two grand theories and entered into similar debates as most other EU scholars. Later, most analysts made the turn toward a domestic politics perspective with the debate centring on the merits of actor-oriented or institutional approaches. Neither of these debates produced a clear winner. But especially the latter discussion produced real value added, as the analysis of this rapidly expanding policy field revealed the multi-faceted and fluid actor and institutional constellations characterizing the EU system of governance.

Many analytically motivated studies of EU policy focus on the making of policy while performance assessments tend to be left to normative commentaries. Arguably, environmental policy research has been a front runner in theory-based performance or output studies. Interestingly, the issue of environmental standards is tackled mostly from a state-centric, rationalist perspective, whereas policy compliance and implementation are approached from an institutional angle. Especially in the latter case, this theory bias has triggered a lively debate also outside the field of environmental policy, inviting comparative policy research in this area.

Furthermore, the performance question has contributed to widening the research perspective beyond mere policy towards governance and beyond Brussels toward impacts on the member states and (to a lesser extent) the international level.

Especially the analysis of different policy instruments and of shifting actor constellations in environmental problem solving revealed not only a close, but also a very dynamic relationship between policy and polity making. In focusing on this interaction, the study of European environmental policy has made a turn from the policy level to the systems level of analysing the EU. This big picture looks highly differentiated and even somewhat messy, more so than either a regime or a federal state. Hopefully, this chapter has shown that (environmental) policy research has made a notable contribution to understanding this complex process and structure of governance in the EU.

Key questions

1 Describe how the focus of EU environmental policy analysis has changed over time.
2 Why has the focus of analysis changed over time? Do you think academic fashions have been the main driver or changes in the 'real world' of policy making?
3 Identify three examples of work in EU environmental policy analysis that have shaped wider debates in EU studies.
4 What analytical topics are likely to appear in the next ten years and why?

References

Andersen, M.S. and Liefferink, D.J. (1997) *European Environmental Policy: The Pioneers*, Manchester University Press, Manchester.

Andersen, M.S. and Rasmussen, L.N. (1998) 'The making of environmental policy in the European Council', *Journal of Common Market Studies*, vol. 36, no. 4, pp. 585–597.

Arp, H. (1993) 'Technical regulation and politics', in J.D. Liefferink, P.D. Lowe and A.P.J. Mol (eds), *European Integration and Environmental Policy*, Belhaven Press, London, pp. 150–171.

Bernauer, T. and Caduff, L. (2004) 'In whose interest? Pressure group politics, economic competition and environmental regulation', *Journal of Public Policy*, vol. 24, no. 1, pp. 99–126.

Bomberg, E. (1998a) *Green Parties and Politics in the European Union*, Routledge, London.

Bomberg, E. (1998b) 'Issue networks and the environment', in D. Marsh (ed.) *Comparing Policy Networks*, Open University Press, Buckingham.

Bomberg, E. and Burns, C. (1999) 'The environment committee of the European Parliament', *Environmental Politics*, vol. 8, no. 4, pp. 173–179.

Börzel, T.A. (2000) 'Why there is no "southern problem": on environmental leaders and laggards in the European Union', *Journal of European Public Policy*, vol. 7, no. 1, pp. 141–162.

Börzel, T.A. (2001) 'Non-compliance in the European Union', *Journal of European Public Policy*, vol. 8, no. 5, pp. 303–324.

Carmin, J. and Vandeveer, S. (2004) 'Enlarging EU environments', *Environmental Politics*, vol. 13, no. 1, pp. 3–24.

Collier, U., Golub, J. and Kreher, A. (eds) (1993) *Subsidiarity and Shared Responsibility*, Nomos, Baden Baden.

Collins, K. and Earnshaw, D. (1993) 'The implementation and enforcement of European Community environment legislation', in D. Judge (ed.) *A Green Dimension for the European Community*, Frank Cass, London, pp. 213–249.

Damro, C. and Méndez, P.L. (2003) 'Emissions trading at Kyoto: from EU resistance to union innovation', *Environmental Politics*, vol. 12, no. 2, pp. 71–94.

De Clercq, M. (ed.) (2002) *Negotiating Environmental Agreements in Europe*, Edward Elgar, Cheltenham.

Dehousse, R. (1992) 'Integration vs. regulation? On the dynamics of regulation in the European Community', *Journal of Common Market Studies*, vol. 15, no. 4, pp. 383–402.

Drezner, D.W. (2001) 'Globalization and policy convergence', *The International Studies Review*, vol. 3, no. 1, pp. 53–78.

Egan, M. (2001) *Constructing a European Market*, Oxford University Press, Oxford.

Eichener, V. (1997) 'Effective European problem-solving', *Journal of European Public Policy*, vol. 4, no. 4, pp. 591–608.

Golub, J. (1996a) 'State power and institutional influence in European integration', *Journal of Common Market Studies*, vol. 34, no. 3, pp. 313–337.

Golub, J. (1996b) 'British sovereignty and the development of EC environmental policy', *Environmental Politics*, vol. 5, no. 4, pp. 700–728.

Golub, J. (1996c) 'Sovereignty and subsidiarity in EU environmental policy', *Political Studies*, vol. 44, no. 4, pp. 686–703.

Golub, J. (ed.) (1998) *New Instruments for Environmental Policy in the EU*, Routledge, London.

Haigh, N. (2004) *Manual of Environmental Policy*, Maney Publishing, Leeds.

Hajer, M.A. (1995) *The Politics of Environmental Discourse*, Oxford University Press, Oxford.

Haverland, M. (2000) 'National adaptation to European integration', *Journal of Public Policy*, vol. 20, no. 1, pp. 83–103.

Heard, J. and Richards, J. (2005) 'European environmental NGOs', *Environmental Politics*, vol. 14, no. 1, pp. 23–41.

Héritier, A. (1996) 'The accommodation of diversity in European policy-making and its outcomes', *Journal of European Public Policy*, vol. 3, no. 2, pp. 149–167.

Héritier, A. (1997) 'Policy-making by subterfuge: Interest accommodation, innovation and substitute democratic legitimation in Europe', *Journal of European Public Policy*, vol. 4, no. 2, pp. 171–189.

Héritier, A. (2002) 'New modes of governance in Europe?', in A. Héritier (ed.) *Common Goods*, Rowman & Littlefield Publishers, Lanham, MD, pp. 185–206.

Héritier, A., Knill, C. and Mingers, S. (1996) *Ringing the Changes in Europe*, De Gruyter, Berlin.

Héritier, A., Mingers, S., Knill, C. and Becka, M. (1994) *Die Veränderung von Staatlichkeit in Europa*, Leske + Budrich, Opladen.

Hey, C. and Brendle, U. (1994) *Towards a New Renaissance: Reversing the Roll-Back of Environmental Policies in the EU*, Eures and EEB, Brussels.

Hey, C., Volkery, A. and Zerle, P. (2005) 'Neue umweltpolitische Steuerungskonzepte in der Europäischen Union', *Zeitschrift für Umweltpolitik und Umweltrecht*, vol. 1, pp. 1–38.

Hildebrand, P.M. (1993) 'The European Community's environmental policy, 1957 to "1992"', in D. Judge (ed.) *A Green Dimension for the European Community*, Frank Cass, London, pp. 13–44.

Holzinger, K. (1994) *Politik des kleinsten gemeinsamen Nenners?* Edition Sigma, Berlin.

Holzinger, K. (2002) 'The provision of transnational common goods', in A. Héritier (ed.) *Common Goods*, Rowman and Littlefield, Lanham, MD, pp. 57–79.

Holzinger, K., Knill, C. and Schäfer, A. (2003) 'Steuerungswandel in der europäischen Umweltpolitik?', in K. Holzinger, C. Knill and D. Lehmkuhl (eds) *Politische Steuerung im Wandel*, Leske+Budrich, Opladen, pp. 103–129.

Homeyer, I. v. (2004) 'Differential effects of enlargement on EU environmental governance', *Environmental Politics*, vol. 13, no. 1, pp. 52–76.

Homeyer, I. v., Carius, A. and Bär, S. (2000) 'Flexibility or renationalization: effects of enlargement on EC environmental policy', in M.G. Cowles and M. Smith (eds) *The State of the European Union*, Oxford University Press, Oxford, pp. 347–368.

Hovden, E. (2002) 'The legal basis of European Union policy: the case of environmental policy', *Environment and Planning C*, vol. 20, no. 4, pp. 535–553.

Huelshoff, M.G. and Pfeiffer, T. (1991) 'Environmental policy in the EC', *International Journal*, vol. 47, no. 1, pp. 136–158.

Hull, R. (1993) 'Lobbying Brussels', in S. Mazey and J. Richardson (eds) *Lobbying in the European Community*, Oxford University Press, Oxford, pp. 82–92.

Imig, D. and Tarrow, S. (2000) 'Political contention in a Europeanising polity', *West European Politics*, vol. 23, pp. 73–93.

Jachtenfuchs, M. (1990) 'The European Community and the protection of the ozone layer', *Journal of Common Market Studies*, vol. 18, no. 3, pp. 261–271.

Jachtenfuchs, M. (1996) 'Regieren durch überzeugen', in M. Jachtenfuchs and B. Kohler-Koch (eds), *Europäische Integration*, Leske+Budrich, Opladen, pp. 429–454.

Jänicke, M. (1998) 'Umweltpolitik: global am Ende oder am Ende global?', in U. Beck (ed.), *Perspektiven der Weltgesellschaft*, Suhrkamp, Frankfurt am Main, pp. 332–344.

Jehlička, P. and Tickle, A. (2004) 'Environmental implications of Eastern enlargement', *Environmental Politics*, vol. 13, no. 1, pp. 77–95.

Johnson, S.P. and Corcelle, G. (1989) *The Environmental Policy of the European Communities*, Graham and Trotman, London.

Jordan, A. (1998) 'Step change or stasis? EC environmental policy after the Amsterdam Summit', *Environmental Politics*, vol. 7, no. 1, pp. 227–236.

Jordan, A. (1999) 'The implementation of EU environmental policy: a problem without a political solution?', *Environment and Planning C*, vol. 17, no. 1, pp. 69–90.

Jordan, A. (2002) *The Europeanization of British Environmental Policy*, Palgrave, Basingstoke.

Jordan, A., Brouwer, R. and Noble, E. (1999) 'Innovative and responsive? A longitudinal analysis of the speed of EU environmental policy making, 1967–97', *Journal of European Public Policy*, vol. 6, no. 3, pp. 376–398.

Jordan, A. and Fairbrass, J. (2001) 'European Union environmental policy after the Nice Summit', *Environmental Politics*, vol. 10, no. 4, pp. 109–114.

Jordan, A. and Liefferink, D.J. (eds) (2004) *Environmental Policy in Europe*, Routledge, London.

Jordan, A., Wurzel, R.K.W. and Zito, A.R. (2003) '"New" instruments of environmental governance: patterns and pathways of change', *Environmental Politics*, vol. 12, no. 1, pp. 1–24.

Judge, D. (1993) 'Predestined to save the Earth? The Environment Committee of the European Parliament', in D. Judge (ed.) *A Green Dimension for the European Community*, Frank Cass, London, pp. 186–212.

Judge, D., Earnshaw, D. and Cowan, N. (1994) 'Ripples or waves: the European Parliament in the European Community policy process', *Journal of European Public Policy*, vol. 1, no. 1, pp. 27–52.

Jupille, J. (1999) 'The European Union and international outcomes', *International Organization*, vol. 53, no. 2, pp. 409–425.

Kasack, C. (2004) 'The legislative impact of the European Parliament under the revised co-decision procedure', *European Union Politics*, vol. 5, no. 2, pp. 241–260.

Kelemen, R.D. (2000) 'Regulatory federalism', *Journal of Public Policy*, vol. 20, no. 3, pp. 133–167.

Knill, C. (1995) *Staatlichkeit im Wandel*, Deutscher Universitätsverlag, Opladen.

Knill, C. (2001) *The Europeanisation of National Administrations*, Cambridge University Press, Cambridge.

Knill, C. and Lenschow, A. (1998) 'Coping with Europe', *Journal of European Public Policy*, vol. 5, no. 4, pp. 595–614.

Knill, C. and Lenschow, A. (eds) (2000) *Implementing EU Environmental Policies*, Manchester University Press, Manchester.

Kohler-Koch, B. (1999) 'The evolution and transformation of European governance', in B. Kohler-Koch and R. Eising (eds) *The Transformation of Governance in the European Union*, Routledge, London, pp. 14–35.

Koppen, I.J. (1993) 'The role of the European Court of Justice', in J.D. Liefferink, P.D. Lowe and A.P.J. Mol (eds) *European Integration and Environmental Policy*, Belhaven Press, London, pp. 126–149.

Lenschow, A. (1997) 'Variation in EC environmental policy integration', *Journal of European Public Policy*, vol. 4, no. 1, pp. 109–127.

Lenschow, A. (1999) 'Transformation in European environmental governance', in B. Kohler-Koch and R. Eising (eds) *The Transformation of Governance in the European Union*, Routledge, London, pp. 39–61.

Lenschow, A. (ed.) (2002a) *Environmental Policy Integration*, Earthscan, London.

Lenschow, A. (2002b) 'New regulatory approaches in "greening" EU policies', *European Law Journal*, vol. 8, no. 1, pp. 19–37.

Lenschow, A. and Zito, A. (1998) 'Blurring or shifting of policy frames?', *Governance*, vol. 11, no. 4, pp. 415–441.

Liefferink, D. and Andersen, M.S. (1998) 'Strategies of the "green" Member States in EU environmental policy-making', *Journal of European Public Policy*, vol. 5, no. 2, pp. 254–270.

Lightfoot, S. and Burchell, J. (2005) 'The European Union and the World Summit on Sustainable Development', *Journal of Common Market Studies*, vol. 43, no. 1, pp. 75–95.

Long, T. (1995) 'Shaping public policy in the European Union', *Journal of European Public Policy*, vol. 2, no. 4, pp. 672–679.

Macrory, R. (1992) 'The enforcement of Community environmental laws', *Common Market Law Review*, vol. 29, pp. 347–369.

Majone, G. (1996) *Regulating Europe*, Routledge, London.

Marks, G. and McAdam, D. (1996) 'Social movements and the changing structure of political opportunity in the European Union', *West European Politics*, vol. 20, pp. 111–133.

Mayntz, R. and Scharpf, F. (1995) 'Steuerung und Selbstorganisation in staatsnähen Sektoren', in R. Mayntz and F. Scharpf (eds) *Gesellschaftliche Selbstregulierung und politische Steuerung*, Campus Verlag, Frankfurt, pp. 9–38.

Mazey, S. and Richardson, J. (1993) 'Environmental groups and the EC', in D. Judge (ed.) *A Green Dimension for the European Community?* Frank Cass, London, pp. 109–128.

Mol, A., Liefferink, D. and Lauber, V. (eds) (2000) *The Voluntary Approach to Environmental Policy*, Oxford University Press, Oxford.

Oates, W.E. and Schwab, R.M. (1988) 'Economic competition among jurisdictions', *Journal of Public Economics*, vol. 35, pp. 333–354.

Peterson, J. (2001) 'The choice for EU theorists: establishing a common framework for analysis', *European Journal of Political Research*, vol. 39, pp. 289–318.

Peterson, J. (2004) 'Policy networks', in A. Wiener and T. Diez (eds) *European Integration Theory*, Oxford University Press, Oxford.

Pollack, M.A. (1997) 'Representing diffuse interests in EC policy-making', *Journal of European Public Policy*, vol. 4, no. 4, pp. 572–590.

Rehbinder, E. and Stewart, R. (1985) *Environmental Protection Policy: Vol. 2*, De Gruyter, Berlin.

Rucht, D. (2001) 'Lobbying or protest?', in D. Imig and S. Tarrow (eds) *Contentious Europe*, Rowman & Littlefield, Lanham, MD, pp. 125–142.

Sabatier, P.A. (1998) 'The advocacy coalition framework', *Journal of European Public Policy*, vol. 5, no. 1, pp. 98–130.

Sbragia, A. (1996) 'Environmental policy', in H. Wallace and W. Wallace (eds) *Policy-Making in the European Union*, Oxford University Press, Oxford, pp. 235–256.

Sbragia, A. (2000) 'Environmental policy', in H. Wallace and W. Wallace (eds), *Policy-making in the European Union*, 2nd edition, Oxford University Press, Oxford, pp. 293–316.

Sbragia, A.M. and Damro, C. (1999) 'The changing role of the European Union in international environmental politics', *Environment and Planning C*, vol. 17, no. 1, pp. 53–68.

Scharpf, F.W. (1997) 'Introduction', *Journal of European Public Policy*, vol. 4, no. 4, pp. 520–538.

Schout, A. and Jordan, A. (2005) 'Coordinated European governance: self-organizing or centrally steered?', *Public Administration*, vol. 83, no. 1, pp. 201–220.

Schreurs, M. (2004) 'Environmental protection in an expanding European Community', *Environmental Politics*, vol. 13, no. 1, pp. 27–51.

Skjærseth. J.B. (1994) 'The climate policy of the EC', *Journal of Common Market Studies*, vol. 32, no. 1, pp. 25–42.

Skjærseth, J.B. and Wettestad, J. (2002) 'Understanding the effectiveness of EU environmental polity', *Environmental Politics*, vol. 11, no. 3, pp. 99–120.

Snyder, F. (1993) 'The effectiveness of European Community law', *Modern Law Review*, vol. 56, pp. 19–54.

Tallberg, J. (1999) *Making States Comply*, Studentlitteratur, Lund.

Töller, A.E. (2002) *Komitologie*, Leske & Budrich, Opladen.

Van Long, N. and Siebert, H. (1991) 'Institutional competition versus ex-ante harmonization: the case of environmental policy', *Journal of Institutional and Theoretical Economics*, vol. 147, pp. 296–311.

Voelzkow, H. (1996) *Private Regierungen in der Techniksteuerung*, Campus, Frankfurt.

Vogel, D. (1995) *Trading Up*, Harvard University Press, Cambridge, MA.

Weale, A. (1992) *The New Politics of Pollution*, Manchester University Press, Manchester.

Weale, A. (1996) 'Environmental rules and rule-making in the European Union', *Journal of European Public Policy*, vol. 3, no. 4, pp. 594–611.

Weale, A. (1999) 'European environmental policy by stealth', *Environment and Planning C*, vol. 17, no. 1, pp. 37–51.

Weale, A., Pridham, G., Cini, M., Konstadakopulos, D., Porter, M. and Flynn, B. (2000) *Environmental Governance in Europe*, Oxford University Press, Oxford.

Weale, A. and Williams, A. (1993) 'Between economy and ecology: the single market and the integration of environmental policy', in D. Judge (ed.) *A Green Dimension for the European Community*, Frank Cass, London, pp. 45–64.

Webster, R. (1998) 'Environmental collective action', in J. Greenwood and M. Aspinwall (eds) *Collective Action in the European Union*, Routledge, London, pp. 176–225.

Wilkinson, D. (1992) *Maastricht and the Environment*, IEEP, London.

Wurzel, R.K.W. (1996) 'The role of the EU Presidency in the environmental field', *Journal of European Public Policy*, vol. 3, no. 2, pp. 272–291.

Young, O.R. and Levy, M.A. (eds) (1999) *The Effectiveness of International Environmental Regimes*, MIT Press, Cambridge, MA.

Zito, A. (1999) 'Task expansion: a theoretical overview', *Environment and Planning C*, vol. 17, no. 1, pp. 19–35.

Zito, A. (2001) 'Epistemic communities, collective entrepreneurship and European integration', *Journal of European Public Policy*, vol. 8, no. 4, pp. 585–603.

Part 2
Actors

5   Member states and the Council

Rüdiger K. W. Wurzel

Summary guide

Member states shape EU policy by working within the Council of Ministers. The Council is thus a central player in EU decision making. There are different Council formations (made up of ministers responsible for particular policy areas), one of which is the Environment Council. Over the years the number of Environment Council meetings has increased significantly. The member governments' top political leaders meet in a different forum – the European Council – which until recently had very little to do with environmental issues. Nowadays the European Council plays an important role in EU climate change policy in particular. The well-known environmental leader–laggard dimension among different member states goes a long way towards explaining the dynamics within the Environment Council.

Introduction

The Council has been called 'the institutional heart of decision making in the EU' (Lewis, 2010: 142). Legally speaking, there is only one Council – or Council of Ministers as it is often also referred to – although the ministers responsible for particular policy areas usually meet separately in different Council formations (e.g. the Agriculture Council or the Environment Council). The inaugural Environment Council meeting only took place in 1973 (although the Council had already been set up by the EU's founding treaties in the 1950s), because the environment was not a salient issue on the EU's political agenda before the 1970s (see Chapter 2). As will be explained below, the ministerial meetings associated with the Council are only the visible tip of the iceberg of a much larger administrative machine. Importantly, it is the Council (together with the European Parliament) which adopts EU laws (see Chapters 8 and 12).

The top political leaders of the member governments (e.g. the British prime minister, the French president and the German chancellor) – usually referred to as heads of state and government in official EU documents – do not meet in the

Council. Instead they gather for summit meetings in the European Council which became institutionalized only in the early 1970s. The European Council does not adopt laws but takes the important strategic decisions such as whether the EU's treaties should be amended (to include, among others, new environmental provisions) or which applicant states should be allowed to join the EU.

The Council and European Council both constitute European institutions *and* negotiating forums for member governments. They therefore exhibit both supranational and intergovernmental features, although the latter tend to be more distinctive for the European Council in particular. Outside the Council and European Council meetings, member governments also exploit numerous bilateral and multilateral contacts on environmental issues with other member governments. For example, the Finnish and Swedish governments frequently discuss environmental issues within the Nordic Council[1] and institutionalized annual bilateral Franco-German environmental minister meetings have been held since the 1980s.[2] European environment ministers also participate in a large number of international environmental negotiations on, for example, climate change and biodiversity. As will be explained below, it is normally the six-monthly rotating Council Presidency which (often together with the Commission) represents the EU in international environmental negotiations (see Chapter 16).

Summary points

- The Council and the European Council are two distinct and very different EU institutions.
- The Council is attended by ministers responsible for a particular policy area such as the environment. Together with the European Parliament, it formally adopts new EU laws.
- The European Council is made up of the heads of state and government who take bigger strategic political decisions on things such as the enlargement of the EU.

The Council

Considering its importance for the EU decision-making process, there is a dearth of studies which focus specifically on the Council, although there are some important exceptions (e.g. Sherrington, 2000; Haynes-Renshaw and Wallace, 2006). One reason for the sparse research on the Council is the fact that most of its meetings are held behind closed doors.

With the perceived need for greater transparency within the EU (see Chapter 18), some ministerial Council meetings are now held in public. However, this is only the case when the Council acts in negotiation mode (in contrast to legislative mode from which the media and public remain excluded) (Hayes-Renshaw and Wallace, 2006: 6). In practice, it is very difficult to differentiate between the two modes and this ambiguity has allowed the Council a lot of discretion over which meetings are held in public. The Council publishes a press release on each meeting, though this merely summarizes the negotiating outcome not the preceding debate among ministers. Council press releases are, for example, wholly silent on the political differences which may have arisen between ministers during negotiations. This allows the ministers to present their own particular versions of events in post-Council press conferences often aimed primarily at their national media and domestic constituencies.

Between the 1970s and the 1990s, there was a proliferation of different Council formations while European integration deepened and the EU moved into new policy areas (including environmental policy). Pinder's assertion that the legal fiction of a single Council has given way to a 'hydra-headed conglomerate of a dozen or more functional Councils' (1991: 25) is still largely correct, although the European Council meeting in Seville in 2002 limited the number of Council formations to nine (after the 1999 Helsinki European Council had already restricted their number to 16) (see Box 5.1).

Box 5.1 Council formations since 2002

General Affairs and External Relations Council (GAERC)
Economic and Financial Affairs (ECOFIN)
Justice and Home Affairs
Employment, Social Policy, Health and Consumer Affairs
Competitiveness (internal market, industry, research and space)
Transport, Telecommunications and Energy
Agriculture and Fisheries
Environment
Education, Youth, Culture and Sport
(Adapted from Council of the European Union, 2011a)

The General Affairs Council, which was merged with the Foreign Affairs Council to form the General Affairs and External Relations Council (GAERC) after 2002, was meant to take on an overall coordination role for the different Council formations. However, it largely failed to fulfil this task (Lewis, 2010). Although there is no formal distinction in terms of importance between different Council formations, General Affairs and External Relations (GAERC) and Economic and Financial Affairs (ECOFIN) are widely seen as the most senior Council formations. The Environmental Council has not reached a similar level of seniority, although it did survive unscathed the merger of the Council formations into the nine listed in Box 5.1.

The Council was set up along functional lines to avoid zero sum games in which the winner seeks to take all. This has helped to depoliticize potentially highly divisive issues, facilitating agreement. However, functionally differentiated

Council formations can lead to disjointed decision making which is unable to take account of the cross-cutting requirements of environmental policy. In the early 1990s, attempts were made to bring about better coordination of EU policies through so-called joint Councils consisting of two different Council formations, which, however, have been largely unsuccessful (Hayes-Renshaw and Wallace, 2006: 63; Wurzel, 2008).

The proliferation of different formations posed a particular challenge for environmental policy because environmentalists believe that its considerations ought to be integrated into all EU policies, and thus all Council formations. In the late 1990s, most Council formations published environmental integration reports. This became known as the Cardiff Process because it was instigated by the European Council meeting in Cardiff in 1998 (Jordan *et al.*, 2008). However, most of the integration reports amounted to little more than symbolic politics and had little, if any, impact on the practical work of the 'non-environmental' Council formations. In the mid-2000s, the integration reports were discontinued (see Chapter 13).

Box 5.2 reproduces the summary and content pages of the press release for the Environment Council meeting on 31 June 2011. It is a fairly typical press release.

Box 5.2 Press release for the Environment Council on 21 June 2011

Main results of the Council

The Council exchanged views and adopted conclusions on the **protection of water resources and integrated sustainable water management.** The conclusions stress that water concerns must be integrated ('mainstreamed') into relevant EU policies. Moreover, extreme weather events should be handled in an integrated way by policies dealing with land use and planning, agriculture, nature conservation and infrastructures.

In addition, the Council adopted conclusions endorsing the **EU biodiversity strategy until 2020.** The strategy is the EU's key instrument for reaching the new EU target for the protection of biodiversity in 2020: the EU intends to halt the loss of biodiversity and the degradation of ecosystem services in the EU by 2020, and restore them in so far as feasible, while stepping up the EU contribution to averting global biodiversity loss.

Finally, the Council examined progress with a proposal that would allow member states to ban or restrict the **cultivation of genetically modified organisms** in their territory.

CONTENTS

PARTICIPANTS   5
ITEMS DEBATED

Major accidents involving dangerous substances	7
Protection of water resources	8
EU biodiversity strategy until 2020	9
Climate change	10
Cultivation of genetically modified organisms	11
OTHER BUSINESS	12
OTHER ITEMS APPROVED	
ENVIRONMENT	
– Biocidal products	15
– European Environmental Accounts	15
ECONOMIC AND FINANCIAL AFFAIRS	
– Excise duties on tobacco	15
CUSTOMS UNION	
– Duties on industrial, agricultural and fishery products	16
– Tariff quotas for certain agricultural and industrial products	16
TRADE POLICY	
– Antidumping – Magnesia bricks – China	16
FISHERIES	
– Financial measures for the common fisheries policy	17
STATISTICS	
– Tourism	17

(Adapted from Council of the European Union, 2011b)
Note: The text in bold appears as in the original.

Importantly, the environment ministers did not actually discuss any of the non-environmental issues (i.e. economic affairs, customs union, trade policy, fisheries and statistics) listed in Box 5.2. Instead they merely adopted – without debate – the agreements on the non-environmental dossiers left over from other Council formations that had reached agreement in principle without, however, having had the time to draft a legally watertight text. The legal fiction of one single Council does therefore have some practical relevance for the smooth running of the Council machinery.

The Council: composition and structure

Council meetings are normally attended by the most senior national politician – a minister or someone who deputizes for the minister (see Box 5.3).[3] Thus agriculture ministers attend the Agricultural and Fisheries Council, environment ministers the Environment Council, and so on. The ministerial meetings are 'at the apex of the Council machinery' (Nugent, 2010: 142), which also consists of the Committee of Permanent Representatives (COREPER), Council working groups and Council committees that are all supported by the Council's secretariat.

The Council secretariat, which has a staff of approximately 3,500, has the task to service the entire Council machinery (ibid.: 147). In 2011, 11 'A-level' staff worked in the Council secretariat on environmental issues. The Council secretariat functions as a conference centre, clearing house, collective memory and advisor to the presidency (Wurzel, 2004: 6). In 2009, the environment Directorate General (DG) of the Council secretariat was split into an environment DG and a climate DG. However, no 'Climate Change Council' was set up. Instead the Environment Council continued to take the lead on most climate change dossiers although it also began increasingly to cooperate closer with other Council formations, particularly with the energy ministers represented in the Transport, Telecommunications and Energy Council. As will be explained below, in the early 2000s, climate change emerged as a 'high politics' issue and thus also attracted increasingly attention from the European Council which issued the Environment Council with political guidelines on how to approach the UN climate change negotiations (Oberthür and Dupont, 2010).

The internal organizational structure of the Council is hierarchical. Thus, all legal dossiers negotiated at ministerial Council meetings will already have been discussed by COREPER and in Council working groups (Hayes-Renshaw and Wallace, 2006: 68–100; Nugent, 2010: 144–147). COREPER meetings are attended by national officials from the Brussels-based permanent representations and national officials from government departments. Permanent representation officials, who work and live in Brussels for several years, acquire a deep knowledge of the EU decision-making process and the views of their opposite numbers from other member states. This explains why permanent representation officials sit beside the Minister at Council meetings (Lewis, 2010: 153).

The Council working groups, which recruit their members from among national ministry officials and permanent representation officials, are 'the workhorse of the Council' (ibid.: 153). Their main purpose is to resolve as many contentious issues in dossiers as possible before they are passed up to the COREPER. Council working groups are, however, also consulted on specific issues in the later stages of the negotiations, 'and can serve as a convenient way to place a proposal in "cold storage" until the political climate is more favourable for an agreement' (ibid.: 153). The Council environment working group is one of approximately 200 Council working groups which have spawned over the years.

If agreement has already been reached between all member states at Council working group and COREPER levels, then the dossier is passed on to the ministers as an 'A' point. Dossiers on which Council working groups and COREPER have made good progress, but failed to find agreement on a number of contested issues, are passed on to the ministers as 'B' points. Importantly, 'A' points are usually adopted by the ministers in the Council without further negotiations (although they can be reopened as 'B' points by any minister present). No hard data is available about the exact number of 'A' points although Hayes-Renshaw and Wallace (2006: 52) quote 'hearsay evidence from Council insiders' who estimated 'that around 85–90 per cent of business was transacted as "A" points, with approximately 70 per cent having been in effect settled at working group level'.

Relations between all levels of the Council and the European Parliament have changed significantly over the years (see also Chapter 8). While the Council often failed to take the European Parliament seriously in the early years of European integration, this is clearly no longer the case. There was a significant increase in legislative powers for the European Parliament after 1987. The co-decision/normal procedure grants it co-legislative powers that are equal to those of the Council. A conciliation committee has to be set up if agreement cannot be achieved between the Council and the European Parliament (see Chapter 8). However, because of the large number of players involved, conciliation committee meetings have proved to be unwieldy affairs. Conciliation negotiations between the Council and European Parliament are therefore conducted primarily during informal trialogues involving small teams of negotiators for each institution, with the Commission playing a mediating role. In trialogue meetings the Council is represented by the permanent representative of the member state holding the presidency, assisted by members of the Council secretariat, including its legal service.

Decision-making rules

The Council takes decisions according to one of three different main decision rules: (1) unanimity; (2) qualified majority; or (3) simple majority. Unanimity used to be the standard decision-making rule in the early years of European integration while simple majority voting was mainly applicable to procedural matters (Nugent, 2010: 154). The formal applicability of the use of qualified majority voting has, however, continuously increased since the late 1980s. It was formally introduced in 1987 for most internal market measures and some other policy areas. Subsequent treaty amendments gradually extended its use to a point that it has become the normal decision-making rule for most common policy areas, including the environment (see Chapter 1). However, there are exceptions (see Chapter 3). For example, the Commission's proposal for a common carbon dioxide/energy tax was never adopted (see Chapter 17), because it was vetoed by the UK on sovereignty grounds (Zito, 2000; McCormick, 2001: 34–35; Jordan *et al.*, 2010; Wurzel and Connelly, 2010).

Box 5.3 Voting in the Council

Under qualified majority voting the votes of the member states are weighted as follows: 29 for Germany, France, Italy and the UK; 27 for Spain and Poland; 14 votes for Romania; 13 for the Netherlands; 12 for Belgium, the Czech Republic, Greece, Hungary and Poland; 10 for Austria, Bulgaria and Sweden; seven for Denmark, Ireland, Lithuania, Slovakia and Finland; four for Cyprus, Estonia, Latvia, Luxembourg and Slovenia; and three votes for Malta. A member state's number of votes corresponds roughly to population size although there are some inconsistencies. Germany has almost

20 million inhabitants more than France, Italy and the UK, while the small member states are somewhat over-represented.

Since 2004, qualified majority voting has required a triple majority within the Council which must be supported by: (1) at least 73.91 per cent of the weighted votes; (2) a numerical majority of member states representing at least 62 per cent of the EU's total population. Formal voting under the triple majority requirement has become so complicated that it is almost impossible to determine the outcome of some Council votes without a pocket calculator. The Council has helpfully made available a voting calculator on its website (Council of the European Union, 2011c).

The 2009 Lisbon Treaty replaced the triple majority voting requirement with a simpler double majority, which protects the large member states from being outvoted by a majority made up of medium-sized and small member states. The double majority requires a minimum of 55 per cent of member states (comprising at least 15 of the 27 member states) which represent at least 65 per cent of the EU's population. This means that the four largest member states can form a blocking minority in the Council. The double majority voting requirement, which will become applicable in 2014, was highly contested by some member states – Poland, in particular – during the Lisbon Treaty negotiations.

In practice, the Council often strives to achieve unanimity even if qualified majority voting is applicable according to the EU treaties. There is a 'consensus reflex' (Hayes-Renshaw and Wallace, 2006: 58) within the Council in which every possible effort is made to persuade reluctant member states to accept a compromise agreement. This explains why many EU laws contain exemptions, derogations, differentiated deadlines and vague phrases which allow for a wide interpretation of legal obligations during the implementation process (Wurzel, 2002, 2008).

The rotating Presidency

The brokering of a compromise agreement is one of the most important tasks assigned to the Council presidency which rotates among all member states every six months, from January to June and from July to December. In addition to its mediator role, the holder of the Council Presidency has to fulfil major administrative, initiator, representative and point of contact functions (Wurzel, 1996, 2004; Talberg, 2006; Schout, 2008). It is not an easy task for the holder of the Presidency to juggle these, at times, conflicting demands.

Over time, the Presidency's mediator role has grown as the EU expanded from six to 27 member states, the number of Council formations and meetings proliferated, qualified majority voting increased and the cooperation/normal procedure was introduced. Moreover, '[t]he tilting of power from the Commission to the

Council began to make the management of Council business a more substantive task' (Hayes-Renshaw and Wallace, 2006: 134).

A good rule of thumb is that holders of the Presidency are more likely to give way on national interests when holding the presidency than when not in office (Wurzel, 1996, 2004: 36). An example which confirms this rule of thumb is the auto oil programme which was adopted under the 1998 UK Presidency by the Council and European Parliament following difficult conciliation negotiations (see Chapter 8). The auto oil programme introduced relatively stringent car emission and fuel standards that were derived from the best available technology principle on which the British government was not keen (Friedrich *et al.*, 2000). However, this is not an axiomatic rule – something illustrated by the 1999 German Presidency's handling of the End-of-Life Vehicles Directive where German national interests where given priority at the expense of the office holder's duty to act as neutral broker and mediator (see Box 5.4; Wurzel, 2000). Germany's actions on the End-of-Life Vehicles Directive show that well-developed informal behavioural norms are sometimes broken because of overriding national interests.

Box 5.4 The End-of-Life Vehicles Directive

The Commission's proposal for an End-of-Life Vehicles Directive required car manufacturers to recycle or reuse a very large part of a scrapped vehicle. It was agreed in principle by all member states (including Germany) at an Environment Council meeting chaired by the 1998 Austrian Presidency. However, after intensive lobbying by the German car industry, and Volkswagen in particular, Germany's Chancellor instructed his Environment Minister to take the proposal off the agenda for the first Environment Council meeting under the German Presidency in 1999. Although Germany's Environment Minister was personally in favour of the End-of-Life Vehicles Directive, he obeyed the Chancellor. The German government then successfully lobbied the British and Spanish governments in order to get a blocking minority for the second Environment Council meeting under its Presidency. The directive was later nevertheless adopted although only in a modified form which largely reflected German concerns.

Germany's behaviour on the End-of-Life Vehicles Directive was uncharacteristic for a pro-integrationist country which has a reputation as an environmental leader; it was also not in line with Germany's otherwise successful handling of most of the other environmental dossiers negotiated under its 1999 Presidency.

The Presidency (often together with the Commission) also represents the EU at the international level (see Chapter 16). Increased international representation demands on the rotating presidency have exposed its limitations. Over the years, the EU has developed into an environmental leader in international climate change politics in particular (Jordan *et al.*, 2010; Wurzel and Connelly, 2010). However, in important international negotiations, such as those at Copenhagen in 2009, it still struggles to speak with one voice. Moreover, the rotating presidency has failed to introduce the expected level of continuity. In order to achieve more continuity, presidencies have informally allocated certain negotiating tasks to member states with strong expertise in particular issues which act as 'lead countries' beyond the term of office of a single presidency (Oberthür and Roche Kelly, 2008; Oberthür and Dupont, 2010). Moreover, team presidencies have been formed where several presidencies work together on a common Presidency work programme (Schout, 2008).

In 2006, the Council's rules of procedure were reformed so that 'every 18 months, the three Presidencies due to hold office shall prepare, in close cooperation with the Commission, and after appropriate consultations, a draft programme of Council activities for that period' (European Council, 2011). The aim of this change was to bring about greater continuity between different Presidency programmes and better representation on the international level. Table 5.1 lists the trio Presidencies until 2020.

Table 5.1 Trio Presidencies, 2007–2020

Year	Member states	Time period
2020	Finland	January–June
2019	Romania	July–December
2019	Austria	January–June
2018	Bulgaria	July–December
2018	Estonia	January–June
2017	United Kingdom	July–December
2017	Malta	January–June
2016	Slovakia	July–December
2016	Netherlands	January–June
2015	Luxembourg	July–December
2015	Latvia	January–June
2014	Italy	July–December
2014	Greece	January–June
2013	Lithuania	July–December
2013	Ireland	January–June
2012	Cyprus	July–December
2012	Denmark	January–June
2011	Poland	July–December
2011	Hungary	January–June
2010	Belgium	July–December
2010	Spain	January–June
2009	Sweden	July–December
2009	Czech Republic	January–June
2008	France	July–December
2008	Slovenia	January–June
2007	Portugal	July–December
2007	Germany	January–June

Germany, Portugal and Slovenia were the first three member states to submit a joint programme under the new procedure. If their experience is anything to go by, then trio Presidencies should work well. There is, however, a danger that large 'old' member states may try to exert undue influence on small 'new' member states. The latter have significantly smaller administrative capacities and lack experience in running the Presidency. They are therefore likely to accept a helping hand from larger and 'older' member states, but their offers may not be driven entirely by altruistic motives. Germany, for example, seconded national Environment Ministry officials to Slovenia to support its presidency while Slovenian Environment Ministry officials were temporarily posted to Germany. The secondment of national environmental ministry officials to other member states also increasingly takes place outside the Presidency. It shows that a considerable degree of trust has developed between member governments. Importantly, holding the Presidency Europeanizes the incumbent to a considerable degree.

Summary points

- The Council is organized along functional lines.
- The integration of environmental concerns into all Council formations is important but difficult to achieve.
- The Council usually strives for consensus although qualified majority voting is now widely applied in practice.

The Environment Council

The inaugural meeting of the Environment Council took place in 1973. In the first four years of its existence only every second Presidency staged an Environment Council meeting. However, since 1977, all Presidencies have organized at least one Environment Council meeting. Since 1989, all Presidencies have held two Environment Council meetings with the exception of the 2009 Swedish Presidency which staged three (Table 5.2). This shows that all member states take the role seriously.

The steady increase in the number of Environment Council meetings per Presidency was necessary because the Council had to adopt a growing number of environmental laws, although recently there has been a slight dip in the legislative output of the Environment Council. The growth of Environment Council meetings also reflects the rise in the political salience of environmental issues on the EU's agenda. It is not only the environment ministers whose Council meetings increased over time. The number of COREPER meetings dealing with environmental dossiers and Environment Council Working Groups has also grown significantly.

Over the years, the Environment Council has matured a lot. It used to be a relatively obscure junior Council formation, which dealt with highly technical dossiers (such as the Directive 75/716/EEC on sulphur content of certain liquid

Table 5.2 Environment Council meetings

Year	Number	Member states holding the Presidency	Dates of the first semester meeting	Dates of the second semester meeting
2011	4	Hungary/Poland	14 March; 21 June	10 October; 19 December
2010	4	Spain/Belgium	15 March; 11 June	14 October; 20 December
2009	5	Czech Republic/ Sweden	2 March; 25 June	21 October; 23 November; 22 December
2008	4	Slovenia/France	3 March; 5 June	20/21 October; 4 December
2007	4	Germany/Portugal	20 February; 28 June	30 October; 20 December
2006	4	Austria/Finland	9 March; 27 June	23 October; 18 December
2005	4	Luxembourg/UK	10 March; 24 June	17 October; 2 December
2004	4	Ireland/Netherlands	2 March; 28 June	14 October; 20 December
2003	4	Greece/Italy	4 March; 13 June	27 October; 22 December
2002	4	Spain/Denmark	4 March; 25 June	17 October; 9 December

Source: Collated by the author from the Council Secretariat's archive in Brussels.

fuels), but now it carries significant political weight, although it cannot possibly match the GAERC and ECOFIN. The EU's ambition to act as a leader in international environmental politics in general, and international climate change politics in particular (Wurzel and Connelly, 2010), has also increased the political standing of the Environment Council.

Table 5.2 lists the formal Environment Council meetings which have taken place from 2002 to 2011. However, nowadays most Presidencies also organize one informal Environment Council meeting during their six months in office. Informal Councils cannot agree legislation, although incumbents may try to adopt Presidency Conclusions (the official documents which summarize the agreements made in the European Council meetings) with the aim of committing the Council to take certain actions in future (Humphreys, 1996: 11). They are used instead for the pooling of ideas and the freest possible exchange of views on general topics (Wurzel, 2004: 4). Informal Council meetings normally take place in the country of the holder of Presidency which tries to create an informal and relaxed atmosphere to allow ministers to get to know each other so that they can talk freely about new initiatives and also major stumbling blocks that might have occurred in formal meetings (Wurzel, 1996). In 1988, the number of informal Council per Presidency was restricted to seven for budgetary reasons but also to stop too much decision making from moving away from Brussels (Wurzel, 2004: 5). However, in practice, the limit is often exceeded although additional informal meetings now have to be paid for by the holder of the Presidency.

The environment ministers have been involved in Joint Council meetings because some Presidencies were keen to champion environmental policy integration by organizing joint Council meetings. Joint Councils were championed in particular by British governments which domestically put a lot of emphasis on joined-up policy making in the 1990s (Jordan *et al.*, 2008; Russel and Jordan, 2008). They flourished in the early 1990s when 30 Joint Councils were organized across all Council formations (Wurzel, 1996: 275; 2004: 5). Theoretically, they tried to break down sectoral barriers, but they 'are difficult to orchestrate, tend to produce general policy statements rather than specific environmental measures and often slow down decision-making' (Wurzel, 1996: 275). In an EU made up of 27 member states, they have ceased to be a viable option for EU decision making because of the large number of ministers who would have to be involved.

While the Environment Council shares legislative powers with the European Parliament, it is the single most important actor shaping the EU's external environmental policy. As Oberthür and Dupont (2010: 75) have pointed out:

> [It] determines the EU's international negotiation position, with active participation and input by the Commission. A working group of the Council develops the positions, which are then usually reflected in Council conclusions. These Council conclusions provide the basis for the Member States and the Commission to coordinate their strategy on a daily basis at international negotiations.

However, on environmental issues with a high level of political salience (such as climate change in the 2000s), the Environment Council receives political guidelines and sometimes even detailed instructions from the European Council which, in recent years, has taken a greater interest in environmental issues (see below).

Summary points

- The first Environment Council meeting took place in 1973.
- The steady increase in the number of meetings over the years reflects its greater workload and increased political standing.
- The Environment Council is the most important actor shaping external EU environmental policy.

The European Council

The European Council is 'the pre-eminent political authority for the EU because it brings together the 27 heads of state and government' (Lewis, 2010: 145). Initially the member governments' top political leaders met only on an informal and ad hoc basis. Since the 1970s, their meetings have become gradually more institutionalized. It was, however, only the 2009 Lisbon Treaty which made it a formal EU institution. Importantly, the Lisbon Treaty created an elected President for the European Council and a High Representative of the Union for Foreign Affairs (while, as was shown above, maintaining the rotating Presidency for the Council). These new posts have complicated the EU's representation in international environmental negotiations.

Prior to the 1990s, the heads of state and government only occasionally dealt with environmental issues. For example, the Paris Summit in October 1972 initiated common environmental policy by instructing the Commission to come up with an Environmental Action Programme. This took place only a few months after the UN Stockholm conference on the human environment at which member states had failed miserably to present a common EU position.

Since the 1990s, environmental issues have been taken more seriously by the European Council (Oberthür and Dupont, 2010). However, the European Council initially failed to make the protection of the environment one of the core aims of the 2000 Lisbon Strategy which aimed to make the EU the most competitive knowledge-based economy by 2020. It was the 2001 Swedish Presidency which raised the profile of sustainable development at the Gothenburg European Council meeting (see Chapter 19). Overall the European Council has provided relatively little leadership on international environmental policy issues, with the possible exception of climate change (Jordan *et al.*, 2010; Oberthür and Dupont, 2010).

A good example of the European Council's increased role in environmental policy and its close cooperation with the Council is provided by the adoption process of the climate change and energy package which positioned the EU firmly as a leader in international climate change politics (Jordan *et al.*, 2010; Oberthür and Dupont, 2010; Wurzel and Connelly, 2010) (see Box 5.5).

Box 5.5 The European Council's role in the adoption of the climate and energy package

In March 2007, the European Council agreed the climate and energy package, the technical details of which had been negotiated and worked out by the Environment Council in close cooperation with the energy and finance ministers. The climate change and energy package proposed a unilateral 20 per cent reduction target for carbon dioxide emissions by 2020 (compared to 1990 levels) and a conditional 30 per cent reduction target, subject to other developed countries undertaking equivalent actions. However, arduous negotiations on the 'effort sharing agreement', which translated the collective 20 per cent EU reduction target into specific national reduction goals for the 27 member states, almost led to the unravelling of the entire package. The firm commitment by all member states under the effort sharing agreement were necessary to give credibility to the

EU's leadership ambitions in international climate change politics. A European Council under the 2009 Swedish Presidency adopted a financial assistance package to support climate adaptation measures in developing countries in order to improve the chances for a global agreement on combatting climate change. The European Council was therefore instrumental in positioning the EU as a leader in international climate change politics.

The European Council cannot adopt EU laws although it may launch new initiatives or try to break the political deadlock in particular Council formations. On the other hand, European Council meetings can also dampen the enthusiasm of environmental ministers or even block certain initiatives altogether. A good example was the European Council meeting in Edinburgh in 1992, which issued a detailed declaration on the correct interpretation of the principle of subsidiarity. This led to the publication of an Anglo-Franco hit list of laws to be scrapped.

Summary points

- The European Council issues guidelines and political instructions to the Council.
- The European Council only occasionally dealt with environmental issues prior to the 1990s.
- Since the 1990s the European Council has taken a more proactive role in international climate change issues.

Member states: leaders and laggards

In environmental policy, member states can be roughly categorized as leaders, laggards or swing states. *Leader states* demand the adoption of ambitious environmental measures at the EU level (and often also the international level). The group of environmental leader states can be subdivided into 'forerunner' states, which aim to maximize their freedom to develop their own ambitious domestic environmental policy, and 'pusher' states which try to export to the EU level (and/or international level) their domestic standards and regulatory philosophies (Liefferink and Andersen, 1998). In order to create a level playing field, Denmark and Sweden have a reputation for often acting as forerunners while Germany is said to have played a pusher role (Liefferink and Andersen, 1998; Wurzel, 2008).

Laggards, on the other hand, drag their feet and may try to use the national veto to prevent the adoption of ambitious EU environmental policy measures (e.g. Haverland, 2000). The reasons why member states act as environmental laggards are multi-faceted and include low domestic political salience of environmental issues and overriding concerns about the negative potential impact of EU policy measures on their domestic economies.

The Central and Eastern European member states as well as the Southern European member states (Greece, Portugal and Spain) and Ireland are often labelled laggard states. However, the domestic environmental problems of these member states differ from those of the more highly industrialized Northern European member states who tend to set the agenda for EU environmental policy (Börzel, 2000; Weale *et al.*, 2000). They often have weaker domestic environmental administrative capacities which makes EU agenda setting (see Chapter 11) and the implementation of EU environmental policy difficult (see Chapter 14). The Southern and Central and Eastern European member states typically have weaker domestic environmental groups and Green Parties and more pressing economic problems than the more affluent Northern European states.

Finally, *swing states* do not hold a strong national preference in environmental policy. They can be swayed (by environmental leaders and laggards) through side payments (e.g. increased EU structural funding), package deals or simply by developing the best arguments in Environment Council and/or European Council negotiations (Wurzel, 2008).

There is relatively wide agreement that the group of environmental leader states initially consisted of a green trio, made up of Denmark, Germany and the Netherlands, that gradually expanded to a green sextet when Austria, Finland and Sweden joined in 1995 (Andersen and Liefferink, 1997; Wurzel, 2008). Although the green sextet still holds a blocking minority (under qualified majority voting), its influence has diminished since 2004 because most of the new Central and Eastern European member states often give a higher priority to economic development.

Importantly, these classifications may vary over time or even from one issue to the next. For much of the 1970s and 1980s, the UK was widely seen as the 'dirty man of Europe' (Weale, 1992), i.e. a laggard. However, since the 1990s, the UK has acted as a leader in EU and international climate change politics (Rayner and Jordan, 2010). Moreover, it developed from a passive 'policy taker' to an active 'policy shaper' (Jordan, 2002, 2004). Partly due to its size (in terms of population and economy), Germany was for long seen as the most important environmental leader state within the EU (Andersen and Liefferink, 1997; Liefferink and Andersen, 1998). However, post-unification it lost some of its penchant for leading while coming under pressure from the EU to modify its regulatory style (Hèritier *et al.*, 1996; Wurzel, 2004). Post unification, Germany has found itself repeatedly on the defensive on EU environmental policy measures (such as environmental impact assessment) which it perceived as costly and incompatible with its regulatory style (e.g. Wurzel, 2004). However, Germany has continued to act as a leader on a range of issues including climate change (ibid.). The Netherlands is another example of an environmental leader which has lost some of its appetite to lead (Liefferink and Birkel, 2010).

Summary points

- Denmark, Germany and the Netherlands as well as Austria, Finland and Sweden have traditionally been portrayed as environmental leader states.
- The environmental priorities of the less prosperous Southern and Eastern European states often differ from the more affluent Northern European states and consequently they tend to behave as laggards.
- Member states' tendency to behave as leader, laggard or swing states may vary over time or even from issue to issue.

Conclusion

The Council and European Council are central actors in EU environmental policy making. These two actors constitute both EU institutions *and* negotiating forums for member governments. The European Council issues the political guidelines while the Council negotiates and adopts EU laws. The environmental leader–laggard dimension goes a long way towards explaining the agreements and stalemates within the Environment Council. However, member states' classification as environmental leaders or laggards may vary over time or even from issue to issue.

It is the role of the rotating Presidency to facilitate compromise solutions within the Council which normally strives to take decisions by consensus even if qualified majority voting is applicable. Over the years the Environment Council has matured into a significant Council formation. Attempts to achieve better integration of environmental requirements into other Council formations have, however, not been very successful (see Chapter 13). Prior to the 1990s, the European Council only occasionally dealt with environmental issues although it gave the starting signal for a common environmental policy at its summit in Paris in 1972. More recently the European Council has developed a greater role in shaping the EU's climate change policy in particular.

Key questions

1. How are decisions arrived at in the Environment Council?
2. Has the European Council become an important actor for EU environmental policy? If so, why?
3. What role does the presidency play in EU environmental policy making?
4. How easy is it to identify environmental leader and laggard states?

Guide to further reading

- Most EU introductory text books (e.g. Cini and Pérez-Solórzano Borragán, 2010; Nugent, 2010; Wallace *et al.*, 2010) include chapters on the Council and the European Council. Hayes-Renshaw and Wallace (2006) offer a superb analysis of the Council and European Council.
- Oberthür and Dupont (2010) provide an excellent analysis of the role which the Environment Council and European Council play in EU climate change politics.
- First-rate assessments of environmental leader states can be found in Andersen and Liefferink (1997) and Liefferink and Andersen (1998).
- The role of the Presidency in EU environmental policy making is analysed by Wurzel (1996; 2004).

Acknowledgements

The research for this chapter benefited from a British Academy grant (SG46048) and draws upon interviews with EU officials. The author would like to thank officials who gave up their precious time to be interviewed. All errors remain the responsibility of the author.

Notes

1   Denmark, Finland, Iceland, Norway and Sweden as well as the three autonomous areas, the Faroe Islands, Greenland and the Åland Islands are members of the Nordic Council.
2   The Franco-German alliance, which in the past has been a major driving force for deeper European integration, does not play an important role in environmental policy. In fact, France and Germany often adopt different views on environmental issues (Héritier *et al.*, 1996).
3   Most continental European member states use the term 'minister' for the political post for which secretary of state is the equivalent post in Britain.

References

Andersen, M.S. and Liefferink, D. (eds) (1997) *European Environmental Policy: The Pioneers*, Manchester University Press, Manchester.
Börzel, T.A. (2000) 'Why there is no "southern problem": on environmental leaders and laggards in the European Union', *Journal of European Public Policy*, vol. 7, no. 1, pp. 141–162.
Cini, M. and Pérez-Solórzano Borragán, N. (eds) (2010) *European Union Politics*, 3rd edition, Oxford University Press, Oxford.
Council of the European Union (2011a) 'Council configurations', available at: www.consilium. europa.eu/council/council-configurations.aspx?lang=en (accessed 1 August 2011).
Council of the European Union (2011b) Press Release. 3103rd Council meeting. Environment. 11827/11 PRESSE 183, press office of the Council of the European Union, Brussels.

Council of the European Union (2011c) 'Voting calculator', available at: www.consilium. europa.eu/council/voting-calculator.aspx?lang=en (accessed 3 October 2011).

European Council (2011) 'Trio presidency', available at: www.eu2007.de/en/The_Council_ Presidency/trio/index.html (accessed 3 August 2011).

Friedrich, A., Tappe, M. and Wurzel, R. (2000) 'A new approach to EU environmental policy-making? The Auto-Oil I programme', *Journal of European Public Policy*, vol. 7, no. 4, pp. 593–612.

Haverland, M. (2000) 'National adaptation to European integration: the importance of institutional veto points', *Journal of Public Policy*, vol. 20, no. 1, pp. 83–103.

Hayes-Renshaw, F. and Wallace, H. (2006) *The Council of Ministers*, 2nd edition, Palgrave, Basingstoke.

Héritier, A., Knill, C. and Mingers, S. (1996) *Ringing the Changes in Europe*, Walter de Gruyter, Berlin.

Humphreys, J. (1996) *A Way Through the Woods: Negotiating in the European Union*, Department of the Environment, London.

Jordan, A. (2002) *The Europeanization of British Environmental Policy: A Departmental Perspective*, Palgrave, Basingstoke.

Jordan, A. (2004) 'The United Kingdom: from policy "taking" to policy "shaping"', in A. Jordan and D. Liefferink (eds) *Environmental Policy in Europe*, Routledge, London, pp. 205–223.

Jordan, A., Huitema, D., van Hasselt, H., Rayner, T. and Berkhout, F. (eds) (2010) *Climate Change Policy in the European Union*, Cambridge University Press, Cambridge.

Jordan, A., Schout, A. and Unfried, M. (2008) 'The European Union', in A. Jordan, and A. Lenschow (eds) *Innovation in Environmental Policy? Integrating the Environment for Sustainability*, Edward Elgar, Cheltenham, pp. 159–179.

Lewis, J. (2010) 'The Council of European Union', in M. Cini and N. Pérez-Solórzano Borragán (eds) *European Union Politics*, 3rd edition, Oxford University Press, Oxford, pp. 141–161.

Liefferink, D. and Andersen, M.A. (1998) 'Strategies of the "green" member states in EU environmental policy-making', *Journal of European Public Policy*, vol. 5, no. 2, pp. 24–70.

Liefferink, D. and Birkel, K. (2010) 'The Netherlands: a case of "cost-free leadership"', in R.K.W. Wurzel and J. Connelly (eds) *The European Union as a Leader in International Climate Change Politics*, Routledge, London, pp. 147–162.

McCormick, J. (2001) *Environmental Policy in the European Union*, Palgrave Macmillan, Basingstoke.

Nugent, N. (2010) *The Government and Politics of the European Union*, 7th edition, Palgrave Macmillan, Basingstoke.

Oberthür, S. and Dupont, C. (2010) 'The Council, the European Council and international climate policy', in R.K.W. Wurzel and J. Connelly (eds) *The European Union as a Leader in International Climate Change Politics*, Routledge, London, pp. 74–91.

Oberthür, S. and Roche Kelly, C. (2008) 'EU leadership in international climate change policy: achievements and challenges', *The International Spectator*, vol. 45, no. 3, pp. 35–50.

Pinder, J. (1991) *European Community: The Building of a Union*, Oxford University Press, Oxford.

Rayner, T. and Jordan, A. (2010) 'The United Kingdom: a paradoxical leader?', in R.K.W. Wurzel and J. Connelly (eds) *The European Union as a Leader in International Climate Change Politics*, Routledge, London, pp. 95–111.

Russel, D. and Jordan, A. (2008) 'The United Kingdom', in A. Jordan and A. Lenschow (eds) *Innovation in Environmental Policy? Integrating the Environment for Sustainability*, Edward Elgar, Cheltenham, pp. 247–267.

Schout, A. (2008) 'Beyond the rotating presidency', in J. Hayward (ed.) *Leaderless Europe*, Oxford University Press, Oxford, pp. 269–287.

Sherrington, P. (2000) *The Council of Ministers: Political Authority in the European Union*, Pinter, London.

Talberg, J. (2006) *Leadership and Negotiation in the European Union*, Cambridge University Press, Cambridge.

Wallace, H., Pollack, M. and Young, A.R. (eds) (2010) *Policy-Making in the European Union*, Oxford University Press, Oxford.

Weale, A. (1992) *The Politics of Pollution*, Manchester University Press, Manchester.

Weale, A., Pridham, G., Cini, M., Konstadakopulos, D., Porter, M. and Flynn, B. (2000) *Environmental Governance in Europe*, Oxford University Press, Oxford.

Wurzel, R.K.W. (1996) 'The role of the EU Presidency in the environmental field: does it make a difference which member state runs the Presidency?', *Journal of European Public Policy*, vol. 3, no. 2, pp. 272–291.

Wurzel, R.K.W. (2000) 'Flying into unexpected turbulence: the German EU presidency in the environmental field', *German Politics*, vol. 9, no. 3, pp. 23–42.

Wurzel, R.K.W. (2002) *Environmental Policy-Making in Britain, Germany and the European Union*, Manchester University Press, Manchester.

Wurzel, R.K.W. (2004) 'Germany: from environmental leadership to partial mismatch', in A. Jordan and D. Liefferink (eds) *Environmental Policy in Europe*, Routledge, London, pp. 99–117.

Wurzel, R.K.W. (2008) 'Environmental policy: EU actors, leader and laggard states', in J. Hayward (ed.) *Leaderless Europe*, Oxford University Press, Oxford, pp. 66–88.

Wurzel, R.K.W. and Connelly, J. (eds) (2010) *The European Union as a Leader in International Climate Change Politics*, Routledge, London.

Zito, A.R. (2000) *Making European Environmental Policy*, Macmillan, Basingstoke.

6   The European Commission

Emmanuelle Schön-Quinlivan

Summary guide

The European Commission has been at the heart of the EU since its creation in the 1950s. Yet it was only in 1973 that it set up a unit dedicated to environmental issues; this did not achieve full Directorate General (DG) status until 1981. Traditionally regarded as rather weak, DG Environment has gradually become more and more assertive, both actively seeking and being empowered by successive treaty changes. The principle of environmental policy integration, which involves the mainstreaming of environmental considerations into the operation of all policy areas gave it an opportunity to intensify cooperation with other DGs. The Commission is now very much at the heart of EU environmental policy. However, it still struggles to deal with its own internal organisational fragmentation as well as poor implementation at the member state level. Nevertheless, it has achieved a huge amount with surprisingly modest resources and little political backing, but important challenges remain, not least with regards to improving policy implementation.

Introduction

The European Commission is now at the heart of EU environmental policy making and enforcement. Not only does it have an exclusive right to propose new environmental policy, but it also has a treaty-based responsibility to ensure the implementation of environmental rules. But this was not always the case. As outlined in Chapter 2, environmental policy started as a collection of disparate rules which had no treaty basis. There was no department dedicated to environmental issues for the first 15 years of the European Commission's existence. It was only in 1973 that an environmental unit was created within Directorate General (DG) for Industry; a fully-fledged Environment DG was only set up in 1981.

This chapter first outlines the structure of the Commission, its administrative services as well as its political component, the College of Commissioners. It also gives a brief overview of recent administrative reforms which have changed the way DG Environment (DG ENV) carries out its everyday business. The second section traces the history of DG ENV and reviews its relationship with DG Climate Action (DG CLIMA). It frames this discussion within the wider context of DG ENV's relations with other DGs in the Commission. In the third section, the functions and power of the Commission are examined to understand its capacity to act coherently in the environmental field. Finally, the chapter reflects on two significant hurdles for EU environmental policy, namely, coordination and implementation. In facing those challenges, it is clear that, contrary to its rather marginal status in the 1980s, the Commission has become a rather proactive 'green actor' which is respected both internally and externally. Through the development of technical and political expertise, as well as the active promotion of principles such as environmental policy integration (EPI), the Commission has placed itself at the heart of EU environmental policy making. However, it still has to rely on member states when it comes to implementation, which tends to produce incomplete and incoherent policy outcomes.

Summary points

- The European Commission is a key institutional actor, operating at the heart of EU environmental policy.
- It has an exclusive right to propose new environmental policy as well as a treaty-based responsibility to ensure the implementation of the EU's environmental rules.
- A fully-fledged Environment DG was, however, only created in 1981, although this was preceded by an environmental unit within DG Industry.

The European Commission: an introduction

Administrative structure

The European Commission was founded in 1958 (see Chapter 2). Neither an international secretariat nor a government of the EU, it is often described as a *sui generis* institution where political–administrative relationships are particularly complex (Egeberg, 2007). Thus, the scope of its power and influence expands beyond the traditional boundaries of an administration. Its political component, the College of Commissioners, whose members can be seen as 'entrepreneurs politiques' (Joana and Smith, 2002: 243), confirms the atypical nature of the Commission. However, the European Commission cannot be equated with a government, even if some literature refers to it as 'the EU's "government in-waiting"' (Warleigh, 2002: 42). It does not operate in a sovereign nation-state and 'it has had up to now no power to raise revenue of its own; it is not based on any electoral or Parliamentary majority; above all – it lacks authority to make decisions on its own' (Coombes, 1970: 101).

Legally, the Commission is one single body. But it is often called a 'unique hybrid' (Peterson and Shackleton, 2006: 82) because the College of Commissioners is composed of political nominees, such as Janez Potočnik (currently the Commissioner for the Environment) or Connie Hedegaard (currently the Commissioner for Climate Action) while the DGs and services are composed of 34,000 administrative staff drawn from the 27 member states (Cini, 1996; Shore, 2000). The administrative branch of the Commission is composed of 44 services and DGs which include horizontal services such as the Legal Service or the Secretariat General and vertical DGs like DG ENV or DG CLIMA. Horizontal services play either a coordinating role or provide support for other services and DGs. Vertical DGs are involved in policy making: they manage a specific policy area such as environment, trade or climate action. Each DG is hierarchically structured into Directorates and Units. DG ENV has six Directorates and shares a Resources Directorate with DG CLIMA.

Political leadership

The Commission is headed by a College of Commissioners, who are appointed by member states after consultation with the President of the Commission. The Commissioner is the political head of the Commission's environmental policy. DG ENV is at her/his service. Cini (1996) demonstrates very well how political leadership from certain Commissioners led to a significant change which was supported and internalised by officials at lower levels. Before looking at the role of Commissioners in the development of DG ENV, it is worth pointing out that Jacques Delors, President of the European Commission from 1985 to 1995, helped to change the image of environmental policy by linking high environmental standards with business opportunities (see Chapter 10). This change in thinking brought the then DG XI out of the political shadows and onto centre stage.

Carlo Ripa di Meana was then appointed Environment Commissioner in 1990 which coincided with increased public interest and awareness in environmental issues. Provocative and controversial, he courted publicity and tried to bypass the Commission's formal procedure by announcing new agenda items in press conferences. Delors did not appreciate Ripa di Meana's way of doing business in the spotlight and their relationship grew tense. Despite his policy-making style, which was far removed from cooperation and discussion, Ripa di Meana's appointment happened at the same time as that of a new Director General, Brinkhorst. They both tried to change the image of DG XI in charge of environmental issues and make it a more mainstream player. Ripa di Meana was eventually replaced by Karel Van Miert for an interim period of six months until a full-time replacement could be found. Yet Van Miert supported what had been done before him and described environmental policy as 'one of our most successful policies, and one of the best understood' (Cini, 2003: 88). Between 1993 and 1995, a cautious Greek Commissioner, Yannis Paleokrassas, took charge. Despite making it clear that he believed in the importance of environmental issues, he did not have a strong public impact.

Between 1995 and 2005, two very outspoken women were appointed as environmental Commissioners, Ritt Bjerregaard and then Margot Wallström. Bjerregaard ended up being marginalised within the College when she publicly criticised her colleagues. Wallström was regarded as a much more active Commissioner; she was instrumental in concluding the ratification process of the Kyoto Protocol. In 2005, the environmental portfolio went back to a Greek Commissioner, Stavros Dimas, who, like Paleokrassas before him, kept a low profile. It is too early to assess the impact of the Slovenian Commissioner, Janez Potočnik.

It is important to remember that the Environment and Climate Action Commissioners are not the only two who can affect the development of the Commission's environmental policy. The College works on the basis of collegiality, which means that each decision made has to be endorsed and defended publicly by *all* Commissioners. Despite Commissioners taking an oath of independence from their country and swearing to defend the EU's public interest rather than their own country's, there have been instances where individual Commissioners have lost sight of this (see Box 6.1).

Box 6.1   The Commission's principle of collegiality . . . or not?

In June 2011, the Polish Commissioner for the EU budget, Janusz Lewandowski, expressed doubts about the reality of global warming in a press interview with a Polish newspaper (Euractiv, 2011). This view seemed to be linked to national political considerations since he was reported as saying that 'the EU's goals . . . [were] too ambitious for the Polish economy'. He concluded that 'Polish politicians have to persuade [the EU] that there cannot be a quick jump away from coal energy. For Poland it would be a disaster'. This incident highlights the internal fighting which goes on within and outside the formal framework of the College which can lead to the watering down of proposals long before they get to the Council of Ministers.

Besides the Commissioner's staff in the DG, a very important cog in the policy process is the *Cabinet* – the Commissioner's political office. It forms the interface between the Commissioner and the services with the aim of improving coordination and communication. But *Cabinets* have been criticised for acting more like a buffer between the Commissioner and his/her service, filtering the DG's message. Crucially, *Cabinets* are the first point of access for lobby groups (see Chapter 9), other European and international institutions as well as national governments to obtain information on a Commission's forthcoming proposals.

Reforming the way the Commission does business

On 15 March 1999, the entire College of Commissioners resigned *en masse* after a report was published by a committee of independent experts who had been appointed by the European Parliament to investigate allegations of fraud, mismanagement and nepotism. In March 2000, the White Paper, *Reforming the Commission* was published (European Commission, 2000). It formed the basis for a 'root and branch' reform of the way of doing business in the Commission and aimed to change the structures, processes and procedures of the European bureaucracy. It was also an opportunity for member states to focus attention on management rather than ever deeper European integration. The reform was divided into three main aspects:

1 Activity-based management which linked planning and programming of the Commission's activities with the allocation of financial and human resources. It also involved the creation of executive agencies dedicated to programme managing so that the parent DG could focus on policy making.
2 Human resources and the modernisation of a system which had hardly been changed since the Commission's creation in 1958. It involved a new career structure, a new staff performance review system, a focus on increased mobility and training as well as flexi-time.
3 Tightening of financial structures and procedures for control. This involved decentralising financial responsibility and creating auditing structures in each DG.

Every year, DG ENV must draft an Annual Management Plan which identifies clear objectives and related impact indicators. For each objective, it states the main policy output as well as the associated expenditure (European Commission, 2011a). Some officials in DG ENV are critical of this exercise which they see as cosmetic. Yet each of them has to reflect about his/her unit's goals for the year ahead and commit it to paper. What they achieve in year 2011 forms the basis for planning and programming in year 2012. It can be argued that willingly or not, this change of practice has impacted on the managerial culture of DG ENV, which has shifted from being input-oriented to being more output-focused. DG ENV is, for example, now directly in charge of its own budget. Financial and human resources planning and programming are central to the Annual Management Plan and have helped DG ENV to take a global view of its resources and match them with its priorities.

Summary points

• The Commission is a hybrid institution composed of a political College of Commissioners and hierarchically structured set of services, staffed with officials from the 27 member states.

- The Commissioner is not the only influence on the output of his/her DG. But the conscious decision of some administrative elites together with Commissioners like Ripa di Meana has changed DG ENV's culture.
- *Cabinets* are the main point of access for lobbies and NGOs to obtain information and/or influence the policy process.
- The Annual Management Plan has impacted on the managerial culture of the Commission, forcing DGs to plan their activities more strategically.

Policy making: the roles of the Commission

The European Commission was put at the heart of the European Community's institutional structure to engage in 'creative thinking'. Jean Monnet, a founding father of the EU, considered it the crux of any successful development of an integrated European political system. Its functions are multi-faceted and representative of its hybrid organisational nature. The Commission's formal roles span agenda-setting, legislative and executive functions.

Agenda setting

Article 17 of the Treaty on the European Union (TEU) attributes the Commission with the exclusive right of legislative initiative within the EU (see also Chapter 11). The Commission is the only institution which can set the agenda through putting forward a policy proposal to be examined by the Council of Ministers and the European Parliament, the two legislative equal partners in the case of the co-decision procedure (and since the Lisbon Treaty known as the ordinary legislative procedure). This very powerful function makes the Commission an internal motor of European integration. However, the reality of politics within the EU means that a legislative proposal does not necessarily follow such a linear route. Other EU institutions as well as member states, lobby groups, regional and local authorities, and private industries, can talk informally to the Commission about a proposal they would like to see put forward. The Commission has the right to ignore their ideas but it also knows that the journey from initiating to passing legislation is a long haul (see also Chapter 12). If a proposal comes from, or is supported, by one or more of these stakeholders, it is be more likely to survive the various stages of the legislative process. The Commission therefore often engages in a game of give and take with other actors. But it remains the ultimate arbiter of what is or is not included in a particular proposal.

The Commission has maximised its influence by developing its contacts with think-tanks. For example, the Bureau of European Policy Advisers, situated within the Commission, connects policy makers with think tanks such as the Centre for European Policy Studies and the Friends of Europe. This input into its thinking gives the Commission a more informal, but nevertheless influential, role in agenda setting. As Pollack (1997: 125) argues, the Commission has been enabled to '"set the agenda" by constructing "focal points" for bargaining in the absence of a unique equilibrium or by constructing policy proposals and matching these to pressing policy problems in an environment of uncertainty and imperfect information'.

Legislative brokering

Together with the European Parliament and the Council of Ministers, the Commission forms what is often referred to as the EU's 'institutional triangle'. However, the Commission is the only institution of the three which is involved in every step of the policy-making process (see Chapter 12), attending meetings in the European Parliament or the Council as well as inter-institutional meetings. The Commission used to have the option of withdrawing its proposal if it was not satisfied with the way other institutions took it forward. Yet the introduction of the ordinary legislative procedure has considerably reduced the Commission's ability to deploy this nuclear option. Indeed, the Commission is no longer allowed to withdraw its proposal once the European Parliament and the Council convene a conciliation meeting. Given that over 75 per cent of legislative decisions in the EU come under the ordinary legislative procedure, the Commission is now most often responsible for 'taking the necessary initiatives with a view to reconciling the positions of the European Parliament and the Council' (Article 294, TEU).

Given the multi-layered, ambiguous and open-ended nature of EU governance (Hooghe, 1997), the Commission is often required to mediate between the various actors in order to smooth out the policy-making process. It also goes further and sometimes tries to lobby those actors to gain support for a particular initiative or policy. The Commission juggles between two main roles: first, as a policy entrepreneur that plays a significant part in policy making towards further European integration; and, second, as a policy manager – a role which has increased with the gradual expansion in the EU's fields of competence.

Finally, and crucially, the Commission also has the exclusive power of drafting the EU's budget. The Preliminary Draft Budget is a key document produced by the Commission in February of the year preceding the budget. It forms the basis for discussion on how the EU's budget is to be spent. The Commission therefore has the first attempt at stating where it sees financial priorities for the advancement of the EU. The 2011 EU budget was €141.9 billion and 41 per cent of this was allocated to 'Preservation and Management of Natural Resources'. The Environment budgetary line increased by 10.9 per cent on the 2010 budget (*Official Journal of the European Union*, L68, Vol. 54, 15.03.2011, pp. 1–1277), which highlights the continuing priority given to environmental protection in the context of scarce resources.

Policy implementation

The Commission relies on the national, regional and local infrastructure to ensure its policies and decisions are implemented (see Chapter 14). The legal tool most commonly used in EU environmental policy is the directive, which unlike regulations, requires transposition into member states' legal systems. Therefore the Commission has to rely on member states' administrative structures and commitment to put directives into practice. Before any policy is implemented, the Commission has to set out the detailed rules which are not included in primary legislation and are required to guarantee consistent implementation. Some 69 per cent of secondary EU legislation passes through this comitology procedure (Blom-Hansen, 2011) (see also Chapter 12).

As explained by Blom-Hansen (2011), recent treaty changes will have significant impacts on the comitology system. The Treaty of Lisbon (see Chapter 3) abolished Article 202 of the Treaty Establishing the European Community (TEC) which formed the legal ground of the old comitology system. Articles 290 and 291 of the new Treaty on the Functioning of the European Union (TFEU) provide that delegated and implementation acts are adopted by the Commission. Furthermore, two new parliamentary control mechanisms were added which allow the European Parliament and the Council either to revoke the delegation of powers to the Commission, or to object to the delegated act within a set period of time. The exercise of implementing powers by the Commission is still under comitology control (Article 291, TFEU). The new rules which will replace the old comitology procedure were adopted by Regulation No 182/2011/EU and entered into force on 1 March 2011. It is as yet uncertain in practice what effect they will have on the distribution of executive power among the EU institutions. However, there will be more motivation for the Council and Parliament to oppose delegated acts because the procedure is simpler and does not require justification (Hardacre and Kaeding, 2011).

The legal guardian of the treaties

The TFEU states that the Commission should act as a legal guardian of the European treaties and any ensuing legislation. Therefore, it plays a supervisory role with regards to implementation and possible infringements of EU primary and secondary legislation (see Chapters 7 and 14). Since the 1993 Maastricht Treaty, the Commission can take member states to court for breach of EU legislation (Article 258, TFEU). Ultimately, however, it is the European Court of Justice which imposes fines on countries for non-transposition. For example, in 2000, Greece was held to be in breach of EU waste directives and was fined €20,000 per day until transposition had been completed (see Chapter 14). Another memorable example was the fining of France at €242,650 per day for non-compliance with EU insurance laws in 2002.

Due to the very large number of directives passed by the Council in the early 1970s, the number of infractions in the environment domain constantly increased in the 1980s. Complaints and cases detected by the Commission's own enquiries increased from 25 in 1978 to 192 in 1986 and 587 in 1992 (Johnson and Corcelle, 1995). Today even DG ENV states on its website that it handles 'the most significant case load of the Commission both in terms of open cases under investigation and in terms of infringement cases' (European Commission, 2011b). This trend continued until 2003 when the number peaked at 570 infringement cases but since 2005 has stabilised around 460 cases per annum. It should also be noted that the Commission has the legal power of follow-up regarding compliance with the judgment of the European Court of Justice under Article 260 TFEU. In 2009, DG ENV was following up on 61 cases.

External representation

The Commission, working together with the Presidency of the EU, is a significant actor in the EU's external policy. As explained in Chapter 16, multilateral environmental agreements are a shared competence between the EU and the member states. As a result, so-called mixed agreements are negotiated by the Commission working together with the Council Presidency. In the past 40 years, the EU has grown to become a leading actor on the international scene as demonstrated by the successful adoption of the Kyoto Protocol. In particular, the Commission is a key actor when it comes to negotiating international environmental agreements (see Chapter 16). For example, DG CLIMA leads the Commission task forces on the international negotiations in the areas of climate change and ozone depleting substances. It also coordinates bi-lateral and multi-lateral partnerships on climate change and energy with third countries. It was the Commission that signed the Cancún Agreement, a package of decisions adopted at the end of the UN Climate Conference in Mexico, which attempt to develop a comprehensive and legally binding framework for climate action for the period after 2012.

Summary points

- The Commission is a central actor in EU policy making because of its sole right of initiative.
- The Commission is also heavily involved in overseeing policy implementation. It can take any member state in breach of European legislation before the European Court of Justice, which has the option of imposing a fine.
- The Commission has worked hard to secure a seat in international policy negotiations, where it works alongside the Council to shape the EU's common position.

The Commission and the historical development of EU environmental policy

DG Environment: a group of 'green fundamentalists'?

In order to understand the power and influence of the Commission in environmental issues, it is necessary to look back at how DG ENV came into being. Path dependency plays a significant role in explaining why DG ENV remained a relatively weak DG in the Commission for several years (Cini, 1997). As already mentioned, DG ENV was only set up in 1973, as a five-person team within DG Industry, 15 years after the European Economic Community (EEC) was created. Since the Community had essentially been established to promote peace as well as economic growth, DGs with strong economic interests such as DG Transport or DG Enterprise had a much stronger voice than DG ENV. They also had more institutional experience and human resources, having been set up 15 years earlier. DG ENV remained a marginal DG for several years as its low staffing levels demonstrate. Having started with five officials in 1973, there were still only about 60 officials in the 1980s. In an organisation such as the Commission where human and financial resources equate to institutional power, a DG with less than 100 officials does not have the same status as other DGs with several hundred staff.

Instead of recruiting internally to the Commission, as is usually the norm when a new DG is created, DG ENV hired specialists with technical knowledge. These new officials were not civil servants and had a different culture to the other Commission's officials which 'gave [it] a reputation for being dominated by . . . "ecological freaks"' (ibid.: 78). The new recruits felt they had an environmental mission to accomplish and produced an enormous amount of legislation in a very short period of time. In the process, they chose speed over inclusion in the policy-making process and operated in a non-cooperative manner towards other DGs and external stakeholders (Cini, 2000: 79–80). They also failed to appreciate the need for local and national implementers to be involved in policy making.

DG ENV: a more mature and settled DG?

Over time, DG ENV matured and settled into the Commission's ways of working. It changed its approach and started focusing on the *politics* of the environment rather than just the technical details. It meant taking politics more into consideration when formulating legislation so that it could be adopted and better implemented (Weale and Williams, 1993). Cini (1997: 82) argues that in order to respond to the perception that DG ENV was a weak player, administrative elites and Commissioners such as Carlo Ripa de Meana (1990–1992) worked to alter 'the underlying assumptions, belief systems and ethos of DG XI officials'. This concerted effort was reflected in the contents of the Fifth Environment Action Programme (EAP) 1993–2000, which, unlike previous environmental programmes, suggested a variety of policy instrument ones (see Chapter 17). In particular, relying on new market-based instruments represented a significant shift in ideological approach to environmental policy making. It aimed 'to internationalize environmental costs by economic and fiscal incentives and disincentives thus helping ensure that environmentally friendly goods and services are not at a disadvantage compared to wasteful and polluting competitors' (Johnson and Corcelle, 1995: 21). This ideology – ecological modernisation – is further discussed in Chapter 10.

The Fifth EAP also departed from previous programmes by implementing a more bottom-up approach to policy making. Legislation was no longer to be made solely behind closed doors, but together with all social and economic partners (Chapter 18). It therefore set up three ad hoc dialogue groups:

1   a General Consultative Forum involving consumer representatives, trade unions, NGOs and businesses;
2   an implementation network comprising representatives of relevant national authorities and of the Commission to facilitate the adequate and smooth implementation of environmental legislation;
3   an Environmental Policy Review Group made up of representatives of the Commission and the member states.

The Fifth EAP represented a more encompassing and shared approach to policy making and implementation. The text highlighted that it was directed not just at environmentalists, but also citizens, consumers and businesses. It argued that '[T]he concept of *shared responsibility* requires a much more broadly-based and active involvement of all economic players including public authorities, public and private enterprise in all its forms, and, above all, the general public, both as citizens and consumers' (*Official Journal of the European Union*, 2011, L68/54, 1993, C138/26; emphasis added).

In 2010, eight years into the Sixth EAP (2002–2012), the Commission acknowledged the growing urgency of the climate issue and set up a DG CLIMA, staffed with 156 officials. In comparison, DG ENV's staff was at 568 in 2011, a significant increase on the average around 60 in the 1980s. DG CLIMA is also involved in policy making and represents the EU in international climate change negotiations together with member states. Since the 2009 Copenhagen climate change conference, where the EU was unable to speak with a single voice, tensions have run high between the Commission, with DG CLIMA taking the lead, together with member states (see Chapter 16). The cooperation between DG ENV and DG CLIMA means that DG ENV's input is to ensure 'that relevant environmental aspects like soil, forests and biodiversity are factored into climate policy' (European Commission, 2010).

Summary points

- DG ENV was created in 1973, as a small unit within DG Industry.
- For a long time DG ENV remained a marginal player within the Commission. There was a widely held perception that it was populated

> by ecological fundamentalists who produced too much legislation, some of which could not be fully implemented.
> • The Fifth EAP marked a sea change in DG ENV's approach to policy-making. It sought to present DG ENV and its policies in a newer and more constructive light.

The Commission: a green voice within the EU?

The problem of organisational fragmentation

Since 1973, the Commission has strived to develop a coherent environmental policy. Yet it has said that EU environmental policymaking is very fragmented (Cini, 1997; Peterson and Bomberg, 1999; Cliquot, 2004) (see also Chapter 13). In part, this is a basic organisational problem. It should also be noted that environmental issues cross-cut almost every other sector of policy making. In 2011, DG ENV listed 13 policies to which the principle of environmental policy integration (EPI) applied. DG ENV, therefore, interacts and negotiates with a large number of other DGs on a daily basis in its policy making. It is very easy to see how it can be drawn into conflict with other DGs (see Cini, 2003: 89).

Organisational fragmentation is not of course limited to DG ENV (see Chapter 13). It exists in any public administration where officials work in separate bureaux and develop different interests (Downs, 1967; Niskanen, 1971; Dunleavy, 1991). However, it is arguably more pronounced in the European Commission which is a multi-national, multi-cultural and multi-lingual organisation. These characteristics led Cram (1994, 1997, 1999) to refer to the Commission as a 'multi-organisation' (see also Caremier, 1997: 238). DG ENV has, however, learnt to cooperate with relevant DGs starting with preparing policy proposals jointly in order to increase their chances of adoption. Other institutions as well as member states, lobby groups, regional and local authorities and businesses talk informally to the Commission about a proposal they would like to see put forward (see Chapter 9).

Since the 1997 Amsterdam Treaty, the principle of EPI has become a legal requirement for all community policies and activities (see Chapters 3 and 13). As a result, a special unit for environmental integration was created within DG ENV (Koch and Lindenthal, 2011). DG ENV has been an active advocate of EPI. This has led Koch and Lindenthal (ibid.: 15) to conclude that:

> DG ENV was an important driving force for the organizational learning of the sectoral DGs as it changed its strategies to encourage environmental integration ... Thereby DG ENV contributed to the perception that the environmental integration principle is a worthwhile internal commitment for the Commission and its DGs.

There has been an acceptance in DG Enterprise (DG ENTR) that 'environmental concerns were a key element of European policy formulation' whereas DG

Transport and Energy (DG TREN) 'was convinced that energy and environment policy could be highly compatible and that the cooperation with DG ENV could produce synergistic effects for both' (ibid.: 12–15). At the organisational level, DG ENV has been pro-active in arguing the need for environmental concerns to be taken into consideration. However, other EU-level actors such as the European Parliament have not been as engaged (European Commission, 2003).

The lack of coordination comes as well from the specific institutional and political context in which the Commission evolves (see Chapter 13). The Commission cannot, as noted above, be compared with a traditional national government. Yet José Manuel Barroso has developed a new strategy since 2005 with the appointment of Catherine Day as the Secretary General. He wants to turn the Secretariat General into a 'Cabinet Office' and advance its policy analysis capacity through processes such as Impact Assessment (see Chapter 12). Since 2005, the Secretariat General has sought to become 'a solution provider' with an enhanced role in networking between services. Information is the crucial primary material which it uses to exert its influence. It is therefore interesting to analyse the deep change in culture within the Secretariat General which has arguably occurred since 2005. Whether this attempt by Barroso proves institutionally successful at EU level remains to be seen. It could, however, be the eventual seed of an EU 'core executive', something which would help with the implementation of EPI at EU level.

The problem of implementation: a proactive but restricted approach?

The implementation of EU environmental policy is systemically poor, in part, due to the multi-level governance system in which the Commission finds itself. It has to rely on member states to comply and has few tools to compel them to do so (see Chapter 14). The Commission's role is limited to monitoring, reporting and carrying out investigations (Nugent, 2003). In an effort to move away from confrontational methods, the Commission has focused on developing networks, such as the Network for the Implementation and Enforcement of Environmental Law (IMPEL). Created in 1992, it is supported by a secretariat located within DG ENV (Martens, 2008: 644). As noted above, the Commission is often required to mediate between various actors in order to facilitate policy-making processes. Yet Commission officials consider themselves as much more than mediators in IMPEL. Because they have a deep knowledge of the EU system and enormous technical expertise, Commission officials are often able to convince national officials of the necessity of a certain course of action. This is particularly the case for new member states which tend to be more eager to comply than older member states and will rely more readily on the Commission's guidance.

The Commission tries to lobby EU-level and national actors to gain support for the effective implementation of environmental acts. Member states as much as the Commission have also got to take into consideration the popularity of the EU environmental policy when not complying. But the Commission cannot push its advantage too much by taking non-compliant states to court because it might trigger a public backlash. That said, member states cannot be seen to be systematically infringing common environmental policies either, hence the highly negotiated style of much implementation and enforcement activity in the EU (see Chapter 14).

Finally, DG ENV has been proactive in seeking to convince the wider public of the importance of environmental issues (Koch and Lindenthal, 2011). However, this does not mean that it feels it has been fully successful in convincing all actors of the benefits and necessity of environmental policy (European Commission, 2003). Ultimately, the main constraints on DG ENV and the Commission in general are systemic. Some businesses, for example, seem wholly unconvinced of the merits of strong environmental policies (see, for example, Chapter 10) and thus cannot easily be overturned. To overcome them would require a major overhaul of the EU's political and administrative system, as well as significant change in political attitudes about the importance of environmental protection vis-à-vis economic and social priorities.

Summary points

- DG ENV has learnt about the importance of cooperating with other relevant DGs from the very beginning of the policy process.
- The Commission has been quite successful in mainstreaming environmental issues throughout the Commission through an organisational learning process driven by DG ENV, but other EU actors have been much less supportive.
- DG ENV has adopted a proactive role with external actors such as transnational implementation networks, but its full effect remains limited.
- Poor implementation is not easy to address because the root causes reside within the structure of the EU's multilevel governance system.

Conclusion

The Commission is only one of several actors in the EU's multi-levelled system of governance but it has established itself at the heart of EU environmental policy. It has developed a deep technical knowledge which makes it a partner to be reckoned with. The changing organisational features of the Commission clearly demonstrate how important environmental policy is in its overall policy portfolio: DG ENV's staffing levels have increased tenfold in 10 years and a second DG dedicated to climate change issues was created in February 2010. Yet organisational characteristics alone cannot fully capture the Commission's environmental influence; some of its most important impacts have to be measured in terms of the emergence of new policy ideas and worldviews within, but also outside Brussels.

Cini (1996, 2003) has explained why DG ENV was regarded as a weak DG that could not impose its views in the face of far bigger DGs defending economic interests. After years of playing in the minor league and developing a reputation for non-implementable legislation, DG ENV consciously reshaped its administrative culture in order to move into the group of mainstream DGs. The turning point was the Fifth EAP and the Amsterdam Treaty which made the integration principle legally binding. Slowly, DG ENV started taking into account the politics of the environment and convinced other DGs that environmental concerns were, in fact, a key element of all policy areas and of European integration more generally. In parallel, public support for EU environmental policy grew as people became more interested, concerned and supportive of environmental issues. It is a measure of the Commission's success in this endeavour that EU environmental policy remains one of *the* most popular of all the EU's policy areas (Chapter 20).

When looking at the Commission and the future prospects for environmental policy, two hurdles remain: one concerns the impact of organisational fragmentation on environmental policy making; the second relates to poor implementation. When looking at organisational fragmentation, EPI gave DG ENV an opportunity to open up a dialogue with other DGs right at the beginning of the policy-making process. The current Commission President and Secretary General are also developing a new culture of service for the Secretariat General which will be the political office of the President and will aim to coordinate and give added weight to EPI.

As for implementation, DG ENV and the wider Commission are caught in a multi-level system which forces them to rely heavily on member states. Solving all implementation problems is next to impossible (see Chapter 14). The Commission has compensated for this by being proactive within new transnational networks. This remains rather a meagre solution to a significant political problem. Since no formal overhaul of the balance of power within the EU is anticipated, pressure for change will have to come from other corners of the political system. The Commission cannot be expected to do everything. The Lisbon Treaty has given a new opportunity for citizens to get more involved (see Chapter 3). The European Commission would certainly value greater public support in its quest to protect the European environment for future generations.

Summary points

- The principle of EPI has facilitated a change in administrative culture within DG ENV and consequently a change in how it is perceived by other DGs.
- The Commission is regarded as a proactive actor within the EU and a leader on environmental issues on the international scene.
- Poor policy implementation is a significant hurdle for DG ENV and the wider Commission.

Key questions

1   Which factors explain the fragmentation of environmental policy making within the European Commission?
2   What impact has the emergence of the EPI principle had on the development of DG ENV and its interactions with other DGs?
3   Why is the implementation of EU environmental policy so problematic for the Commission?
4   To what extent is the European Commission the most proactive 'green actor' at EU level?

Guide to further reading

• For an in-depth analysis of the Commission and its politico-administrative dynamics, see Stevens and Stevens (2001; a new edition is in preparation) and Spence and Edwards (2006).
• A more specific understanding of the Commission's environmental role can be gained from Johnson and Corcelle (1995), Cini (2003), Martens (2008) and Koch and Lindenthal (2011).
• For a better understanding of administrative reforms and their impact on the Commission's everyday business, see Schön-Quinlivan (2011).

References

Blom-Hansen, J. (2011) 'The EU comitology system: taking stock before the new Lisbon regime', *Journal of European Public Policy*, vol. 18, no. 4, pp. 607–617.

Caremier, B. (1997) '"L'Eurocratie": une fonction publique à la croisée du politique et de l'administratif', *Revue de la Recherche Juridique, Droit Prospectif*, vol. 1, no. 68, pp. 229–286.

Cini, M. (1996) *The European Commission: Leadership, Organisation and Culture in the EU Administration*, Manchester University Press, Manchester.

Cini, M. (1997) 'Administrative culture in the European Commission: the cases of competition and environment', in N. Nugent (ed.) *At the Heart of the Union: Studies of the European Commission*, St Martin's Press, New York.

Cini, M. (2000) 'Administrative culture in the European Commission: the cases of competition and environment' in N. Nugent (ed.) *At the Heart of the Union; Studies on the European Commission*, 2nd edition, Macmillan Press, Basingstoke.

Cini, M. (2003) 'Actors and institutions in environmental governance', in A. Weale *et al. Environmental Governance in Europe*, Oxford University Press, Oxford.

Cliquot, N. (2004) *Un Van Gogh de la Politique? La Capacité d'Entrepreneur Politique de la Commission Européenne dans la Genèse de la Directive Responsabilité Environnementale*, Mémoire de DEA, IEP, Paris.

Coombes, D. (1970) *Politics and Bureaucracy in the European Community*, Sage, Beverly Hills, CA.

Cram, L. (1994) 'The European Commission as a multi-organisation: social policy and IT policy in the EU', *Journal of European Public Policy*, vol. 1, no. 2, pp. 195–217.

Cram, L. (1997) *Policy-making in the European Union*, Routledge, London.

Cram, L. (1999) 'The Commission', in L. Cram, D. Dinan and N. Nugent (eds) *Developments in the European Union*, Macmillan, Basingstoke.

Downs, A. (1967) *Inside Bureaucracy*, Little Brown, Boston.

Dunleavy, P. (1991) *Democracy, Bureaucracy and Public Choice: Economic Explanations in Political Science*, Harvester Wheatsheaf, London.

Egeberg, M. (2007) 'The European Commission', in M. Cini (ed.) *European Union Politics*, Oxford University Press, Oxford.

Euractiv (2011) 'Poland's EU commissioner in surprise climate denial move', available at: www.euractiv.com/en/climate-environment/polands-eu-commissioner-surprise-climate-denial-move-news-505869 (accessed 23 June 2011).

European Commission (2000) *Reforming the Commission: A White Paper, Part I*, (COM (2000) 200), European Commission, Brussels.

European Commission (2003) *2003 Environmental Policy Review*, (COM (2003) 745), European Commission, Brussels.

European Commission (2010) 'DG Environment factsheet', September 2010, available at: http://ec.europa.eu/environment/pubs/pdf/factsheets/dg_environment.pdf (accessed 14 October 2011).

European Commission (2011a) 'Annual Management Plan', European Commission, available at: http://ec.europa.eu/dgs/environment/pdf/management_plan_2011.pdf (accessed 14 October 2011).

European Commission (2011b) 'Legal enforcement', *Europa*, available at: http://ec.europa.eu/environment/legal/lawa/statistics.htm (accessed 23 June 2011).

Hardacre, A. and Kaeding, M. (2011) 'Delegated and implementing acts: the new world of comitology – implications for European and national public administrations', *Eipascope*, no. 2011, pp. 29–32.

Hooghe, L. (1997) 'A house with differing views: the European Commission and cohesion policy', in N. Nugent (ed.) *At the Heart of the Union: Studies of the European Commission*, 2nd edition, Macmillan, Basingstoke.

Joana, J. and Smith, A. (2002) *Les Commissaires Européens: Technocrates, Diplomates ou Politiques?*, Presses de Sciences Po, Paris.

Johnson, S.P. and Corcelle, G. (1995) *The Environmental Policy of the European Communities*, 2nd edition, Kluwer Law International, London.

Koch, M. and Lindenthal, A. (2011) 'Learning within the European Commission: the case of environmental integration', *Journal of European Public Policy*, vol. 18, no. 7, pp. 1–19.

Martens, M. (2008) 'Administrative integration through the back door? The role and influence of the European Commission in transgovernmental networks within the environmental policy field', *European Integration*, vol. 30, no. 5, pp. 635–651.

Niskanen, W.A. (1971) *Bureaucracy and Representative Government*, Aldine-Atherton, Chicago.

Nugent, N. (2003) *Government and Politics of the European Union*, Palgrave, Basingstoke.

Peterson, J. and Bomberg, E. (1999) *Decision-making in the European Union*, Palgrave, Basingstoke.

Peterson, J. and Shackleton, M. (eds) (2006) *The Institutions of the European Union*, 2nd edition, Oxford University Press, Oxford.

Pollack, M.A. (1997) 'Delegation, agency and agenda-setting in the European Community', *International Organization*, vol. 51, pp. 99–134.

Schön-Quinlivan, E. (2011) *Reforming the European Commission*, Palgrave, Basingstoke.

Shore, C. (2000) *Building Europe: The Cultural Politics of European Integration*, Routledge, London.

Spence, D. and Edwards, G. (2006) *The European Commission*, John Harper Publishing, London.

Stevens, A. and Stevens H. (2001) *Brussels Bureaucrats? The Administration of the European Union*, Palgrave, Basingstoke.

Warleigh, A. (2002) *Understanding European Union Institutions*, Routledge, London.

Weale, A. and Williams, A. (1993) 'Between economy and ecology? The single market and the integration of environmental policy', in D. Judge (ed.) *A Green Dimension for the European Community: Political Issues and Processes*, Frank Cass, Portland, OR.

7　The European Court of Justice

Ludwig Krämer

Summary guide

Since 1976, the European Court of Justice (ECJ) has delivered more than 700 judgments on environmental matters, the vast majority being initiated by the European Commission against a member state. Most of them have dealt with the omission to transpose the requirements of EU environmental law into the national provisions, or the incomplete or incorrect transposition of EU environmental law. Cases of bad practical application of EU law in the member states are less frequent. In general, the ECJ has tended to side with the environment; it has developed a considerable number of innovative arguments in order to have EU environmental law and principles applied. Most of its judgments have managed to strike the right balance between the diverging economic and ecological interests. However, it is difficult for individual persons and environmental organizations to bring cases before the ECJ themselves.

Structure and function of the ECJ

The Court of Justice of the European Union (see Box 7.1) serves two main functions: (1) to oversee the lawful interpretation of the EU treaties; and (2) to provide effective legal protection in the fields covered by EU law (Article 19, Treaty on the European Union [TEU]). It is the last and final arbiter on the interpretation of EU law and its judgments create precedents in all 27 member states. In environmental law, the judgments contributed to making EU legislation and legal principles more precise and to ensuring uniform application of these provisions.

Box 7.1   What is the European Court of Justice?

The Court consists of three parts: (1) the Court of Justice; (2) the General Court; and (3) an EU Civil Service Tribunal. The Civil Service Tribunal will not be discussed in this chapter. The Court of Justice is composed of one judge per member state who is appointed by agreement between the governments of the member states. It has a number of main functions: it deals with disputes between EU institutions as well as actions taken by the EU Commission against a member state; it also gives preliminary rulings on the interpretation of EU law in cases which are submitted by the courts of the 27 member states and it decides on appeals against decisions by the General Court. The Court of Justice is assisted in its work by Advocates-General who present opinions on the cases submitted to the Court. The General Court is composed of at least one judge per member state. The Advocates-General do not give opinions in cases before it. The General Court is mainly competent for cases submitted by private persons or companies, as well as in competition matters.

The present structure of the EU judiciary system favours economic interests over environmental interests, which is illustrated by the following example. Where two companies in the EU make an unlawful agreement which restricts or distorts competition within the internal market (e.g. according to Article 101 of the Treaty on the Functioning of the European Union [TFEU]), the European Commission (if indeed it even becomes aware of this situation) may send its inspectors to the companies, enter premises, interview persons, seize documents, examine books and records, and take other appropriate measures. At the end of the investigation procedure, the Commission will take a decision. It may impose financial sanctions of up to 10 per cent of the total turnover of the companies. The companies may appeal against this decision to the General Court and then, if necessary, they may appeal against the judgment of the General Court to the Court of Justice.

Where the same companies breach environmental legislation, for example, by discharging cadmium-containing waste water so that a river exceeds the maximum admissible concentrations (see Directive 83/513/EEC), and the Commission learns of it, it may address a letter to the member state in which the company discharged the water. Where it is not satisfied with the member state's answer, the Commission may begin formal proceedings by sending a formal letter to that member state. Should this answer again not be adequate, the Commission may issue a reasoned opinion. Should the member state's answer still not satisfy the Commission, the latter may then appeal to the Court of Justice. The Court may, at best, state that the member state in question has infringed its obligation under EU environmental law. No financial sanctions may be imposed. Only when the member state in question does not take the necessary measures to comply with the Court's judgment, may the Commission initiate further proceedings – again with a letter of formal notice and a reasoned opinion preceding the application – and the Court then impose a financial sanction (for details, see Chapter 14).

The difference is amazing: in the first example where competition law has been broken, there is a three-level procedure: the Commission decision; application to the General Court; and appeal. However, where environmental law has been broken, only one judicial level is available. No immediate sanction may be imposed by the Commission or the Court. And the action is taken against the relevant member state, not against the polluter.

The next section of this chapter describes the official and unofficial statistics on environmental Court cases. The remaining sections then set out some of the most relevant features of the ECJ's jurisdiction in environmental matters. This starts with a discussion of who can bring a case to the Court, i.e. who has legal 'standing'. The next section then sets out some of the most innovative cases where the Court has played an important role in interpreting EU environmental law in order to protect the environment in the spirit, if not the exact letter, of the law. How the Court attempts to balance the interests of the EU (i.e. its objectives of environmental protection) and those of member states is the subject of the next section. The following section examines how the court balances environmental and economic interests. Then, the Court's attempts to increase the transparency of EU environmental law and to strengthen citizen rights are discussed. This is followed by an outline of cases which appear to have political character. A comparison is made between the Court of Justice and the General Court before the final section draws together some conclusions on the role of the Court in the development of EU environmental policy.

Summary points

- The ECJ is responsible for interpreting and applying EU law for the whole of the EU.
- The ECJ has 27 judges and the General Court has another 27 judges.
- The present structure of the EU judiciary system favours economic interests over environmental interests.

Statistical data

There are no specific statistics on environmental cases held by the Court of Justice. The Court's annual statistics of judicial activity lists cases on environmental matters together with consumer cases, under the heading 'environment and consumers' (Court of Justice, no date). Furthermore, there are many circumstances where important cases concerning environmental directives or regulations are categorized under another heading. For example, where a case is important with regard to the participation of the European Parliament or the residual competencies of member states, it will be treated under the heading 'law governing the institutions', as will cases concerning access to environmental information. Alternatively, cases concerning Environmental State Aid are classified as competition cases, etc.

The author's own statistics, made since 1992, considers all these cases as environmental cases – though even then there always remain cases which are hard to classify. According to these data, between 1976 and until the end of 2010, the Court of Justice issued more than 700 judgments on environmental matters (Krämer, 1995; 1998; 2000; 2002a; 2004; 2006; 2008).[1] Around three-quarters of these judgments were cases submitted to the Court by the European Commission which took action against a member state for not, or not correctly, transposing EU environmental legislation into national law, or less frequently in recent years, for poorly applying EU environmental law. The remaining cases were principally preliminary judgments on cases submitted by national courts and, in few cases, actions by private persons or environmental organizations. Significantly, in not one case has a member state taken action against another member state for not having complied with its obligations under EU environmental law.

The duration of the procedure before the Court in environmental cases is, on average, just less than two years (Krämer, 2008; see also Chapter 14). However, this does not include the pre-judicial phase between the Commission and the member state, where a letter of formal notice and a reasoned opinion is given. The overall time for this whole procedure is closer to 47 months on average.

Summary points

- There are detailed statistics on competition or internal market Court cases, but no specific official statistics on environmental cases.
- Environmental procedures before the Court generally take about two years to be completed.
- Where the Commission takes action against a member state, the whole procedure, including the pre-judicial stage, on average, takes almost four years.

The ECJ as an arbiter of diverging interests

EU environmental law has developed progressively since the mid-1970s with an environmental chapter only inserted into the treaty in 1987 (see Chapter 2). EU environmental legislation was at first drafted to a large extent as framework legislation, which left a considerable amount of discretion to the different legal cultures in member states. However, the general terms of EU environmental legislation required a uniform interpretation, in order to ensure their coherent application in all member states, including by their national, regional and local administrations and by their courts. It was the Court of Justice which had to ensure this uniform interpretation (Krämer, 1992; 1993).

An example illustrates how far this interpretative role of the Court in environmental matters had to go. As late as 1993, the United Kingdom argued in a case before the Court (Case C-56/90) that an environmental directive 'merely requires the member states to take all practicable steps to comply' with the directive's provisions (European Court Report, 1993: paragraph 40). The Court had to indicate that a directive imposed the obligation on member states to achieve a specific result.

Vested interests have long aimed at preventing the adoption of precise EU environmental legislation. They prefer, if legislation could not be avoided altogether, to see general provisions adopted which impose 'best available techniques', 'best practices', 'good ecological quality', 'no significant risk' or similar obligations. Opposing environmental lobby groups are often thought to be less influential than these vested interests (see Chapters 9 and 10). Therefore, it is not surprising that several member state governments have preferred not to impose very strict environmental obligations on economic operators in order to promote economic growth, albeit sometimes at the expense of the environment. The Commission has a tendency of submitting only cases to the Court, when it has a high chance of winning. Therefore, the Court had, until recently, few opportunities to interpret and sharpen such general provisions. Overall, it is fair to say that where such opportunities were offered, the Court normally interpreted EU environmental law in a pro-environmental way. The following text tries to illustrate the Court's interpretative efforts with a number of examples.

Standing

Under Article 258 TFEU, the European Commission may take action against a member state which fails to fulfil an obligation under the TFEU Treaty or under secondary EU legislation. The Commission has discretionary power, whether it brings such a case, and need not have an interest in bringing it. This discretion cannot be controlled by the Court of Justice.

Under Article 263(4) TFEU, any person may institute proceedings against a decision addressed to that person or against a decision which, although addressed to another person, is of 'direct and individual concern' to it, with the argument that the decision infringes EU law. This provision is the key provision for court actions. In practice, though, court actions by NGOs have never been held admissible. The general rule is that NGOs and citizens have no standing in environmental matters.

The first reason for this situation lies in the drafting of the EU treaties. Indeed, while the treaties allow economic operators to initiate actions before national or the EU courts, where they are of the opinion that a legislative or an administrative measure creates obstacles to the free trade within the European Union, environmental NGOs or citizens do not have the same possibility when they are of the opinion that a measure pollutes or otherwise damages the environment. With regard to the free trade within the EU, Article 34 TFEU provides that 'quantitative restrictions on imports and all measures having equivalent effect, shall be prohibited between member states'.[2] The Court of Justice ruled in numerous judgments that the individual producer or trader could claim in court that a legislative provision or a measure is incompatible with Articles 34 TFEU, as he was directly and individually concerned by such measures; national courts ruled, under their national provisions, in the same way.

In contrast, there is no provision in the EU treaties which prohibits the pollution of the environment. All the provisions of the treaties which deal with environmental issues (e.g. Articles 191 to 193 and 11 TFEU), are drafted in a rather neutral way, but do not have the purpose or the effect of protecting the interests of citizens or NGOs.

The Court of Justice has interpreted Article 263(4) TFEU rather restrictively. The leading case was Case C-321/95P. In that case, Greenpeace and other applicants opposed a decision by the Commission to grant financial assistance from the European Regional Development Fund to enable the construction of two power stations in the Canary Islands of Spain. The decision by the Spanish authorities which authorized the construction projects had been taken without an assessment of their direct and indirect effects on the environment. Such an impact assessment was obligatory under the Environmental Impact Assessment Directive (85/337/EEC). In addition, Regulation EEC No. 2052/88 also provided that financial assistance by the Regional Development Fund could only be given when the project in question was in conformity with EU law and policy. The General Court held the application by Greenpeace and the other applicants to be inadmissible because the Commission decision did not affect them in a way that differentiated them from all other persons (Case T-585/93); they were thus not directly and individually concerned by it. On appeal, the Court of Justice confirmed the inadmissibility of the application. It argued that the applicants always had the possibility to appeal to a Spanish court, in order to have the construction permit annulled. The Spanish court might then, if necessary, put a preliminary question to the Court of Justice on the interpretation of EU law. This jurisprudence was confirmed in numerous later judgments (e.g. Case T-94/04; Case C-355/08P; Case C-444/08P). In particular, all applications of environmental organizations and individual persons against legislative provisions, decisions or measures in environmental matters were held inadmissible. The EU Courts considered that the protection of the environment was a matter of *general* interest, so that their applicants were not *individually* concerned.

The General Court once tried, in a case on fisheries policy, to change the interpretation of Article 263(4) TFEU, arguing that it was not compatible with the human right of effective judicial protection. However, on appeal, the Court of Justice argued (in Case T-263/02P) that it was up to the member states 'to establish a system of legal remedies and procedures which ensure respect for the right of effective judicial protection' (European Court Report, 2004; paragraph 31); it held that the existing system of Article 263(4) TFEU could only be changed by an amendment of the EU Treaty.

In 2010, the Lisbon Treaties amended Article 263(4) TFEU. For 'a regulatory act which is of direct concern to [natural or legal persons] and does not entail implementing measures', an individual concern is no longer necessary. The Court of Justice has not yet given rulings on this new and rather obscure provision.[3] It is likely that it will only have a minor importance in environmental matters. The Court has not yet pronounced on this issue. Specifically, is a person whose individual human right to health or safety is threatened by a measure directly and individually concerned by that measure? As the Lisbon Treaty gave the rights laid down in the Charter of Fundamental Rights of the European Union (which include the right to life and health) the same legal value as the EU treaties themselves, this question may, eventually influence future Court jurisprudence.

Summary points

- Individuals and environmental NGOs have almost no access to the ECJ, as most environmental legislation and measures are of no direct and individual concern to them.
- The vast majority of environmental cases submitted to the ECJ are brought by the Commission, by member states or by national courts.
- The lack of standing for individuals and NGOs is a severe impediment to enforcing the application of EU environmental law.

Innovative court judgments

As EU environmental law landed largely on virgin grounds within the member states, the Court had the opportunity to develop a very innovative interpretation of this law which largely corresponded to the spirit of the law even if it was not always reflected in its letters. The very first judgment in an environmental case showed the Court's innovative capacity. This case concerned French waste discharges into the Rhine River which contaminated Dutch farmland and greenhouse agriculture (Case C-21/76). A question arose: could Dutch farmers claim compensation before Dutch courts where the damage occurred? Or, alternatively, should they address French courts, where the damaging event had taken place, but where their chances of compensation were considered to be less good? The Court decided that the victims could choose to apply either to Dutch or to French courts.

Another important innovative Court judgment came in the 1980s. Before the terms of 'environment', 'environmental policy' or 'environmental protection' ever appeared in the EEC Treaty, the Court declared in a judgment of 1980 that the provisions on the free trade of goods did not prevent the EU from adopting measures which had the objective to protect the environment (Case C-92/79). In 1985, the Court took a further, very decisive step in Case C-240/83 when it declared that 'environmental protection . . . is one of the Community's essential objectives' (European Court Report, 1985: 531, paragraph 13).

When majority voting in the Council for environmental legislation was introduced into the EU Treaty (see Chapter 2), it became the normal decision-making form. However, unanimous Council decisions were still required, among others, for 'the management of water resources' (Article 130s[2] Maastricht Treaty on European Union). The Court decided that unanimous decisions were only required for the *quantitative* management of water resources which left the great majority of all decisions in the water sector to majority decisions (Case C-36/98). Subsequently, the EU Treaty was amended by states to align to this judgment.

The Court was also quite innovative in the use of the environmental principles of precaution and polluter-pays in its jurisdiction. In 1998, it had to decide on an export ban which the European Commission had imposed on British beef, in order to prevent the spreading of the 'mad cow disease', Bovine Spongiform Encephalopathy. British farmers and the UK Government argued that such a ban was illegal, as the exact cause of the disease was not yet scientifically established. The Court held that, as there was scientific uncertainty with regard to the origin of the disease, the Commission was entitled, based on the principle of precaution, to take preventive measures. The problem, though, was that the precautionary principle was laid down in the environmental section of the EU Treaty, whereas the export ban was an agricultural measure. The Court solved this problem by declaring that the treaty also provided that environmental requirements had to be integrated into the other EU policies (see also Chapter 13); for this reason, agricultural measures could also be based on the precautionary principle (Case C-157/96). Since then, this interpretation of the precautionary principle and its use in the context of other EU policies have become standard practice by the Court as well as by the other EU institutions.

The Court referred to the polluter-pays principle in particular in the waste sector, where it had expressly been laid down in several directives and regulations. In a Belgian case, it dealt with hydrocarbons which had leaked from a petrol service station to an adjacent ground. The Court held that the hydrocarbons, spilled by accident, constituted 'waste' in the legal sense of the term. The manager of the service station was responsible for the soil contamination by the hydrocarbons. However, the owner of the service station, Texaco, had supplied the hydrocarbons to the service station. If it had disregarded its contractual obligations and thereby contributed to the soil contamination, it also could be considered to be the 'polluter' and be held responsible (Case C-1/03). This construction would allow the damaged land owner to recur to Texaco and not have to try to recover his damage from the service station manager.

The Court took a similar line in another judgment of 2008. In this case (Case C-188/07), a tanker accident off the French coast had contaminated large parts of the shoreline with heavy fuels. A French municipality asked for compensation, among others from another petroleum company – Total. This company had contractually excluded all its own liability for any damage, and argued in court that the carrier of the heavy fuel should be held responsible. The Court found that hydrocarbons which were accidentally spilled at sea and contaminating the coast of a member state did constitute waste. Where the producer of the heavy fuel had contributed, by its conduct, to the risk that the pollution caused by the shipwreck would occur, it could, in application of the polluter-pays principle, be held responsible for the damage of the municipality.

In the area of nature conservation, EU legislation is essentially concentrated in two directives: on the protection of birds (2009/147/EC) and of natural habitats and species of fauna and flora (92/43/EEC). These legal texts were intensively interpreted by the Court that has erected a whole system of interpretation and protection, largely siding with the environment. For example, the Court declared that, where a member state had not designated a protected bird area, though it was legally obliged to do so, it would let itself be treated as if it had designated the area (Case C-355/90). When member states and the European Commission disagreed whether enough areas had been designated as protected habitats, the Court accepted evidence from a private environmental organization and argued that the burden of proof that this association's findings were incorrect would fall on the member state in question (Case C-3/96). The Court issued a great number of judgments to annul member states' hunting legislation and hunting practice that did not conform with the requirements of EU law, in particular in Southern European member states. And the Court took numerous decisions to protect natural habitats or protected species against infrastructure projects or other measures which intended to threaten them or their habitats.

In public procurement issues, EU legislation requires public authorities to accept, in general, the most economically advantageous tender. Although taking environmental criteria into consideration was not mentioned, the Court pointed out that the criteria did not necessarily have to be 'of a purely economic nature' (European Court Report, 2002: paragraph 55). It interpreted Article 11 TFEU (according to which environmental requirements have to be integrated into the elaboration and implementation of the other EU policies) as to mean that national authorities were allowed to consider ecological criteria, provided that these criteria were: linked to the subject matter of the contract; did not give an unrestricted freedom to the authorities; were expressly mentioned in the public tender documents; and complied with all fundamental principles of EU law (Case C-448/01). This jurisprudence led to a complete change in the EU's public procurement legislation which aligned with the Court's jurisdiction and thus gave member states' authorities the possibility of inserting ecological criteria into their public procurement activities.

Citizen rights in environmental issues were considerably strengthened by the Aarhus Convention on access to information, participation in decision making and access to justice in environmental matters. This Convention was ratified by the EU in 2005 and thus became part of EU law. The Court has further strengthened these rights. For example, it held a Swedish legislative provision, which provided for environmental organizations to have standing in Swedish courts only when they had at least 2,000 members, incompatible with EU law, as such a high number would not give efficient judicial protection to environmental organizations – one of the objectives of the Convention (Case C-263/08). In another case (Case C-266/09), it held that the results of tests on pesticide residues on vegetables, made for the application of a permit for that pesticide, constituted 'environmental information' and therefore could not be kept confidential.

Summary points

- The ECJ has developed a considerable number of innovative inter-pretations of environmental provisions, in order to ensure effective environmental protection.
- The ECJ normally goes beyond the wording of a provision, interpreting it according to its objectives and purpose.
- Human rights issues have not yet played a role in the Court's environmental jurisdiction, but they might do so in future.

Balancing EU and member states' interests

In a number of decisions, the Court of Justice was asked to decide whether the EU or the member states were primarily responsible for addressing certain environmental problems. This question was of particular importance in the area of product-related provisions, as the treaties provide that there should be a free circulation of products within the EU. Thus, once the EU has established common EU-wide rules, member states may not, in principle, add supplementary rules which impede free trade. However, in the environmental area, when the EU has established EU-wide rules, member states may introduce or maintain provisions which give better protection to their environment.

The Court was asked whether the trade in waste should follow the provisions of free trade or the provisions of environmental protection. The Court decided that the environmental provisions should apply (Case C-155/91). This had the consequence, for example, that member states were allowed to prohibit imports of hazardous wastes from other states (Case C-2/90; Case C-228/00; Case C-458/00). In contrast, provisions on air emissions from cars were considered to affect the free trade in cars, so that member states could not, as a rule, deviate from the EU-wide standards which had been fixed (Case T-234/04). As this jurisdiction appeared rather rigid, the Court encouraged the EU to develop legislation which was, for some articles, based on the free-trade rules, and for other provisions of the same legislative act, on the environment rules (Case C-178/03).

Member states and the EU discussed for a long time whether the EU could adopt provisions on the protection of the environment through criminal law. Finally, the Court decided that the EU was allowed to adopt such rules (Case C-176/03). However, in a second judgment, the Court found that the type and level of criminal penalties were the responsibility of member states, i.e. the EU could not adopt rules on them (Case C-440/05).

The Court also had to decide whether rules on genetically modified organisms (GMOs) came under free trade rules, or whether member states, regions or local authorities were allowed to go further than EU law and prohibit GMOs altogether. While provisions on species of fauna and flora undoubtedly are environment-related provisions, the Court found that organisms which were genetically modified were to be seen as products (joined Cases C-439/05P and C-454/05P). The rules which had been fixed at EU level therefore applied, independently of the local or regional environment. Finally, in an interesting judgment, the Court stated that member states were obliged to respect the rules of an international environmental agreement even when they had not signed up to that agreement; it was sufficient that the EU had signed it, provided that there already existed EU legislation in the sector covered by the agreement (Case C-213/03; Case C-239/03).

Generally speaking, the Court's decisions to balance the interests of member states and those of the EU were cautious, prudent and were acceptable to member states. In the vast majority, its decisions have shown considerable concern for the environment. The Court is probably well aware that in many areas, when the EU is prevented from adopting provisions on the protection of the environment, only a few member states will adopt relevant national protection measures. The judgments on competence in criminal matters might have been influenced by the heavy reaction of member states to the first judgment (C-176/03 – see above).[4] The second judgment (Case C-440/05) greatly satisfied member states, but the Court did not explain, with one single word, why the EU should not be allowed to decide on the type and level of penalties.

Summary points

- The ECJ normally interprets EU law in a way that promotes EU integration.
- Generally, the ECJ tries to ensure effective environmental protection, even against public administrative interests.
- Where fundamental national interests are at stake (e.g. criminal law, waste infrastructure), the ECJ is cautious and tries to find acceptable solutions.

Balancing economic and environmental interests

On several occasions, the Court has had to deal with questions concerning whether the free trade in materials should prevail or whether the member states should be allowed to restrict the free circulation of goods in order to protect their local, regional or national environment. With regard to pesticides, the Court decided that member states were allowed to restrict or ban the use of a specific pesticide because of environmental reasons, at least as long as the EU legislation on pesticides had not been completely harmonized (Case C-272/80; Case C-94/83). In a landmark decision of 1988, the Court decided that member states were allowed to restrict the import of waste in order to set up efficient waste recovery systems at national level (Case C-302/86). In contrast, the export of waste material to other member states for recovery purposes (i.e. recycling or incineration with energy recovery) in order to have the recovery process reserved for national installations could normally not be prohibited (Case C-172/82; Case C-118/86; Case C-203/96).

When Germany tried to protect its farmers by declaring that ordinary agricultural practice was compatible with EU nature conservation provisions, the Court prohibited this measure (Case C-412/85). In contrast, when Germany tried to promote alternative energies by giving financial incentives to producers, but limited these incentives to national producers of alternative energies, the Court found that the free trade in electricity was not unduly hampered by this measure, as the electricity market was not yet sufficiently harmonized (Case C-379/88).

Summary points

- The ECJ tries to maintain a fair balance between trade and environmental interests.
- The jurisprudence is result-oriented and normally weighs carefully the purpose of the environmental provision.

Rights of citizens and environmental organizations

Since its early judgments on environmental matters, the Court has tried to increase the transparency of EU environmental law and to strengthen citizen rights. Indeed, in the 1970s and the 1980s, member states generally only adopted internal circulars or other instruments requesting local, regional or national administrations to observe this or that practice. These internal instruments were not available for citizens to use in their discussions with the administration or in court.

The Court held this practice to be incompatible with the general principles of EU law. It was of the opinion that citizen and economic undertakings had a right to know what exactly their environmental rights and obligations were. EU environmental directives had therefore normally to be transposed into the national legal order by a legislative measure. Administrative circulars or similar measures which could be amended at the discretion of the administration at any time were deemed to be incompatible with this principle (see case C-59/90 above). An exception could only be made, where a specific provision of a directive exclusively addressed the national administration, for example, when a competent authority had to be appointed or when a report had to be sent to the European Commission. This jurisdiction led to the progressive disappearance of most administrative decrees or circulars.

In a similar way, the Court addressed the problem of 'tacit permits'. This was an administrative practice in several member states where if the administration did not react within a specific time-span to an application for an administrative permit, the permit was deemed to be granted. The Court held that where EU environmental law provided for the granting of a permit, this permit had to be given expressly; a 'tacit permit' did not provide for the necessary legal security for applicants and the public in general.

Of particular importance was the Court's jurisdiction with regard to EU legislation on air or water pollution. The Court held that:

> Whenever the failure to observe the measures required by the directives which relate to air quality and drinking water, and which are designed to protect public health, could endanger human health, the persons concerned must be in a position to rely on the mandatory rules included in these directives.
>
> (Case C-237/07, paragraph 38)

The Court had held in earlier judgments that EU directives which fixed emission standards or quality values (concentration values) for the air or for water, aimed at the protection of human health. Therefore its jurisdiction is likely to apply to most directives on air pollution or water contamination. It means that citizen or environmental organizations may apply to the national courts in order to have the provisions of the respective directive fully complied with. Thus they may force the administration to take the necessary measures in order to keep the pollution within the limits fixed by EU legislation. The principles of this jurisdiction are not limited to air pollution and drinking water. They also apply to health-related noise legislation, provisions to protect the soil and groundwater and other water legislation. The Court has not yet had an opportunity to pronounce itself on such cases.

The efforts to allow individual citizens to contribute to the protection of the environment might in future even lead to a change in the above-mentioned Court's position on the standing of citizens and NGOs. Indeed, in 2011, the Court was asked about the interpretation of Article 9(3) of the Aarhus Convention which allowed citizens and NGOs, under certain conditions, to have standing in environmental matters. The Court discussed the objective of that provision and concluded:

> If the effective protection of EU environmental law is not to be undermined, it is inconceivable that Article 9(3) of the Aarhus Convention be interpreted in such a way as to make it in practice impossible or excessively difficult to exercise rights conferred by EU law. It follows . . . that it is for the national court in order to ensure effective judicial protection in the fields covered by EU environmental law, to interpret its national law in a way which, to the fullest extent possible, is consistent with the objectives laid down in article 9(3) of the Aarhus Convention.
>
> (European Court Report, 2011: paragraphs 49 and 50)

This judgment applies to the courts of the EU member states and asks them to ensure 'to the fullest extent possible' that the objectives of Article 9(39) of the Aarhus Convention are respected, i.e. that citizens and NGOs have access to national courts. However, as mentioned above, access for citizens and NGOs to the EU courts in environmental matters is, in practice, impossible as no such application has ever been successful. The question, which will inevitably have to be raised, is why does the EU Court of Justice not interpret Article 263(4) TFEU in a way that allows 'to the fullest extent possible' access to the EU Court, in order to ensure effective judicial protection of EU environmental law? In addition, would such an interpretation not have to lead to a change in the Court's position with regard to standing? The Court will certainly rather soon be asked this question.

Summary points

- The ECJ has tried to enlarge citizens' rights for effective environmental protection.
- Human rights do not yet play a role in the jurisprudence of the ECJ.
- The Lisbon Treaties and the Aarhus Convention of 1998 might bring about some changes in the Court's jurisprudence.

Political judgments

Among the numerous environmental judgments by the Court are also some where the reader has the impression that more than purely legal reasons motivated the decision, but that political considerations also influenced the outcome of the case. Of course, such an assessment is necessarily subjective and will depend on the position of the external observer. No hard evidence can be found in any of the cases discussed hereafter.

In a case on the hunting of birds in France, the Court rejected the Commission's application. The case concerned some forms of traditional hunting which involved lime trees and threads. This form of hunting had a considerable social importance in particular in rural France. The Court held that the Commission had not proven that the hunting measures were non-selective and that they did not correspond to the requirements of the Birds Directive. It seems that the Court in no other hunting case put the requirements on the burden of proof at such a high level. Then in a Spanish case, the Court held that under certain conditions animal excrements – pig slurry – did not constitute 'waste' but a traded product (Case C-416/02). This was a judgment which was obviously influenced by the objective to amend the EU waste legislation.

The Court allowed Belgium to adopt regional legislation which banned the import of (hazardous) waste from other EU member states, but exempted the import of hazardous waste from other Belgian regions (Case C-2/90). Also, the Court allowed Germany to grant financial incentive to producers of wind energy, though these incentives were limited to German producers (Case C-379/98). In both cases, the Court omitted to discuss whether the principle of non-discrimination was not disregarded by the respective legislation.

In a case where an environmental organization had asked for access to a letter from the German chancellor concerning the construction of a private airport in a protected natural habitat, the Court refused access. The Court's argument was that the disclosure of the letter in the year 2011 (more than ten years after it was written) would undermine the German economic policy (Case T-362/08).[5] The Court did not consider that the provisions of the Aarhus Convention applied to this case – which did not allow the disclosure of information to be refused on the grounds that the economic policy of a member state was undermined.

Some other cases were already mentioned above. Both judgments with regard to the polluter-pays principle had the side effect of allowing recourse for damage against the large companies which owned the petrol service station or which had the heavy fuels shipped.[6] The judgment stating that the EU had no competence to fix the type and level of criminal sanctions, unexplained, can also be categorized as a political judgment. And the Court's findings on standing also belong to this category: it has an obvious interest to restrict access to justice as far as possible.

Summary points

- In some cases, the political character of judgments appears obvious.
- Such cases mainly concern issues where public opinion in a particular member state threatens to affect the acceptance of the judgment.
- Overall, though, the number of 'political' judgments is very small; the vast majority of judgments are well argued and legally convincing.

The Court of Justice and the General Court

It was mentioned in the Introduction that the 'European Court of Justice' consists of the General Court and the Court of Justice. While the General Court mainly deals with environmental cases which are brought by an individual person or a company against an EU institution, the Court of Justice deals essentially with environmental cases which are brought by the Commission against a member state. Furthermore, the Court of Justice deals with environmental cases which are submitted to it by national courts, and on appeal against a judgment of the General Court. The question then is whether there is a difference between the two courts with regard to environmental protection. The appeal procedure does not show any difference in this regard. In only two of the 13 environmental cases, against which an appeal was introduced since 1989, was the appeal successful (Cases C-64/05P, C-405/07). These cases concerned general questions and did not address specific environmental questions.

Generally speaking, the Court of Justice is more innovative and creative in its attempt to protect the environment; a role which the Lisbon Treaties grants to it (see Articles 191–193 and 11 TFEU). These consist of: a high level of protection; the integration of environmental requirements into all other EU policies; the application of the precautionary and polluter-pays principles; and the possibility for member states to adopt even stricter environmental protection measures than those decided by the EU (see Chapter 3 for details). The General Court appears to view the environment as one factor in society among many, rather than a general interest which cannot be placed at the same level as vested interests (Krämer, 2009).

The more reserved attitude of the General Court towards environmental protection might at least partly be due to the fact that it deals with actions brought by private persons against EU institutions and bodies. However, the General Court always, and systematically, accepts the interpretation of EU environmental law given by the Court of Justice without continuing to defend its earlier differing position.

Summary points

- Generally, the Court of Justice is more innovative and creative in its attempt to protect the environment – a role given to it by the Lisbon Treaty.
- The General Court appears to view the environment as one factor in society among many due, in part, because it deals with actions brought by private persons against EU institutions and bodies.

Conclusion: the Court's role in the development of environmental law

The Court's role in shaping EU environmental law cannot easily be overestimated. From the very beginning of its extensive jurisprudence on environmental law, the Court has tried to translate the far-reaching objectives and principles of the EU treaties into daily administrative and economic practice, namely, a high level of environmental protection; the improvement of environmental quality; economic development that takes environmental considerations into due account (sustainable development); precaution and prevention; and making the polluter pay. The jurisprudence of the Court on environmental issues has opened up new paths in the interpretation of EU law in general and often influenced the making of EU secondary environmental law (Jans, 2009). The general understanding of the Court has been that EU law, where the 23 different linguistic versions have the same legal value, has to be interpreted according to the objective and aim of the provisions rather than according to its wording. Building on this understanding, the Court has shown itself throughout more than 35 years of environmental jurisprudence, to be creative and innovative in constantly trying to strike a balance between the diverging interests on environmental matters. A small reservation has to be made with regard to the questions of standing, where the Court has persisted in treating access to justice in environmental matters in exactly the same way as access to justice in other areas of law, not taking into account the specificity of environmental protection as a general interest.

The areas of nature conservation and public procurement stand out. In matters of nature conservation, the Court embodied EU legislation with more precise legal obligations for public administrations and economic operators. As a result, its case law is taken into consideration in almost every administrative decision concerning a natural habitat or a specific species. In the area of public procurement, the Court's jurisprudence made it possible to include ecological criteria in the public tenders of local, regional or national administrations. This was despite the fact that the EU legislation had explicitly rejected this possibility up to this point and thus subsequently had to be aligned to the Court's judgments.

The majority of innovative and progressively integrating ideas in environmental law are found in the preliminary judgments issued by the Court. This might further encourage judges in the 27 EU member states to submit more cases to the Court, with a view to allowing the Court to further contribute to the development of environmental law in the whole of the EU.

Summary points

- The ECJ has played and continues to play an outstanding role in interpreting and, in that way, shaping and fine-tuning EU environmental law, which is often originally formulated in general and vague terms.
- ECJ jurisprudence is often creative and innovative and tries, overall, to do justice to the environment.
- In the areas of nature conservation and public procurement, the ECJ jurisprudence has particularly strongly marked the development of the law, and influenced national legislation, administrative practice and court jurisdiction.

Key questions

1. Who has standing in the ECJ and what are the implications for EU environmental law?
2. Describe four of the most innovative cases for the interpretation of EU environmental law and explain their repercussions.
3. How, in general, has the Court balanced environmental protection with economic or member states' interests?
4. What role has the Court played in the transparency and rights of citizens with regard to environmental policy? How might the Lisbon Treaty and the Aarhus Convention change its role?
5. What different roles do the Court of Justice and the General Court play in EU environmental policy?

Guide to further reading

- A more in depth exploration of EU environmental law can be found in Krämer (2011).
- For details of important Court cases and judgments on EU environmental law, see Krämer (2002b).
- A systematic analysis of the entire body of EU environmental law, i.e. over 500 directives, decisions and regulations, can be found in an online manual edited by Farmer (2011).

Notes

1   Following the author's classification system, there were 55 environmental judgments in 2008, 54 in 2009 and 38 in 2010.
2   Article 36 TFEU states, in the same sense that 'Quantitative restrictions on exports, and all measures having equivalent effect, shall be prohibited between member states.'
3   The TFEU does not define what a 'regulatory act' is.
4   It is known that the judgment in case C-176/03 was adopted by the Court with seven votes against six.
5   Case T-362/08, *IFAW v. Commission*, judgment of 13 January 2011, the case is under appeal.
6   In US law, such judgments are sometimes qualified as 'deep pocket' judgments: a person is held responsible who is economically in the best position to cover the damage.

References

Court of Justice (no date) *Annual Statistics of Judicial Activity*, available at: http://curia.europa.eu/jcms/jcms/Jo2_7032/ (accessed 20 September 2011).

European Court Report (1985) Case C-240/83, *Association de Défense des Brûleurs d'Huiles Usagées*, p. 531.

European Court Report (1993) Case C-56/90, *Commission v. United Kingdom*, pp. I–4109.

European Court Report (2002) Case C-513/99, *Concordia Bus Finland*, pp. I–7123.

European Court Report (2004) Case T-263/02P, *Commission v. Jégo-Quéré*, pp. I–3425.

European Court Report (2011) Case C-240/09, Lesoochranárske, judgment of 8 March 2011.

Farmer, A. (ed.) (2011) *Manual of European Environmental Policy*, Taylor & Francis. London, available at: www.europeanenvironmentalpolicy.eu/ (accessed 5 October 2011).

Jans, J. (2009) 'The effect of the ECJ judgments in environmental cases for other areas of EU law', in G. Bándi (ed.) *The Impact of ECJ Jurisprudence on Environmental Law*, Szent István Társulat, Budapest, pp. 83–94.

Krämer, L. (1992) *Casebook on EU Environmental Law*, Hart Publishing, Oxford and Portland, OR.

Krämer, L. (1993) *European Environmental Law Casebook*, Sweet & Maxwell, London.

Krämer, L. (1995) 'Die Rechtsprechung des Gerichtshofs der Europäischen Gemeinschaft zum Umweltrecht 1992 bis 1994', *Europäische Grundrechte Zeitschrift 1995*.

Krämer, L. (1998) 'Die Rechtsprechung der EG-Gerichte zum Umweltrecht 1995 bis 1997', *Europäische Grundrechte Zeitschrift 1998*.

Krämer, L. (2000) 'Die Rechtsprechung der EG-Gerichte zum Umweltschutz 1998 und 1999', *Europäische Grundrechte Zeitschrift 2000*.

Krämer, L. (2002a) 'Die Rechtsprechung der EG-Gerichte zum Umweltrecht 2000 und 2001', *Europäische Grundrechte Zeitschrift 2002*.

Krämer, L. (2002b) *European Environmental Law Case Book*, Hart Publishing, Oxford and Portland, OR.

Krämer, L. (2004) 'Data on environmental judgments by the EC Court of Justice', *Journal for European and Environmental Planning & Law*, vol. 1, no. 4, pp. 127–135.

Krämer, L. (2006) 'Statistics on environmental judgments by the EC Court of Justice', *Journal for European and Environmental Planning & Law*, vol. 18, no. 3, pp. 407–421.

Krämer, L. (2008) 'Environmental judgments by the Court of Justice and their duration', *Journal for European and Environmental Planning & Law*, vol. 5, no. 3, pp. 263–280.

Krämer, L. (2009) 'On the Court of First Instance and the protection of the environment', in G. Bándi (ed.) *The Impact of ECJ Jurisprudence on Environmental Law*, Szent István Társulat, Budapest, pp. 95–123.

Krämer, L. (2011) *EU Environmental Law*, 7th edition, Sweet & Maxwell, London.

8   The European Parliament

Charlotte Burns

Summary guide

The European Parliament established a reputation in its early years as a champion of environmental interests within the EU. The EU's only directly elected institution, it provided an access point for those excluded from decision making and a voice for green political parties. However, it was a reactive and relatively weak institution. In more recent times, the Parliament has benefited from treaty changes that have made it a co-legislator with the Council of Ministers. However, the empowerment of the Parliament seems to have blunted its environmental radicalism: it now appears less willing to adopt green amendments.

Introduction

The European Parliament (hereafter 'the Parliament') is the only directly elected EU institution. Following the first elections of 1979, it rapidly established a reputation as a standard bearer for the environment. It has consistently benefited from the various EU Treaty reforms (see Chapters 2 and 3), seeing both its policy competence and formal powers increase over the years. Over time it has shifted from being a relatively weak institution, often derided as a mere 'talking shop', to a co-legislator that crafts legislation jointly with representatives of the member states in the Council of Ministers. However, an increase in formal power does not necessarily lead to the exercise of greater influence. It has been suggested more recently that as the Parliament's powers have increased, its willingness and ability to adopt radical environmental amendments and to set the wider EU environmental policy agenda have waned (see Burns and Carter, 2010a; Burns *et al.*, 2012) (see also Chapter 11). Moreover the emergence of climate change as a key issue on the EU and wider international policy agenda has exposed the Parliament's relative weakness on the international stage. Notwithstanding these concerns, the Parliament remains an important environmental actor on the European stage with the ability to make a substantive contribution to policy outputs. This chapter describes the Parliament's structure and powers, explains how and why it has come to be regarded as a key environmental actor, and explores the future challenges it faces. While the 2004 and 2007 enlargements were less disruptive than predicted in some quarters, they have nevertheless ushered in a new approach to policy making and a more diverse range of actors and interests that may act to undermine the Parliament's hard-won reputation as the EU's environmental champion.

Composition

The European Parliament is composed of 736[1] members who sit in seven cross-national political groups. As Table 8.1 illustrates, no one group controls a majority. Therefore in order to adopt amendments to legislation the political groups must cooperate with one another to achieve an absolute majority. However, before they can reach an inter-group consensus, the groups must also reach intra-group agreement which can sometimes be challenging, particularly since the 2004 and 2007 enlargements, which have seen the political groups absorb a wider range of political parties from up to 27 states. Within the groups, each national delegation gets a certain number of positions of responsibility, which are decided via the D'Hondt system of proportional representation. Thus, the largest national delegation within the largest political group gains the most posts of importance, but there is an opportunity for small groups and small national delegations within groups to gain some key posts within the Parliament.

The Greens in Parliament sit in the Group of Greens/European Free Alliance. The system for allocating positions of responsibility within the Parliament means that the Greens have been able to secure key posts of responsibility. For example, after the 2009 election Belgian Green, Isabelle Durant, was appointed as a Vice-President, French Green, Eva Joly, was appointed Chair of the Development Committee, and the group secured a further five Vice-Chair positions (see Box 8.1).[2] It might be supposed that the heterogeneity that characterizes the Parliament makes achieving consensus difficult, with numerous defections from group

Table 8.1 Composition of the European Parliament as of July 2011

Political group	Number of members
European Peoples' Party (EPP)	265
Group of the Progressive Alliance of Socialists and Democrats (S&D)	184
Group of the Alliance of Liberals and Democrats for Europe (ALDE)	84
European Conservatives and Reformists Group (ECR)	56
Group of the Greens and European Free Alliance (Greens/EFA)	55
Confederal Group of European United Left/ Nordic Green Left (EUL/NGL)	35
Europe of Freedom and Democracy Group (EFD)	32
Non-Affiliated Members (NA)	27
TOTAL	736

Source: European Parliament (2011a).

positions by national delegations. However, successive studies have shown that the Parliament behaves along ideological rather than national lines, i.e. British Green MEPs vote with the Green group rather than with British Labour and/or Conservative Members of the European Parliament (MEPs) (see Hix *et al.*, 2007). Indeed, the Green/EFA group is the most cohesive of all the political groups with few defections from the group line in the 2004–2009 Parliament (see Votewatch, 2011, for cohesion scores). The most successful coalition in the Parliament is a grand EPP/SD coalition, as it carries the most votes. It was the dominant coalition from 1979 to 1999. However, since 1999 when the EPP was elected as the largest political group, a right-of-centre coalition between the Liberals (ALDE) and the Christian Democrats (EPP) has emerged. Following the 2004 and 2007 enlargements, this centre-right coalition has entrenched its strong position within the Parliament (Hix and Noury, 2009: 166; Hagemann, 2009: 20–22).

Box 8.1 The Greens in the European Parliament

The Greens were first elected to the European Parliament in 1984. However, they only secured 11 seats, so, following fraught negotiations, chose to sit in a rainbow collation with regionalists and the Danish movement against the EU (Bomberg, 1998: 90, 104). In 1989, the Greens formed the Green Group in the European Parliament which was replaced in 1999 by the Green/EFA Group which saw the Greens combine again with regionalists (for example, the Scottish National Party and Plaid Cymru). In the 2004 and 2009 elections, the Green/EFA group secured sufficient numbers to become the fourth largest group in the Parliament, but the European Conservatives and Reformists Group (ECR) increased its group sufficiently by July 2011 to overtake the Greens and become the fourth largest group overall (see Table 8.1). Table 8.2 shows that the majority of the Green MEPs are drawn from parties in Northern Europe with no representatives from the EU12 states that acceded in 2004 and 2007. A key challenge for the Greens, therefore, is to be able to reach beyond their traditional bases to reach voters in Southern, Central and Eastern Europe.

This need to cooperate and form coalitions means that the Parliament rarely adopts a radical position on legislation. For example, although the Parliament has been prepared to propose environmental amendments that impose significant costs upon the member states and industries, broadly speaking, it has adopted the ecological modernization agenda of the Commission, based upon greening capitalism and furthering growth in the EU (see Chapter 10 for further details). While this trend towards consensus affects all the political groups, from an environmental perspective, it most obviously impacts upon the Greens, who find it difficult to secure the adoption of radical amendments. Indeed, the Greens find themselves in a dilemma:

Table 8.2 Greens in the European Parliament, 2009–2014

Country	Number of Green Members of the European Parliament
Austria	2
Belgium Groen	1
Belgium Ecolo	2
Denmark	2
Finland	2
France	13
Germany	14
Greece	1
Luxembourg	1
Netherlands	3
Spain	1
Sweden	2
United Kingdom	2
TOTAL	46

Source: Carter (2010: 296).

going along with the larger groups means that [their] . . . ideas are swallowed up and become indistinguishable from those of the mainstream parties. Yet to hold out often leaves the[m] . . . isolated, marginalized, and no nearer achieving their goals.

(Bomberg, 1998: 141)

Realistically, the Greens cannot afford to be purist on a regular basis; they need to form coalitions to have any chance of seeing their amendments adopted. Hence the consensus politics of the Parliament has had a deradicalizing effect upon what both the Greens and the Parliament as a whole can achieve.

The Parliament organizes its work through standing committees which mirror the ideological composition of the wider Parliament. In addition, it sometimes appoints temporary committees to consider pressing or controversial issues. For example, in 2007, it appointed a Temporary Committee on Climate Change (CLIM) to help to prepare the legislative proposals for the Climate and Energy Package and to determine the Parliament's position in the run up to the 2009 Copenhagen Conference of the Parties (see Box 8.2). When the Commission proposes legislation (see Chapter 6), responsibility for drafting the Parliament's opinion is allocated to the most relevant committee. Inevitably, given the cross-sectoral nature of environmental policy, sometimes there is an overlap of competence between committees. Under these circumstances, affected committees can offer an opinion or committees may be given joint responsibility for drafting the Parliament's opinion (European Parliament, 2011b: rules 49 and 51). Under this process the draftsmen for each committee coordinate their work and the reports are adopted jointly by all the committees together. Thus, for example, during the consideration of the regulation upon the registration and evaluation of chemicals

(REACH), a vast and complex law of legislation that sought to harmonize existing chemicals legislation (see also Chapter 10), responsibility for drafting the report for consideration by the plenary was shared between no less than three committees (Smith, 2008). Such sharing of responsibility can lead to coordination problems (Judge and Earnshaw, 2011). Smith (2008: 76) suggests that in the case of REACH, the sharing of competence ultimately led to the adoption of a weaker report by the Parliament. Certainly the Green Group has opposed the move in the 2009–2014 Parliament to see more reports considered jointly by committees, on the grounds that the Industry Committee will dominate decision making on key environmental policies (Taylor, 2009). However, the sharing of responsibility can also aid the process of crafting a consensus that is acceptable to the whole plenary (see Settembri and Neuhold, 2009).

Box 8.2 The Temporary Committee on Climate Change (CLIM)

The Parliament's Temporary Committee on Climate Change (CLIM) had a mandate from May 2007 to January 2009. It was composed of 60 MEPs drawn primarily from the Environment, Industry and Transport committees. It provided a venue to bring together personnel from committees affected by the issues of climate change, reflecting the wider trend that has emerged of creating cross-cutting climate bodies such as the new DG on Climate Action in the Commission. CLIM's primary responsibility was to draw up the Parliament's recommendations on the future direction of EU Climate Policy. Its report therefore sought to shape the wider EU climate policy agenda but it had no legislative force. Burns and Carter (2010b) suggest that because the committee's report had a limited legislative impact, it contained stronger statements about the actions needed to combat climate change than were included in legislative reports negotiated between the Council and the Parliament.

Within committees, individual members are allocated responsibility for drafting opinions: they are then known as the rapporteur for the particular piece of legislation. Each rapporteur is responsible for consulting with the Commission and Council, affected interest groups and representatives from the other political groups within the Parliament in order to devise amendments that can command the support of the committee in the first instance and then, subsequently, the wider plenary. Committee members can propose amendments to the draft report, and once the committee has adopted it, it is referred to the plenary. At this point, amendments to the report can be offered by committees, political groups, or groups of at least 40 MEPs. Plenary votes can be recorded at the request of a political group or at least 40 MEPs. Such votes are termed roll call votes and are made publicly available; they show how each MEP voted. They are called either for disciplinary purposes or so that groups can make a political point about how they are voting by making it a matter of public record.

The work of each committee is coordinated by its bureau, composed of the committee chair and vice-chairs in consultation with the political group co-ordinators, who are the equivalent of party whips. The coordinators allocate the committee reports and the decision as to which political group gets a particular report is normally decided via a bidding system under which each group is given a certain number of points according to group size. Coordinators use their points to bid for reports. This system more or less ensures a fair distribution and allows smaller groups and/or non-aligned members the opportunity to bid for and some-times to draft important reports. For example, the Greens secured responsibility for drafting the report on fuel quality as part of the landmark auto-oil package that regulated both car engine design and fuel quality (see Friedrich *et al.*, 2000; Warleigh, 2000; Wurzel, 2002), and ushered in a new kind of policy instrument – a voluntary agreement (see Chapter 17). They also secured responsibility for the effort-sharing report as part of the 2008 Climate and Energy Package. The rapporteurs are aided in their work by the shadow rapporteurs who are drawn from another political group.

The Environment Committee

The main committee dealing with environmental policy in the Parliament is the Committee of Environment, Public Health and Food Safety (ENVI). With 64 members, it is one of the largest committees and has always borne a heavy legislative workload, which has given it a high profile. Between 1979 and 1999, it was characterized by remarkable continuity of leadership, as for 15 years one man, the British Labour MEP, Ken Collins, acted as its chair. He crafted a formidable reputation for himself and the committee as leading entrepreneurs in the field of environmental policy. As Weale *et al.* (2000: 91) note, the committee and the wider Parliament came to be regarded as the defender of the environmental interest within the EU. This reputation was maintained under the leadership of UK Conservative MEP Caroline Jackson from 1999–2004. However, in the 2004–2009 session, this pattern was disrupted. The chairmanship passed initially to a popular long-standing member of the committee Karl-Heinz Florenz, a German EPP member. However, in order to satisfy the need for a representative from the ECR delegation within the EPP to hold a post of importance, Florenz was replaced by Miroslav Ouzky, a member of the Czech Civic Democrats in 2007 (see Burns and Carter, 2010b: 66; Burns *et al.*, 2012). Ouzky's appointment was a surprise, given his inexperience both as a politician and in relation to environmental policy. He had a poor attendance record at committee meetings prior to his appointment. Moreover, as a doctor by training, he was possibly more concerned with the Committee's health remit (O'Donnell, 2007). Certainly during his tenure as chair, the committee's reputation as being a key environmental actor fell into abeyance (see Burns *et al.*, 2012; Burns and Carter, 2010a). After the 2009 elections, the Socialist Group regained control of ENVI with well-respected German Social

Democrat Jo Leinen taking the Chair. He has sought to re-establish the Committee's reputation as an important environmental actor by challenging the Commission on core issues such as the need to include oil from tar sands in the EU's oil quality directive (Rankin, 2011). However, despite this change in leadership, it has been suggested that there has been a long-term shift in the behaviour of the plenary in relation to environmental legislation, i.e. as the Parliament has become more powerful, it has become less radical (see Burns and Carter, 2010a). The following section discusses the evolution of the Parliament's powers and evaluates the extent to which it has been able to shape environmental policy.

Summary points

- The European Parliament is a transnational institution that votes along ideological rather than national lines.
- The Greens comprise the fifth largest group in Parliament and hold key positions of responsibility and take the lead on important legislative reports.
- The Committee for the Environment, Public Health and Food Safety is the main actor responsible for drawing up Parliament opinions on environmental legislation, but it must secure the support of the plenary for its amendments.

Powers and policy influence

When the Parliament was first elected in 1979, its legislative powers were relatively limited. It had the right to be consulted by the Commission on the content of proposals prior to the Council delivering its verdict. Thus, the Commission would propose legislation, the Parliament could offer amendments before the Council reached its common position. The Council, however, would often adopt its opinion before the Parliament delivered its opinion or just ignore the Parliament's amendments. Following the isoglucose judgement of 1980, the Parliament was able to delay the adoption of legislation under consultation (see Box 8.3), but remained a reactive institution with limited legislative power. However, from 1986 onwards, it fought for and was the recipient of successive increases in its powers and a widening of its policy competences. As detailed in Chapter 2, the Single European Act (SEA) introduced a more solid legal base for environmental policy. Crucially it also introduced qualified majority voting in the Council of Ministers. Hitherto, the Council had adopted legislation by unanimity, which resulted in a legislative log-jam whereby Commission proposals could not be adopted due to the opposition of key member states acting as veto-players. The introduction of qualified majority voting (QMV) broke this log-jam and freed up the legislative process. The SEA also launched the Internal Market programme and with it a whole host of new legislation. The Parliament thus had much greater opportunity to amend legislative proposals. Moreover, the SEA increased the Parliament's powers via the cooperation procedure so that the chance of its amendments being incorporated into the final version of policy also increased.

Box 8.3 The isoglucose ruling

Two isoglucose producers, who were supported by the Parliament, took a case to the ECJ claiming that a Council regulation should be declared invalid on the grounds that the Council failed to obtain the Parliament's opinion prior to adopting the regulation (Kirchner and Williams, 1983: 173). The Court's ruling gave the Parliament a *de facto* delaying power which the Parliament exploited to the full by introducing a new rule of procedure that allowed it to postpone the final vote on a Commission proposal until the Commission had taken a position on Parliament amendments. If the Commission did not accept the Parliament's amendments, the matter could be referred back to committee for reconsideration, thereby delaying the Parliament's opinion and holding up the whole policy process (Corbett, 1998: 119). Thus, as Corbett (ibid.: 120) notes, the Parliament had 'a strong bargaining position to fall back on' and as a result was able to exert more legislative influence in such situations.

Under cooperation, the Parliament had up to two readings of legislation and a conditional veto of legislation, i.e. it could reject legislative proposals but a unanimous Council could overturn its rejection. It also secured a conditional agenda-setting power (Tsebelis, 1994) where the term 'agenda-setting power' is taken to mean the power to make proposals that others find easier to adopt than to amend. So if the Commission supported the Parliament's amendments, the Council could adopt them by QMV but could only reject them by unanimity. Thus if the Parliament satisfied the condition of securing the support of the Commission and a qualified majority of the Council, it was able to secure the adoption of its amendments into legislation (ibid.).

The introduction of the cooperation procedure was a key turning point for the Parliament; for over a decade it was the major vehicle used by the Parliament to secure its policy preferences. Moreover its introduction heralded the start of an era of closer collaboration between the Commission and Parliament (Judge, 1992; Earnshaw and Judge, 1997). In order to exercise this influence the Parliament needed to secure the support of relevant personnel in the European Commission, especially those in DG Environment. The cooperation procedure was used for the adoption of harmonization measures necessary to complete the Single European Market under Article 100a of the SEA. Consequently, proposals seeking to harmonize national environmental standards in order to facilitate the completion of the Internal Market were adopted under cooperation. However, all other environmental measures were adopted under Article 130s of the SEA, which carried the consultation procedure (Judge, 1992: 195). The Parliament therefore had a double interest in improving relations with the Commission: first, in order to persuade the Commission to propose legislation under Article 100a so that the cooperation procedure would be used; and second, when cooperation was used, to secure the Commission's support for the Parliament's amendments.

DG Environment started to view the Parliament's Environment Committee as a natural ally against both the Council and colleagues in the Commission who were unsympathetic to environmental concerns (Judge, 1992: 199–200). There is some evidence to suggest that DG Environment was prepared, where possible, to bring forward proposals under Article 100a. For example, between 1989 and 1992, 15 out of the 29 environmental proposals brought forward by the Commission were based on Article 100a (ibid.: 195). Council officials began to suspect that there was 'an incestuous relationship' between the Parliament and DG Environment (DG Environment Official, quoted in ibid.: 199). Indeed, Ken Collins established regular meetings between himself and the Commissioner as a key means of keeping the dialogue between the Commission and Parliament open. Overall, the cooperation procedure allowed the Parliament to insert itself into the traditional dialogue between the Commission and Council, replacing it with a trialogue involving the Commission, the Council *and* the Parliament (Earnshaw and Judge, 1997: 560).

The cooperation procedure is no longer used in the EU. Nevertheless, its introduction paved the way for an increase in the Parliament's formal and informal powers. These were augmented again by the Maastricht Treaty, which introduced the Parliament's long-desired co-decision procedure, now known as the 'ordinary legislative procedure' (OLP) (see Table 8.3; see also Chapter 3). Initially, the procedure applied to only 15 treaty articles, but its scope was subsequently extended, and now covers 85 policy areas, including most areas of environmental policy (European Parliament, 2010: 36–40). The OLP makes the Parliament a genuine co-legislator with the Council: the agreement of both institutions is necessary for legislation to be adopted. It introduces: a third reading; an unconditional right of rejection for the Parliament; and a conciliation procedure, which is triggered after the Parliament's second reading if the Council cannot accept the Parliament's amendments (see Table 8.3). The conciliation process involves a committee composed of delegations of equal size from both the Council and Parliament, who negotiate a compromise that both sides are both prepared to accept. The Commission is also present and acts as a facilitator. If either institution fails to adopt the compromise text negotiated by the conciliation committee, then the proposal falls.

There is no doubt that since its introduction in November 1993, the OLP has had a profound effect upon inter-institutional relations. While the introduction of cooperation increased informal contacts between the Commission and Parliament, the OLP has facilitated the development of direct informal relations between the

Table 8.3 The ordinary legislative procedure

Stage of decision making	Options
Commission Proposal	
EP First Reading Opinion	Accept, amend or reject Commission proposal
Commission Opinion	Accept, amend or reject the Parliament's first-reading amendments
Council Common Position	Accept or reject the Parliament's amendments. If all the Parliament's first-reading amendments are accepted, legislation is adopted
EP Second Reading	Accept, amend or reject Council Common Position. If Common Position is accepted, legislation is adopted
Commission Opinion	Accept, amend or reject the Parliament's second-reading amendments
	Council needs QMV for the Parliament's amendments with Commission support, and unanimity for amendments rejected by Commission
Council Position	Accept or reject the Parliament's second-reading amendments
	If the Parliament's amendments are accepted, legislation is adopted
	If the Parliament's amendments are rejected, a Conciliation Committee is convened
Conciliation Committee in order to negotiate a compromise on those European Parliament amendments that the Council cannot accept	If co-legislators (European Parliament and Council) cannot reach agreement, the proposal falls. If co-legislators do reach agreement, the legislation is adopted

Council and Parliament. In the early years these informal relations emerged as a response to the difficulties of negotiating an agreement with 30 or more people present in a full-blown conciliation meeting. They were initiated under the German Presidency in 1994, when Environment Committee chair, Ken Collins, met his counterpart from the Council, Jochen Grünhage, privately to discuss amendments to the packaging waste directive (Garman and Hilditch, 1998: 274–275). The success of these meetings, along with others held between Grünhage and representatives from the Culture Committee, led, over time, to a more regular use of trialogues, which are typically attended by the rapporteur, the competent committee chair, the delegation chairs from the Council and the European Parliament, and a representative of the Commission (Shackleton, 2000). As trialogues are easier to arrange and manage than full conciliation meetings, they are widely used, with conciliation meetings reserved for all but the most intractable issues. Thus, for example, such informal meetings were used extensively during the complex auto-oil negotiations (see Box 8.4).

Box 8.4 The Auto-Oil Programme

The Auto-Oil Programme sought to regulate car emissions via legislation aimed at both the oil and car industries. It represented a departure from the traditional approach to car emission policy in the EU as previously, for example, small car emission limits had been tightened incrementally in line with the development of the Best Available Technology (Friedrich *et al.*, 2000: 593). By contrast, when drawing up the auto-oil proposals, the Commission sought to develop environmental quality objectives through the adoption of cost effective regulation. The Commission also adopted a new approach to policy making by consulting closely with the automobile and oil industries when drawing up the legislation, while excluding member states, NGOs and the European Parliament (ibid.: 593–594). Unsurprisingly, none of these excluded actors were content with the Commission proposals, and a huge lobbying campaign followed, which eventually resulted in the European Parliament adopting 36 amendments at its second reading. Those amendments principally aimed to tighten the legislation's emission standards and to introduce strict deadlines, both of which would be mandatory (ibid.: 600–602). Given the enormous complexity of the dossiers and the large number of proposed amendments, the then chair, Ken Collins, with the cooperation of officials from the UK Presidency, arranged a series of informal meetings in his own office to allow the rapporteurs and Council officials to start negotiating with one another. These important and small-scale encounters made it easier to reach agreement (ibid.: 603–605). Friedrich *et al.* (2000: 604) argue that the European Parliament emerged as the clear winner from the conciliation process. Collins in turn claimed that it was the 'biggest success story' of his time in office (Wurzel, 1999: 22).

The nature of these informal meetings between the co-legislators has continued to evolve over time. As Table 8.3 indicates, the European Parliament and the Council are able to conclude the legislative process at first reading if both sides have committed themselves to agree as early as possible in the procedure (European Parliament, Council and Commission, 1999; 2007). To facilitate early agreements, the Council of Ministers' representatives (drawn from the Presidency) meet with the rapporteur and others from the Parliament with a view to finding common ground. There was initial resistance to such contacts in the Parliament on the grounds that negotiations should only take place once the Parliament had given its formal opinion in the plenary (see Shackleton and Raunio, 2003). However, over time such doubts were allayed and the use of so-called fast-track readings started to increase; thus, in the 1999–2004 session, 28 per cent of OLP dossiers were agreed at first reading, increasing to 72 per cent in the 2004–2009 session (European Parliament, 2010: 8). A key turning point was the run-up to the 2004 enlargement when there was a concerted effort on the part of all institutional actors to adopt as much legislation as possible in view of the forthcoming enlargement, which it was felt could slow down decision making (House of Lords, 2009: 39–40). However, the advent of enlargement does not appear to have either reduced the number of pieces of environmental legislation proposed or slowed down the pace at which policy proposals are agreed (Burns *et al.*, 2012). Part of the reason for this is the willingness of all three institutions to continue to use the fast-track approach to agreeing legislation (Baier, cited in House of Lords, 2009: 40). However, the process is not without its problems.

As noted above, there was initial resistance within the European Parliament to the use of fast track processes: it was felt the plenary should offer its opinion before the rapporteur opened negotiations. Moreover, there is the issue of who should be included in negotiations with the Council (see Judge and Earnshaw, 2011) and whether the rapporteur and the negotiating team could open negotiations before the committee had delivered its opinion. In some instances, negotiations have opened without a formal mandate being given to the rapporteur by the committee. In one such instance (in the negotiations over CO_2 emissions from cars), the rapporteur, Guido Sacconi (Social Democrat), presented a set of amendments to the environment committee that he had negotiated with the Council only to see them voted down by the committee, which was disgruntled with the rapporteur for ignoring the committee's legislative prerogative (Burns and Carter, 2010b).

The European Parliament instituted a working group on inter-institutional relations in response to concerns about the potential lack of transparency of informal negotiations between MEPs and Council representatives without a proper mandate from either the committee or the plenary. Following the recommendations of the working group, the European Parliament changed its rules of procedure to introduce a new rule (Rule 70) that states that before the rapporteur opens negotiations with the Council, the committee should in principle adopt a mandate to inform those negotiations (European Parliament, 2011b). However, the inclusion of the term 'in principle' still leaves open the possibility of rapporteurs forging ahead without having had a proper debate in committee or garnering the wider support of their committee peers (Judge and Earnshaw, 2011). The increased use of informal meetings also potentially excludes smaller groups such as the Greens. As noted above, rapporteurships are normally decided via an auction with the number of points allocated according to group size. Smaller groups and non-aligned members secure fewer reports and can struggle to secure important reports as they are likely to be more 'expensive'. Nevertheless, in principle, the small groups can make their views known during committee deliberations and in plenary. However, if committee meetings and plenaries are increasingly used to rubber stamp agreements negotiated by a few actors behind closed doors, the scope to have one's views considered during the legislative process is much lower. Moreover, the European Parliament's reputation as an environmental champion has rested partly upon its openness to outsider interests (see Chapter 18), which in the early days was particularly useful for environmental NGOs that were more likely to be excluded from the decision-making process in the Commission and Council (see Chapter 9). The shift towards backroom deals potentially excludes such actors from the decision-making process, which is problematic for the European Parliament, which has tried to present itself as the most open and representative EU institution.

The process of informal negotiation also means that the amendments adopted by the plenary are the subject of compromise – their content has been through a process of intra- *and* inter-institutional negotiations. As noted above, this consensual approach to politics has a potentially negative effect of de-radicalizing the content of the European Parliament's amendments – a process that is heightened if there are two layers of compromise through which amendments are being filtered. This shift in the norms of decision making may explain the finding that over time the European Parliament's amendments to environmental legislation appear to have become less 'green' (Burns and Carter, 2010a; Burns *et al.*, 2012; see Box 8.5). There are of course other potential explanations for this shift in the Parliament's behaviour. One of Burns and Carter's key findings is that post 1999, the Parliament appeared less environmentally radical (2010a: 136–139). One obvious explanation for that shift was the changing ideological composition of the Parliament as the EPP became the largest political group and, by combining with the ALDE, was able to shift the centre of gravity of the European Parliament to the centre-right, which is traditionally less sympathetic to environmental concerns than the centre-left (Carter, 2010). In their further study of amendments adopted by the European Parliament's plenary to 112 pieces of environmental legislation adopted under the OLP between 1999 and 2009, Burns *et al.* (2012) found that this process of de-radicalization appeared to be continuing. The 2004 and 2007 enlargements are likely to have been central to that process for three reasons. First, the enlargements have further consolidated the grip of the centre-right upon the Parliament. Second, they have brought in a range of states with lower environmental ambitions. For example, there has yet to be a Green MEP elected from the EU12 (see Box 8.1). Third, it is clear that the intensification of the use of informal negotiations under the OLP was in part a response to the coordination challenges posed by enlargement. Burns *et al.* (2012) also suggest that there is some evidence that MEPs from the enlargement states may have played a role in weakening the European Parliament's position on the 2008 Climate and Energy Package, but urge caution in blaming the EU12 alone, noting that German and Italian MEPs also called for lower standards.

Box 8.5 How environmental is the European Parliament?

How should academics measure the European Parliament's influence? One way is to analyse the extent to which the Parliament is able to shape legislation through its amendments by tracking whether and to what extent the amendments are included in the final legislation (see, for example,

Kreppel, 1999; Tsebelis and Kalandrakis, 1999; Tsebelis *et al.*, 2001). However, for such analysis to be meaningful, a distinction needs to be made between trivial amendments that merely clarify the wording of the text and those that seek to make a real difference by, for example, requiring further cuts in CO_2 emissions in cars (Kreppel, 1999: 522). In order to make such a judgement, Burns and Carter (2010a) have established a typology based upon the principles of ecological modernization. They have used this typology to rank over 7,000 amendments adopted between 1999 and 2009 and then analyse whether there is a relationship between how green an amendment is and its likelihood of adoption (Burns *et al.*, 2012). Unsurprisingly, they find that greener amendments are less likely to be adopted by the Council. But, significantly, they also find that over time the European Parliament has proposed fewer green amendments.

Summary points

- The principal process by which environmental policy is adopted is the ordinary legislative procedure, also known as co-decision. It has transformed the process of decision making by creating a three-way dialogue between the Parliament, Commission and Council.
- The use of informal negotiations is now common practice under the ordinary legislative procedure with the vast majority of legislation being agreed at first reading.
- These informal processes raise challenges for transparency and participation in decision making, particularly for smaller groups such as the Greens and outside interests, such as environmental NGOs.

Future challenges

In many respects, the European Parliament has been on an upward trajectory since 1979. It has now secured its treasured right of co-decision under the OLP, which applies to many areas of environmental policy as well as important cognate domains such as agriculture, energy and development. This extension of policy competence may eventually strengthen the European Parliament's ability to advance environmental policy integration (see Chapter 13) and sustainability (see Chapter 19). Although, as noted above, the move to involve a wider range of committees in legislative decision making may equally lead to a more business-oriented position being advanced by the European Parliament. Moreover, the Parliament still has no power of co-decision in relation to environmental measures with fiscal and energy supply implications, land use, town and country planning and the quantitative management of water resources (Article 175(2), TEU) – areas that still require unanimity in the Council (see Chapter 3). The European Parliament also still plays an incredibly limited role in common foreign, security and trade policies (see Chapter 16); key areas that remain dominated by the Council and Commission. Therefore, it is difficult for the European Parliament to exert any impact upon the positions adopted by the EU in important international environmental and trade negotiations such as those on ozone, climate change and trade. The Parliament's role is limited to assenting to agreements reached by the Council and Commission and offering its opinion upon their implementation (see Chapter 14), rather than being able to shape their content in any meaningful way. However, increasingly it may be able to influence such negotiations through its legislative role under the OLP by shaping legislation adopted in the EU that has a bearing upon such negotiations, such as the Climate and Energy Package (see Burns and Carter, 2010b).

The increases in the European Parliament's powers have also meant a massive increase in its workload. For example, between 1993 and 1999, it dealt with 164 OLP dossiers (European Parliament, 1999), which increased to 405 between 1999 and 2004 (European Parliament, 2004: 10–11) and approximately 480 between 2004 and 2009 (European Parliament, 2010: 6–7). Such an expansion puts a strain upon the Parliament. For example, an ongoing source of concern has been the lack of in-house expertise and an over-reliance upon interest groups for data and research materials. Moreover, the Parliament has been unable to undertake impact assessments on legislative proposals (see Chapter 12). In 2004, and in recognition of the growing need for the Parliament to be able to draw upon wider expertise, the European Parliament established its own Policy Departments, which either commission or undertake research on behalf of the European Parliament's committees (European Parliament, 2011c). In addition, there has been the challenge of enlargement. All the institutions have coped well with the increase in size of the EU, but some trade-offs have had to be made. The decision to use informal meetings to lubricate the process of decision making in order to prevent policy stasis has achieved that goal, but at a cost: transparency and participation have to some degree been sacrificed. Moreover, the changing ideological composition of the European Parliament has shifted the chamber's centre of gravity. While the SD has secured the chairmanship of the environment committee, ultimately it is the plenary that decides on amendments to legislation. The challenges of securing agreement on environmental legislation in a heterogeneous chamber were well illustrated in July 2011 when the SD and Green groups forged an alliance to vote down an environment committee report which had originally called for the Commission to bring forward a proposal to increase the level of CO_2 cuts from 20 to 30 per cent. However, members of the EPP and ECR amended the proposal in plenary to thwart the EU's climate change targets that had been originally agreed in 2008. Thus the Greens and SD voted against a report they had originally endorsed (Brand, 2011). This example highlights the key challenge for the European Parliament in the coming years: how to maintain internal cohesion in the face of the worst recession of modern times.

Summary points

- Despite the increase in its formal powers, the Parliament still has limited ability to influence key areas such as international negotiations or domestic fiscal policy.
- The Parliament also has limited in-house expertise and has struggled to cope with the increase in its workload.
- A key challenge for the coming years is to develop a coherent position that enables the European Parliament to strengthen Commission proposals.

Conclusion

The European Parliament has, in little over 30 years, undergone a significant metamorphosis; it is no longer a weak talking shop limited to making the Council wait for its opinion. It is a genuine co-legislator that can set the wider EU policy agenda. Its political groups have overcome national differences to find common ideological cause, and the Green Group has, over time, increased its representation to become a serious political force within the Parliament. The European Parliament has secured a reputation as a key environmental actor that has forced its way into the traditional bipartite relationship between the Commission and Council. However, as its powers and heterogeneity have increased, the Parliament has encountered new challenges. The cumulative strain of a greatly increased workload and a greater number of member states within the wider EU has seen new informal processes of decision making emerge. While these have clear advantages, they also carry risks that are particularly acute in the environmental policy field. The European Parliament has traditionally been able to represent the views of small groups such as the Greens and marginalized interests such as environmental NGOs, but these groups face being excluded as decision making once again takes place behind closed doors.

Summary points

- In little over 30 years the European Parliament has metamorphosed from a weak talking shop to a genuine co-legislator that can shape the wider policy agenda in the EU.
- The European Parliament has secured a reputation as a key environmental actor that has forced its way into the traditional bipartite relationship between the Commission and Council.
- However, as its powers and internal heterogeneity have increased, the European Parliament's ability to represent the views of small groups, such as the Greens, and marginalized interests, such as environmental NGOs, may have been compromised.

Key questions

1 What is the principal procedure used for adopting environmental legislation in the European Parliament?
2 What impact has enlargement had upon the European Parliament as an environmental actor?
3 What are the implications of the consensual processes of decision making in the Parliament?
4 What are the principal challenges facing the Green Group in the European Parliament?

Guide to further reading

- Corbett *et al.* (2011) and Judge and Earnshaw (2008) provide excellent introductions to the European Parliament in general. For an analysis of the evolution of the party system and voting behaviour of the European Parliament, see Hix *et al.* (2007).
- Bomberg (1998) provides a fascinating account of the early years of the European Greens. For a more up-to-date analysis of the fate of the 'Greens in Brussels', see Bomberg and Carter (2006).
- For an analysis of the European Parliament's environmental behaviour across different procedures and between 1999 and 2009, see Burns and Carter (2010a) and Burns *et al.* (2012).
- On MEP voting behaviour (including roll call votes), see the Votewatch website (Votewatch, 2011).
- For information on the Greens' electoral performance, see the regular profiles in the *Journal of Environmental Politics* (e.g. Carter, 2010).

Notes

1 Post Lisbon, the number of MEPs was supposed to increase to 751. However, the treaty was agreed after the 2009 elections and at the time of writing the number of MEPs remains at 736 (see Chapter 3).
2 On the Committees for Agriculture and Rural Development, Regional Affairs, International Trade, Environment, Public Health and Food Safety, and Employment and Social Affairs.

References

Bomberg, E. (1998) *Green Parties and Politics in the European Union*, Routledge, London.
Bomberg, E. and Carter, N. (2006) 'The Greens in Brussels', *European Journal of Political Research*, vol. 45, no. S1, pp. 99–125.

Brand, C. (2011) 'MEPs reject climate change report', *European Voice*, 5 July, available at: www.europeanvoice.com/article/2011/july/meps-reject-climate-change-report/71542.aspx (accessed 4 August 2011).

Burns, C. and Carter, N. (2010a) 'Is codecision good for the environment?' *Political Studies*, vol. 58, no. 1, pp. 128–142.

Burns, C. and Carter, N. (2010b) 'The European Parliament and climate change: from symbolism to heroism and back again', in R.K.W. Wurzel and J. Connelly (eds) *The European Union as a Leader in International Climate Change Politics*, Routledge, London.

Burns, C., Carter, N. and Worsfold, N. (2012) 'Exploring the implications of enlargement for the European Parliament's environmental record', *Journal of Common Market Studies*, vol. 50, no. 1, pp. 54–70.

Carter, N. (2010) 'The Greens in the 2009 European Parliament election', *Environmental Politics*, vol. 19, no. 2, pp. 295–302.

Corbett, R. (1998) *The European Parliament's Role in Closer Integration*, Macmillan, London.

Corbett, R., Jacobs, F. and Shackleton, M. (2011) *The European Parliament*, 8th edition, John Harper Publishing, London.

Earnshaw, D. and Judge, D. (1997) 'The life and times of the European Union's co-operation procedure', *Journal of Common Market Studies*, vol. 35, no. 4, pp. 543–564.

European Parliament (1999) *Activity Report 1 November 1993 to 30 April 1999 of the Delegations to the Conciliation Committee*, European Parliament, Brussels.

European Parliament (2004) *Activity Report 1 May 1999 to 30 April 2004 of the Delegations to the Conciliation Committee*, European Parliament, Brussels.

European Parliament (2010) *Activity Report 1 May 2004 to 13 July 2009 of the Delegations to the Conciliation Committee*, European Parliament, Brussels.

European Parliament (2011a) European Parliament website, available at: www.europarl.europa.eu (accessed 28 July 2011).

European Parliament (2011b) 'Rules of Procedure of the European Parliament, seventh parliamentary term, July 2011', available at: www.europarl.europa.eu/sides/getLast Rules.do?language=EN&reference=TOC (accessed 4 August 2011).

European Parliament (2011c) 'Studies page', available at: www.europarl.europa.eu/activities/committees/studies.do?language=EN (accessed 4 August 2011).

European Parliament, Council and Commission (1999) 'Joint declaration on the practical arrangements for the new codecision procedure', *OJC*, no. 148, pp. 1–2, *Official Journal of the European Communities*, Brussels.

European Parliament, Council and Commission (2007) 'Joint declaration on the practical arrangements for the new codecision procedure', *OJC*, no. 145, pp. 5–9, *Official Journal of the European Union*, Brussels.

Friedrich, A., Tappe, M. and Wurzel, R. (2000) 'A new approach to EU Environmental policy-making? The Auto-Oil I programme', *Journal of European Public Policy*, vol. 7, no. 4, pp. 593–612.

Garman, J. and Hilditch, L. (1998) 'Behind the scenes: an examination of the importance of the informal processes at work in conciliation', *Journal of European Public Policy*, vol. 5, no. 2, pp. 271–284.

Hagemann, S. (2009) 'Strength in numbers? An evaluation of the 2004–2009 European Parliament', EPC Issue Paper No. 58, available at: www.epc.eu/pub_details.php?cat_id=2&pub_id=479&year=2009 (accessed 25 August 2011).

Hix, S. and Noury, A. (2009) 'After enlargement: voting patterns in the Sixth European Parliament', *Legislative Studies Quarterly*, vol. 34, no. 2, pp. 159–174.

Hix, S., Noury, A. and Roland, G. (2007) *Democratic Politics in the European Parliament*, Cambridge University Press, Cambridge.

House of Lords (2009) *Codecision and National Parliamentary Scrutiny: Report with Evidence*, European Union Committee, 17th Report of Session 2008–2009, Stationery Office Limited, London.

Judge, D. (1992) 'Predestined to save the Earth: the Environment Committee of the European Parliament', *Environmental Politics*, vol. 1, no. 4, pp. 186–212.

Judge, D. and Earnshaw, D. (2008) *The European Parliament*, 2nd edition, Palgrave Macmillan, Basingstoke.

Judge, D. and Earnshaw, D. (2011) '"Relais Actors" and codecision first reading agreements in the European Parliament: the case of the advanced therapies regulation', *Journal of European Public Policy*, vol. 18, no. 1, pp. 53–71.

Kirchner, E. and Williams, K. (1983) 'The legal, political and institutional implications of the isoglucose judgments 1980', *Journal of Common Market Studies*, vol. 22, no. 2, pp. 173–190.

Kreppel, A. (1999) 'What affects the European Parliament's legislative influence? An analysis of the success of EP amendments', *Journal of Common Market Studies*, vol. 37, no. 3, pp. 521–538.

O'Donnell, P. (2007) 'House doctor', *European Voice*, 8 March, available at: www.europeanvoice.com/article/imported/house-doctor/56934.aspx (accessed 4 April 2011).

Rankin, J. (2011) 'Row over green status of oil from tar sands', *European Voice*, 3 March, available at: www.europeanvoice.com/article/imported/row-over-green-status-of-oil-from-tar-sands/70112.aspx (accessed 4 April 2011).

Settembri, P. and Neuhold, C. (2009) 'Achieving consensus through committees: does the European Parliament manage?', *Journal of Common Market Studies*, vol. 47, no. 1, pp. 127–151.

Shackleton, M. (2000) 'The politics of codecision', *Journal of Common Market Studies*, vol. 38, no. 2, pp. 325–342.

Shackleton, M. and Raunio, T. (2003) 'Codecision since Amsterdam: a laboratory for institutional innovation and change', *Journal of European Public Policy*, vol. 10, no. 2, pp. 171–188.

Smith, M.P. (2008) 'All access points are not created equal: explaining the fate of diffuse interests in the EU', *British Journal of Politics and International Relations*, vol. 10, no. 1, pp. 64–83.

Taylor, I. (2009) 'Greens attack European Parliament reforms', *European Voice*, 5 May, available at: www.europeanvoice.com/article/2009/05/greens-attack-european-parliament-reforms/64787.aspx (accessed 4 April 2011).

Tsebelis, G. (1994) 'The power of the European Parliament as a conditional agenda setter', *American Political Science Review*, vol. 88, no. 1, pp. 128–142.

Tsebelis, G. and Kalandrakis, A. (1999) 'The European Parliament and environmental legislation: the case of chemicals', *European Journal of Political Research*, vol. 36, no. 1, pp. 119–154.

Tsebelis, G., Jensen, C., Kalandrakis, A. and Kreppel, A. (2001) 'Legislative procedures in the European Union: an empirical analysis', *British Journal of Political Science*, vol. 31, no. 4, pp. 573–599.

Votewatch (2011) 'Votewatch.eu', available at: http://www.votewatch.eu/ (accessed 5 October 2011).

Warleigh, A. (2000) 'The hustle: citizenship practice, NGOs and "policy coalitions" in the European Union: the cases of Auto Oil, drinking water and unit pricing', *Journal of European Public Policy*, vol. 7, no. 2, pp. 229–243.

Weale, A., Pridham, G., Cini, M., Konstadakopoulos, D., Porter, M. and Flynn, B. (2000) *Environmental Governance in Europe*, Oxford University Press, Oxford.

Wurzel, R.K.W. (1999) 'The role of the European Parliament: interview with Ken Collins', *Journal of Legislative Studies*, vol. 5, no. 2, pp. 1–23.

Wurzel, R.K.W. (2002) *Environmental Policy-making in Britain, Germany and the European Union*, Manchester University Press, Manchester.

9 Lobby groups

Camilla Adelle and Jason Anderson

Summary guide

Over the past 40 years the EU has attracted the interest of a vast number of lobbying groups as well as a sizeable literature describing and evaluating their role. In this chapter we argue that in recent years this situation has started to mature, and that now is a good time to reflect again on the activities and wider roles of lobby groups. We find that there has been a professionalization of lobbying activities in the EU. The Commission in particular has reacted to the increased importance and number of lobby groups by changing the way it governs its relationship with them. However, it is questionable if lobby groups are willing or able to reduce the EU's alleged democratic deficit.

Introduction

Lobbying – the practice of trying to influence policy making – is an integral part of life in Brussels. The number and scope of lobby groups now operating in Brussels are vast. As national governments have ceded more and more power to the EU institutions, it is natural that the activities of lobby groups have also shifted (Mazey and Richardson, 2006). Lobby groups are simply 'shooting where the ducks are' (Coen and Richardson, 2009: 344). Besides, European institutions, especially the European Commission, provide relatively easy access compared to some national ministries and parliaments. The European Commission has even actively encouraged the participation of such groups by setting up consultative committees and other bodies, and providing funds to establish and maintain certain core groups (Eising and Lehringer, 2010). The large number of lobby groups in Brussels also encourages others to follow, fearful that they will be left out. While it is not (yet) possible to verify the exact number of lobby groups in Brussels, Greenwood (2009: 11) calculates that in 2006 there were 2,478 groups. Of these, business interests (see Chapter 10) constitute around one half of the total while one-third represent citizens' interests (including environmental lobby groups), up from around a fifth of the total in 2000 (Greenwood, 2009).

As a consequence, there has been increasing pressure on the European Commission in particular to broaden its contacts even further while at the same time standardizing them and making them more transparent. In addition, the EU has recently emphasized the potential role that public interest lobby groups (as opposed to private interest or business lobby groups), could play in enhancing the EU's democratic credentials (Eising and Lehringer, 2010).

The context in which environmental lobby groups operate in Brussels, therefore, has changed and continues to change over time as the lobby groups, and their relationship with the EU institutions, as well as the role they play in the policy making-process, evolve. These developments have been summarized in a sizeable academic literature, which had its heyday in the 1990s. This was the period when Brussels-based lobby groups surged in number. However, over the past two decades, the situation has gradually matured. After 40 years of EU environmental policy making, it is important to reflect on the roles lobby groups now play in the policy process, and how has this changed over time? We attempt to address this question by breaking it down into a number of more specific questions that form the structure of the rest of this chapter:

- Who are the main lobby groups and what context do they operate in?
- What lobbying targets and strategies have environmental lobby groups adopted?
- How influential are environmental lobby groups when compared to those representing 'big business'?
- How has the EU sought to govern the increasing number and size of lobby groups?
- How are environmental lobby groups linking the EU to its citizens and thus enhancing the EU's democratic credentials?

Summary points

- The number and importance of lobby groups operating in Brussels have increased over recent decades; at the same time, the context in which they operate has also significantly evolved.
- There has been political pressure on the EU, and particularly on the European Commission, to interface with these groups in a more consistent and transparent way.
- After a period of intense change in the 1990s, the patterns of lobbying have matured somewhat.

The main actors and contexts of lobbying

The first environmental lobby group to establish itself in Brussels was the European Environmental Bureau (EEB) which opened an office in 1974 (Hontelez, 2005). At the end of the 1980s, the EEB was joined in Brussels by a number of the larger international environmental lobby groups, such as the World Wide Fund for Nature (WWF), Friends of the Earth Europe (FOEE), Birdlife International and Greenpeace (Long, 1995). This second wave was partly a response to the enormous expansion in the volume and scope of EU environmental legislation in the 1980s following the introduction of a new environment 'title' to the EU treaties in the Single European Act (ibid.) (see Chapter 2). There are now ten core environmental lobby groups operating in Brussels which coordinate and collaborate in a loose network – the so-called 'G10' (Green Ten) (a parody of the name given to the economic summits of the G7 states) (Wurzel and Connelly, 2010: 214) (see Table 9.1).

These environmental lobby groups strive to influence EU decision making by exploiting the same complex and dynamic 'opportunity structure' exploited by other lobby groups (Mazey and Richardson, 2003). There is at least one lobby group in Brussels to represent almost every likely aspect of EU life, including: business groups (see Chapter 10); trade and professional associations; employer federations; trade unions; law firms; and international organizations. To this list can also be added public affairs consultants, who lobby on behalf of their clients.

The relationship between these groups and the EU is a symbiotic one. The Commission, and to a lesser extent the European Parliament and Council of Ministers, are reliant on technical information and advice to produce successful policy proposals (Coen and Richardson, 2009). Contrary to popular belief, the European Commission is a relatively small administration with limited resources and has a particular need for reliable information about all 27 member states (Mazey and Richardson, 2003). Pan-European umbrella groups and international networks (including the majority of the main environmental lobby groups) are

Table 9.1 The G10 environmental lobby groups

Organization (acronym)	Year Brussels office established	Outreach office, number of members*
European Environment Bureau (EEB)	1974	143 organizations in 31 countries
World Wide Fund for Nature (WWF)	1989	Outreach office
Friends of the Earth Europe (FOEE)	1989	Outreach office
Greenpeace	1988	Outreach office
Transport and Environment (T&E)	1989	44 organizations in 24 countries
Birdlife International	1993	Outreach office
Climate Action Network Europe (CAN-Europe)	1989	149 European members
Friends of Nature International (IFN)	n/a	50 organizations in 46 countries
CEE Bankwatch Network	n/a	Prague-based network
Health and Environmental Alliance (HEAL)	2003	65 members globally

*Note: Environmental lobbying groups in Brussels generally fit into two types: (1) outreach offices of wider global movements; or (2) offices representing international networks of (member) organizations.
Source: Greenwood (2009) and websites of individual organizations.

particularly good at providing access to this important 'on the ground' information. Lobby groups can also provide valuable support for EU policies and institutions, including particular Directorate Generals (DGs) within the European Commission (Wurzel and Connelly, 2010). It is therefore in the interests of the EU institutions to assemble and maintain their key clientele so that its services become valuable to the users.

More recently, these functional, interest-driven incentives to build enduring relationships have been strengthened by political incentives for the EU as a whole to be open to scrutiny in order to enhance its own legitimacy (Mazey and Richardson, 2003). EU lobby groups are now thought to have an important role in linking the EU institutions to European citizens and thereby enhance their democratic credentials (Eising and Lehringer, 2010). In the words of the European Commission (2002: 5):

> By fulfilling its duty to consult, the Commission ensures that its proposals are technically viable, practically workable and based on a bottom-up approach. In other words, good consultation serves a dual purpose by helping to improve the quality of the policy outcome and at the same time enhancing the involvement of interested parties and the public at large.

According to this argument, interest groups contribute 'functional representation' to improve the legitimacy of EU policies already provided by representation of citizen interests through European Parliament and of territorial interests through the EU Council (Eising and Lehringer, 2010: 194).

Summary points

- A group of ten main environmental lobby groups operating in Brussels coordinate and collaborate in a loose network known as the 'Green Ten'.
- The relationship between lobby groups and the EU is a symbiotic one.
- The EU now portrays lobby groups as having an important role in linking the EU institutions to EU citizens.

Lobbying the EU: targets and strategies

Targets

Lobby groups need to focus their activities on multiple targets to maximize their influence. This includes targeting actors through all the stages of the policy-making process from agenda setting (see Chapter 11) and policy formulation, through to decision making (see Chapter 12) and implementation (see Chapter 14). However, it is often easier and less resource-intensive to attempt to influence decisions at an early stage of policy making where the views and options of policy makers are still relatively malleable (Mazey and Richardson, 1992). Environmental lobby groups are thought to be particularly good at bringing issues onto the agenda in these very early stages of the policy process (Grant *et al.*, 2000; Greenwood, 2003).

As a consequence, the European Commission is generally believed to be the most important target for EU lobby groups (Greenwood, 2003; Eising and Lehringer, 2010). The Commission's exclusive right to initiate policies gives it a vital role in agenda setting as well as policy formulation. Mazey and Richardson (2003: 222) distinguish between two types of formal consultation employed by the Commission: (1) 'thin' consultation through large open gatherings bringing together all the potential stakeholders in a forum, seminar or conference; and (2) the 'thick' consultation of expert committees and advisory bodies containing the 'key players'. However, environmental lobby groups complain that their inclusion in these committees is more varied across the different DGs than that enjoyed by business lobby groups (Coen, 2007). Even when they are invited to join such committees, their interaction does not necessarily translate into influence. John Hontelez, a very long-serving Secretary General of the EEB, relates a cautionary tale about the participation of his group in the consultative committees of certain DGs:

> In many cases, the main purpose of our presence is to supply balance to a predominantly business attendance . . . dialogue can also become ritual, a theatre to show transparency and a willingness to listen without having any impact on policies.
>
> (Hontelez, 2005: 403)

As a consequence, the EEB, like all lobbying groups, seeks to target informal channels, technical experts and higher-level officials at particular key points in time. Hontelez (2005) argues that this approach is widely recognized as being far more influential than relying on the formal consultation exercises (see Chapter 18). Increasingly, lobby groups also target comitology committees where the details of policies are thrashed out between representatives of the member states and the Commission (see Box 9.1).

Box 9.1 Lobbying in Brussels: Indirect Land Use Change

The Renewable Energy Directive (2009/28/EC), which was part of the Climate and Energy Package, requires 10 per cent of transport fuels to come from renewable energy by 2020. This primarily means increasing the use of biofuels. However, the directive left decisions about the long-term sustainability of the main sources to the comitology process and to further co-decision (see Chapter 12). This includes the issue of Indirect Land Use

Change (ILUC), which arises because increasing the land used to grow biofuels could lead to environmentally detrimental impacts (including increased greenhouse gas emissions) through the displacement of other activities. This issue is, however, controversial and 'the facts' remain deeply contested.

Leadership on transport issues among environmental lobby groups in Brussels lies with Transport and Environment (T&E), an association of 50 European organizations. However, many other groups are also active in this area, including Birdlife International, the EEB, FOEE, Greenpeace, and the WWF. The main relevant industry groups include companies dedicated to biofuels and related technologies, oil companies with biofuels investments, and those representing specific crops like sugar cane.

The Commission is mandated by the Renewable Energy Directive to use the 'best available evidence' to review the issue of ILUC and, if necessary, make a legislative proposal amending the directive to account for it. The environmental lobby groups argue that the ILUC effects can be so large as to rule out the use of several popular crop types. However, as with any result based on complex modelling, the predicted effects can vary significantly (according to a range of factors. The main industry groups tend to argue, therefore, that the ILUC studies were too broad-brush to apply to any single crop type.

Studies by EEB, Birdlife and T&E have tried to keep the issue in the public eye. Lobby groups have also amplified the messages issued by other actors. The WWF continued working with both lobby groups and certain industry players, seeking to elicit broader support for dealing with ILUC. Lobby groups were also invited to specialist workshops, as well as having access to officials in private meetings.

Although a report with policy options was due by December 2010, the European Commission only offered a status report. The Impact Assessment on the options, which was expected in July 2011, was also delayed and eventually the Commission decided to postpone it until 2014 – the last year of its mandate. Delays probably indicate that the Commission has little choice but to acknowledge the severity of the problem, but hopes to find a way out of offering a solution which in part meets the interests of large economic and political groups.

The European Parliament is also an increasingly attractive target for environmental lobby groups (see Chapter 8). Successive treaty changes have increased its power (see Chapters 2 and 3), and it has a well-known reputation for supporting environmental causes (Eising and Lehringer, 2010). Gullberg (2008b) reports that some environmental lobby groups have now begun to target it in preference to other EU institutions. Members of the relevant parliamentary committees who first consider the Commission's proposals are a popular target, especially the rapporteurs who prepare the draft reports (Greenwood, 2003). Informal inter-groups made up of both Members of the European Parliament (MEPs) and stakeholders (including lobby groups) are another useful target (de Jesus Butler, 2008).

Arguably the most difficult EU institution for lobby groups to influence is the Council of Ministers. By the time proposals reach this point, the issues and most actors' positions have already been concretized (Greenwood, 2003: 32). In addition, the closed and confidential nature of intergovernmental negotiations means that there is less chance to monitor, let alone influence, policy developments (see Chapter 5). For this reason, the Council is usually accessed by lobby groups (especially umbrella and confederate groups) via national governments (Mazey and Richardson, 1992; 2003; Eising and Lehringer, 2010).

Strategies

Within the EU institutions, lobby groups have a choice between lobbying 'friends' or 'foes' (Gullberg, 2008a). Environmental lobby groups can target decision makers who are already sympathetic to their views, for example, DG Environment or members of the Parliament's Environment, Public Health and Food Safety Committee. While lobbying policy makers with opposing views may seem more rational, it can be resource-intensive and extremely difficult to influence them. On the other hand, providing support for 'their' DG can be a useful approach for environmental lobby groups as it can provide cover for a 'green' stance which could not be openly declared otherwise (Warleigh, 2000). Long and Lorinczi (2009: 176) report a DG Environment official saying that for the REACH proposals for regulating chemicals in the EU 'without the persistent and very strong lobbying from the environmental lobby groups, it would not have been possible for the Environmental Commissioner to put forward such a proposal with such consequences for industry'.

The literature differentiates between 'insider' lobbying groups, which are consulted and granted greater access to EU institutions, and 'outsider' groups which employ a more aggressive approach to lobbying (e.g. Grant *et al.*, 2000: 60). In practice, environmental lobby groups dispute the idea that these two strategies are mutually exclusive (Wurzel and Connelly, 2010) (see Box 9.2). However, it is clear that some 'light-green' (i.e. less radical) environmental lobby groups, such as WWF and Birdlife International, prefer a more insider lobbying strategy (Greenwood, 2003: 194). It requires considerable financial and human resources to collect advanced intelligence of policy proposals and to provide policy officials with information. Other, more 'dark-green' environmental lobby groups (ibid.: 194), such as the FOEE and especially Greenpeace, deliberately take a more confrontational stance (Grant *et al.*, 2000). By mobilizing their massive membership networks and attracting media attention, these groups can organise formidable direct action campaigns such as boycotts. In reality, both strategies are often adopted to varying degrees by environmental lobby groups able to combine institutional politics with traditional social movement (Greenwood, 2003). A combination of strategies was used by environmental lobby groups in their campaign on tar sands described in Box 9.2. However, Greenwood (ibid.: 194–195) suggests that even the most aggressive groups such as Greenpeace engage in policy making at a technical level in Brussels and that over time are tamed as they become 'incorporated in, and influenced by the routines of, institutional political decision-making'.

Box 9.2 Lobbying in Brussels: tar sands

The Fuel Quality Directive was revised in 2009 (2009/70/EC) to include a provision (Article 7a) that the lifecycle greenhouse gas emissions of European transport fuels should fall by 6 per cent by 2020 per unit of energy sold. However, the details of how this would be implemented were left to comitology (see Chapter 12). In particular, the default emission values for tar (oil) sands still needed to be decided.

A draft proposal by the European Commission seen by lobby groups in 2009 included a separate default value for tar sands higher than for 'conventional' oil. However, this was dropped from a version seen in early 2010. A broad coalition of environmental lobby groups jointly sent a briefing to the Commission, Parliament, and members of the Commission's consultative committee. It drew on a review of existing research by the US Natural Resources Defense Council, which indicated that tar sands were significantly more polluting to extract than conventional fuels. This information was contested by the Canadian government, supported by oil companies, with significant investments there. The European Commission then commissioned its own 'independent' paper, which essentially backed the position of the environmental lobby groups.

Another strategy employed by the environmental lobby groups was the use of coalitions both in and beyond the 'Brussels bubble'. A coalition on the issue of tar sands had already formed in the UK between 'The Cooperative' a group of cooperatively owned businesses, WWF UK's toxic fuels campaign and Greenpeace. A strong national campaign brought significant additional resources and another perspective to the EU campaign. There was also a high level of communication and trust between EU environmental groups. T&E and Greenpeace led detailed work in Brussels, backed by WWF and FOEE. In addition, close ties internationally (including to Canada, the United States, and Madagascar), reinforced by decades of cooperation on environmental matters, led to information flowing across borders.

The environmental lobby groups also employed more high-profile 'outside' tactics. For example, the Cooperative, WWF UK and Greenpeace placed the 'Tarnished Earth' photography exhibition in front of the European Parliament in March 2011 at the same time as handing in a petition of 20,000 signatures to MEPs.

Finally, building alliances, coalitions and networks has become an important part of how Brussels works and can improve the chances of success for 'bread and butter lobbying' (Long and Lorinczi, 2009: 168–169). Warleigh (2000: 240) argues that issue-specific coalition formation is the 'principal dynamic' of lobby groups. Over the years 'policy clusters' have therefore emerged of lobby groups drawn together for collective organization and action on specific topics (Wurzel and Connelly, 2010: 216). Warleigh (2000) argues that the key motivation to join such coalitions is to secure a marginal political advantage rather than because of deeply held values. In other words, many coalitions are quite opportunistic. This is reflected in the fact that some of the coalitions involve both environmental lobby groups and wider public interest groups. For example, the European Public Health Alliance joined with environmental lobby groups in a single issue organization, the 'Zero Mercury Campaign', which lobbied (successfully) for the EU to ban the export of mercury from the EU (Zero Mercury Campaign, 2011) (see Chapter 16).

Summary points

- The European Commission is traditionally considered to be the most important lobbying target for environmental lobby groups, but the attractiveness of the European Parliament is rapidly increasing.
- Environmental lobby groups have a choice between focusing their lobbying activities on 'friends' or 'foes'.
- Environmental lobby groups can employ 'insider' and/or more confrontational 'outsider' strategies.
- Building alliances, coalitions and other networks has become an important part of the lobbying process in Brussels.

Measuring the impacts of lobbying

The sheer number of lobbyists and lobby groups present in Brussels indicates that they think they exert some influence over the EU policy-making process. If they did not, why would they take the trouble to be there (Lelieveldt and Princen, 2011)? However, it is difficult to measure the precise extent of their influence (but see Woll, 2006). The counterfactual (i.e. what would have happened in the absence of the lobbying?) is, after all, almost impossible to assess. Policies can be shaped by a number of different factors, including other lobby groups, member states, MEPs, etc. (Michalowitz, 2007; Lelieveldt and Princen, 2011). Much of the early literature on lobby groups therefore focused on identifying simple proxies for overall influence such as access to the policy process, or which strategies were most successful (Woll, 2006). There are also studies which tell us something about the relative differences between the level of influence of different interest groups. It is to these studies which we now turn.

Some authors have argued that the most powerful European lobbyists are producer or business lobby groups (e.g. Mazey and Richardson, 2003). The interests and views of these groups are thought to be deeply embedded within the Commission in particular (Mazey and Richardson, 2003; Coen, 2007). Private business lobby groups still significantly outnumber public lobby groups (Greenwood, 2009). However, this does not necessarily indicate that they wield greater influence. A number of intrinsic characteristics of environmental lobby groups work in their favour. First, the lack of competition between environmental lobby groups which share a common 'cause' is thought to make it easier for them to reach a common policy position than business groups (Wurzel and Connelly, 2010). Second, as groups representing public (as opposed to private) interests, they are seen as being 'on the side of the angels' (Greenwood, 2003: 183) – something which can encourage policy makers to take them more seriously than business groups (Grant *et al.*, 2000). On the other hand, some characteristics of environmental lobby groups can weaken their impact. For example, an excessive focus on DG Environment can be a real limitation (Mazey and Richardson, 1992; Hontelez, 2005). While environmental lobby groups have good contacts with DG Environment, business groups have strong contacts across the whole of the Commission (Grant *et al.*, 2000).

The apparent inequality of access is not, however, the main barrier facing environmental lobby groups. For a long time environmental lobby groups have complained that they are under-resourced compared to business lobby groups (e.g. Long, 1995; Hontelez, 2005), something which has been incorporated into the literature on EU lobbying (e.g. Grant *et al.*, 2000; Mazey and Richardson, 2003). However, while there may still be a level of inbuilt bias in the EU policy process, overall a more mixed picture is beginning to emerge. Greenwood (2003) points out that the larger environmental lobby groups are mainly outreach organizations of wider global movements which have very significant resources to draw on. This helps them engage policy makers at a more detailed scientific level (ibid.). WWF in particular is reported to have a significant level of resources compared to other environmental groups which allow it to lobby on more issues and engage in more general long-term lobbying (Gullberg, 2008b) than the rest. In such cases, the idea of 'David against Goliath' probably underrates the resources and influence enjoyed by environmental lobby groups (Greenwood, 2003; Gullberg, 2008b).

Summary points

- It is difficult to measure the influence of any lobby group on decision making.
- Some authors argue that business groups are the most powerful, but a number of intrinsic characteristics of environmental lobby groups serve to enhance their effectiveness.
- Environmental lobby groups have long complained that they are under-resourced compared to business groups. In practice, there are some large and very influential environmental lobby groups.

The governance of lobbying

The management of lobby groups by the Commission, the Parliament and the Council has, until recently, not been approached in a consistent manner. While efforts by the Commission have received the most attention in the literature, it is the European Parliament that first implemented a mandatory registration system for lobby groups. Traditionally, the European Parliament has had a rather different attitude to the Commission. As elected representatives of the European citizens, the European Parliament maintains that it, together with national parliaments, 'constitutes the basis for a European system with democratic legitimacy' (European Parliament, 2001: point 8). Therefore the Parliament had fewer qualms about making its registration scheme mandatory in exchange for annual entry permits into its buildings (Obradovic, 2009). The Council, on the other hand, continues to have no framework for managing its relations with lobby groups. This difference is even more significant if one recalls that it is the most closed of the three EU institutions and hence also the most difficult to monitor externally.

The Commission, by contrast, has always been a very accessible institution (Greenwood, 2003: 54), preferring self-regulation of lobbying through voluntary codes of conduct and existing administrative rules (European Commission, 2006: 9). It feared that tighter mandatory measures might limit its access to the kinds of lobby groups that it relies on for expertise. Throughout the 1990s, therefore, the Commission rejected any accreditation system for lobby groups. A voluntary and self-regulatory code of conduct was in place, but this only set minimum standards and was only really adhered to by public affairs consultancies, who comprise a relatively small proportion of the total population of lobbying groups in Brussels (Obradovic, 2009). Then, in 2001, the Commission published a White Paper on Governance (European Commission, 2001) which put forward recommendations on how to enhance the legitimacy of the EU institutions. In this paper, interest groups and their role in linking citizens with EU institutions were seen as playing a critical role. As a consequence, measures intended to improve the way in which the EU approached its contacts with these groups were set out. This was followed up a year later by the adoption of a set of 'general principles and minimum standards for consultation of interested parties' (European Commission, 2002).

In 2005, the Commission went further still, launching the 'European Transparency Initiative'. This was intended to enhance the financial accountability of EU funding, strengthen the independence and integrity of EU institutions and make the controls on lobbying activities stricter (European Commission, 2005). In particular, the Green Paper on the European Transparency Initiative in 2006 called for a more structured framework for the activities of lobby groups and for the disclosure of information on who benefits from EU funding (European Commission, 2006). This ultimately led to the creation of an online 'Register of Interest Representatives' which was launched in June 2008. This register was voluntary but all groups which undertook 'activities carried out with the objective of influencing the policy formulation and decision-making processes of the European institutions' were encouraged to sign up (European Commission, 2008: 3). Registered groups had to comply with a code of conduct and contraventions led to the temporary suspension of access rights and even the expulsion of some groups from the register (although only a handful of contraventions ever reached this stage). The Commission claimed that sufficient incentives to join the register would come from providing registered groups with automatic alerts of relevant Commission consultations. However, this thinking was criticized because many, if not most, of the main lobby groups in Brussels already followed the Commission's activities on a daily basis (Obradovic, 2009: 310).

In June 2011, the Commission's register was combined with the longer-standing register of the European Parliament in a new 'Transparency Register' (European Commission, 2011). The Parliament's original incentive to register (i.e. in exchange for an entry pass) was carried over into this new joint system, adding an important additional motivation that the Commission's original scheme lacked (European Commission, 2011).

Summary points

- Throughout the 1990s, the Commission rejected several requests for a formal accreditation system for lobby groups, preferring instead to keep access as open as possible.
- The 2001 White Paper on Governance set out recommendations for changing the EU's contacts with lobby groups.
- The Commission and the European Parliament launched a combined 'Transparency Register' in June 2011.

The role of lobby groups in EU democracy

The EU's increased efforts to improve the transparency and accountability of its interactions with lobby groups have underlined the potential role of consultation and lobby groups in enhancing the EU's democratic credentials. A debate on the EU's so-called 'democratic deficit' has been underway since the late 1980s. It is based on a number of claims (Hix, 2005: 178). First, that EU decision making is concentrated in the executive of the Commission and the Council, with the powers of the European Parliament being too weak to compensate for the loss of national parliamentary control. Second, there are no European elections, just European *parliamentary* elections, which more often than not are dominated by national issues. This bias is aggravated by the fact that EU citizens find it hard to understand the complex and remote policies and processes of the EU.

Other authors, however, claim that the EU does not need to be democratic in quite the same way as national governments; rather, the EU should only be more transparent and professional in its decision making (ibid.: 178). Moravcsik (2002; 2003) goes even further, pointing out that the power of the European Parliament has increased considerably and that decision making in the EU is more transparent than most domestic policy-making systems. These academic controversies aside, the Commission's White Paper on Governance (European Commission, 2001) portrayed lobby groups as representatives of 'civil society' and laid out plans to improve the transparency and accountability of their activities. On this view, lobbying can bring alternative viewpoints to the attention of the policy maker; viewpoints which may be shared by many citizens but which might otherwise escape the attention of policy makers (Lelieveldt and Princen, 2011). They may also facilitate greater political engagement among excluded and/or alienated citizens (Warleigh, 2001). The EU, therefore, now sees lobby groups as playing an important role in bringing EU decision making closer to the people and thus reducing the 'democratic deficit' (ibid.).

Long and Lorinczi (2009) argue that the umbrella or confederal structure of many of the main environmental lobby groups (something which is actively preferred by the Commission) exists precisely to give a voice to smaller nationally or regionally based organizations. Through organizations like the EEB, the environmental lobby groups claim to represent millions of EU citizens. The EEB (2011) maintains it is the 'environmental voice' of 15 million European citizens while the Green Ten (2011) reports to have a collective grassroots membership of more than 20 million. More generally, Eurobarometer surveys show a high level of public support both for EU environmental policy and for environmental lobby groups (Eurobarometer, 2011). Thus, the environmental lobby groups can play an important role both in linking environmentally minded citizens to the EU institutions as well as a supporting role for the EU's portrayal of itself as an international environmental leader (Grant *et al.*, 2000: 64).

The confederal structure of some of the lobby groups, however, has also been criticized for being remote from the grassroots interests of many citizens (Greenwood, 2003). Warleigh (2000; 2001) argues that the internal governance of lobby groups is far too dynamic and specialized to allow their supporters a direct role in shaping policy: lobby groups are by their very nature 'elite driven' rather than 'membership-led' (Warleigh, 2000: 230). They usually make little or no effort to inform their supporters about the need to engage with the EU. Indeed, the need for a sophisticated understanding of the issues in hand can cause them to act against the wishes (or even without the awareness) of their members (ibid.). In addition, he concludes that most grassroots members have little interest in the EU and are happy to serve a passive role (Warleigh, 2001). In other words, it may not only be the EU institutions that are struggling with a 'democratic deficit'.

Summary points

- Lobby groups have increasingly been portrayed as representatives of civil society and are now regarded by the EU as playing a critical role in enhancing the EU's democratic credentials.

- Many environmental lobby groups have an extensive grassroots membership which makes them an attractive link for the EU to its citizens in member states.
- Environmental policy processes in Brussels are highly complex and lobby groups have in turn been criticized for being remote from their supporters.

Conclusion

After 40 years of environmental policy making, the world of lobbying in Brussels has matured. Consequently, now is a good time to reflect on what role lobby groups play in this process and how has this changed over time. Various trends can be detected. First, over the past 20 years there has been a steady professionalization of lobbying strategies and approaches and with them an emergence of a distinct EU lobbying style (Coen and Richardson, 2009). Second, trust and credibility through an 'insider' strategy have emerged as the most effective lobbying strategy in Brussels. Third, although the Commission remains perhaps the most important target at EU level, the European Parliament, and particularly its committees, are increasingly being targeted (Lelieveldt and Princen, 2011). Finally, building issue-specific coalitions and networks has become one of the most prominent features of the contemporary world of lobbying.

Through these well-honed strategies, it is apparent that environmental lobby groups are now able to play an important role in the policy process (Warleigh, 2000). They can, at times, heavily influence standards, help select policy instruments as well as act as watchdogs in the implementation of environmental policy. However, measuring the extent of their influence is difficult. Exercising power should not be judged narrowly: sometimes it is enough for lobby groups to be seen by their supporters to be 'fighting their corner' in Brussels. Such a strategy may be enough to secure the political and financial support that they need from their supporters. In addition, if a long-term view of the impact of lobby groups is taken – a view which takes into account their influence on the broader ways of thinking in civil society – their influence is seen to be more significant than is sometimes assumed (Greenwood, 2003). They *are* able to influence policy outcomes, even if this is often less obvious or extensive than the reach of industry (Warleigh, 2000). Moreover, what environmental lobby groups are lobbying for – essentially a wholly different direction for European integration – is arguably more difficult to achieve than what industry wants (i.e. a better functioning single market to create a level playing field for competition) (Grant *et al.*, 2000; Hontelez, 2005). Indeed, given that the basic *raison d'être* of the EU is to promote economic growth through trade liberalization, the fact that so much of environmental legislation is on the statute books at all must count as a major success, even though a lot of it is not that radical or completely implemented.

The rise in the number, professionalism and perhaps influence of lobbying groups has been accompanied by efforts to improve the way the EU governs its contacts with lobby groups. However, the Commission in particular faces a basic dilemma: whether to promote openness or effective governance. It is certainly anxious not to 'create new bureaucratic hurdles [that] . . . restrict the number of those that can participate in consultation processes' (European Commission, 2002: 11). Obradovic (2009: 311), however, points out that the Commission may have found 'the golden formula' by excluding from the registration requirements those interest groups which have been invited by the Commission to input their expertise on particular issues and/or to participate in public hearings, consultative committee, or in similar influential fora. The Commission is also under no obligation to incorporate ideas contributed in the course of its consultations into its proposals or to ensure the balanced participations of all interested parties (ibid.). Therefore, it is possible for the European Commission to pursue greater legitimacy through attempting to ensure the equitable and ethical inclusion of a plurality of interests, while at the same time consistently favouring certain powerful groups.

However, what can realistically be achieved in this regard by only one EU institution – the Commission – is questionable. It seems unlikely that the Commission's recent efforts to govern its contacts with lobby groups will be able to solve the EU's democratic deficit. After all, it is far from certain if the structural bias built into the system of EU lobbying can be ameliorated while still ensuring that the policy process continues, greatly lubricated, it should be remembered, by information provided by lobby groups. It is also very questionable whether lobby groups are even currently *able* to play a key part in enhancing the democratic legitimacy, caught as they are in the ever more technical 'insider' world of policy making in Brussels.

Summary points

- The strategies and targets of environmental lobbyists have changed over time, as has the way the Commission governs its relationship with them.
- Despite many challenges, environmental lobby groups are now able to play a significant role in EU policy making.
- The EU's expectation that lobby groups can help to solve its democratic deficit, appears rather optimistic.

Key questions

1   What general approaches and strategies to lobbying have environmental lobby groups adopted?

2 What influence do the environmental lobby groups now enjoy (especially when compared to 'big business')?
3 Why and how has the EU sought to govern the increasing number of lobby groups?
4 What role (if any) do environmental lobby groups play in connecting the EU to its citizens?

Guide to further reading

- A key text on EU lobby groups is Greenwood's (2011) book, which is now in its third edition.
- Obradovic (2009) gives a detailed account of how the EU has regulated lobbying in the EU.
- A number of interesting 'insider' accounts of lobbying from the environmental movement exist. Two of the most recent are by Long and Lorinczi (2009) and that by John Hontelez (2005).

References

Coen, D. (2007) 'Empirical and theoretical studies in EU lobbying', *Journal of European Public Policy*, vol. 14, no. 3, pp. 333–345.

Coen, D. and Richardson, J. (2009) 'Learning to lobby the European Union: 20 years of change', in D. Coen and J. Richardson (eds) *Lobbying the European Union: Institutions, Actors, and Issues*, Oxford University Press, Oxford, pp. 3–15.

De Jesus Butler, I. (2008) 'Non-governmental organisation participation in the EU law-making process: the example of social non-governmental organisations at the Commission, Parliament and Council', *European Law Journal*, vol. 14, no. 5, pp. 558–582.

Eising, R. and Lehringer, S. (2010) 'Interest groups and the European Union', in M. Cini and N. Pérez-Solórzano Borragán (eds) *European Union Politics*, Oxford University Press, Oxford, pp. 189–206.

Eurobarometer (2011) 'Attitudes of European citizens towards the environment', Special Eurobarometer 365, available at: http://ec.europa.eu/environment/pdf/EB_summary_EB752.pdf (accessed 28 August 2011).

European Commission (2001) *European Governance: A White Paper* (COM (2001) 428), Commission of the European Communities, Brussels.

European Commission (2002) *Towards a Reinforced Culture of Consultation and Dialogue: General Principles and Minimum Standards for Consultation of Interested Parties by the Commission* (COM (2002) 704), Commission of the European Communities, Brussels.

European Commission (2005) 'Communication to the Commission from the President, Ms Wallstrom, Mr Kallas, Ms Huber and Ms Fischer Boel proposing the launch of a European Transparency Initiative', available at: http://ec.europa.eu/civil_society/interest_groups/docs/etik-communication_en.pdf (accessed 31 May 2011).

European Commission (2006) *Green Paper: European Transparency Initiative* (COM (2006) 194), Commission of the European Communities, Brussels.

European Commission (2008) *European Transparency Initiative: A Framework for Relations with Interest Representatives (Register and Code of Conduct)* (COM (2008) 323), Commission of the European Communities, Brussels.

European Commission (2011) 'Transparency Register', available at: http://europa.eu/transparency-register/index_en.htm (accessed 22 June 2011).

European Environment Bureau (EEB) (2011) 'About EEB: the environmental voice of European citizens', available at: http://www.eeb.org/index.cfm/about-eeb/ (accessed 31 May 2011).

European Parliament (2001) 'Resolution on the Commission White Paper on European governance', A5-0399/2001, European Parliament, Brussels.

Grant, W., Matthews, D. and Newell, P. (2000) *The Effectiveness of European Union Environmental Policy*, Macmillan Press, Basingstoke.

Green Ten (2011) 'About the Green-10', available at: http://green10.org/ (accessed 31 May 2011).

Greenwood, J. (2003) *Interest Representation in the European Union*, Palgrave Macmillan, Basingstoke.

Greenwood, J. (2009) *Interest Representation in the European Union*, 2nd edition, Palgrave Macmillan, Basingstoke.

Greenwood, J. (2011) *Interest Representation in the European Union*, 3rd edition, Palgrave Macmillan, Basingstoke.

Gullberg, A.T. (2008a) 'Lobbying friends and foes in climate policy: the case of business and environmental interest groups in the European Union', *Energy Policy*, vol. 36, pp. 2964–2972.

Gullberg, A.T. (2008b) 'Rational lobbying and EU climate policy', *International Environmental Agreements*, vol. 8, pp. 161–178.

Hix, S. (2005) *The Political System of the European Union*, 2nd edition, Palgrave Macmillan, Basingstoke.

Hontelez, J. (2005) 'The impact of European non-governmental organisations on EU environmental regulation', in F. Wijen, K. Zoeteman and J. Pieters (eds) *A Handbook of Globalization and Environmental Policy: National Government Interventions in a Global Arena*, Edward Elgar, Cheltenham.

Lelieveldt, H. and Princen, S. (2011) *The Politics of the European Union*, Cambridge University Press, Cambridge.

Long, T. (1995) 'Shaping the public policy in the European Union: a case study of the structural funds', *Journal of European Public Policy*, vol. 2, pp. 672–679.

Long, T. and Lorinczi, L. (2009) 'NGOs as gatekeepers: a green vision', in D. Coen and J. Richardson (eds) *Lobbying the European Union: Institutions, Actors, and Issues*, Oxford University Press, Oxford.

Mazey, S. and Richardson, R. (1992) 'Environmental groups and the EC: challenges and opportunities', *Environmental Politics*, vol. 1, no. 4, pp. 109–128.

Mazey, S. and Richardson, R. (2003) 'Interest groups and the Brussels bureaucracy', in J. Hayward and A. Menon (eds) *Governing Europe*, Oxford University Press, Oxford, pp. 208–227.

Mazey, S. and Richardson, J. (2006) 'Interest groups and EU policy-making: organizational logic and venue shopping', in J. Richardson (ed.) *European Union: Power and Policy-Making*, Routledge, London, pp. 247–265.

Michalowitz, I. (2007) 'What determines influence? Assessing conditions for decision-making influence of interest groups in the EU', *Journal of European Public Policy*, vol. 14, no. 1, pp. 132–151.

Moravcsik, A. (2002) 'In defense of the "Democratic Deficit": reassessing the legitimacy of the European Union', *Journal of Common Market Studies*, vol. 40, no. 4, pp. 603–634.

Moravcsik, A. (2003) 'The EU ain't broke', *Prospect*, March, pp. 38–45.

Obradovic, D. (2009) 'Regulating lobbying in the European Union', in D. Coen and J. Richardson (eds) *Lobbying the European Union: Institutions, Actors, and Issues*, Oxford University Press, Oxford, pp. 298–333.

Warleigh, A. (2000) 'The hustle: citizenship practice, NGOs and "policy coalitions" in the European Union – the cases of auto oil, drinking water and unit pricing', *Journal of European Public Policy*, vol. 7, no. 2, pp. 229–243.

Warleigh, A. (2001) '"Europeanizing" civil society: NGOs as agents of political socialization', *Journal of Common Markets Studies*, vol. 39, no. 4, pp. 619–639.

Woll, C. (2006) 'Lobbying in the European Union: from *sui generic* to a comparative perspective', *Journal of European Public Policy*, vol. 13, no. 3, pp. 456–469.

Wurzel, R. and Connelly, J. (2010) 'Environmental NGOs: taking a lead?', in R. Wurzel and J. Connelly (eds) *Leader in International Climate Change Politics*, Routledge, London, pp. 214–231.

Zero Mercury Campaign (2011) 'Zero Mercury Global Campaign', available at: www.zeromercury.org/index.html (accessed 24 June 2011).

10 Business

Wyn Grant

Summary guide

Business interests are widely represented in the EU but are also potentially the greatest constraint on the development of effective environmental policies, which can challenge both their markets and profitability. Weak versions of ecological modernization adopted in practice by the EU envisage a 'win–win' outcome in terms of the relationship between business and environmental policy. The climate change debate, however, poses many new challenges to this relationship and has led to further divisions both between different business sectors and even between firms within a particular sector. The economic downturn serves to emphasize these challenges as well as highlight some new opportunities in relation to business and environmental policy in the EU.

Introduction

Exactly what constitutes a business is not a straightforward matter. Many 'third sector' organizations such as charities are run on business-like lines and have brands that are stronger than many commercial businesses, while organizations such as producer or retail cooperatives compete in the market place with privately owned companies. There are still publicly owned enterprises throughout Europe, even if their number and displacement have diminished.

However, the focus in this chapter is on privately owned companies, partnerships or individuals (e.g. trading on eBay) who sell goods and services with the intention of generating a surplus from their trading activities. The place of primary business (agriculture, forestry and fishing; mining and extraction) has declined as a share of the modern economy, although many of these activities are of key importance in terms of the pursuit of sustainability (see Chapter 19). In 2010, services accounted for 63.6 per cent of world gross domestic product (GDP), manufacturing 30.7 per cent and agriculture 5.7 per cent (CIA, 2011). Manufacturing has also declined as a share of economic activity, but more so in some member states (e.g. the UK) than others (e.g. Germany). Construction is an important activity in all member states and the materials it uses and the way in which it constructs structures have important environmental implications. The transport of passengers and freight has very significant environmental implications. Civil aviation, in particular, has escaped some forms of regulation until recently and there is still no taxation on aviation fuel. Services are growing their share of the economy and their environmental impact may be more subtle but important nonetheless.

As trade unions have weakened, business interests have come to see environmental NGOs as one of the main challenges to their activities (see Chapter 9). Environmental policy can potentially prohibit the use of particular substances, processes or products, but more usually it produces regulations which constrain the way in which certain production activities are undertaken or which at least impose transaction costs on firms in terms of demonstrating that they are complying with them. There has, of course, been a move away from 'command and control' regulation, which is often difficult and costly to enforce, to a greater advocacy of the use of taxation, which has not been deployed in practice except through measures such as pesticide taxes in particular member states, trading mechanisms that create markets in externalities, or voluntary agreements (Golub, 1998).

It should be emphasized that business is not necessarily always opposed to environmental regulation. Businesses that have brands to maintain and develop are very conscious of the costs of damage to their reputation:

> Up to 70 per cent of a firm's earnings can be attributed to brands . . . whilst the average British and American company is valued by the stock market at twice net balance sheet assets, companies with strong brands are valued at four times net assets.
>
> (Bridgewater, 2010: 1)

If the public loses trust in a company's products and processes, the financial consequences can be considerable in terms of loss of share value, declining profitability and vulnerability to takeover. Senior managers can lose their jobs if they are seen to mishandle an environmental problem, e.g. BP and the Gulf of Mexico oil spill in 2010.

Of course, one response to challenges about a company's environmental impact is to engage in 'greenwash', i.e. emphasizing environmentally friendly aspects of a company's business which in fact form only a small part of its total activities. Anyone passing through a European airport and looking at the adverts could, for example, gain the impression that oil companies are primarily engaged in renewable energy. Nevertheless, companies do have an interest in ensuring that regulations apply to all firms in a sector to set a level playing field so that competition is not distorted and in particular that reputational damage is not caused by 'cowboy' operations that ignore environmental good practice.

There is also a growing market for various forms of environmental technology, either to control emissions or to provide substitutes for carbon-intensive forms of production. Some member states have been particularly effective at developing these 'green industries', notably Germany or Denmark in the case of wind turbines. Germany has followed a strategy of technological integration which has created a new environmental industry with high growth rates which is 'highly competitive with a dominant position in the world market. Germany's market share for environmentally friendly energy supply technologies is about 30 per cent' (Jänicke, 2011: 139).

However, it should be noted that political displacement in terms of organizational representation and links with decision makers can lag behind economic growth, with more mature sectors exerting greater influence.

Business is not a homogeneous whole politically any more than it is in terms of its environmental impact. In terms of the environment, different sectors face different challenges which require different policy responses. Mitigating and adapting to climate change are, of course, a unifying narrative in environmental policy which did not exist in the earlier years of EU environmental policy. Although the six Environmental Action Programmes have sought to give a unity and coherence to the EU's programme of work, often they were the aggregation of different programmes of work, relating, for example, to ground-level air pollution, pollution of rivers or the sea or waste disposal. This encouraged 'end-of-pipe' technological fixes for specific environmental problems 'that only shifted industrial-related problems between environmental media' such as the air or water (Horlings and Marsden, 2011: 444). Climate change affects different sectors in different ways. It is particularly important for the energy production industries because it will lead to changes in the generation mix, but it is also important for energy-intensive industries because the real costs of energy are likely to rise over time in part because of climate change mitigation efforts. Above all, it is important for the transport industry, particularly the production and use of motor vehicles, but also the airline industry. Attempts to bring it within the scope of climate change mitigation have been particularly contested.

There is an inherent puzzle in the story of the development of environmental policy in the EU. On the one hand, business has had substantial influence on the policy and has been able to block, delay or modify some policy initiatives. On the other hand, the EU has developed a coherent and in many respects effective environmental policy that has made a real difference to environmental standards. Part of the key to this puzzle is an understanding of the role the theory of ecological modernization has played in guiding policy; something which is examined in the next section. This chapter then goes on to use the theoretical perspective of informational lobbying to help understand the influence exerted by business and reviews some of the main business lobbying groups. It discusses the 'Registration, Evaluation, Authorization and restriction of Chemicals' (REACH) legislation as an example of a conflict between business and environmental groups, and then reviews a counter-example where environmentalists have been more successful.

Summary points

- Business is not a homogeneous whole and its response to environmental policy initiatives can vary considerably.
- Business interests see environmental groups as their main political adversaries.
- A central puzzle in understanding EU environmental policy is why business influence has not prevented the emergence of a coherent and effective policy.

Ecological modernization

Ecological modernization sometimes seems close to being the official environmental ideology of the EU. 'Ecological modernisation provides the framework within which the EU marries economic growth to its environmental protection policies' (Baker, 2007: 297). It assumes that there is a win–win relationship between the economy and environmental protection. 'Instead of seeing environmental protection as a burden upon the economy, the ecological modernist sees it as a potential source for future growth' (Weale, 1992: 76). It is an approach that the more progressive sectors of business can comfortably sign up to. As Weale (ibid.: 31) noted in an early account of ecological modernization: 'a cleavage begins to open up not between business and environmentalists, but between progressive, environmentally-aware business on the one hand and short-term profit takers on the other'.

The UK adopted ecological modernization as a guiding principle for environmental policy 'sometimes even at the instigation of industry' (Wurzel and Connelly, 2010a: 281). 'Interestingly, at times it has been industry – or at least sections of it – that have been the most emphatic exponents of ecological modernization' (Rayner and Jordan, 2011: 103). In part, this is because some sections of business stand to benefit from policies designed to promote climate protection policies, for example, those manufacturing, installing or using wind turbines or solar power, or the insurance industry which is concerned about the additional and unpredictable risks associated with climate change. It also reflects the way in which ecological modernization offers an attractive normative discourse in terms of its 'combined notions of development and modernity and . . . ecological critique' (Horlings and Marsden, 2011: 444). It pushes a lot of political buttons and provides an umbrella under which potentially divergent interests and perspective can shelter, although that strength is also potentially a weakness.

As Weale points out (1992: 75), 'There is no one canonical statement of the ideology of ecological modernization as *The General Theory* is a source for Keynesianism'. Horlings and Marsden (2011: 444) nevertheless summarize the main characteristics of ecological modernization as follows:

- Qualitative, economical growth [a proposition that chimes with efforts to complement conventional gross domestic product measures with indicators of well-being in the population].
- Realization of ecological goals.
- Modern technologies which can have an enormous potential for stretching the ecological boundaries and reduce negative environmental effects [in other words a rejection of the anti-technology and romantic backward-looking stance that can occur in some environmental thinking].
- A steering governmental role . . . market and governance need each other, compensate and limit each other.
- A further 'scientification' of society [which implies that experts and epistemic communities play an important role in policy formation and implementation].

The Stern Review (2006) on climate change in the UK is a classic piece of ecologically modernist writing which stated the case for intervention to mitigate climate change in terms of economics, thus injecting a new discourse into the debate and reaching out to different audiences, including those in business. It 'framed the issue firmly within the bounds of ecological modernization by presenting ambitious climate change policy measures as a pro-growth strategy' (Wurzel and Connelly, 2010a: 278).

Nevertheless, there are limitations to how far ecological modernization can function as an ideology that promotes sustainable policy solutions. As Baker notes, 'It does not address the underlying contradiction in capitalism: a logic of ever-increasing consumption in a world characterised by material resource limitations' (2007: 313). Admittedly, the EU does not, unlike the US, have significant numbers of politicians in leadership positions who question whether global warming is caused by human activities, let alone whether policy measures should be taken to mitigate it. Even so, it is Germany, the Netherlands and the Nordic countries who have signed up most unequivocally to ecological modernization. France has more reservations because of its commitment to nuclear power. '"Ecological modernisation" theory has arisen outside of France and does not cite nuclear power as a reference technology, while within France the theory per se is little known' (Szarka, 2011: 117). The idea is less well embedded in Southern Europe while 'the accession of the poorer East European states in 2004/07, together with the 2008 credit crunch, created doubts over the commitment to ecological modernization within the [European Parliament], widely regard as the "greenest" of the European institutions' (Wurzel and Connelly, 2010a: 280). It is therefore perhaps not surprising that when the European Commission set out a 'road map' in 2011 for moving to a low-carbon economy by 2050, it drew back from the more radical suggestion of a 25 per cent cut in carbon emissions by 2020, even though that would be more efficient in the long run. Some environmentally ambitious businesses had actually backed a 30 per cent, but any increase was resisted by heavy manufacturing businesses.

It may be that ecological modernization theory applies clearly where a firm's actions have a specific and identifiable geographical impact which may lead them to experience reputational damage or even subject them to regulatory sanctions. As well as these costs, a firm may derive benefits from acting in a more environmentally friendly way. It may well make financial sense to use energy efficiently, to find uses for by-products or to recycle as much as is practicable. In the case of climate change, one is dealing with a global public bad and it is more difficult to trace a link between action and outcome. Actions taken by any one firm are generally not likely to have a major impact on climate change, nor will the firm derive any specific benefits.

Weak forms of ecological modernization have tended to prevail, thus addressing environmental problems through technocratic and corporatist modes of policy making. While they may decrease environmental problems, they can also lead to negative side effects by pursuing an insufficiently holistic picture of the ecosystem as a whole. Nevertheless, business, as a potential veto player, is comfortable with such approaches and is not surprisingly uncomfortable with stronger versions which envisage 'restructuring the capitalist political economy' (Horlings and Marsden, 2011: 444). 'The danger is that the need for business consent risks diluting EU climate change policy to the point where it no longer reflects the idea of ecological modernization' (Wurzel and Connelly, 2010a: 282).

Summary points

- Ecological modernization provides an ideological framework that the EU and progressive businesses can sign up to, but it could encourage the dilution of policy so that it becomes ineffective.
- Member states differ in their commitment to ecological modernization.
- Firms vary in the extent to which their activities are consistent with ecologically modernist ideas.

The business lobby

In order to understand the role of business lobbying in EU environmental policy making, it is important to appreciate the distinction that has developed in the literature between rent-seeking (or distributional) lobbying and informational lobbying. 'Traditional models of rent-seeking view lobbying activities as a straightforward quid-pro-quo exchange of money for favourable political decisions' (Lohmann, 1995: 267). It offers a straightforward model of pressure politics, although resources other than money may be exchanged which would apply more clearly to the US. Business has relatively limited opportunities to conduct this kind of lobbying, particularly given great emphasis on the regulation of lobbying and the transparency register (see Chapter 9), so the emphasis here will be on the newer literature on informational lobbying which has a particular relevance to the case of the EU.

By contrast, informational models of interests assume asymmetrical knowledge with the private interests having greater knowledge than the public actors or environmental lobby groups, which is particularly relevant in an unpredictable and unstable system like that of the EU, as identified in Chapter 9. 'An environmental group, for example, may know the costs and benefits of scrubber devices, knowledge that would be valuable to a policy maker in establishing an environmental standard' (Grossman and Helpman, 2001: 23). Public actors could seek to develop that knowledge themselves and to some extent this is the function of research commissioned by the EU. They could also go to a well-informed NGO like Climate Change Europe, which in the earlier phase of the climate change debate, when knowledge within the institutions was more limited, was 'for most policy-makers . . . the first point of contact on climate related matters' (Newell and Grant, 2000: 246). Nevertheless, 'private actors involved in a specific economic policy area often possess a very high level of expertise that would be very costly for political actors to develop' (Broscheid, 2006: 93).

One might ask why business actors would not lie or at least distort information in such an information provision process. Decision makers certainly face a verification problem which could incur transaction costs. 'Whenever a policy maker has even a slightly different objective than the . . . [special interest group], she must guard herself against exaggeration and misrepresentation by the lobbyist' (Grossman and Helpman, 2001: 105). This entails verification costs for the decision maker. It should be noted, however, that the relationship with lobbyists is normally a repeated exchange so that any participant that provided misleading information would suffer future penalties such as downgrading reliance on their information or exclusion from the information exchange process altogether. There is thus an incentive to lobbyists to create and maintain credibility. Such adherence to the informal 'rules of the game' is a feature of insider groups in interest group activity (see Chapter 9).

Business has a particular strength in information lobbying. Businesses often have the resources to invest in acquiring and communicating credible information. However, it should be noted that environmental NGOs are increasingly developing the skills to provide the Commission with such information. Informational lobbying is also seen as a legitimate and even helpful form of intervention which does not incur reputational damage. 'In the European context, the European Commission has a strong demand for outside information, due to its own limited informational resources' (Broscheid, 2006: 105). Business has to rely on informational lobbying more than other actors and this does rely on access to relevant decision makers, although that has not generally been a problem for business at the EU level. Hence, the literature on informational lobbying would lead one to expect business to be an influential lobbyist at the EU level.

The literature on the structural power of business (Lindblom, 1977) that derives from its ability to deliver economic success would lead to a similar conclusion. This is also borne out by the strength of economic actors within the Commission, e.g., DG Enterprise. Barroso's own appointment and influence are relevant here, as are that of other commissioners such as Verheugen (see Chapter 6). Olson (1965) notes the ability of business to overcome free rider problems by forming 'privileged' groups where it is rational for one actor to provide all of the collective good.

However, a note of caution is necessary here. 'Olson's assumption that smaller groups face fewer free-riding problems and hence are more likely to act collectively is rejected by most empirical studies of business associations' (Lang *et al.*, 2008: 50).

Key actors in the business lobby

Box 10.1 deals with the leading cross-sectoral organizations representing business at an EU level. However, in many respects, some of the most effective organizations are to be found at a sectoral level. The prime example of this is the organization representing the chemical industry, the European Chemical Industry Council, known by the French language acronym CEFIC. With a staff of around 120, CEFIC is easily the largest European-level business association (Greenwood, 2002: 13).

Box 10.1   Cross-sectoral business organizations in the EU

Business Europe has 41 member federations and claims to represent 20 million companies from 35 countries. Its slogan in 2011 was 'Go for Growth', although it emphasized that this meant sustainable growth. Environment and climate action is one of its themes, but is not in the title of any of its seven main committees.

The *European Round Table of Industrialists* is an informal but highly influential forum that brings together 45 selected chief executives and chairmen of major multinational companies of European parentage with total sales exceeding €1,000 billion. It gives climate change a high priority, arguing that drastic policy changes are needed at the regulatory and technical level, operating through an Energy and Climate Change Working Group.

AmCham (the American Chamber of Commerce to the European Union) is regarded as a highly influential body and has a Climate Change Task Force, although its stance is less overtly progressive than the European-led Round Table.

Associations representing environmentally sustainable industries often have more limited resources (see Box 10.2). Perhaps more important than its size is the way in which potentially diverse interests are managed within one broad umbrella group. In terms of membership, it organizes the leading European companies as corporate members alongside national chemical associations, thus explicitly recognizing the key role of the big companies in this industry. European-level product associations dealing with, for example, chlorine operate under CEFIC's umbrella structure.

Box 10.2   The International Biocontrol Manufacturers' Association

The International Biocontrol Manufacturers' Association (IBMA) is a European-level association representing the generally small firms that develop and produce biological control products as alternatives to synthetic pesticides. They have a potentially important contribution to make to the EU's Integrated Pest Management strategy. The IBMA has, however, been hampered by a lack of political sophistication, reflecting the natural science background of its member firms and limited resources. Its current income is around \$220,000–\$240,000 a year. The IBMA's lobbying efforts were limited to a part-time lobbyist operating in Brussels. From 2010, however, it has employed a full-time executive director who has an industry background.

As well as being organized on a horizontal, product and subsector level, CFIC is also structured to deal with major issue areas such as the environment. CEFIC is a proficient user of working parties within the inter-sectoral employers' organization, BusinessEurope and the European Confederation of Business, formerly known as UNICE. It is able to get many of its 'own positions carried forward in the name of UNICE. In order to work this route, an association needs to be sufficiently endowed with monitoring capacity to spot opportunities, and to arrange the personnel to contribute to the working party' (Greenwood, 2002: 52). In this task, CEFIC is aided not only by its permanent staff, but also by the staff seconded by its leading companies.

In terms of the terminology deployed by Streeck and Schmitter (1981), CEFIC is very much an organization oriented towards the *logic of influence*. In other words, the chemical industry has developed broad-based associations that have a sophisticated approach to policy making. The political leaders of the chemical industry are aware that, in accordance with the principles of informational lobbying, the interests of their members are best served by developing an understanding of the policy positions of decision makers. They are able to articulate a clear policy position for the industry that takes account of what is politically possible. They can evolve strategies of accommodation to threats to the legitimacy and functioning of the industry without conceding too much. What is eventually agreed may represent a second best position from the perspective of the industry, but may still be more satisfactory than the outcome that would have occurred without any systematic industry intervention.

Summary points

- Business is well organized at both a cross-sectoral and a sectoral level.
- Informational styles of lobbying, in which information is supplied to the Commission, tend to favour business.
- Environmentally sustainable industries are often less effectively represented than other industries.

Business influence on environmental policy: the REACH programme

In 1998, the EU Environment Council asked the Commission to review the set of existing chemicals legislation (REACH, Registration, Evaluation, Authorization and restriction of Chemicals). In February 2001, the European Commission published a White Paper setting out the strategy for a future EU policy for chemicals. The then Environment Commissioner Margot Wallström claimed, 'This is one of the most important initiatives the Commission has taken in the context of sustainable development' (European Commission, 2001a: 1). Even allowing for a certain amount of political hyperbole, there is no doubt that the contents of the White Paper represented a major challenge to the chemical industry. NGOs were also very interested in the outcome, although there were some divisions of opinion among them. It was noted in Chapter 9 that without lobbying from environmental NGOs, REACH would probably have not been proposed in the first place.

There was broad agreement that EU chemicals policy, which had developed over a period of some 20 years, had become too complex and cumbersome to be effective. By the end of the twentieth century it was made up of more than three hundred directives, regulations and decisions. The main deficiency of the arrangements existing in 2001 was the failure to provide equivalent information about the hazards of 'existing' and 'new' substances. A system of chemicals control was originally introduced in September 1981 and EU testing rules had only been applied to products developed after that date. It has been estimated that existing substances accounted for over 99 per cent of the total volume of all substances on the market. The number of existing substances marketed in volumes above one tonne in 2001 was estimated at 30,000 (European Commission, 2001b: 6).

The legislative process was very protracted, reflecting the complexity of the policy. The European Parliament commenced its first reading in February 2005, completing it in November. After lengthy 'trialogue' negotiations involving the Council and Parliament, but also the Commission, a compromise was reached in December 2006 and the REACH regulation entered into force in 2007. It was 2008, ten years after the original request for a review, before the new system started to operate. The European Chemicals Agency (ECA), located in Helsinki, started accepting registrations from June 2008 with the first registration phase ending in November 2010. REACH is not expected to cover all chemicals until 2018.

The influence of public concern

It is evident that in developing the chemicals policy, the Commission was influenced by growing public concern that far too little is known about chemical substances. In line with its agenda-setting role on environmental issues, this concern was shaped by Greenpeace which took the leading role in the campaign to require firms to explain their products' effects on health and the environment. The health effects are generally of more immediate concern to the general public and were emphasized by Greenpeace. The key point is that the health concerns filtered through to the White Paper, albeit expressed in more cautious language than Greenpeace would use:

> The incidence of some diseases, e.g. testicular cancer in young men and allergies, has increased significantly over the last decades. While the underlying reasons for this have not yet been identified, there is justified concern that certain chemicals play a causative role for allergies.
>
> (European Commission, 2001b: 4)

The White Paper presented sustainable development as its 'overriding goal' (ibid.: 4). This led to an emphasis on the fundamental importance of the precautionary principle, which states that:

> Whenever reliable scientific evidence is available that a substance may have an adverse impact on human health and the environment but there is still scientific uncertainty about the precise nature or the magnitude of the potential damage, scientific decision-making must be based on precaution in order to prevent damage to human health and the environment.
>
> (ibid.: 5)

The emphasis on safeguarding human health in the White Paper was, however, balanced by an expression of the need to ensure the competitiveness of the chemical industry:

> EU chemicals policy must ensure *a high level of protection of human health and the environment* as enshrined in the Treaty both for the present generation and future generations while also ensuring the efficient functioning of the internal market and the competitiveness of the chemical industry.
>
> (ibid.: 5; original emphasis)

One of the key elements of the White Paper, anticipated in the Council Conclusions of June 1999, was the shift of the burden of proof and responsibility to the chemical industry and to the downstream industries which use its products. The main responsibility was to be placed on manufacturers, importers, formulators and industrial users to generate and assess data, prepare risk assessment reports, as well as give adequate information on safety to the public. Greenpeace welcomed this principle of the reversal of the burden of proof.

One of the areas of difficulty was the proposed registration procedure for existing chemicals. The White Paper suggested that the timing of the submission of registration dossiers would depend on production volumes. Where more than 1,000 tonnes of an existing chemical were produced, registration would have to take place by 2005, but deadlines could be extended to 2018 for products produced in small quantities. What concerned environmentalists was the absence of mechanisms and sanctions to ensure that the deadlines for registration and evaluation were met. This remains an issue, given that staffing the ECA has not been easy.

A division of opinion among NGOs about the use of animal testing complicated the politics of the REACH process. It is an open question whether animal protection organizations form part of the environmental movement, although most analysts would treat them as a separate category. The general view is that the animal protection movement 'has different organizational and ideological roots from the broader environmental movement' (Garner, 2000: 119). In any event, the British Union for the Abolition of Vivisectionists claimed that up to ten million animals could be used in laboratory tests if the White Paper was implemented. The Eurogroup for Animal Welfare stated that animal tests required for the safety assessment of new chemicals involved the use of approximately 60 rats, 40 guinea pigs, six rabbits and 50 fish for each chemical.

The Commission tried to sit on the fence on this politically difficult issue, arguing that '[p]rotection of human health and the environment, including wildlife, should be balanced against the protection of the welfare of laboratory animals' (European Commission, 2001b: 7). CEFIC, possibly seeing the opportunity of driving a wedge between different NGOs, argued that animal protection must be taken into consideration in relation to testing. It argued that testing would use up to 13 million animals. It has continued to take an interest in animal welfare issues, supporting research into animal welfare and organizing an Animal Alternatives Issue Management Team.

The strategy of CEFIC

It was evident that there was considerable high-level political support for the chemicals strategy and that it would eventually be introduced in some form. However, as always, the devil was in the detail. CEFIC's (2002: 1) strategy was first to argue that 'all of the political objectives set out in the White Paper should be equally met'. In particular, this would mean giving equal weight to the protection of human health and the environment and the maintenance and enhancement of the competitiveness of the EU chemical industry. Given such contradictory goals, some prioritization is unavoidable and public sentiment favours effective action to protect health in particular.

More realistically, CEFIC has emphasized the need for a 'practical approach' to the proposals, a phrase that recurs in its composite statement. In the meetings of the six working groups, e.g. on 'Testing, Registration and Evaluation', set up by the Commission which met between October 2001 and March 2002, CEFIC 'proactively contributed to the working group discussions by providing pragmatic input, information and solutions to the issues raised' (CEFIC, 2002: 1). This detailed and highly technical consideration of the implications of policy is where CEFIC, with all the specialist resources at its disposal, is at its strongest.

In particular, CEFIC became involved in an argument with the Commission about the cost of risk assessment. The Commission estimated the cost to the industry at €2.1 billion. CEFIC conducted its own parallel impact assessment (a procedure described in Chapter 12) and estimated that testing would cost €7–10 billion. According to CEFIC, the discrepancy in part arose from the Commission's failure to account for industrial chemicals that are not marketed as final products, a substantial proportion of total industry output (*European Voice*, 2001: 16). In May 2002, the Commission organized a conference to present a report on the cost impact of the EU chemicals policy conducted by a consultant, Risk and Policy Analysts (RPA). CEFIC argued that: 'The RPA study shows that missing chemical data can be collected at an estimated cost of €7 billion. These figures are in line with those presented by the chemical industry one year ago' (CEFIC, 2002: 1).

There was thus plenty of scope for CEFIC to question the details of the proposals and the form and timing of their implementation. The cumulative effect of a number of detailed interventions could undermine the achievement of the strategy's goals by moderating its impact and slowing down its implementation. As has been noted, in its original form it represented much less than environmentalists wanted. From one perspective, this could represent another demonstration of the political power of capital. From another, it could represent a pluralist balancing out of different political forces with the Commission acting as an arbiter of the process.

Outcomes

Environmentalists were less happy with the outcome than the chemical industry. In part, this was a reflection of the Commission's intention to adopt more business-friendly policies reflecting the wider importance of the Lisbon Process. The German government was a key ally for the chemical industry throughout the negotiations and the then industry minister, Michael Glos, commented, 'Our position was accepted in all areas essential to us' (Buck, 2006). The final compromise involved the Parliament accepting a heavily watered down clause on substitution. This meant it will be left to companies to identify whether safer alternatives exist to the 1,500–2,000 most dangerous substances, and then to come up with a 'substitution plan'.

The chemical industry would have preferred a more risk-based approach, but was particularly pleased that companies would not have to elaborate a Chemical Safety Report for substances below ten tonnes. For the Greens, Caroline Lucas MEP argued that the industry had been rewarded 'for the relentless lobbying which has successfully torn the guts out of the package' (Lucas, 2006). The Brussels office of the World Wide Fund for Nature (WWF) which had run a very sophisticated DetoX campaign on the issue from 2003–2006 took a more measured approach, characterizing the new law as a modest step towards a new approach on chemicals. WWF considered that at least having one of the most comprehensive environmental laws passed in Europe was a step forward, given that the industry would have preferred not to have legislation at all. The manufacturers of the 3,000 chemicals considered most dangerous will have to apply for authorization which will only be given if no alternative exists, and then only for a limited period while the manufacturer pays for research to identify an alternative. Nevertheless, the compromise reached on balance favoured the industry, showing that it has developed a highly effective lobbying capacity at the EU level to match that which it has always enjoyed at member state level.

Summary points

- The fact that new chemicals legislation was considered at all was a success for environmental groups.
- Environmentalists made some gains in the REACH legislation on chemicals, but business got more of what it wanted in part because of its greater resources that enabled it to influence detailed provisions.
- The outcome was also influenced by the business-friendly climate associated with the Lisbon Strategy.

Lessons from REACH and a counter-example

The example of REACH might suggest that the conditions in which informational lobbying takes place tend to benefit business but this cannot be explained just in terms of informational lobbying. Another important factor was the priority given to economic objectives in the EU, especially at the time of the Lisbon Strategy (see Chapter 3). The defeat of the carbon tax proposal in the early 1990s provides another example of business influence on environmental policy (Newell and Paterson, 1998). In the case of the carbon tax, one saw the influence that could be exerted by a 'formidable alliance [of] coal, oil, motor, road, petrochemical and heavy industry lobbies, all major employers in the EU, and with the financial backing and channels of access to effectively press their case' (Grant *et al.*, 2000: 124). Nevertheless, over time the EU has subsequently developed a climate change strategy which is far more advanced than has been achieved anywhere else in the world.

However, business does not always get what it wants, even in the short term. A counter-example is offered by the example of genetically modified (GM) crops. These are extensively grown in North America, South America and China. In the United States, almost all US-grown soybeans are now produced using GM seeds and nine out of ten farmers there are planting such crops. In the EU, however, there have been strict controls on the planting and import of GM crops which have meant that very small commercial quantities have been grown in the EU.

Following a challenge by the US in the World Trade Organization dispute settlement mechanism, the EU sought to end the *de facto* moratorium on approving such crops but the European Parliament voted in July 2011 to widen the scope of options for member states to ban GM crops on their territories to include environmental as well as moral grounds.

Why has the campaign against GM crops, led by Greenpeace, been so success- ful when so many other environmental campaigns have failed or had limited success? Part of it was a question of timing as GM crops were proposed for introduction at a time when public trust in regulation had been shaken by the Bovine Spongiform Encephalopathy crisis and other food safety episodes. Although there has never been any sound scientific evidence that such crops pose a health threat, their framing as 'Frankenstein foods' resonated with a distrustful public. The multinational companies such as Monsanto that were developing the products handled their public relations campaigns in a clumsy fashion. It is generally accepted that Monsanto followed 'a deeply misguided approach to introducing GMOs into the western European market . . . Monsanto moved into western Europe like a bull in a china shop' (Schurman and Munro, 2010: xxiii). GM crops have acquired a wider political significance, being seen

> as a signifier of resistance to or support for agri-industrial models. Although not always clearly articulated, the technology is seen as a prop to shore up homogenized, intensive, concentrated models of agricultural production; to sustain the unsustainable agri-industrial model.
>
> (Marsden *et al.*, 2010: 45)

Perhaps one lesson that emerges from the GM story is that '[i]f the business community does not speak with a unified voice, political space for civil society and public actors emerges' (Fuchs and Clapp, 2009: 293). As has been emphasized throughout this chapter, business is often divided. EU attempts to bring the airlines within the scope of its climate change policies have provoked much controversy, but within the industry, Virgin Atlantic, for example, has taken a very different stance on climate change from Ryanair.

> On the other hand, if the only remaining enemy of business influence is business itself, the strategies and likelihood of success for civil society in cases in which such business conflict is absent and cannot be clearly created are limited.
>
> (ibid.: 293)

One could also argue that some progress has been made in 'greening' the Common Agricultural Policy (CAP), even if it falls short of what many critics want. The second 'pillar' of the CAP contains a number of measures to support more environmentally friendly forms of agriculture. Cross-compliance requires farmers to meet basic environmental standards to claim their principal form of subsidy, the Single Farm Payment, and it is envisaged that these requirements will be tightened after 2014. The extent to which agriculture is a source of water pollution has been dealt with through a number of measures such as the creation of nitrate-vulnerable zones. The debate about climate change is having an increasing influence on the CAP, particularly as livestock is a potent source of a major greenhouse gas, methane.

Summary points

- The 1992 decision not to adopt an EU-level carbon tax was a major setback for the environmental movement.
- GM crops are an example of successful environmental influence and suggest that when business is divided or acts clumsily, its influence may be more limited.
- The CAP has been modified to make it more environmentally friendly despite the presence of a powerful farming lobby.

Conclusion

At the beginning of the chapter we posed a puzzle: business clearly has a substantial influence on EU environmental policy, but has not prevented the EU from developing an increasingly effective and coherent set of environmental policies that impose significant costs on it. In part, that is because some parts of business have welcomed environmental policy for a variety of reasons such as new business opportunities, raising the entry price for new entrants into the sector or enhancing their reputation. Divisions within business can create opportunities for other actors, but business will also seek to exploit divisions among NGOs, for example, between the animal protection movement and environmentalists, as in the case of REACH. Ecological modernization has provided an ideology that has allowed the European institutions and business to work together, but it may have also set limits on what can be achieved in terms of radically protecting the environment.

There is also a story about public opinion that needs to be considered. Public interest in environmental issues fluctuates considerably and attention may be focused on a particular aspect of environmental policy following a significant event. However, a number of member states have green parties that have significant legislative representation and all of them have more or less strong environmental movements. The EU needs to legitimize itself in the eyes of its citizens and one way of reaching out to them is to show that it can take more effective action on environmental issues than the member states could acting by themselves.

The economic downturn since 2008 provides some reinforcement for those who argued that strong environmental policies and regulations can be a drag on economic growth and the creation of employment. This may have had some effects on the development of a more ambitious climate change policy, e.g. the reluctance to go beyond the conditional commitment to a 30 per cent reduction in emissions. However, environmental policy is now well embedded in the EU and business knows that it has not just to react to it, but also be proactive. The stance of business towards environmental policy, particularly climate change, is generally more welcoming than in the US where there is less acceptance of the reality or significance of important environmental problems such as climate change and of the need for government and business to work together to find feasible solutions.

Summary points

- Business interests have considerable advantages over other interest groups in terms of resources and access to decision makers.
- Yet real progress has still been made towards a coherent and effective environmental policy.
- This can be partly explained by the fact that public pressure for change can be significant and businesses care about their reputations.

Key questions

1   How influential are business interests on EU environmental policy?
2   Why is business not always a homogeneous interest?
3   What is ecological modernization and why is it so important in debates about EU environmental policy?
4   Why does informational lobbying often work well for business?
5   In what circumstances is business likely to be less influential?

Guide to further reading

- Coen *et al.* (2010) offer an overview of the relationship between government and business including the environmental dimension.
- Greenwood (2011) provides an overview of the system of interest representation in the EU.
- Kraft and Kamieniecki (2007) give an authoritative account of the relationship between business and environmental policy in the US.
- Wurzel and Connelly (2010b) examine the leadership offered by a range of actors in relation to climate change policy in the EU.

References

Baker, S. (2007) 'Sustainable development as symbolic commitment: declaratory politics and the seductive appeal of ecological modernisation in the European Union', *Environmental Politics*, vol. 16, no. 2, pp. 291–317.

Bridgewater, S. (2010) *Football Brands*, Palgrave Macmillan, Basingstoke.

Broscheid, A. (2006) 'Public choice models of business lobbying', in D. Coen and W. Grant (eds) *Business and Government: Methods and Practice*, Barbara Budrich, Opladen.

Buck, T. (2006) 'EU secures compromise to bring in new hazardous chemicals law', *Financial Times*, 2 December.

CEFIC (The European Chemicals Industry Council) (2002) 'CEFIC composite statement on EU Commission's White Paper Working Group discussions', March, CEFIC, Brussels.

CIA (Central Intelligence Agency) (2011) *The World Factbook*, available at: www.cia.gov/library/publications/the-world-factbook (accessed 17 August 2011).

Coen, D., Grant, W. and Wilson, G. (eds) (2010) *The Oxford Handbook of Business and Government*, Oxford University Press, Oxford.

European Commission (2001a) 'Commission sets out the path towards sustainable use of chemicals', press release IP/01/201, 13 February.

European Commission (2001b) *White Paper: Strategy for a Future Chemicals Policy* (COM (2001) 88), Commission of the European Communities, Brussels.

European Voice (2001) 'Chemical industry based for fresh battle over testing', *European Voice*, 5 July, p. 16.

Fuchs, D. and Clapp, J. (2009) 'Corporate power and global agrifood governance: lessons learned', in J. Clapp and D. Fuchs (eds) *Corporate Power in Global Agrifood Governance*, MIT Press, Cambridge, MA.

Garner, R. (2000) *Environmental Politics: Britain, Europe and the Global Environment*, 2nd edition, Macmillan, Basingstoke.

Golub, J. (ed.) (1998) *New Instruments for Environmental Policy in the EU*, Routledge, London.

Grant, W., Matthews, D. and Newell, P. (2000) *The Effectiveness of European Union Environmental Policy*, Macmillan, Basingstoke.

Greenwood, J. (2002) *Inside the EU Business Associations*, Palgrave and Ernst and Young Association Management, Basingstoke.

Greenwood, J. (2011) *Interest Representation in the European Union*, Palgrave Macmillan, Basingstoke.

Grossman, G.M. and Helpman, E. (2001) *Special Interest Politics*, MIT Press, Cambridge, MA.

Horlings, L.G. and Marsden, T.K. (2011) 'Towards the real green revolution? Exploring the conceptual dimensions of a new ecological modernization of agriculture that could "feed the world"', *Global Environmental Change*, vol. 21, no. 2, pp. 441–452.

Jänicke, M. (2011) 'German climate change policy: political and economic leadership', in R.K.W. Wurzel and J. Connelly (eds) *The European Union as a Leader in International Climate Change Politics*, Routledge, London, pp. 129–146.

Kraft, M.E. and Kamieniecki, S. (eds) (2007) *Business and Environmental Policy*, MIT Press, Cambridge, MA.

Lang, S., Schneider, V. and Werle, R. (2008) 'Between politics, economics and technology: the changing environments of business associations', in J. Grote, A. Lang and V. Schneider (eds) *Organized Business in Changing Environments: The Complexity of Adaptation*, Palgrave Macmillan, Basingstoke, pp. 1–14.

Lindblom, C.E. (1977) *Politics and Markets: The World's Economic Systems*, Basic Books, New York.

Lohmann, S. (1995) 'Information, access and contributions: a signalling model of lobbying', *Public Choice*, vol. 85, pp. 267–284.

Lucas, C. (2006) 'REACH: there was a better alternative', *European Voice*, 14 December.

Marsden, T., Lee, R., Flynn, A. and Thankappan, S. (2010) *The New Regulation and Governance of Food. Beyond the Food Crisis?*, Routledge, London.

Newell, P. and Grant, W. (2000) 'Environmental NGOs and EU environmental law' in H. Somsen (ed.), *Yearbook of European Environmental Law*, Vol. 1, Oxford University Press, Oxford, pp. 231–237.

Newell, P. and Paterson, M. (1998) 'A climate for business: global warming, the state and capital', *Review of International Political Economy*, vol. 5, no. 3, pp. 679–703.

Olson, M. (1965) *The Logic of Collective Action: Public Goods and the Theory of Economic Groups*, Harvard University Press, Cambridge, MA.

Rayner, T. and Jordan, R. (2011) 'The United Kingdom: a paradoxical leader?', in R.K.W. Wurzel and J. Connelly (eds) *The European Union as a Leader in International Climate Change Politics*, Routledge, London, pp. 95–111.

Schurman, R. and Munro, W.A. (2010) *Fighting for the Future of Food: Activists Versus Agribusiness in the Struggle over Biotechnology*, Minneapolis, University of Minnesota Press.

Stern, N. (2006) *The Stern Review: The Economics of Climate Change*, Cambridge University Press, Cambridge.

Streeck, W. and Schmitter, P.C. (1981) 'The organization of business interests: a research design to study the associative action of business in the advanced industrial societies of Western Europe', *International Institute of Management Labour Market Policy Discussion Papers*, International Institute of Management, Berlin.

Szarka, J. (2011) 'France's troubled bids to climate leadership', in R.K.W. Wurzel and J. Connelly (eds) *The European Union as a Leader in International Climate Change Politics*, Routledge, London, pp. 112–128.

Weale, A. (1992) *The New Politics of Pollution*, Manchester University Press, Manchester.

Wurzel, R.K.W. and Connelly, J. (2010a) 'Conclusion: the European Union's leadership role in international climate change policies reassessed', in R.K.W. Wurzel and J. Connelly (eds) *The European Union as a Leader in International Climate Change Politics*, Routledge, London, pp. 271–290.

Wurzel, R.K.W. and Connelly, J. (eds) (2010b) *The European Union as a Leader in International Climate Change Politics*, Routledge, London.

Part 3

Policy dynamics

11 Agenda setting

Sebastiaan Princen

Summary guide

This chapter looks at the formation of the EU's environmental policy agenda. After discussing what is meant by the term 'agenda' and what types of agenda can be discerned at EU level, it presents a theoretical framework for understanding agenda-setting processes. This framework highlights the interplay of issue frames and institutional venues as the main driver of agenda formation. It then discusses seven key characteristics of EU environmental agenda setting, which help to understand why issues come onto the EU agenda and what challenges and opportunities political actors face when they try to bring an issue onto the EU agenda.

Introduction

When Al Gore released his movie *An Inconvenient Truth* in 2006, climate change became the 'talk of the town' in Europe and North America. An issue that had hitherto interested a relatively small circle of experts and environmentally conscious citizens suddenly became a hot topic in public debate. Politicians in several European countries, including the British Prime Minister Tony Blair, embraced the issue of climate change, propelling it to the top of the political agenda in many countries. The public and political profile climate change intensified even further when Al Gore, together with the Intergovernmental Panel on Climate Change, received the Nobel Peace Prize in 2007. The issue also received a boost at the EU level, with recurring discussions in the European Council and new initiatives being launched in subsequent years. In 2010, a separate DG for Climate Action was created to institutionalize policy making on the topic within the European Commission. Even though the 'hype' around climate change abated after a few years, the issue had obtained a fixed place among the EU's political priorities, having been discussed at lower levels and in more specialist circles as long ago as the late 1980s.

The story of the rise of climate change as an issue is a story of agenda setting. At any given point in time, some issues are considered important, given attention and priority, while other issues are considered less important and hence are neglected. The set of issues that receive considerable attention in a political system is called the political agenda (Kingdon, 2003: 3). Political agendas change over time. Issues may receive a lot of attention at one point in time (e.g. climate change in the years after 2006), but much less attention in other periods, it is true for environmental protection more generally: in some periods this issue is considered to be politically 'hot', while in others it is seen as secondary to other concerns.

Studying (political) agendas is interesting and worthwhile for two reasons. First, being on the agenda is a necessary precondition for policy-making activity and decision making. Only when issues receive attention (i.e. when they are being actively considered and policy makers devote effort and time to them) will they be subjected to decision making (see Chapter 12). As a result, agendas are politically highly consequential. Second, the content of the political agenda is neither a 'given' nor directly related to objective measures of the importance of problems. Whether or not an issue receives attention is the result of political processes and political decisions in which some issues are 'played up' while others are 'played down'. Therefore, agenda setting is a fundamentally *political* process.

In this chapter, I will take a closer look at agenda setting on environmental issues in the EU. How are political agendas formed? And what determines whether or not environmental issues come onto the EU agenda? To answer these questions, I will first discuss in greater detail what is meant by 'an agenda'. Then, I will present a theoretical framework that can be used to understand agenda-setting processes. On the basis of this conceptual and theoretical foundation, the second part of the chapter will focus on the dynamics of environmental agenda setting in the EU, going through seven key characteristics that may help us understand why and how environmental issues come onto the EU agenda.

Summary points

- The political agenda consists of the set of issues that receive considerable attention in a political system.
- The content of the agenda determines which issues will be subjected to policy making and decision making.
- Which issues are on the agenda at a given point in time is determined by political processes.

What are political agendas?

In the Introduction, the concept of a 'political agenda' was used as if there is only one agenda in a political system. However, different types of agenda can be discerned, depending on who is giving attention. The political agenda can be defined as the set of issues that receive attention from politicians and policy makers. In addition, there is also a 'public agenda' (the set of issues that are considered important in public opinion) and a 'media agenda' (the set of issues that receive a lot of attention in the media). These agendas affect each other. For example, the main reason why politicians embraced climate change as an issue after Al Gore's documentary was that the issue had become important among the public, which in turn was partly the effect of media coverage. Nevertheless, they are not identical. At any given point in time, some issues may be important for politicians and policy makers that do not necessarily loom large in public opinion or receive much attention in the media, and vice versa. Therefore, it is important to distinguish between them.

In each of these main types of agenda, different sub-agendas can be discerned. If we limit ourselves to the political agenda in the EU, there may be an overall set of EU priorities (the EU's political agenda), but each of the EU's institutions also has its own agenda. Thus, the European Parliament's agenda may not be identical to the agenda of the European Council or the European Commission. And within those institutions, even further subdivisions exist. Within the European Commission, for instance, the agenda of DG Environment will be different to DG Trade's (for details, see Chapter 6). Hence, what we have is not one 'agenda', but a range of partly overlapping, partly hierarchically ordered agendas, which affect each other, but also have their own internal dynamics.

In addition to the variety of agendas, it is also important to keep in mind that 'the agenda' is not a fixed set of issues. According to the definition given above, an issue is 'on the agenda' if it receives 'serious' or 'considerable' attention. If it does not, it is 'off the agenda'. In reality, the dividing line between being 'on' and 'off' the agenda is not always clear. Moreover, attention for issues that are said to be 'on the agenda' may also differ, with some receiving more attention than others or specific levels of attention varying over time (as we saw for climate change, above). Hence, rather than trying to define some (arbitrary) threshold to distinguish between issues that are on and issues that are off the agenda, it is more useful to think of an agenda as a continuum, with issues ranging from less to more attention. The main political struggle over agendas is concerned with moving issues higher or lower on the agenda.

Summary points

- Different types of agenda can be discerned, including the political agenda, the media agenda and the public agenda.
- Within the EU's overall political agenda, specific agendas can be identified for each of the EU's institutions and also for units within those institutions.
- Agenda processes revolve around attempts to move issues higher up and lower down agendas.

Frames and venues in agenda setting

Why do some issues go up the agenda while others go down or are ignored altogether? This section presents a theoretical framework that can be used to answer that question. It is based on the work of two American political scientists, Frank Baumgartner and Bryan Jones (in particular Baumgartner and Jones, 2009). Although it was developed in the context of domestic (i.e. US) agenda setting, it is equally applicable to agenda setting in the EU (for a more detailed discussion, see Princen, 2007).

The basic idea of their theoretical framework is that the rise and fall of issues on the political agenda are determined by the interplay of two factors: issue frames and institutional venues. By using or manipulating these two factors, political actors seek to affect the scope of participation on an issue by involving actors who are supportive of their cause and keeping out their opponents. In that way, they try to reach the most receptive audience for their claims.

The first element in agenda setting is framing. Framing is the process of defining an issue, and the problem underlying it, in more certain terms. Framing is important because most issues can be framed in different ways. Take the example of genetic modification in food crops. What is at stake in this issue? Depending on one's point of view, possible answers include:

- developing more efficient methods of growing crops in order to increase the competitiveness of the agricultural sector;
- creating better tasting or more nutritious crops that improve the health of consumers;
- finding ways to increase agricultural production in developing countries, thus decreasing hunger and poverty in the world;
- misleading consumers by inserting artificial genes into their food, whose effects on human health are uncertain;
- creating novel crops that have the potential to crowd out other species and thereby reduce biodiversity;
- tampering with Nature in a show of human hubris vis-à-vis the natural order of things.

All of these perspectives on genetic modification have been highlighted by participants in the debate on the technology. They represent many different frames of 'the issue' of genetic modification. Note that the political tone of the six frames presented above is very different. The first three frames stress the positive potential of genetic modification, whereas the final three frames emphasize the potential negative consequences.

Much of the debate on this issue has revolved around attempts by proponents and opponents to promote their frame at the expense of others. In doing so, frames are used to stir up interest in an issue and to alter the balance of proponents and opponents around it. When environmental NGOs evoke the spectre of health threats and a large-scale loss of biodiversity, they hope to achieve two things. First, they hope to raise interest in the issue among people who are not (yet) concerned about it (for other examples, see Chapter 9). Second, they hope to convince people to oppose the technology by making the negative potential consequences more salient. Proponents of the technology take exactly the opposite approach: they try to convince people there is little to worry about ('the technology is scientifically tested and safe in our hands') and they try to give it a positive connotation ('cheaper, healthier food for you').

Frames are politically significant because they have very different policy implications. The first three (positive) frames all imply a wider use and further spread of genetically modified crops. The other three (negative) frames, by contrast, imply a containment of or even a ban on using genetic modification in food crops. Therefore, once a certain frame becomes dominant and is not seriously contested, it largely determines the type of policy to be pursued (Rochefort and Cobb, 1994).

The effect of framing is both mediated and reinforced by the second element in the theoretical framework: the existence and characteristics of institutional venues. Policy making does not take place in an institutional void. In modern political systems, policy making takes place within distinct institutional loci, such as government departments and parliamentary committees. These are called policy-making 'venues'. Venues differ in terms of the types of issue they are likely to take up; generally speaking, they focus on issues that tie in with their institutional remit (Princen, 2009: 35).

As a result, venues will tend to give attention to issues that are framed in terms that relate to their remit and ignore issues that are framed in terms that have nothing to do with their remit. This offers room for moving issues between venues. After all, as we saw above, whether or not an issue is an 'environmental issue' or an 'economic issue' depends on the way it is framed. If genetic modification is seen as a relatively risk-free technology that has great economic potential, policy making will most likely take place in an economic policy venue, such as the European Commission's DG Enterprise and Industry. Yet, if genetic modification is seen as an inherently risky technology that may adversely affect the environment, then policy making will take place in an environmental venue such as DG Environment. Hence, if an issue is framed in a certain way, it is more likely that it will be taken up by some venues and not by others. The choice of venues deeply affects subsequent policy processes (see Chapter 2).

An important part of agenda setting consists of attempts to steer an issue towards a certain venue. Actors in certain venues may do this for themselves, for example when they try to gain a foothold over policy making in a certain field. It may also be a strategy by outside actors, who frame an issue in a certain way in order to target the venue that they believe is most favourable to them. The latter strategy is called 'venue shopping' (Baumgartner and Jones, 2009: 36).

In the end, then, agenda setting revolves around the interplay of framing and venues. By framing issues in a certain way, it becomes more (or less) likely that a given venue will pick up that issue. Conversely, when a certain venue deals with an issue, it is likely to define it in terms that fit its own remit and preoccupations. As long as there is one dominant issue frame and a stable set of venues dealing with it, an issue will not gain much attention and be low on the agenda. However, when an issue frame is contested and/or attempts are made to shift policy making from one venue to another, the issue will become more salient and rise up the political agenda.

This theoretical framework applies to the EU in two ways. First, the EU itself can be seen as a venue vis-à-vis the member states and other international organizations. One can then analyse how and why issues move from those other venues to the EU and vice versa. Second, the EU in turn consists of a range of venues (the institutions and units within those institutions). Agenda setting in the EU can be understood in terms of the dynamics between those different venues.

Summary points

- Agenda setting can be understood in terms of the interplay between different issue frames and institutional venues.
- Framing consists of attempts to define an issue in certain terms, so as to stir up or deny attention for that issue and thus change the balance of support and opposition.
- Institutional venues are more receptive to issues that relate to their remit. They will deal more positively with issues that are defined in terms of that remit.

The characteristics of agenda setting in the EU

In the previous section, a general theoretical framework for understanding agenda-setting processes was presented. In the remainder of this chapter, we will take a closer look at the dynamics of environmental agenda setting in the EU. This discussion will be structured along the lines of seven key characteristics of EU environmental agenda setting:

1 the EU as a multilevel system;
2 the interlinkages between the EU and other international organizations;
3 agenda setting amidst variety;
4 the limited role of public opinion;
5 the role of focusing events;
6 links with other policy areas;
7 from new issues to ongoing concerns.

Together, these characteristics provide a way to understand the context in which agenda setting on environmental issues takes place, and of the kind of challenges and opportunities that political actors face when they try to bring environmental issues onto the EU agenda.

The EU as a multilevel system

The EU is part of a multilayered system of governance, which is often described as a system of 'multilevel governance' (Hooghe and Marks, 2001). A crucial characteristic of a system of multilevel governance is that issues are dealt with at several levels simultaneously. Thus, the different levels of government do not simply specialize in specific issues but one and the same issue is taken up at different levels at the same time.

EU environmental policy is an area of multilevel governance *par excellence* (Fairbrass and Jordan, 2004). One reason for this is that many environmental issues occur at multiple geographical scales, which are often intertwined. For instance, air pollution is partly a local problem, with large variation in air quality between parts of Europe and local sources of pollution (such as car emissions). Yet, it is also linked with other parts of the continent and even the wider world, because pollutants are carried over long distances from this original source to other regions.

Hence, the effects and causes of environmental issues are sometimes local, sometimes European and sometimes global. Moreover, cause and effect are sometimes closely linked geographically (more household waste leads to more pollution on local garbage dumps), but sometimes they lie far apart (pollution of a river in one country leads to poorer water quality in another country). Where exactly one level begins and another ends is often unclear, hence the continuing debate about task allocation in the EU (see Chapters 3 and 4).

The EU's multilevel character, coupled with the almost intrinsic multilevel character of environmental problems, has a number of consequences for agenda setting on environmental issues. These consequences involve both challenges and opportunities for actors who want to place an environmental issue on the EU agenda. The main challenge revolves around the question: why should this issue be dealt with at the EU level? In a unitary political system, as are most European countries, it is self-evident that the central government can take up any issue it wishes to. In a system of multilevel governance, by contrast, the allocation of issues to different levels is not self-evident and is often contested.

Within the EU, the general rule for allocating issues is given by the principle of subsidiarity, which states that the EU can only act if the issue cannot be dealt with at least equally well by the member states. However, this is far from a hard and fast rule. After all, when is an issue 'better' or 'equally well' dealt with at the member state level? How does one measure this and what is the threshold for saying the EU does a better job than member states? Nevertheless, the principle provides an argumentative challenge for prospective agenda setters, and it provides ammunition for actors opposed to the inclusion of an issue on the EU agenda. Therefore, actors who want to place an issue on the EU agenda convincingly have to argue that the EU is a suitable level for dealing with their issue. In other words, they have to frame the issue in European terms because of the EU's institutional remit (Princen, 2009: 39–40). For some issues, this is fairly easy, in particular if the causes and/or effects of the environmental problem can be argued to be cross-border. For other issues, however, such a link is more difficult to make.

Having said this, the EU's multilevel character also offers incentives to and opportunities for political actors who want to place an issue on its agenda. Since issues are often dealt with at multiple levels, actors who are unsuccessful at one level may try again at another level, i.e. a form of venue shopping. The EU level is particularly attractive for actors (e.g. politicians, civil servants and interest groups) who have difficulties getting things on agendas and/or having their pre-ferred policies adopted domestically. If the political context is more receptive to their issue at the EU level than at the domestic level, they can use the EU to bypass domestic resistance and have policies considered or even adopted at EU level that would be unfeasible domestically. This is known as uploading (see Chapter 3) (see also Beyers and Kerremans, 2011). This strategy is particularly powerful because the distinction between what 'belongs' at the EU level and what is 'better' dealt with at the member state level is often fuzzy, leaving room for pushing issues at either or even both levels. This has been one of the drivers of the EU's political agenda on environmental (and other) issues.

The interlinkages between the EU and other international organizations

The multilevel character of environmental issues is not restricted to the EU. Many environmental issues are also dealt with at the global level (see Chapters 16 and 19). As a result, the EU is part of an even wider multilevel system, which includes the local, regional, national, European and global levels. Many of the dynamics that were described above also apply between the EU and global levels. Political actors can strategically and selectively 'plug' issues with global institutions in order to have their voice heard domestically (Keck and Sikkink, 1998) or at EU level.

Chapter 16 shows how the global level is an important driver of the EU's political agenda. In its 2001 report on better lawmaking, the European Commission estimated that some 30 per cent of all its legislative proposals were 'conditioned' by international obligations (European Commission, 2001: 8). In the field of environmental policy, this percentage is likely to be even higher, given the density of international environmental institutions and agreements (see Chapter 16). Although the Commission likes to present international obligations as 'external constraints' on its activity, the global environmental agenda is shaped by the activities of political actors from within states and regions, including the EU. This means that global environmental institutions offer opportunities for European actors (including the Commission's DG Environment itself) to influence the EU environmental agenda.

This is illustrated by the attempts to 'green' the EU's fisheries policies, which are presented in Box 11.1. This example shows how developments within environmental institutions at the global level influence the EU agenda.

> ## Box 11.1 Global environmental institutions and the greening of EU fisheries policy
>
> A good example of how global environmental venues affect the EU agenda is formed by the debates on the 'greening' of the EU's fisheries policy (Princen, 2009; 2010). Fisheries activities are regulated under the EU's Common Fisheries Policy (CFP). The original rationale behind the CFP was formed by a fisheries management logic: fish stocks had to be protected in order to ensure continued fish yields in the future. This policy frame was strongly institutionalized in the EU, as decision making on fisheries issues took place in a policy community centred on the Commission's DG Fisheries, member state fisheries ministers, and representatives of the fisheries industry.
>
> However, from the early 1990s onwards, fisheries issues received increasing attention from environmental policy makers. This was a result of the rise of the concept of 'biodiversity' in global environmental policy making after the 1992 United Nations summit in Rio de Janeiro and especially the 1992 Convention on Biological Diversity. From a biodiversity perspective, overfishing and destructive fishing techniques were not merely problematic because they jeopardized the existence of fish stocks, but also because they caused damage to the ecosystems surrounding and linked to the fish stocks.
>
> On the basis of this new understanding of fisheries issues, a separate work programme on marine and coastal biodiversity was developed under the Convention on Biological Diversity. Fuelled by this global shift in attention, the Commission's DG Environment and member state environmental ministers began to show a more sustained interest in fisheries issues from the mid-1990s onwards. This has led to the wider application of environmental policy instruments in EU fisheries policy and to a more ecosystems-based approach to fisheries management in the CFP.

Agenda setting amidst variety

Agenda setting revolves around identifying and defining problems. In environmental politics, much depends on one's perceptions of actual environmental conditions, and the relative importance of environmental protection as compared to other values and objectives. On both accounts, great diversity exists within the EU, because of differences in natural conditions, levels of economic development, cultural understandings of environmental issues and political systems between (and sometimes within) the member states.

As a result, the overall importance attached to environmental protection as well as the attention for specific environmental issues vary across the European continent, much more so than in any of its member states (but more similar to what can be found in the USA or Canada). Since actors from the EU member states (be they politicians, civil servants or interest groups) play an important role in defining the EU agenda, this has also affected the EU agenda.

Traditionally, the literature on environmental policy making in the EU distinguished between a number of (Northern European) 'environmental leaders' (most notably Denmark, Germany and the Netherlands) and another set of (Southern European) 'laggards' (Vogel, 1995: 56ff.; Sbragia, 1996: 237; Liefferink and Andersen, 1998: 254) (see also Chapters 4 and 5). Agenda-setting dynamics around environmental issues were then explained in terms of the struggle between these blocs, and in particular the initiatives taken by the 'green' member states. Although this North–South divide appears to have become less marked since the mid-1990s, and the EU has since been enlarged toward the East, differences between more and less environmentally conscious member states continue to exist (see Chapter 5).

Environmentally conscious member states exert a particular influence on the EU's environmental agenda because they are both more willing and able to invest time and effort in developing an issue. They are more willing to invest in environmental issues because member state governments tend to concentrate on those issues that are closest to their country's interests and ignore issues they care less about. Moreover, it is easier for political actors to play an active role on an issue if they have sufficient expertise and manpower. The member states that have the most progressive environmental policies are often the member states that have most experts and officials working on environmental issues. As a result, in most cases only a subset of member states is actively involved in the process of agenda setting – and these tend to be those member states for which environmental issues are most important.

Despite the important roles of member states in environmental agenda setting, one should not focus exclusively on differences between member states. Equally significant are differences within member states. For instance, right-wing parties and left-wing parties within a member state normally have very different ideas about the relative importance of environmental protection and specific environmental problems. The same is true for environmental groups and industrial interests within a member state. These different approaches can also be found within the EU institutions. As we saw above, the Commission is not a unified institution, but consists of different DGs, each with its own institutional interests and agenda. In actual policy-making processes, the crucial political dividing line is therefore often between competing 'advocacy coalitions' (Sabatier and Weible, 2007), which bring together like-minded actors. One advocacy coalition may consist of DG Environment, environmentally-minded Members of the European Parliament (MEPs), and environmental policy makers and NGOs from a number of member states, while another may consist of DG Industry, trade-oriented MEPs, and economic policy makers and interest groups from those same member states. This arrangement changes the political playing field compared to a situation in which member states are pitted against each other.

The limited role of public opinion

In democratic domestic political systems, public opinion is an important source of agenda setting. When an issue becomes important in public opinion, it is likely also to move higher up on the political agenda. Our running example of climate change after 2006 is a good case in point. The reason for this is that politicians have an incentive to respond to public opinion. If an issue is important to citizens, they can gain public support by taking up that issue. This, in turn, may improve their chances of success in the next elections.

In the EU, public opinion plays a smaller role when compared to each of its member states and other democratic countries (see Chapter 18). There are two reasons for this (Imig and Tarrow, 2000; Princen, 2009: 37–38). The first reason is that EU decision makers are less dependent on public opinion than are domestic politicians. Unlike governments in presidential or parliamentary systems, the Commission is 'elected' neither directly nor indirectly. Member state ministers in the Council of Ministers (and heads of government in the European Council) answer to their parliaments and voters, but because there are 27 participants, it is very difficult to hold individual participants to account for what is decided. The European Parliament, finally, is directly elected, but studies of voting behaviour show that European Parliament elections are decided on national issues, not European ones (e.g. Schmitt, 2005). All in all, therefore, the EU's political system is structured in such a way that EU decision makers do not need to worry as much about public opinion as domestic politicians.

Second, it is more difficult to mobilize public opinion at EU level than within one member state. As we saw above, member states vary in the overall importance attached to environmental issues and to the specific environmental issues they worry about. In addition, it is difficult to mobilize public opinion in all member states at the same time because the EU's public sphere is highly fragmented, if only because media systems are organized along national lines. As a result, it is rare for a single issue to become important in most member states at the same time. Climate change was an example of such cross-border public mobilization, but it was quite exceptional in this regard.

This is not to say that public opinion plays no role at all in the EU. However, its effects are more indirect and, when it comes to environmental issues, occur most strongly around issues that have widespread appeal in a large number of member states.

The role of focusing events

Apart from general swings in public opinion, environmental issues can also be propelled up the political agenda in response to highly salient, much-publicized events that draw attention to a given issue. The quintessential example in environmental policy was the Chernobyl disaster in 1986, which drew strong attention to the risks of nuclear energy. Other examples were the large-scale oil spill caused by the sinking of the oil tanker *Prestige* off the coast of Spain in 2002 and the major industrial accident in a chemical plant near the Italian town of Seveso in 1976. Each of these disasters eventually led to EU responses and legislation.

These events have been important and have left an indelible mark on policy. For instance, the chemical accident in Seveso led to a directive aimed at the prevention of industrial accidents and limiting their impact, which is still known as the 'Seveso Directive'. Likewise, the 'Erika Package', consisting of a range of directives and regulations aimed at improving the safety of oil transport by sea, was adopted after a major oil spill in the Bay of Biscay caused by the oil tanker *Erika* in 1999. It was further strengthened after the *Prestige* accident.

Such events have been dubbed 'focusing events' by the American scholar John Kingdon (2003: 94–100) (see also Birkland, 1998). Focusing events are powerful because they put one particular (aspect of an) issue in the spotlight, while simultaneously detracting attention from other (aspects of) other issues. As a result, they increase the awareness of a particular problem, so people will tend to give greater priority to that problem. For a (brief) period of time, that problem seems to be much more important than other problems, catapulting it up the political agenda as calls for action to remedy it mount.

Focusing events do not speak for themselves. An important role in interpreting them is played by political actors who seek to frame the focusing event in such a way as to support their preferred cause. For political actors, crises and disasters are opportunities that they can use to sway the opinion of (other) policy makers and the general public in their direction. To that end, they actively try to frame events in ways that fit with their own interests. Lobby groups in particular devote huge amounts of their time to framing problems.

They can do this because the causes, consequences and implications of major crises are not always clear. To give another nuclear energy-related example: what were the implications of the meltdown in the Fukushima nuclear power plant in Japan after the tsunami of March 2011? Did it show that nuclear energy is inherently unsafe and should therefore be phased out in Europe? Or did it merely show that nuclear power plants should not be built in earthquake-prone areas, which does not include most of Europe? During and after the crisis, it was exactly this political debate that was being waged, with different actors in different countries promoting arguments that best fitted their interests and preconceived positions.

Focusing events may lead to activity at EU level because domestic politicians can use EU action as a way to address the concerns of their (domestic) constituencies. Moreover, large-scale environmental disasters have the potential to focus attention and public opinion in a wide range of member states at the same time, overcoming the limits of the EU's fragmented linguistic and media landscape. As a result, focusing events can affect the public agendas of a large number of member states simultaneously, which pushes the issue onto the EU agenda.

Links with other policy areas

Environmental issues are closely linked with other policy areas, not just in the EU but anywhere. For instance, if one wants to reduce air pollution, any proposal one can come up with (e.g. switching from fossil fuel power plants to renewable energy sources, taxing the use of cars, or strengthening emission standards for trucks) will have implications for other areas, such as economic development, urban planning and transport. Often, these implications are negative: higher taxes on fossil fuels may hamper economic development, make it more expensive for people to use their cars or require costly investments by government (e.g. development of alternative energy sources) or firms (e.g. installing new pollution-abatement devices).

In the EU, the many links between the environment and other issue areas both pose challenges and offer opportunities for would be agenda setters. The main challenge consists of gaining attention for the environmental aspects of an issue vis-à-vis other aspects, in particular, economic development. In the EU, this struggle is reinforced by the EU's institutional remit. The EU started as an economic union, and economic issues still form the core of the EU's *raison d'être* (see Chapter 1). Institutionally, this is reflected by the fact that the Commission's economic DGs (Enterprise, Internal Market, Competition) are considered the most important and powerful within the Commission (see Chapter 6 for details). Since promoting the economic development of its member states is a core task for the EU, issues and arguments that relate to economic development have a much greater chance of reaching the EU agenda than issues and arguments that do not.

For this reason, a classic strategy in EU agenda setting has been to present an issue in economic terms (see Chapter 10), even when it is not overtly economic in nature. Guignier (2004), writing on health policy in the EU, called this an 'economicized' approach to issues. The key in such an approach is to frame an issue as a contribution to economic development. An example is the argument that stricter environmental protection measures will yield economic benefits because they create an incentive for firms to develop and invest in innovative technologies, which will strengthen their position on world markets vis-à-vis competitors from outside the EU. Whether or not this is a really valid argument, what is important for understanding agenda-setting processes is to recognize the strategic value and use of this argument. By presenting environmental protection not (just) as a benefit to the environment but as a contribution to economic development ('ecological modernization'), the potential trade-off between environmental protection and economic development is reversed. This makes the issue appeal to policy makers and venues that are interested in economic development, which in turn increases the chances of it climbing up the political agenda.

Above, we saw how linking environmental protection to another issue area can both present a hurdle (when environmental protection is perceived to go against another cherished political objective) and offer opportunities (when environmental protection is perceived to contribute to another cherished political objective). This type of strategic issue linkage can also occur with other areas than economic development. A classic strategy, often employed by the Commission, for bringing issues to the EU agenda has been to link them to the internal market (see Chapter 2). The argument then is that an issue needs to be dealt with because it involves barriers to trade. This argument was particularly important in the early years of EU environmental policy, before a separate legal basis was included in the Single

European Act (see Chapters 2 and 4). Even today, however, links to the internal market can be used strategically to increase the chances of agenda access for an environmental issue.

From new issues to ongoing concerns

EU environmental policy in the 1970s and 1980s was marked by the rapid build-up of a body of legislation that covered a range of issues previously not dealt with at EU level (see Chapter 2). Since the 1980s, other new issues have been taken up but in addition an increasing proportion of the environmental agenda has been taken up by debates on the revision of existing legislation. As a result, the proportion of EU environmental legislation that amends previous laws has steadily increased over time (see McCormick, 2001: 64, for the period 1973–1999).

As a result, agenda-setting processes have taken on a somewhat different character. For most environmental issues, the key question no longer is: 'Should the EU be involved?' but 'What should the EU be doing?' And the point in getting the issue on the EU agenda is no longer to make the EU take it up, but to change existing policies (strengthening or weakening them, depending on a political actor's objectives). This change in both the stakes of and the key struggle in agenda-setting strategies marks a shift from 'new issues' to 'ongoing or recurring concerns'.

Some debates on existing legislation concern fundamental aspects of an issue, such as the debate on the basic approach in fisheries conservation highlighted in Box 11.1. Most amendments, however, concern very specific and often highly technical updates of existing regulatory standards. Table 11.1 lists all 12 official Commission documents (so-called COM documents) published in the first six months of 2011 for which DG Environment was responsible. It gives a feel for the kind of environmental issues that are currently on the EU agenda.

Crucially, all of these documents relate to issues that were already subject to EU policies and legislation. Some documents concern issues that are relatively broad and strategic in scope, such as the thematic strategy on the prevention and recycling of waste and an EU biodiversity strategy. Most, however, deal with relatively narrower issues such as the proposal to include creosote as an active substance in an Annex to Directive 98/8/EC on biocidal products, the proposal to sign a supplementary protocol to the Cartagena Protocol, or the proposal on 'specific criteria for the storage of metallic mercury considered as waste'.

Little publicized as they may be, these issues, too, are part of the EU environmental agenda – and they form an increasingly large part of it. As a result, the agenda dynamics around EU environmental policy have become focused more on updating existing policies than on building up the EU's role in environmental policy (the focus of the standard European integration literature) (for a more detailed summary, see Chapter 4).

Table 11.1 COM documents from DG Environment published between 1 January and 30 June 2011

COM number	Title
COM(2011)13	Report on the Thematic Strategy on the Prevention and Recycling of Waste
COM(2011)49	Proposal for a Council Decision on the signing of the Nagoya Protocol on Access to Genetic Resources and the Fair and Equitable Sharing of Benefits Arising from their Utilization to the Convention on Biological Diversity
COM(2011)50	Proposal for a Council Directive amending Directive 98/8/EC of the European Parliament and of the Council to include creosote as an active substance in Annex I thereto
COM(2011)67	Proposal for a Council Decision establishing the position to be adopted on behalf of the European Union at the Fifth Conference of the Parties to the Stockholm Convention on Persistent Organic Pollutants (POPs) with regard to the proposal for an amendment of Annex A
COM(2011)130	Proposal for a Council Decision on signing the Nagoya-Kuala Lumpur Supplementary Protocol on Liability and Redress to the Cartagena Protocol on Biosafety
COM(2011)133	Third Follow-Up Report to the Communication on water scarcity and droughts in the European Union COM (2007) 414 final
COM(2011)244	Our life insurance, our natural capital: an EU biodiversity strategy to 2020
COM(2011)245	Proposal for a Regulation concerning the export and import of dangerous chemicals (recast)
COM(2011)297	Report on the implementation and review of Directive 2004/42/EC of the European Parliament and of the Council on the limitation of emissions of volatile organic compounds due to the use of organic solvents in certain paints and varnishes and vehicle refinishing products and amending Directive 1999/13/EC
COM(2011)299	Proposal for a Council Directive amending Council Directive 1999/31/EC as regards specific criteria for the storage of metallic mercury considered as waste
COM(2011)316	Proposal for a Council Decision establishing the position to be adopted on behalf of the European Union with regard to proposals for amendment of the Appendices of the Convention on the conservation of migratory species of wild animals with a view to the tenth meeting of the Conference of the Parties
COM(2011)321	Report on the implementation of the Environmental Noise Directive in accordance with Article 11 of Directive 2002/49/EC

Source: PreLex (2011).

Summary points

- Agenda setting on environmental issues in the EU takes place within a multilevel system, which spans local, regional, national and global levels.
- Environmental agenda setting in the EU is strongly affected by the EU's specific geographic, institutional and political characteristics.
- Over time, the EU's environmental agenda has focused less on completely new issues and more on the revision of existing policies and legislation.

Conclusion

This chapter has highlighted the dynamics of agenda setting in EU environmental politics. It has sought to provide an understanding of how and why (certain) environmental issues come onto the EU's political agenda. Agenda setting is a relatively fluid part of the policy-making process, because issues and participants have not yet crystallized. In fact, agenda setting is exactly about determining what issues will be dealt with and by whom. This makes agenda setting an elusive phenomenon, which is strongly affected by idiosyncratic factors, such as the occurrence of media 'hypes' and focusing events.

Nevertheless, there is order in these seemingly chaotic processes. As this chapter has shown, environmental agenda setting in the EU reflects the institutional and political characteristics of the EU's political system. As a result, agenda-setting processes in the EU show similarities with agenda-setting processes that can be observed elsewhere, but there are nonetheless a number of specificities that flow from the way the EU has been organized and operates.

Although it remains extremely difficult to predict precisely which issues will be on the top of the EU (environmental) agenda a few years from now, the order in EU agenda-setting processes can help to understand what is happening and why. In addition, the analysis of agenda-setting dynamics presented in this chapter has clear implications for the kinds of agenda-setting strategies that political actors use and the challenges they face (see also Princen, 2011). As a result, attempts to influence the agenda, either by bringing issues onto it or by keeping them off, have become an integral part of the activities of actors in EU environmental policy making.

Summary points

- Since agenda-setting processes are relatively unstructured, their outcome is often difficult to predict in advance.

- Nevertheless, EU agenda-setting processes show a number of regularities and recurring dynamics, which reflect the characteristics of the EU's political system.
- The analysis of agenda-setting dynamics has implications for the strategies that are used by prospective agenda setters, and their strengths and weaknesses.

Key questions

1 Why is an understanding of agenda-setting processes so important for understanding environmental policy making in the EU?
2 How does issue framing and institutional venues affect the likelihood that a given issue will come onto the EU's political agenda?
3 What consequences does the multilevel character of environmental policy making have for agenda-setting processes in the EU?
4 Under what conditions would you expect public opinion to play a small/large role in agenda setting on environmental issues in the EU?
5 What does the shift from new issues to ongoing concerns mean for agenda-setting processes on environmental issues in the EU?
6 Overall, do you think it is easier or more difficult for environmental issues to come onto the EU's political agenda than onto the political agenda of the country you live in?

Guide to further reading

- Kingdon (2003) has written one of the most influential books on agenda setting. It proposes a framework based on three 'streams' of policy making.
- Baumgartner and Jones (2009) develop and apply an agenda-setting theory based on the interplay of frames and venues.
- Princen (2009) develops a theoretical framework for analysing agenda setting in the EU and applies it to two policy areas: environment and health.
- Princen (2011) gives an overview of the various strategies used by political actors to bring issues onto the EU agenda.

References

Baumgartner, F.R. and Jones, B.D. (2009) *Agendas and Instability in American Politics*, 2nd edition, University of Chicago Press, Chicago.

Beyers, J. and Kerremans, B. (2011) 'Domestic embeddedness and the dynamics of multi-level venue-shopping in four EU member states', *Governance*, vol. 25, no. 2, pp. 263–290.

Birkland, T.A. (1998) 'Focusing events, mobilization, and agenda setting', *Journal of Public Policy*, vol. 18, no. 1, pp. 53–74.

European Commission (2001) *Commission Report to the European Council: Better Lawmaking 2001* (COM (2001) 728), European Commission, Brussels.

Fairbrass, J. and Jordan, A. (2004) 'Multi-level governance and environmental policy', in I. Bache and M. Flinders (eds) *Multi-Level Governance*, Oxford University Press, Oxford.

Guignier, S. (2004) 'Institutionalizing public health in the European Commission: the thrills and spills of politicization', in A. Smith (ed.) *Politics and the European Commission: Actors, Interdependence, Legitimacy*, Routledge, London.

Hooghe, L. and Marks, G. (2001) *Multi-Level Governance and European Integration*, Rowman and Littlefield, Lanham, MD.

Imig, D. and Tarrow, S. (2000) 'Political contention in a Europeanising polity', *West European Politics*, vol. 23, no. 4, pp. 73–93.

Keck, M.E. and Sikkink, K. (1998) *Advocates Beyond Borders: Advocacy Networks in International Politics*, Cornell University Press, Ithaca, NY.

Kingdon, J.W. (2003) *Agendas, Alternatives, and Public Policies*, 2nd edition, HarperCollins College Publishers, New York.

Liefferink, D. and Andersen, M.S. (1998) 'Strategies of the "green" member states in EU environmental policy making', *Journal of European Public Policy*, vol. 5, no. 2, pp. 254–270.

McCormick, J. (2001) *Environmental Policy in the European Union*, Palgrave, Basingstoke.

PreLex (2011) 'Monitoring of the decision-making process between institutions', http://ec.europa.eu/prelex/apcnet.cfm?CL=en (accessed 26 September 2011).

Princen, S. (2007) 'Agenda setting in the European Union: a theoretical exploration and agenda for research', *Journal of European Public Policy*, vol. 14, no. 1, pp. 21–38.

Princen, S. (2009) *Agenda Setting in the European Union*, Palgrave, Basingstoke.

Princen, S. (2010) 'Venue shifts and policy change in EU fisheries policy', *Marine Policy*, vol. 34, no. 1, pp. 36–41.

Princen, S. (2011) 'Agenda setting strategies in EU policy processes', *Journal of European Public Policy*, vol. 18, no. 7, pp. 927–943.

Rochefort, D.A. and Cobb, R.W. (eds) (1994) *The Politics of Problem Definition: Shaping the Policy Agenda*, University Press of Kansas, Lawrence, KS.

Sabatier, P.A. and Weible, C.M. (2007) 'The advocacy coalition framework: innovations and clarifications', in P.A. Sabatier (ed.) *Theories of the Policy Process*, 2nd edition, Westview Press, Boulder, CO.

Sbragia, A. (1996) 'Environmental policy: the push-pull of policy-making', in H. Wallace and W. Wallace (eds) *Policy-Making in the European Union*, Oxford: Oxford University Press, pp. 235–255.

Schmitt, H. (2005) 'The European Parliament elections of June 2004: still second-order?', *West European Politics*, vol. 28, no. 3, pp. 650–679.

Vogel, D. (1995) *Trading up: Consumer and Environmental Regulation in a Global Economy*, Harvard University Press, Cambridge, MA.

12 Policy making

*Camilla Adelle, Andrew Jordan
and John Turnpenny*

Summary guide

This chapter examines the process through which legislative proposals are selected and adopted at EU level. In the past, this process, which brings together many different actors operating at different levels of governance, has tended to be rather open and unpredictable. In the 2000s, attempts were made to introduce greater formality and predictability by employing the 'standard operating procedure' of Impact Assessment (IA). This chapter outlines the two main parts of the policy-making process (namely policy formulation and decision making) and analyses how far IA has succeeded in imposing a more formal procedure on them. It reveals that while the European Commission has made greater use of IA, the other EU institutions have not. Furthermore, it is still unclear if IA can completely proceduralize policy making, given the very many sources of unpredictability.

Introduction

This whole book is about 'policy making' in one way or another. This chapter, however, focuses on the steps leading to the adoption of a particular policy. Policy making comes after the point at which a political issue has been placed on the policy agenda (see Chapter 11), but before the process of implementation kicks in (Chapter 12). It is the stage in the policy process when policy makers have to decide what to do about a particular issue, assuming, of course, that they have decided to do something. There will usually be a range of possible policy options to choose between, some of which may bear upon policies developed in other sectors (Chapter 13). Although many of these options will be investigated and subsequently negotiated over, only one will be eventually selected. For the sake of convenience, this long and at times highly recursive choice process is often divided into two main steps: policy formulation and decision making. These two steps provide the main focus of this chapter, although the same material is also examined by the authors of the chapters in Part 2 (and specifically, Chapters 5, 6, 8 and 9).

More specifically, this chapter examines the process through which legislative proposals are selected and adopted in the EU. Special attention is given to the role of an Impact Assessment (IA), a procedure introduced by the European Commission in 2002 to assess the likely positive and negative impacts of policy proposals *before* they are decided upon. The next section describes the two phases of the EU's policy-making process, namely, policy formulation and decision making, in greater detail. Then the mixed providence of IA is discussed, showing how IA in the EU arose from both the better regulation agenda and contemporaneous calls for sustainability issues (see Chapter 19) to be incorporated in policy-level assessments. At the same time, there were a number of more subtle reasons for the growing popularity of IA which are also outlined and discussed. This section then goes on to explain how IA fitted into the pre-existing patterns of policy making. It finds that, while IA has quickly become an established procedure within the Commission in the policy formulation stage, this does not appear to be the case with respect to the decision-making stage involving the European Parliament and the Council. The following section reviews the many evaluations of the new IA procedure that have been conducted in the EU. These have revealed the difficulties associated with trying to proceduralize something as fluid and complex as EU-level policy making. The concluding section reflects on the extent to which IA has proceduralized EU policy making, given the very many sources of unpredictability in the EU system.

Before proceeding, it is very important to be aware that the EU routinely engages in a number of different types of policy making, each of which has different characteristics. Lelieveldt and Princen (2011: 229) differentiate between three different main types: (1) history making; (2) policy setting; and (3) policy shaping. They argue that the vast majority of decisions are not the 'history-making decisions' surrounding the renegotiation of the treaties, which shape the legal structure of the EU (see Chapters 3 and 4). More common and arguably more important are the 'policy-setting decisions' concerning high-level targets and strategies in specific policy areas, and the 'policy-shaping decisions', which deal with the fine detail (the precise targets to be aimed at; the instruments to be used; issues to do with implementation and enforcement, etc.). This chapter mostly deals with policy-setting and policy-shaping decisions.

Furthermore there is not a single method for making decisions in the EU but a number of different ones. Wallace (2010: 90) mentions four in particular (see Box 12.1). Of these, the regulatory method is the most common way in which most environmental policy is made. The Monnet Method used to be more common (see Chapter 3), and the open method of coordination (see Box 12.1) is becoming more significant, but this chapter mainly focuses on how the EU employs the regulatory method to formulate and decide upon most of its environmental policies. This method is perceived to have worked well in relation to trade liberalization especially via the use of regulations to harmonize standards governing traded products. Within the regulatory method, there are a number of different 'procedures' which determine the relationship between the Council, the Parliament and the Commission in this phase of policy making. The most common procedure for environmental policy making is the 'ordinary legislative procedure' (see below) but another procedure – the 'comitology procedure' – is becoming more prominent (see Box 12.2).

Box 12.1 The four policy-making methods used in the EU

Helen Wallace (2010) sets out four different methods for making policy in the EU:

1   *The classic Monnet or community method*: this was the predominant way of making policy in the early years of the EU. It involved the Commission and the Council working together in a closed and technocratic manner with only limited opportunities for the European Parliament to intervene. Named after one of the founding fathers of the EU, Jean Monnet, it advanced European integration 'by stealth' through focusing on incremental change (Jordan *et al.*, 2010: 36). One of the classic examples of a policy developed through this method is the Common Agricultural Policy (Wallace, 2010: 91). This method is now thought to be in decline (Majone, 2006).

2   *The 'regulatory method'*: involves the Commission, Council and the Parliament working together on a more equal basis, and emerged in the mid-1980s. It was driven in part by the single market programme and the consequent need to harmonize standards for traded products. It turned out that the EU was particularly well suited to generating an overarching regulatory framework that could incorporate some inter-country differences (Wallace, 2010: 95).

3   *The 'policy coordination method'*: also known as the open method of coordination, this involves member states coming together in a much less formal decision-making setting in areas where cooperation is desirable but the EU lacks competence and/or political support. This method is increasingly applied in areas such as employment and social policy (Jordan *et al.*, 2010: 36).

4   *The 'intergovernmental method'*: mainly relies on direct interaction between relevant national policy makers with little impact from EU institutions. It is usually used in the most delicate policy areas such as foreign affairs, defence and fiscal policy. It can, however, be a precursor to deeper EU involvement (ibid.).

Box 12.2 The comitology procedure

After the formal adoption of a piece of legislation, often certain practical issues still need to be decided; such as reporting requirements and technical specifications (Farmer, 2011). The Commission can sometimes decide these issues (in the form of a Commission Decision) with the help of committees chaired by the Commission and composed of member state experts. This type of decision making, whereby committees 'assist' the Commission in the exercise of its implementation powers as delegated by the EU legislator (i.e. the Council and Parliament), is referred to as 'comitology'. Although a highly technical and at times convoluted process, comitology is becoming increasingly important at the EU level. During the Barroso 1 Commission (2004–2009) no less than 14,522 legally binding implementing measures were decided in this way (Hardacre and Kaeding, 2011).

Initially, this procedure was developed on an *ad hoc* basis by the Council. Its process was later formalized through the adoption of Council Decisions, with concessions gradually being made for engagement by the European Parliament. The Lisbon Treaty (Article 290–291, TFEU) also introduced significant modifications, which have not yet been fully implemented (see also Chapter 6). The Lisbon Treaty split comitology into two types of delegation of executive power to the Commission: 'delegated' acts and 'implementing' acts. Delegated acts address sensitive matters that amend, delete or supplement non-essential elements of a legislative act (e.g. adding a substance to an annex of banned products). The main changes introduced by the Lisbon Treaty are related to this new category of delegated acts, where committees are no longer used and the legislators have equal rights to object to individual delegated acts or to revoke the delegation to the Commission entirely (Hardacre and Kaeding, 2011). Implementing acts correspond to the continuation of 'traditional' comitology procedures in which the Commission is empowered to implement EU legislation under the supervision of comitology committees.

Policy making in the EU can be highly complex; much more complex in fact than that at national level. At EU level, 'the institutional structures are more in flux, the allocation of authority is more contested and multiple levels of government engage a multitude of actors' (Young, 2010: 46). The existing literature suggests that the policy-making process is too densely populated with veto players (i.e. actors whose agreement is necessary for a policy to be adopted) for any single actor or group of actors (including the EU member states) to consistently dictate the direction of policy making. More often than not, EU environmental policies are 'the aggregate and transformed standards of their original champions modified under the need to secure political accommodation from powerful veto players'

(Weale, 2005: 136). The resulting picture resembles less a grand master plan and more a complicated 'policy patchwork' (Héritier, 2002). The need to secure the agreement among so many players also means that in the past there has been incentive for actors to point out the full implications of their policy proposals to other actors. In the past even some member states have not always been fully aware of what they are signing up to when they 'make' EU environmental policy (Weale, 2005).

The European Commission is a key player in the EU policy process (see Chapter 6) and not surprisingly, it has come under the most pressure to develop 'standard operating procedures' for processing policy (Mazey and Richardson, 1992: 110). For example, it has increased openness and transparency by adopting minimum standards of consultation (see Chapter 9), and it has improved its strategic planning through the earlier publication of its work programmes (Chapter 6). These steps are part of a worldwide trend towards forms of 'better regulation'. Radaelli (2007: 191) claims that better regulation puts 'emphasis on standards and rules which, instead of governing specific sectors or economic actors, steer the process of rule formulation, adoption, enforcement, and evaluation'. A crucial element of the Commission's better regulation reforms is policy level IA (see Box 12.3) which, when it was introduced, sought to 'improve the quality and coherence of the policy development process' (European Commission, 2002a: 2). The remainder of this chapter asks if IA has provided the EU policy process with the stronger standard operating procedure that it was reportedly previously lacking.

Box 12.3 The six steps of Impact Assessment

Impact Assessment attempts to formalize the policy-making process. It is a procedure designed to guide officials through the basic steps involved in developing a policy proposal. The steps are to:

1   Identify the problem to be addressed by the proposed policy.
2   Define the objectives which correspond to this problem.
3   Identify the different policy options to pursue these objectives.
4   Analyse the economic, social and environmental impacts of each option.
5   Compare the options by weighing up the negative and positive impacts of each.
6   Outline plans for monitoring and evaluating the policy once it has been implemented.

The output of this process is usually a document (an IA report) describing each step, together with any supporting information such as economic costs. This report is then submitted to decision makers alongside the policy proposal for their eventual approval.

The EU policy-making process

The policy-making process in the EU can be split into two main phases: 'policy formulation' and 'decision making'.

Policy formulation

The Commission has the formal right of policy initiation for all policy areas where the EU has 'exclusive' or 'shared' competencies including environmental policy (see Chapter 6). The Commission is the 'centrepiece' of much of what goes on in this phase (Versluis *et al.*, 2011: 134). Once an issue has been placed on the agenda (see Chapter 11), it is inserted into the Commission's Work Programme, which is prepared in November every year. Work planning has increased in recent years to make policy making in the Commission less 'opaque and incoherent' (Jordan and Schout, 2006: 217). At the level of day-to-day planning, the Commission also prepares a 'list of planned Commission initiatives' which gives a more detailed overview of planned activities; this list is updated every month (European Commission, 2011a). Whether a policy proposal makes it onto this list depends on the political priorities of the Commission and the other EU institutions (Jordan and Schout, 2006: 217–218).

Once drafting begins, one lead Directorate General (DG) is given overall responsibility and appoints a *chef de dossier* for the proposal. This person is normally a middle-ranking staff member with a relevant expertise. Drafting is usually done in close cooperation with a number of working groups, composed of national officials, experts from the Commission, representatives of interest groups and external experts (see Chapter 9). At the same time, the Commission also conducts more open, and at times, large-scale consultation exercises in accordance with its minimum standards of consultation. Both the working groups and the wider consultations serve to smooth out any technical and legal difficulties which might hinder agreement in the Council and/or with the European Parliament (Knill and Liefferink, 2007: 86).

Proposals are also discussed between the different DGs within the Commission. The internal rivalries between individual DGs are the stuff of folklore in Brussels and can shape proposals just as heavily as interactions with external actors, such as member states and the Parliament (Versluis *et al.*, 2011). Conflicts between DGs can be negotiated informally in inter-service committees, convened by the *chef de dossier*, or bilaterally by unit heads, directors, DGs or Commissioners. Any contentious issues are raised more formally at weekly meetings of DGs and their deputies or ultimately in the College of Commissioners (which consists of the 27 Commissioners – one from every member state). However, the substantial workload of the College means that where possible, issues are resolved at the lowest level possible. Before a proposal is officially adopted by the Commission, it is sent around all the DGs in an Inter-Service Consultation in which the DGs have ten days to respond. After this formal step, the proposal is put on the agenda of the College. The *Cabinet* (i.e. the office of each European Commissioner) discusses the proposal beforehand, if necessary, referring to the Cabinet *chefs.* The

College is prepared by the *Hebdo* (a team of Cabinet *chefs*) which may send proposals back to their *chef de dossier* or onward for discussion in the College. If there are still severe controversies, the Secretariat General of the Commission can call in the relevant parties for a discussion, but the final decision lies with the College. Officially decisions can be made here by majority, but in practice unanimity is preferred.

Decision making

Once a policy proposal has been adopted by the Commission, it is sent to the Council of Ministers (see Chapter 5) and the European Parliament (see Chapter 6) which continue to engage in policy formulation activities (Knill and Liefferink, 2007: 87). Within the regulatory method of decision making (see above), various different 'legislative procedures' determine the relationship between the Council and the Parliament in this phase of policy making. The vast majority of EU policy areas (including most environmental policy) follow the procedure which used to be known as the 'co-decision procedure' but since the Lisbon Treaty has become known as the 'ordinary legislative procedure' (Lelieveldt and Princen, 2011: 85). In this procedure, both the Council and the Parliament must agree on the proposal and can adopt amendments through a series of 'readings' in order to arrive at a final text. The Commission plays a smaller role, but can give an official opinion on the acceptability of the Parliament's amendments. Crucially, it can modify or withdraw its proposal at any time.

Summary points

- In the policy formulation phase of policy making, policy options are identified and shaped mainly within the European Commission.
- Input to this phase comes from many different actors both inside and outside the Commission.
- During the decision-making phase, policy proposals are fine tuned and the content agreed through political negotiation with the Council and the Parliament.

The introduction of Impact Assessment in the EU

At first sight, the EU always had procedures for making policy. The previous section described those that existed in the Commission. In practice, political factors always intruded, particularly in the decision-making stages. Here, a functional or problem-solving mentality tended to give way to political bargaining over national (Knill and Liefferink, 2007) and even inter-institutional interests (McCormick, 2001). It is hardly surprising that, as noted above, the resulting policies bore a closer resemblance to a patchwork than a carefully ordered framework. In the late

1990s, attempts were made to further proceduralize the policy-making process, principally through the use of IA.

A mixed providence

Better regulation – and with it the IA – emerged in the EU as a topic for discussion in the early 1990s propelled by concerns, voiced by some member states and pressure groups, over the quality and quantity of legislation emanating from Brussels (Radaelli, 2007; Radaelli and Meuwese, 2010). In the 1990s, the Commission started to experiment with different forms of policy appraisal, including the 'Green Star initiative' which sought to assess the potential environmental impacts of all new Commission proposals. However, it was never used much in practice (Wilkinson, 1997). In 2001, an expert group of national officials established by the European Ministers of Public Administration produced a 'blueprint' for pursuing better regulation in the EU (Radaelli, 2007: 192). It was at this point, following the recommendations of the group's report (named the Mandelkern Report after its chair, Dieudonné Mandelkern) that the Commission's activities evolved into a 'comprehensive, consistent and fully fledged' better regulation strategy (Allio, 2007: 73).

A number of other high-level EU initiatives reinforced the trend towards greater proceduralization. First, in March 2000, the European Council launched the 'Lisbon Strategy' which, among other things, sought to 'simplify the regulatory environment, including the performance of public administration (European Council, 2000: point 17). Better regulation also formed an integral part of the Commission's 2001 White Paper on Governance (European Commission, 2001). These developments culminated in the launch of the Commission's action plan on 'better law-making' in June 2002 (European Commission, 2002b). Eight Communications on specific actions supported this plan, including one outlining a new approach to IA (European Commission, 2002a). IA, it was claimed, would act as an 'instrument to improve the quality and coherence of the policy development process' (European Commission, 2002a: 2).

Better regulation, however, was not the only driver of IA in the EU. Sustainability Impact Assessment was also mentioned in the Gothenburg Presidency Conclusions in June 2001 as an instrument to implement the EU's new Sustainable Development Strategy (European Council, 2001) (see also Chapter 19). In fact when the Commission's IA system was unveiled in 2002, it was envisaged as an instrument to cover the potential economic, social *and environmental* consequences of all major policy proposals (European Commission, 2002a). For environmentalists, IA presented both an opportunity (it was stronger than the failed 'Green Star initiative'), but also a threat: there was, after all, still potential for environmental and social impacts to be downplayed relative to the economic impacts of new proposals. In many ways IA represents a perfect illustration of how policy agendas are shaped in the EU (see Chapter 11).

The mixed origins of IA were certainly visible in the wording of the guidance issued to Commission officials who were to conduct IA. This stated that IA would 'contribute to an effective and efficient regulatory environment and, further, to a more coherent implementation of the European Strategy for Sustainable Development' (European Commission, 2002a: 3). The technical guidelines went further by placing an excerpt from the Sustainable Development Strategy on the front cover (European Commission, n.d.: 1). The EU's preferred approach to IA was rather different to that used in the USA. Dubbed Regulatory Impact Assessment (RIA), the variant used in the USA mainly concentrates on economic impacts and, in particular, reducing regulatory burdens. In the early 2000s, RIA was rolled out in several EU member states including the UK and Ireland.

There were other more subtle reasons why IA and RIA became so popular in the 2000s. These include the desire to emulate what neighbours were doing (i.e. copy international best practice), changes in public management styles (i.e. the shift towards an 'audit culture'), and a wish to enhance the political control over bureaucrats. Radaelli (2010) argues that IA in the EU was forced upon the Commission by a group of member states who were anxious to control its policy-making activities. They believed that IA would slow down and open up the policy-making process, in a way that would alert them to when something 'politically dangerous' might be happening (ibid.: 92).

The early days of Impact Assessment

Whatever the precise motivations for its introduction, an obvious question to ask is, has IA delivered what was expected of it? Following the Commission's 2002 Communication, IA was gradually rolled out. It was originally applied in a two-stage process: first, a preliminary IA briefly setting out the policy problem, available options, likely impacts, etc.; and, second, by an 'extended IA' if the impacts were deemed to be significant. In the first year (2003), 21 extended IAs were completed; the number subsequently rose to 31 in 2004. The Commission felt that it had learnt valuable lessons in these early years (European Commission, 2004). However, external evaluations were much more critical of both the IAs and the functioning of the entire system, and suggested numerous improvements (see below).

In the spring of 2005, there was a high-profile relaunch of the Lisbon Strategy for growth and jobs (European Commission, 2005a; 2005b). Around this time, better regulation was presented as a means of improving the EU's economic performance and increase its competitiveness. The downgrading of sustainable development also had implications for the design of IA, henceforth, the Commission would highlight the importance of assessing the impact of all new legislation on *competitiveness* (Radaelli, 2007). Environmental commentators felt uneasy about what they saw as a focusing of the better regulation agenda on the reduction of 'red tape' (Lofstedt, 2007).

As a result of these developments, the IA system was revised. New guidelines were published in 2005 and further modified in 2006 (European Commission, 2005c; 2005d; 2005e). In particular, a greater focus was placed on reducing administrative burdens and the compliance costs of regulation borne by small and medium-sized enterprises. An Impact Assessment Board, comprised of high-level

Commission officials, was established inside the Commission in 2006 to quality check all IAs. Those that were deemed to be sub-standard would be issued with an unfavourable opinion from the board as well as advice on any necessary changes.

Since then, the number of IAs has increased: 264 IA reports were produced between the beginning of 2008 and the end of 2010 (European Commission, 2011b). The IA guidelines have also continued to be revised: they were last updated in 2009 (European Commission, 2009a). The powers of the Impact Assessment Board have also increased over time (European Commission, 2009b; European Commission, 2011c), such that it now has the power to reject sub-standard IAs and ask for them to be resubmitted only after significant changes have been made.

Impact Assessment and policy formulation

An IA is necessary for all of the Commission's most significant proposals. These include legislative proposals contained in the Commission's Work Programme as well as other proposals but which have clearly identifiable economic, social and environmental impacts (European Commission, 2009a). Non-legislative initiatives (such as White Papers, Action Plans, etc.) also require an IA, as do certain implementing measures (so-called 'comitology' items). The question of which proposals to subject to an IA is decided each year by the Secretariat General and the Commission's Impact Assessment Board, based on suggestions from the lead DG.

All policy initiatives placed on the Commission's Work Programme or which are otherwise identified as needing an IA must be accompanied by a 'roadmap' setting out the anticipated scope, contents and timetable of the IA (European Commission, 2009a). These roadmaps are circulated to the relevant DGs as well as posted on the Commission's IA website. The next step is to set up an Impact Assessment Steering Group. This comprises a representative from each DG with an interest in the policy proposal (ibid.). This group is intended to be involved in all stages of the IA as well as review the IA before it is submitted to the Impact Assessment Board – the minutes of the final meeting of the group are attached to the IA report when it is submitted. The bringing together of interested parties is seen as an important part of an IA (European Commission, 2009a). In this way, the more open and large-scale consultation which is conducted in the normal course of the proposal drafting phase (see above) is incorporated into the framework of IA while the working groups inform the IA in a less structured manner. It also prevents individual DGs from incubating proposals out of the public eye and then at the last possible moment presenting them to the rest as a *fait acompli* – once common practices associated with the Monnet Method.

As far as possible, the analysis of impacts in the IA is quantified and, if possible, monetized. The *chefs de dossier* are supported in this by IA units (usually containing economists) within their DG. When the draft is ready, and at least eight weeks before the policy proposal is to be discussed at Inter-Service Consultation, the draft IA report is submitted to the Impact Assessment Board. Assuming the IA report is not rejected on the grounds of poor quality (see above), the Impact

Assessment Board gives a written opinion on each IA which is then published on the Commission IA webpage as well as submitted to the College of Commissioners along with the IA report (European Commission, 2009b). The Commission estimates that it takes at least one year to progress from the roadmap to this, the final stage of an IA (European Commission, 2009a).

Impact Assessment and decision making

Once the College has approved a proposal, it is circulated to the European Parliament and the Council, along with the IA report. An inter-institutional agreement between the Commission, the European Parliament and the Council commits the European Parliament and the Council to assess the impact of any substantial amendments they make to a Commission proposal (European Commission, European Parliament and the EU Council, 2005). However, this rarely happens in practice (European Court of Auditors, 2010). Neither the European Parliament nor the Council conduct IAs on their amendments even though some of them can have significant effects. Moreover, there is little evidence that the Parliament or the Council use the Commission's IAs in their discussions (European Court of Auditors, 2010; Radaelli and Meuwese, 2010). Thus, IA remains very much a procedure used by and for the Commission.

Summary points

- IA has a very mixed providence arising from things as diverse as desire for, among other things, better regulation, more sustainable development and less 'red tape'.
- Bureaucrats in the Commission have therefore found themselves using IA for many different and at times contradictory purposes.
- The Parliament and the Council do not conduct an IA to inform their own decisions. Neither do they routinely use the Commission's IAs to inform their deliberations.

Evaluations of Impact Assessment in practice

At first sight, the EU's new IA system appeared to be more systematically applied than many existing systems (e.g. those in the US and the UK) (Renda, 2006). However, gaps soon emerged between the stated aims and everyday practices.

First steps in Impact Assessment

The Institute of European Environmental Policy (commissioned by the UK Department of the Environment) was the first to report its findings (Wilkinson *et al.*, 2004). Together with subsequent studies (e.g. Hertin *et al.*, 2004; Lee and

Kirkpatrick, 2004), it presented a mixed picture. A number of common symptoms of 'poor' quality were identified, not least of which was an inadequate and unbalanced treatment of impacts, with notably less attention given to environmental and/or social issues (Lee and Kirkpatrick, 2004; Wilkinson *et al.*, 2004). Other criticisms of the early IAs included: the narrow range of policy options considered (Lee and Kirkpatrick, 2004); the uneven coverage of the system with very few or no IAs being undertaken in some policy areas (Hertin *et al.*, 2004); the narrow framing of the problem to be addressed (Wilkinson *et al.*, 2004); an asymmetry in stakeholder engagement, with industrial groups tending to be more involved in the IA process than environmental or social actors (ibid.); and a marked lack of transparency in the whole process (Lee and Kirkpatrick, 2004; Wilkinson *et al.*, 2004). Some of these criticisms were echoed in the Commission's own report (European Commission, 2004). Most, if not all, of these studies offered recommendations on how to improve the performance of IA. This eventually led to the IA system being revised in 2005 and 2006 (see above).

A second wave of studies

A second wave of studies investigated the IA procedure when it was in a more mature state. Many of the same early criticisms and recommendations were raised again, perhaps giving an early indication that improving the quality of IA would be more difficult than policy makers had at first assumed. Poor quantification was widely reported, especially of long-term environmental and/or social impacts (Jacob *et al.*, 2008; Nielsen *et al.*, 2006; Renda, 2006). In addition, a lack of clarity about what counted as 'proportionate' analysis was also evident (Nielsen *et al.*, 2006; Renda, 2006). However, another internal evaluation of the EU's IAs system commissioned by the European Commission found that half the IAs it examined were adequate and proportionate (TEP, 2007). This evaluation informed yet another revision of the IA guidelines in 2009 (European Commission, 2009a).

Recent evaluations

Since 2007, the Impact Assessment Board has reported on its work each year, and on each occasion issued more recommendations on how to improve the IA system. In recent years it has moved on from discussing the 'basic structural elements' of the IA system, such as the identification of policy options and problem definitions to more 'substantial analytical issues', such as the consideration of specific types of impacts (European Commission, 2009b: 2). Despite this, the resubmission rate for IAs with serious deficiencies has steadily increased (from 33 per cent in 2008 to 42 per cent in 2010) (European Commission, 2009b; 2011c). However, the Impact Assessment Board claims that this is more to do with the strengthening of standards than reflection of poor quality (European Commission, 2011c). In general, the Impact Assessment Board maintains that the quality of IA is improving (ibid.). In addition, the European Court of Auditors published a report on the EU's IA system in September 2010 which found that compliance with the IA guidelines was good (European Court of Auditors, 2010: 17). However, the report identified a number of specific areas for further improvement, and noted the need for better integration into the EU's decision-making process. In particular, the need to update the IAs as proposals progressed through the legislative procedure in the European Parliament and Council was again emphasized, as was the need to implement *ex post* evaluations (European Court of Auditors, 2010). In other words, rather than improving the quality of the IA reports (which were now seen to be mostly satisfactory), something much more fundamental was now being highlighted: the need to systematically integrate the findings of IAs into the policy-making process. In this, the Board was starting to voice criticisms that had routinely been made by academics and pressure groups.

A wider academic literature on IA has sprung up, some of it searching not for measures of compliance with bureaucratic rules set out in handbooks, but whether or not appraisal actually leads to policy change via processes of learning. Hertin *et al.* (2009: 1196), for example, found IA only really informed 'policy designs at the margins' and that the (little) learning that did take place occurs despite, rather than because of, the design of appraisal procedures. This literature has been relatively silent on issuing practical recommendations for the improvement of IA systems in the EU or beyond. What it did do was challenge the whole notion that there are simple solutions to the problem of poor 'quality' (Adelle *et al.*, 2012). In fact, other 'problems' might be much more salient.

There have, however, been some other interesting consequences of IA. The Commission had attempted to initiate internal administrative reforms before, but with very mixed success (see Chapter 6). Radaelli (2010) argues that the Commission's DGs saw IA as an opportunity to revitalize these efforts, and invested human resources and expertise to conduct more and more IAs. In turn, these created new coordinating networks within the Commission. These have provided an opportunity for DGs to challenge each other's proposals, thus increasing the transparency and internal coordination (Radaelli, 2010: Radaelli and Meuwese, 2010) (see also Chapter 6). In addition, the Secretariat General of the Commission, which traditionally had played only an arbitration role, was able to function more like a cabinet office, supporting and in many ways overseeing the delivery of the priorities of the Commission's President (Radaelli, 2010: 100). So although the member states may have originally viewed IA as a means to control the Commission, the Commission has been able to use it to bolster its own internal coordinating capacity.

Summary points

- Early evaluations of the practice of IA in the EU revealed gaps between the stated aims and the everyday practices of IA; a rosier picture has emerged in more recent evaluations.

- Some academics question whether IA quality can be equated with 'better' policy. Their studies have revealed that IA only rarely leads to significant changes in policy.
- IA appears to have led to an (unintended) increase in the administrative capacity of the European Commission, in effect, making it more like a national 'cabinet office'.

Conclusion

The EU's policy-making process has traditionally lacked 'standard operating procedures' (Mazey and Richardson, 1992: 110). EU policy making in the environmental sphere has been widely depicted as being especially unpredictable, unstable and at times even chaotic. To an extent, this has facilitated the development of strong environmental rules. The design of IA, with its six-step process, appeared to offer a framework with which to proceduralize policy making. In many respects, these hopes have been realized. For example, IA has opened up the policy making process to other stakeholders and other policy makers. Inside the Commission, it has reduced the ability of one DG to catch the rest off guard. It is much more difficult nowadays for a policy proposal with significant impacts on another DG to appear 'out of the blue' at an Inter-Service Consultation. IA has thus increased the Commission's internal coordination capacity (Radaelli, 2010: 147) and arguably reduced DGs' ability to generate radical new environmental policies.

It is questionable, however, if IA has really imposed order on the 'messy reality' of policy making at EU level or made policy more evidence-based. First, the numerous weaknesses which have been extensively reported with regards to the quality of IA practice appear to bear this out. Second, the strong and continued political support for the better regulation agenda in the EU has resulted in IA becoming firmly institutionalized in the day-to-day activities of the Commission (European Court of Auditors, 2010: 6). However, IA has hardly been taken up in the European Parliament or the Council. It has also yet to be fully embedded across the entire policy-making cycle by linking it to *ex post* evaluation of policy implementation, as recommended by the European Court of Auditors (2010). IA is therefore very much the *Commission's* approach to policy appraisal, not the EU's. Consequently it is focused on one phase of the policy making – policy formulation – while almost entirely ignoring other important stages of the process, namely decision making, implementation and *ex post* evaluation. This would seem to lend support to the view that IA is more about controlling and managing the Commission than 'improving' the quality of EU policy making *per se*.

Perhaps more fundamentally, academic research continues to ask whether IA will ever really promote longer-term policy learning. As it is conceived and practised in the EU, IA is far too heavily based on a linear and rational model of policy making to achieve this. This model assumes that policy making occurs as a series of discrete and logical steps and that 'knowledge directly informs concrete decisions by providing specific information on the design of policies' (Hertin *et al.*, 2009: 1187). However, many academics sense that another model might be more applicable to IA: one where 'knowledge "enlightens" policy makers by slowly feeding new information, ideas and perspectives into the policy system' (ibid.: 1187). According to this model, the role of IA is not to identify the overall 'best' option through rational and linear assessment of objective information, but rather to inform and facilitate debate and critical reflection among many different players. The problem with this model is that it appears to assume away the existing power structures in the EU (i.e. many veto players working at different levels). In this context it is not at all surprising that IA has provided a new venue in which all the age-old tensions between economic, social and environmental objectives – the ones that have been present since the dawn of EU environmental policy – are constantly played out.

Summary points

- It is questionable whether IA has been able to impose a new 'standard operating procedure' on EU policy making.
- IA has bolstered the administrative capacity of the European Commission.
- However, the linear model of decision making on which IA is premised has not been able to fundamentally re-orientate the underlying power structures of the EU; policy making at EU level is still relatively messy and unpredictable.

Key questions

1 How does IA correspond to the two main phases of the EU's decision-making process?
2 How have tensions between the EU's better regulation and sustainable development agendas affected the design and everyday functioning of IA?
3 Why has the potential for IA to contribute to stronger environmental objectives not been fully realized?

Guide to further reading

Somewhat surprisingly, the literatures on EU's decision making and IA have evolved somewhat separately:

- Versluis *et al*. (2011) give a very readable account of policy making in the EU.
- Allio (2007) details the history of the EU's better regulation agenda and its influence on the spread of IA practices across Europe.
- For a review of the rapidly growing literature on IA, see Adelle *et al*. (2012).
- The European Commission (2011b) provides a website containing most relevant EU documents relating to IA, including all published IA reports, opinions and reports from the Impact Assessment Board as well as guidelines on how to conduct IAs.

References

Adelle, C., Jordan, A., and Turnpenny, J. (2012) 'Proceeding in parallel or drifting apart? A systematic review of policy appraisal research and practices', *Environment and Planning C*, 30, 3, 400–414.

Allio, L. (2007) 'Better regulation and impact assessment in the European Commission', in C. Kirkpatrick and D. Parker (eds) *Regulatory Impact Assessment: Towards Better Regulation?*, Edward Elgar, Cheltenham.

European Commission (2001) *White Paper on European Governance*, (COM (2001) 428), Commission of the European Communities, Brussels.

European Commission (2002a) *Impact Assessment*, (COM (2002) 276), Commission of the European Communities, Brussels.

European Commission (2002b) *European Governance: Better Law-Making*, (COM (2005) 275), Commission of the European Communities, Brussels.

European Commission (2004) *Impact Assessment: Next Steps in Support of Competitiveness and Sustainable Development*, (SEC (2004) 1377), Commission of the European Communities, Brussels.

European Commission (2005a) *Communication to the Spring European Council: Working Together for Growth and Jobs – A New Start for the Lisbon Strategy – Communication from President Barroso in Agreement with Vice-President Verheugen*, (COM (2005) 24), Commission of the European Communities, Brussels.

European Commission (2005b) *Better Regulation for Growth and Jobs in the European Union*, (COM (2005) 97), Commission of the European Communities, Brussels.

European Commission (2005c) *Impact Assessment Guidelines, 15 June 2005*, (SEC (2005) 791), Commission of the European Communities, Brussels.

European Commission (2005d) *Impact Assessment Guidelines, 15 June 2005 with 15 March 2006 Update on Procedural Rules*, (SEC (2005) 791), Commission of the European Communities, Brussels.

European Commission (2005e) *Impact Assessment Guidelines, 15 June 2005 with 15 March 2006 Update of Annex 10 Assessing Administrative Costs Imposed by Legislation*, (SEC (2005) 791), Commission of the European Communities, Brussels.

European Commission (2009a) *Impact Assessment Guidelines*, (SEC (2009) 92), Commission of the European Communities, Brussels.

European Commission (2009b) *Impact Assessment Review Board Report 2009*, (SEC (2009) 1728), Commission of the European Communities, Brussels.

European Commission (2011a) 'Strategic planning and programming', available at: http://ec.europa.eu/atwork/strategicplanning/index_en.htm (accessed 11 July 2011).

European Commission (2011b) 'Impact assessment', available at: http://ec.europa.eu/governance/impact/index_en.htm (accessed 22 July 2011).

European Commission (2011c) *Impact Assessment Review Board Report 2010*, (SEC (2011) 126), Commission of the European Communities, Brussels.

European Commission (n.d.) *Impact Assessment: Technical Guidelines*, European Commission, Brussels.

European Commission, European Parliament and the EU Council (2005) 'Common approach to impact assessment', available at: http://ec.europa.eu/governance/better_regulation/documents/ii_common_approach_to_ia_en.pdf (accessed 12 July 2011).

European Council (2000) *Presidency Conclusions, Lisbon European Council, 23–24 March 2000*, European Council, Brussels.

European Council (2001) *Presidency Conclusions, Gothenburg European Council, 15–16 June 2001*, European Council, Brussels.

European Court of Auditors (2010) *Impact Assessments in the EU Institutions: Do They Support Decision-Making?*, Special Report No. 3 2010, European Court of Auditors, Luxembourg.

Farmer, A. (ed.) (2011) *Manual of European Environmental Policy*, Taylor & Francis, London, available at: http://www.europeanenvironmentalpolicy.eu/ (accessed 10 October 2011).

Hardacre, A. and Kaeding, M. (2011) 'Delegated and implementing acts: the new world of comitology – implications for European and national public administrations', *Eipascope*, no. 2011, pp. 29–32.

Héritier, A. (2002) 'The accommodation of diversity in European policy-making and its outcomes: regulatory policy as a patchwork', in A. Jordan (ed.) *Environmental Policy in the European Union*, Earthscan, London, pp. 180–197.

Hertin, J., Turnpenny, J., Jordan, A., Nilsson, M., Russel, D. and Nykvist, B. (2009) 'Rationalising the policy mess? Ex ante assessment and the utilisation of knowledge in the policy process', *Environment and Planning A*, vol. 41, pp. 1185–1200.

Hertin, J., Wilksinson, D., Bartolomeo, M., Jacob, K. and Volkery, A. (2004) *Making EU Policies Sustainable? The New Impact Assessment Procedure in the European Commission*, SPRU, University of Sussex, Brighton.

Jacob, K., Hertin, J., Hjerp, P., Radaelli, C., Meuwese, A., Wolf, O., Pacchi, C. and Rennings, K. (2008) *Improving the Practice of Impact Assessment*, EVIA (Evaluating Integrated Impact Assessments), Project No. 028889, European Commission Sixth Framework Programme, European Commission, Brussels.

Jordan, A. and Schout, A. (2006) *The Coordination of the European Union: Exploring the Capacities of Networked Governance*, Oxford University Press, Oxford.

Jordan, A., Huitema, D., van Asselt, H., Rayner, T., and Berhout, F. (2010) *Climate Change Policy in the European Union: Confronting the Dilemmas of Mitigation and Adaptation?* Cambridge University Press, Cambridge.

Knill, C. and Liefferink, D. (2007) *Environmental Politics in the European Union: Policy-Making, Implementation and Patterns of Multi-Level Governance*, Manchester University Press, Manchester.

Lee, N., and Kirkpatrick, C. (2004) 'A pilot study of the quality of European Commission Extended Impact Assessments', Impact Assessment Research Centre, Working Paper Series, Paper No. 8, Institute for Development Policy and Management, Manchester.

Lelieveldt, H. and Princen, S. (2011) *The Politics of the European Union*, Cambridge University Press, Cambridge.

Lofstedt, R. E. (2007) 'The "plateau-ing" of the European better regulation agenda: an analysis of activities carried out by the Barroso Commission', *Journal of Risk Research*, vol. 10, no. 4, pp. 423–447.

Majone, G. (2006) 'The common sense of European integration', *Journal of European Public Policy*, vol. 13, no. 5, pp. 607–626.

Mazey, S. and Richardson, J. (1992) 'Environmental groups and the EC: challenges and opportunities', *Environmental Politics*, vol. 1, no. 4, pp. 109–128.

McCormick, J. (2001) *Environmental Policy in the European Union*, Palgrave, Basingstoke.

Nielsen, U., Lerche, D.B., Kjellingbro, P.M. and Jeppesen, L.M. (2006) *Getting Proportions Right: How Far Should EU Impact Assessment Go?*, Environmental Assessment Institute, Copenhagen.

Radaelli, C.M. (2007) 'Whither better regulation for the Lisbon Agenda?', *Journal of European Public Policy*, vol. 14, no. 2, pp. 190–207.

Radaelli, C.M. (2010) 'Regulating rule-making via impact assessment', *Governance: An International Journal of Policy, Administration, and Institutions*, vol. 23, pp. 89–108.

Radaelli, C.M. and Meuwese, A.C.M. (2010) 'Hard questions, hard solutions: proceduralisation through impact assessment in the EU', *West European Politics*, vol. 33, pp. 136–153.

Renda, A. (2006) *Impact Assessment in the EU: The State of the Art and the Art of the State*, Centre for European Policy Studies, Brussels.

TEP (The Evaluation Partnership) (2007) *Evaluation of the Commission's Impact Assessment System*, report written for the European Commission, Contract Number SG-02/2006, European Commission, Brussels.

Versluis, E., van Keulen, M. and Stephenson, P. (2011) *Analyzing the European Union Policy Process*, Palgrave Macmillan, Basingstoke.

Wallace, H. (2010) 'An institutional anatomy and five policy modes', in H. Wallace, M.A. Pollack, and A.R. Young, *Policy Making in the European Union*, 6th edition, Oxford University Press, Oxford, pp. 69–104.

Weale, A. (2005) 'Environmental rules and rule-making in the European Union', in A. Jordan (ed.) *Environmental Policy in the European Union*, 2nd edition, Earthscan, London, pp. 125–140.

Wilkinson, D. (1997) 'Towards sustainability in the European Union? Steps within the European Commission towards integrating the environment into other European Union policy sectors', *Environmental Politics*, vol. 6, no. 1, pp. 153–173.

Wilkinson, D., Fergusson, M., Bowyer, C., Brown, J., Ladefoged, A., Monkhouse, C. and Zdanowicz, A. (2004) *Sustainable Development in the European Commission's Integrated Impact Assessment for 2003*, IEEP, London.

Young, A. (2010) 'The European policy process in comparative perspective', in H. Wallace, M.A. Pollack and A.R. Young, *Policy Making in the European Union*, 6th edition, Oxford University Press, Oxford, pp. 45–69.

13 Policy coordination

*Andrew Jordan, Adriaan Schout
and Martin Unfried*

Summary guide

The EU has made a significant effort to engage in a particular type of policy coordination, namely, the integration of environmental thinking into the operation of all policy sectors. The potential of environmental policy integration is undoubtedly ambitious: economically powerful sectors such as agriculture, energy and transport should 'design out' environmental problems in the development of their own policies. However, it has proven much harder to implement than many had originally expected, not least those working in the European Commission's Environment Directorate General. A significant causal factor here has been the EU's fragmented institutional and political structure, which, on the one hand, has facilitated the adoption of visionary policy coordination objectives, but, on the other, has also undermined their implementation.

Introduction

There are several good reasons to expect the EU to be relatively good at one particular aspect of policy coordination, namely the integration of an environmental dimension into the work of all policy sectors. It has a very extensive and innovative system of environmental policy dating back over 30 years. It has also done a great deal to popularize the idea of environmental policy integration at a global level (Lenschow, 2002; Jordan and Lenschow, 2010). Indeed, environmental policy integration (or EPI) is a long-standing aim of EU policy – older even than that of sustainable development (see Chapter 19). The EU's political commitment to EPI is relatively strong and precisely expressed in the heading of the 1997 Amsterdam Treaty. Article 6 states that 'environmental protection requirements *must* be integrated into the definition and implementation of . . . Community policies . . . *in particular with a view to promoting sustainable development*' (emphasis added). Lawyers believe that Article 6 represents 'the only constitutional document' in the world where EPI has been given 'explicit expression in law' (Macrory, 1999: 173).

However, this quasi-constitutional commitment to EPI has proven to be much harder to implement than many people had originally expected. The European Commission has openly conceded that many of the EU's most important sectoral policies (e.g. transport, agriculture and energy) fundamentally undermine EPI (COM (2004) 394 final: 5–8). From the environmental side, the verdicts have been similarly critical. One eminent EU environmental lawyer has concluded that Article 6 remains 'an empty shell which has not had much substantive content' (Krämer, 2005: 555) and Weale and Williams (1992: 49) have described the EU's implementation of EPI as a 'faltering and haphazard affair'. The head of the European Environment Bureau of environmental pressure groups, John Hontelez (2005: 397), believes that 'actual EPI' in the EU is 'still in its infancy'. And having completed a more comprehensive assessment of environmental trends in the EU, the European Environment Agency (EEA) (2003: 7) has suggested that the 'implementation of more integrated approaches . . . needs to be accelerated if Europe is . . . to meet its aspirations on sectoral integration and sustainable development'.

This chapter seeks to describe what the EU has – and has not – done to implement EPI over the past 30 years, and searches for underlying causes for the overall pattern of (in)activity. Although the relationship between national and EU level EPI initiatives is one of deep interdependence (Jordan and Schout, 2006), we primarily will focus on what the EU has done to nurture EPI at EU level.

The rest of our argument unfolds as follows. The next section describes the political and institutional situation in the EU. We then chart the changing ways in which the EU has thought about and sought to apply the EPI principle. We show that the EU's response can be broken down into five phases. In the following section, we describe the various instruments that the EU has deployed, and then assess how effectively this has been done. In the final section, we summarize the most noteworthy features of the EU involvement with the EPI principle and draw together some concluding thoughts.

History

The EU: a unique institutional and political setting?

The EU does not find it at all difficult to make ambitious political and legal commitments to things like EPI and sustainability (see Chapter 19). But when it comes to implementing EPI, there are a number of reasons why it has struggled more than some other political systems (Jordan and Lenschow, 2008; 2010). According to two experts in administrative and policy coordination (Peters and Wright, 2001: 158), 'Managing the problems of fragmentation, sectoralization and policy interdependence is not peculiar to Brussels, but the extent and nature of these problems in Brussels are of a different order from that prevailing in the member states'. One cannot possibly begin to understand why this is the case without first understanding the history and institutional make-up of the EU.

First and foremost, one needs to be aware of the very complex way in which legal competences are shared across different sectors and levels of governance in the EU, the relatively weak capacity for central leadership, and the presence of deeply 'pillarised' (Peterson, 1997: 5) policy-making structures (Peters and Wright, 2001: 161). Whether one regards the EU as a political system (Hix, 2005), a proto federal nation state (Moravcsik, 2005: 1) or a deeply integrated international organization, one thing is now almost universally accepted – it is not 'a state'. It is very telling that the term 'multi-level governance' was originally coined to describe the *sui generis* nature of the EU (Jordan, 2001). The EU does not, for example, have a coherent 'core executive' or coordinating centre like most sovereign states. The European Commission may be the font of most formal policy initiatives (see Chapter 6) and it may also administer many important aspects of the EU's day-to-day activities (e.g. policy implementation), but it operates 'without the government – the prime minister, cabinet – which gives meaning to the core executive in a traditional governmental structure with a public administration as traditionally understood' (Sbragia, 2002: 3). If the EU has a 'cabinet', it is the European Council (see Chapter 5). But this body meets too infrequently to secure a firm grip on the detail of policy making (Bomberg, 2004: 70). Political leadership (a *sine qua non* of effective coordination – Peters, 1998), therefore, is fragmented across a number of different locations – the Commission, the Presidency and of course the European Council itself. In theory, there is one Council of Ministers, but in practice most of its activities are strongly divided into different sectoral formations and this 'has tended to work against the effective integration of environmental considerations across the EU's main policy sectors' (Haigh, 2005: 3.11–17). Therefore, the basic institutional impediments to EPI at national level are not simply reproduced at EU level, but appear there in an even more accentuated form. In the absence of a core executive, 'turf battles' are 'frequent' and the sectoral 'firewalls' are 'high and often impermeable' (Peterson, 1997: 5).

Second, the EU is undeniably a very strong force for higher environmental standards at national (Jordan and Liefferink, 2004) and international levels (Sbragia, 2005), but at heart it remains a system of 'economic governance' (Bomberg, 2004: 62). Although the quest for a single integrated market in Europe has forced policy makers to develop common environmental rules (Weale *et al.*, 2000; Lenschow, 2005), the core principles – what Sbragia (2000: 223) terms its 'constitutional order' – are those of international economic competitiveness, market liberalization and, ultimately, economic growth. Bomberg's (2004: 89) argument that these 'render any dramatic shift' to sustainability 'unlikely', is equally applicable to the (intimately interlinked) principle of EPI.

Finally, the EU's legal capacity (or competence) to develop environmental rules has gradually evolved over the past 30 years (see Chapter 7), to the extent that most if not all national policy is developed by or in close collaboration with EU actors. By contrast, many of the so-called 'driving force' sectors of environmental damage such as transport or energy production are not nearly as deeply controlled by the EU institutions (Jordan and Lenschow, 2000). Consequently, the EU's competence to intervene in the social, economic and environmental spheres of sustainability is asymmetrically distributed (Wurzel, 2001: 14). So, when the EEA reports that 'much more needs to be done to achieve an effective integration of environmental actions into the "driving forces" of economic sectors' (EEA, 1998: 285), there is only so much that the EU can do to respond. Crucially, therefore, the EU is handicapped by its fragmented institutional structure when it comes to implementing (as distinct from committing itself to) EPI (OECD, 2001: 47; European Commission, 2004: 15).

Summary points

- The EU finds it relatively easy to adopt ambitious political and legal commitments to things like EPI.
- However, in practice, the EU struggles to coordinate its own policy activities; at heart, it remains a systems of economic not environmental governance.
- Policy coordination in the EU is a shared challenge – it requires actors at different levels of governance and in different sectors to work together.

Responding to EPI

1970–1987: from awareness raising to legal codification

The history of the EU's engagement with the EPI principle dates back at least as far as the First Environmental Action Programme (EAP) in 1973 (Lenschow, 2002: 3). Of all the EU institutions, the Commission stands out as having been the most consistently forceful advocate of EPI. At first, however, DG Environment struggled to sell even the principle of better integration to other parts of the Commission, let alone the rest of the EU. EPI was, for instance, mentioned in the Fourth EAP. This formally committed the Commission to developing internal procedures to institutionalize EPI, but these were not announced until the next EAP (the Fifth) in 1992 (Wilkinson, 1997: 157). Undaunted, DG Environment drew fresh political support from the publication of the Brundtland Report in 1987. An important step had, however, already been taken in 1985, when EPI was incorporated into the draft text of the 1987 Single European Act (Article 130r), largely it has to be said, at DG Environment's insistence.

1987–1996: deeper institutionalization of the EPI principle

As several member states began to explore different ways of incorporating EPI into their own national policy systems (see Jordan and Schout, 2006), DG Environment was able to muster political support to get the EU's quasi-constitutional commitment to EPI tightened up. This was eventually achieved via a new treaty (the Maastricht Treaty), which stipulated that 'environmental protection *must* be integrated into the definition and implementation of other Community policies' (Article 130r [2]) (emphasis added). EPI's transformation into a fully-fledged political objective of European political integration was completed in 1999 when this form of wording was inserted into Article 6 of the Amsterdam Treaty (see also Chapter 3).

Lawyers regarded the adoption of Article 6 as a very significant legal and policy development (Macrory, 1999: 173), elevating EPI from being just a narrow, 'environmental' concept, into an overarching legal principle of European integration. Well before this, however, DG Environment had tried to develop internal procedures to implement EPI internally. The Fifth EAP outlined a number of internal reforms including a new integration unit and a policy appraisal system covering all new legislative proposals (see Chapter 12). However, for reasons that are more fully elaborated below, the outcome of these reforms was rather disappointing (Wilkinson, 1997). Moreover, other than issue declarations in the European Council stressing the political importance of EPI, the member states did very little to ensure that their national EPI systems were adequately coordinated with the EU's (Schout and Jordan, 2005).

1996–1998: integration programmes and strategies

In the mid-1990s, the accession into the EU of three new advocates of EPI (namely the post-1995 member states of Sweden, Austria and Finland), gave the debate about how to implement EPI a strong fillip. With their assistance, DG Environment was able to produce a very ambitious Communication in 1998, entitled a 'Partnership for Integration' (COM [98] 333: 3). This marked a new and much more purposeful phase in the life of EPI in the EU. Henceforth, many new actors, most notably the Heads of State, the European Parliament and the Council of Ministers, were drawn into a common process of sectoral reporting, reviewing and target setting known as the Cardiff Process, a reference to the location of the June 1998 European Council. Initially, it was a partnership involving just three sectors, but was later expanded to include another six.

1998–2001: a proliferation of coordination strategies?

At first, hopes were high that the self-imposed discipline of writing and sharing integration strategies would generate new information, intra-sectoral learning and, eventually, a new and pervasive sense of commitment in the sectors to own environmental problems, one that had previously been very weak (Wilkinson *et al.*, 2002: 5). Crucially, DG Environment found itself playing a different role. That is to say, rather than prescribe standards from the outside, the Cardiff Process aimed to initiate a self-sustaining process of inter-sectoral and inter-institutional learning and acting. But as is now widely known, the resulting strategies eventually failed to live up to these high expectations.

2001–2006: retrenchment and regulatory reform

In response to these problems as well as a growing political appetite for 'Better' (that is less environmental) EU regulation (see below), DG Environment began to channel its energies away from Cardiff (which was perceived to be failing) to the EU's emerging Sustainable Development Strategy (SDS), its Sixth EAP and processes of regulatory streamlining. Published by the Commission in the run-up to the 2002 Johannesburg summit, the SDS was not produced in a particularly coordinated manner (see Chapter 19). Hinterberger and Zacherl (2003: 15) argue that key inconsistencies – such as the ecologically harmful subsidies paid by the EU to the energy, fisheries and agricultural sectors – were glossed over, and the promise to include ambitious targets and timetables dropped (Wurzel, 2001: 14). Moreover, insufficient thought was given to how it would eventually dovetail with the other main strands of the EU's wider sustainability programme, namely the Sixth EAP, the Lisbon and, of course, the Cardiff Processes. The relationship was clarified somewhat during a review of the EU SDS in 2005, but there have been few attempts to assess the extent to which it – or its successor (published in 2006) – contribute to – or even undermine – EPI (Pallemaerts *et al.*, 2007: 6).

Summary

Already, a number of underlying themes should be obvious in relation to the overall pattern of response in the EU. First, while the *principle* of EPI has achieved greater legal force and clarity over the past 30 years, it is by no means obvious who or what is primarily responsible for implementing it. Jans (2000: 22), for example, argues that Article 6 has no direct legal consequences for member states, because it refers only to '*Community* policies and activities' (emphasis added). But later, he concedes that there may be important *indirect* consequences for member states in relation to the implementation of EU legislation. By contrast, Kraemer *et al.* (2001: 44) argue that states must *de facto* accept some responsibility for Article 6, because they implement the policies decided centrally in the EU. It is also unclear whether Article 6 could ever be used to mount a legal challenge against environmentally damaging activities pursued by the sectoral formations of the Council or a particular member state (Grimeaud, 2000). This lack of legal clarity has undoubtedly made it easier for different parts of the EU selectively to reinterpret EPI to suit their purposes.

Second, strong *conceptual* links between EPI and sustainable development have been made in various EAPs as well as the founding treaties of the EU (most specifically in Article 6 – see above). In one recent review of the implementation of the EPI principle, Wilkinson (1998: 113) concluded that it was a 'fundamental prerequisite for sustainable development'. Bomberg (2004: 72) similarly concludes that EPI is 'the' key substantive principle of sustainability in the EU. In practice, the EU has (as we shall explain more fully below) tended to treat EPI and sustainability as somewhat separate policy challenges. Thus, EPI is addressed by the Cardiff Process and its various reports, strategies and stocktakes, on the one hand, whereas sustainability is chiefly a matter for the SDS. According to

Pallemaerts *et al.* (2007: 34), the most positive thing that can be said about the relationship between EPI and the EU SDS is that it is 'ambivalent'.

Third, very few EU-level actors are anywhere as committed to EPI as DG Environment. In fact, many parts of the Commission regard it at best as essentially unimportant and at worst as something to be neutered. Crucially, the dominant axis of political and administrative support continues to run from the (environmental parts of the) Commission through to the (Environment) Council. It is especially strange that the European Parliament has only been very partially engaged in the Cardiff and Lisbon Processes, despite being one of the most consistent and forceful champions of higher environmental standards in the EU (see Chapter 8), and the main architect of its green budgeting system (see Wilkinson *et al.*, 2008). It has, for example, never initiated an internal review of the steps it could in principle take to facilitate greater EPI (Jordan and Schout, 2006). A similar pattern of (dis)engagement is apparent across the various policy sectors. Agriculture, energy, industry and transport were the initial targets of the Cardiff Process. These sectors were also identified by the Fifth EAP. By contrast, the financial, fisheries, social, tourism and employment sectors were either not initially identified or have never been formally targeted by either initiative.

Summary points

- The EU has been struggling to implement the principle of EPI since the 1970s.
- These efforts reached a high point in the late 1990s, when the EU adopted the Cardiff Process of cross-sectoral integration.
- However, in the 2000s, doubts began to set in about who was really responsible and whether the EU's ambitions were really achievable.

EPI in practice

Administrative instruments

Only a relatively small number of administrative instruments have been deployed at EU level. There is, for example, no high-level environmental cabinet committee in the EU. There is, of course, the European Council, but other than issue political declarations that either stress the continuing political importance of EPI or request other EU-level actors to respond, it has not played a direct role. There is also no high-level committee or department in the EU overseeing the implementation of EPI. The General Affairs Council was given a loose coordinating role in relation to Cardiff, but 'this has consisted of little more than the development of a road map setting out the relevant policy issues where the environment is relevant' (EEA, 2005b: 29). As enthusiasm for the Cardiff Process waned in the driving force sectors, environmentalists called for new administrative capacities to be created in the apex of the EU. These included an 'Article 6 Committee' to coordinate and inform the Council of Ministers (Kraemer *et al.*, 2002: 5; Kraemer *et al.*, 2001: 45–46). At the time of writing, none of these suggestions on how to green the EU's 'core executive' has been formally adopted.

Consequently, the closest that the EU has to a high-level environment cabinet committee is probably the Environment Council. However, this is primarily sectoral in nature (it comprises national environment ministers) (see Chapter 5) and as such, is not really in an ideal position to pursue EPI. In fact, Sbragia (2000: 300) argues that its sectoral isolation has allowed (environment) ministers to adopt much more ambitious environmental legislation at EU level than they could have in their respective cabinets back home: that is, by behaving in precisely the same poorly coordinated manner as other Councils. There is a tradition of two or more councils meeting informally (e.g. transport and environment), but as this normally depends on support from a particular Presidency, it is not an especially robust or enduring means of pursuing EPI (Wurzel, 2001).

The EU-level actor which has done the most to utilize administrative and bureaucratic instruments in pursuit of EPI is, perhaps not surprisingly, its main administrative body – the European Commission. These measures have included the creation of a sustainable development/integration unit in DG Environment and a network of environmental correspondents spanning the various DGs (Wilkinson, 1997: 162). How effective have these been? The integration unit has never been that well resourced or politically supported by the apex of DG Environment. The upper echelons of DG Environment do not appear to have ever favoured a 'policing' role, perceiving their primary role to be that of producing new environment policy. Moreover, EPI implies frequent intervention in the work of other DGs, but this goes against the tradition of respecting 'turf' boundaries in the Commission. The unit has not even enjoyed consistent leadership – there have been frequent changes of head of unit. Meanwhile, the correspondents were supposed to make the organization more transparent and reduce coordination costs, but they found it hard to promote EPI in battles between different DGs.

It is fair to say that neither initiative has ever commanded sufficient support from the apex of the Commission. They were part of a package of internal measures listed in the Fifth EAP that were allegedly adopted after 'very little discussion' among the various DGs. Consequently, 'most Commissioners seem not to have properly absorbed their full implications' (ibid.: 160). And even if they had worked perfectly, they would not have been sufficient because EPI at EU level is a multi-actor challenge. The Commission can try all that it likes to produce perfectly coordinated proposals for new legislation (see Chapter 12), but EPI will fail to take root in the EU if other actors continue to have ample opportunities to unpick them later on in the policy process.

Green budgeting

Because around 80 per cent of the EU's annual budget is spent on agriculture and regional development, the opportunities for employing this particular instrument are potentially quite good. In 1975, the European Parliament (or more correctly, its budgetary committee) was given a number of powers, including the right to approve, or not to approve the way in which the Commission spends this money (Judge and Earnshaw, 2004: 37). Following an environmental pressure group campaign in the 1980s, DG Environment and the European Parliament started to work together to turn this 'power of the purse' (Wilkinson, 1997: 166) to environmental ends. One of the most obvious effects has been to ensure that all projects and programmes funded by the Cohesion and Structural Funds now require an environmental appraisal. If the Parliament feels these are not satisfactory, it has the power to block spending (see Lenschow, 1999).

In a more recent development, EU financial support for regional and agricultural projects was tied to adequate compliance with the Habitat, Nitrates and Birds Directives (this conditionality is known as 'cross-compliance'). From 2000, approval of Structural Funding was made contingent upon adequate implementation of the Habitats and Birds Directives (Haigh, 2005: 3.11–14). This was subsequently extended to agricultural spending under the Rural Development Regulation (ibid.: 3.11–14). For a more detailed summary of green budgeting activities in the EU, see Wilkinson *et al.* (2008).

Strategies and/or strategy developing processes

Four strategic EU-level initiatives fall under this sub-heading: (1) the Fifth EAP; (2) the Cardiff Process; (3) the Lisbon Process; and (4) the Sixth EAP.

The *Fifth EAP* was adopted just three months before the Rio conference (Wilkinson, 1997: 158) and was subsequently re-badged as the EU's response to the sustainability agenda. It laid out some medium- and long-term targets for reducing key pollutants, and recommended some appropriate instruments, including some new environmental policy instruments such as eco-taxes. However, its targets were not binding. In fact, it was not even completely clear to whom the entire programme was formally addressed. See, for example, the ambiguous wording of the Council's Resolution on the Fifth EAP (*Official Journal* C138/1 17-5-93). The UK Environment Ministry produced an implementation report (DoE, 1994) and a number of other member states initiated national sustainable development strategies, but they were in the minority and the Commission lacked the power to improve the situation. A 1994 review concluded gloomily that 'sustainable development essentially continues to be seen as the business of those who deal with the environment' (COM [94] 453). In 1996, the Commission approved a progress report (COM [95] 624, final), which revealed how little had been achieved across the EU. A range of other stakeholders reached much more critical assessments during a wide-ranging review process organized by DG Environment, dubbed 'the Global Assessment'. In his assessment, Wilkinson (1997: 164) concluded that any integration generated during this period was 'as much the consequence of exogenous factors [e.g. the global competitiveness pressures on the Common Agricultural Policy] as of [DG Environment's] measures'.

The adoption of the *Cardiff Process* is symptomatic of a wider change in the EU towards 'soft' or networked forms of coordination (Stubb *et al.*, 2003: 152; see also Jordan and Schout, 2006). These typically involve states mimicking one another's best practices via peer review, benchmarking and policy learning activities in a way that induces *voluntary* policy coordination (Scott and Trubek, 2002: 5–6). They seek to build upon the EU's existing coordinating capacity not by legislating (as in the Community Method), but via more '*networked*' forms of multi-level governance (Stubb *et al.*, 2003: 148). When it was launched, the Cardiff Process was vaunted as 'one of the EU's "big ideas" on environment' (ENDS *Europe Daily*, No. 1679, 3 June 2004). But the initial strategies produced by the sectors were very poorly received (Fergusson *et al.*, 2001; Jordan and Schout, 2006). The sectors presented their policies as 'given' and hence not open to any substantial change (i.e. integration) to achieve EPI. By late 2002, the production of new strategies and/or the updating of existing ones had all but ceased, as the entire process began to fall into the long shadow cast by the newly emerging *Lisbon Process* on social and economic reform. The EEA (2003: 272) subsequently concluded that 'the [Cardiff] process . . . lacked urgency and has yet to have a significant impact on sectoral policy making, let alone on improvements on the ground'. A stocktake undertaken by DG Environment in 2003–2004 concluded that that EPI was 'still largely to be translated into further concrete results for the environment . . . [and] . . . has failed to deliver fully on expectations' (COM (2004) 394, final: 31).

With hindsight, failure was always the most likely outcome because a number of hugely important issues had not been properly clarified at the start. For example, the process failed to fully engage several key actors, namely the European Parliament and the member states. It also relied heavily upon the different sectors of the Council producing and evaluating their own strategies. DG Environment was an obvious candidate to fulfil the role of network manager (that is a *primus inter pares* capable of leading from the front, resolving conflicts and maintaining momentum), but neither it nor the Environment Council were asked to take on this job by the European Council. Worse still, no one was really sure if the process had an end point or how (or by whom) its performance would eventually be assessed. Formally, the Cardiff Process is still alive, but politically speaking it is dead in the water.

Established in 2000, the *Lisbon Process* aims to make the EU 'the most competitive and dynamic knowledge-based economy in the world, capable of sustainable economic growth with more and better jobs and greater social cohesion'. Its appearance reflected a growing concern among some of the larger member states that what the EU needed most was 'old-fashioned' economic growth to provide more jobs, not EPI or, for that matter, sustainable development. To the very great disappointment of many environmentalists, at first the Lisbon Process made only very passing references to environmental protection. In 2003, DG Environment complained that 'to many actors the environment still appears as an "add-on"' to the annual synthesis reports that are submitted to the European Council each Spring (COM (2003) 745, final). The 2001 Swedish Presidency eventually succeeded in retrofitting Lisbon with an environmental dimension (Hinterberger and Zacherl, 2003). So, rather late in the day, DG Environment started (in 2003) to produce the first of what has become an annual Environmental Policy Review to feed into the production of the Lisbon synthesis reports. Nonetheless, the Lisbon Process continues to be skewed heavily in the direction of economy and growth. The current list of 14 indicators of progress includes only one direct environmental indicator (greenhouse gas emissions) and two indirect ones (energy intensity and transport volume).

Finally, the EU's EAPs have taken the form of 'lists of proposed legislation often selected in response to events' (Wilkinson, 1997: 158). Traditionally, they had no legal force; instead they sought to identify new strategic directions for EU environmental policy to follow. By contrast, *the Sixth EAP*, which covers the period 2002–2012, was shorter and had legal force, but contained no new targets and timetables. The Commission said that they would be elaborated in a series of Thematic Strategies drawn up after extensive negotiation with different stake-holders, and covering broad, thematic topics such as marine areas, soil and air quality. The Thematic Strategies could be seen as another step in the direction of more inclusive and networked forms of EPI, i.e. they seek to build better linkages between different policies by bringing together all the relevant DGs to support their design and implementation. DG Environment hoped they would provide a 'test bed for [more] innovative approaches' to EPI (COM (2004) 394 final: 35). However, their publication was repeatedly delayed during 2005, as DG Environment came under intense pressure from other DGs to water them down (Wilkinson *et al.*, 2005). At the time of writing, it is still too early to reach a definitive judgment on their overall quality, but the early indications are that the participation of many stakeholders and sectors has 'contributed to a reduction in the level of ambition of the EU's environment policy' (Wilkinson, 2007: 23).

In the mid-2000s, the Commission tried to dovetail these and several other strategy processes into the Lisbon Process, which in 2005 was re-launched as the EU's Partnership for Growth and Jobs (COM (2005) 24) – a title which appeared to further downplay the environmental dimensions of sustainability. In June 2005, the Director General of environmental protection in DG Environment openly admitted that while 'the idea of integration is very much alive . . . the Cardiff Process is not going anywhere' (ENDS Ltd., No. 365: 24).

Policy appraisal systems

Formal policy appraisal did not take root in EU environmental policy making as early as it did at the national level (Pearce, 1998) (see Chapter 12). However, as part of the package of measures adopted in the early 1990s (see above), the Commission pledged to appraise all new proposals for environmental impacts (COM (97) 1844/1 and 2). In a wide-ranging assessment, Wilkinson (1997: 163) struggled to find a single DG that had produced an environmental appraisal of one of its proposals. The lead DGs in the sectors evidently saw no reason to produce them, and in any case DG Environment had not put in place the relevant methodologies and support systems.

In the early 2000s, the Commission sought to learn from these problems by moving onto what has come to be known as Impact Assessment (IA) (see Chapter 12). The Gothenburg European Council in June 2001 had originally called upon the Commission to subject all major new policy processes to a *Sustainability* Impact Assessment. A few months later, the Commission issued a Communication (COM (2001) 726) setting out the basic approach it intended to follow. But when it finally issued a set of formal proposals (COM (2002) 276), it was simply referred to as 'impact assessment', the 'S' having been ditched during internal, inter-DG negotiations (see Chapter 12).

Despite some critical early reports on its performance (Wilkinson *et al.*, 2004), the new IA system does have a much higher political profile outside DG Environment than its predecessor, Green Star. According to the Commission's own assessment, it successfully contributes to a culture of greater transparency and more formalized policy planning and evaluation (SEC (2004) 1377: 4). But whether it leads to greater EPI at the level of individual sectoral policy proposals is still far from clear. In 2004, the regime was 'refocused to give greater attention to factors that are widely considered to be important to productivity and hence to the competitiveness of the EU' (COM SEC (2004) 1377: 5). Even more importantly, it remains primarily an EU-level instrument. There are, for example, no structured arrangements for involving member state authorities in the production of IAs, even though they may possess far more detailed information on the likely impact of particular proposals than Commission officials working centrally in Brussels (Wilkinson *et al.*, 2004: 33). And even if policy appraisal in the Commission was perfect (the early indications are that it is not – Wilkinson *et al.*, 2004: 5), it will never be a panacea when EPI is a multi-actor and multi-levelled problem.

Strategic environmental assessment

The EU does have a formal system of Strategic Environmental Assessment (SEA), but it applies to member state not EU-level activities and, even then, primarily to projects rather than policies and programmes. Meanwhile, the EU does not formally subject all its policies to SEA. Nonetheless, many EU-level activities have been identified as needing SEAs. Trans-European Transport Networks (TEN-T, a key element of the European transport policy) were seen as good candidates for SEA. However, despite significant debate in the European Parliament, the Commission and at member state level, an SEA of the TEN-T has yet to be carried out. Some DGs have chosen to undertake sustainability impact assessments on their policy activities (e.g. on international trade agreement, see Lee and Kirkpatrick, 2001), but generally the EU seems to have turned its back on SEA in favour of IA, presumably because it provides a better coverage of the politically important social and the economic dimensions of sustainability.

Summary points

- The EU has employed a whole host of different mechanisms to achieve greater EPI.
- However, most of these have been of a relatively 'soft' format, such as strategies development and reports.
- One of the early hopes – sustainability impact assessment – covering all new policy proposals (see Chapter 12), was systematically undermined by more powerful policy DGs.

Discussion

There are a number of points that emerge from our analysis of the various ways in which the EU has sought to implement EPI. The first is that the main drivers of EPI have mostly been environmental in nature, namely environmental pressure groups, environmental agencies and environmental ministries at national level. Chief among these has been the Commission's DG Environment, whose crowning achievement was probably the adoption of Article 6. But as the sectors have gradually become more aware of the potential long-term implications of Article 6, so they have made ever-stronger attempts to neutralize it. In many ways, the political debate in the EU has moved in their favour, now that many influential actors see increasing global economic competition as the most significant threat to Europe's continuing prosperity and way of life. ENDS *Europe Daily* (No. 1679, 3 June 2004) concluded that 'The debate [is now] ... less of integrating environment into sectoral policies, and more of reverse integrating competitiveness into EU environmental policies'. In this sense, the debate in the 1990s (which was essentially about integrating environment into the sectors) has turned around: now, DG Environment finds itself under growing pressure to fight its corner in a three-way battle with those representing the economy and social pillars of sustainability. In some cases, it has had its work cut out simply to defend the existing environmental *acquis communautaire* against those arguing that it threatened employment prospects and economic growth (SEC (2005) 1530; COM (2006) 70). Many of these arguments have been marshalled under the banner of 'Better Regulation', which in practical terms has meant the streamlining, simplification and possible repeal of existing environmental laws (Wilkinson *et al*., 2005; COM (2005) 535; COM (2005) 462). The 2000s witnessed the decline of the Cardiff Process, the re-focusing of the Lisbon Process onto jobs and growth, and DG Environment searching ever harder for less intrusive ways to implement EPI. Cardiff tried to push the sectors into 'owning' their environmental problems, but failed to make much headway. The EU SDS has since emerged to take its place, but 'seems rather remote to sectoral policy makers' (Pallemaerts *et al*., 2007: 34). Whichever way one looks at it, the environmental sector has largely failed to get the sectors to 'own' (let alone implement) EPI.

External political pressure – particularly that generated by the environmental pressure groups – played a successful part in raising the political and legal profile of EPI, but there are clear limits to what it can achieve when EU policy making is so spatially and temporally expansive. There is simply too much going on in the EU for the environmental groups to campaign on everything: they have to be selective. This brings us to our second point, which is that, apart from DG Environment (which is a relatively small and politically weak part of the Commission), there is still no clear and consistent political leadership on EPI coming from the EU's 'core executive' (EEA, 2005a: 34): DG Environment is essentially being left to fight its own corner in battles with the other sectors. It is certainly hard to think of a Commission President or head of state in the past decade who has powerfully and consistently championed the twin causes of EPI and sustainability. Far from it: many parts of the EU expect Commission officials to act as the legal and political guardian of EPI, because they often lack the time or the incentives to do this for themselves. The Commission – and principally DG Environment – has sought to develop this guardianship role, for example, through the EAPs and Article 6. However, DG Environment has discovered (to its great cost) that if it does the running on EPI, the other actors tend not to feel so compelled to pay attention to it. In practice, the only significant source of political leadership has had to come from the member state holding the EU Presidency. The problem here is that some Presidencies (e.g. Sweden and the UK) have been much more proactive on environmental and EPI-related matters than others (Wurzel, 2001). Consequently, important initiatives like Cardiff and the SDS have tended to proceed in fits and starts, depending on the political ambitions and energy of the state holding the Presidency.

One way to address this might be to embed EPI more deeply in the institutions and administrations of policy making (OECD, 2002: Chapter 2) to ensure it is consistently applied. However, our third point is that the EU's administrative structures are relatively weaker than those at national level (Kassim, 2003). Therefore, the EU finds itself having to rely heavily on a relatively small number of fairly weak coordination instruments. Administrative instruments are particularly weakly applied at EU level. Regulation, meanwhile, is no longer regarded as an effective or legitimate means of compelling the sectors to integrate environment into their thinking (Knill and Lenschow, 2000). The Commission believes that the use of market-based instruments such as eco-taxes offers 'one of the fastest', most flexible and cost-effective routes for environmental integration (COM (2004) 394 final: 35). However, markets do not yet constitute a viable means of facilitating EPI at EU level because of, *inter alia*, political opposition from polluters and member states' principled objection to vesting the EU with (environmental) tax-raising/harmonizing powers (see Chapter 17). The environment is one of a small number of EU policy areas in which the adoption of 'new' modes such as voluntary agreements and eco-management standards has been the most conspicuous (Héritier, 2001), but the total number remains very small (Jordan *et al.*, 2005). Consequently, the EU continues to rely very heavily on its mostly untried and untested Impact Assessment system and the gamut of high-level strategic approaches described above: all things considered, a rather fragile basis.

This leads on to our fourth point, which is that there is now a '*piling up* of strategies . . . that are insufficiently harmonized with one another' (Hinterberger and Zacherl, 2003: 32). For instance, the EU now has not one, but *two* long-term environmental strategies (the SDS and the Sixth EAP), and two integration processes – Lisbon and Cardiff. There are also other important strategic activities with a strong sustainability dimension which could be mentioned (the Commission is, for example, reforming key instruments such as the Common Agricultural Policy and the Structural Funds). Some have argued that these activities 'need to be brought together in an overarching EU environmental strategy or road map' (Wilkinson *et al.*, 2002: 17). The idea of a super-coordinated 'strategy of strategies' sounds appealing, but unless it is adequately supported by coordination capacities (that is, instruments to exchange information, consult and arbitrate, etc.), it will 'be superficial and vulnerable to the disruption of unresolved conflicts and the emergence of unforeseen problems' in daily policy making at lower levels (Metcalfe, 2000: 832).

DG Environment appeared to have accepted this point, when it conceded that 'the institutional and top down approach of [the Cardiff] process, [now] needs to be complemented by more practical steps at both Community and national levels' (COM (2004) 394, final: 34). Our final point, therefore, is that despite widespread agreement that EPI has both a horizontal *and* a vertical dimension (OECD, 2001: 47), the EU does not actually conceptualize (or tackle) it in a holistic way (EEA, 2005a: 35). For instance, the Cardiff integration strategies pay very little attention to vertical relationships, including the issue of capacities for coordination at EU and national levels (Schout and Jordan, 2005). National and EU policy appraisal systems are similarly weakly connected. Finally, national administrative capacities could, in theory, be pooled or in some way better coordinated to compensate for the 'management deficit' (Metcalfe, 2000) at EU level. However, there appears to be precious little appetite for this either within the Commission or among the member states.

Summary points

- The original, radical intention of EPI has been blunted: environmental parts of the EU gradually now find themselves under growing pressure to fight their corner in a three-way battle with those representing the economic and social pillars of sustainability.
- Political leadership from member states and the European Council has been highly variable.
- Despite widespread agreement that EPI is a shared problem, the EU does not actually conceptualize (or tackle) it in this holistic way.

Conclusion

The EU presents a rather puzzling case in that it is both a leading advocate of EPI, but also (via its sectoral funding and policy decisions) a significant cause of unsustainable development in Western Europe. As with sustainability more generally (see Chapter 19), the EU's willingness to advocate EPI both within and outside its borders continues to outstrip its capacity to translate its political promises and legal principles into practice (Bomberg, 2004: 61). A significant causal factor here is the EU's basic institutional structure, particularly the divisions between the EU institutions at the EU level and the 27 member states. These are simultaneously a source of strength and weakness. The weak horizontal co-ordinating links between these actors in the past has paradoxically made it easier for DG Environment and other pro-environment actors in the EU to achieve an ambitious legal and political commitment to EPI at EU level. However, they have made the implementation of this ambitious commitment extremely difficult to achieve, not least because DG Environment has been forced to rely heavily on 'persuasion rather than power' (Wilkinson, 1998: 113).

These difficulties have been compounded by the fact that the Commission and the European Parliament – the two most environmentally focused institutions in the EU and hence natural allies in the pursuit of sustainability – have often not seen eye to eye on EPI. Thus, the Commission now has a functioning policy appraisal system; the Parliament does not; the Commission has reviewed and upgraded its internal coordination capacities, but the Parliament has not; the Commission developed an innovative implementing mechanism in the 1990s (the Cardiff Process), but the Parliament never felt the need to join; and the Commission has tried to develop more internally integrated ways of working (Jordan and Schout, 2006: Chapter 9), but the Parliament's committees are still structured in a very vertical fashion. Meanwhile, the links between EU-level and national EPI activities are still not formally coordinated, although the Commission has started to show an interest in indirectly coordinating (via benchmarking type activities) national sustainability strategies.

Another equally important underlying issue is the political unwillingness of states to subject policy making in 'driving force' sectors to more EU involvement (hence the significant reliance on non-hierarchical or 'new' modes of governance such as the Cardiff Process and the Thematic strategies), or to grant the Commission a stronger role in pursuing EPI in a holistic manner, e.g. linking green budgeting with greener revenue raising measures such as environmental taxes. In the past, DG Environment has arguably tried to overcome this structural weakness by pursuing EPI 'by stealth' (Weale *et al.*, 2000), i.e. developing strong environmental policies within the environmental parts of the EU and then 'imposing' them on the sectors. This has led to significant implementation deficits and in any case did not tackle the root causes of unsustainable development (Jordan, 2002). In the past ten years, there has been a discernible shift away from this approach towards new, less hierarchical modes, starting with the Fifth EAP and the Cardiff Process, through to the Sixth EAP and Impact Assessment. In so doing, DG Environment has seen the focus of environmental policy dissipate as the sectors have taken on a stronger policy defining and development role in relation to environmental and sustainability matters. The problem is that DG Environment has still not fully worked out what to do when – as now appears to be the case – the sectors are slow to accept ownership of environmental problems, or develop practical interpretations of EPI and sustainability that are wholly inconsistent with its preferred interpretation of Article 6.

Summary points

- The EU is puzzling in that it is both a leading advocate of EPI, but also (via its sectoral funding and policy decisions) a significant cause of unsustainable development trends.
- These difficulties have been compounded by the fact that the Commission and the European Parliament have not always worked together on EPI; support from member states has also been rather episodic.
- In the 2000s, the Commission changed tack seeking instead to progress EPI in a less comprehensive fashion, through action in particular issue areas such as climate change ('climate policy integration' or climate mainstreaming), biodiversity protection ('ecosystem services') and reform of the Common Agricultural Policy reform.

Key questions

1 Why did the EU commit itself to such a strong reading of the EPI principle?
2 What kinds of mechanisms and tools has the EU employed to achieve greater EPI?
3 On balance, does the structure of the EU make it harder or easier to engage in cross-policy coordination?
4 Compare the EU's experience with EPI with other comparable multi-level governance systems such as Australia and the USA.
5 Explore the relationship – both theoretical and empirical – between the EU's pursuit of sustainable development and its pursuit of EPI. Are they mutually compatible or does one undermine the other?

Guide to further reading

- For a useful summary of the EPI principle and a state of the art review of the accompanying literature, see Jordan and Lenschow (2010).

- Jordan and Lenschow (2008) analyse the various mechanisms to coordinate policy and review their use in different parts of the EU, Australia and the US.
- For a more detailed diagnosis of why the Cardiff Process went wrong, and a review of the wider implications of the EU's attempts to govern via networks ('networked governance'), see Jordan and Schout (2006).

References

Bomberg, E. (2004) 'Adapting form to function? From economic to sustainable development governance in the EU', in W. Lafferty (ed.) *Governance for Sustainable Development*, Edward Elgar, Cheltenham.

DoE (Department of the Environment) (1994) *Towards Sustainability: Government Action in the UK*, Department of the Environment, London.

EEA (European Environment Agency) (1998) *Europe's Environment: The Second Assessment*, EEA, Copenhagen.

EEA (European Environment Agency) (2003) *Europe's Environment: The Third Assessment (Full Report)*, EEA, Copenhagen.

EEA (European Environment Agency) (2005a) *Environmental Policy Integration in Europe: State of Play and an Evaluation Framework*, EEA Technical Report No. 2/2005, EEA, Copenhagen.

EEA (European Environment Agency) (2005b) *Environmental Policy Integration in Europe: Administrative Culture and Practices*, EEA Technical Report No. 5/2005, EEA, Copenhagen.

ENDS (Environmental Data Services) Ltd. (various years) *Environmental Data Services Report*, ENDS, London.

ENDS *Europe Daily* (various years) *ENDS Europe Daily*, ENDS, London.

European Commission (2004) *National Sustainable Development Strategies in the EU: A First Analysis by the European Commission*, Commission Staff Working Document, April 2004, European Commission, Brussels.

Fergusson, M. *et al.* (2001) *The Effectiveness of EU Council Integration Strategies and Options for Carrying Forward the 'Cardiff' Process*, IEEP, London.

Grimeaud, D. (2000) 'The integration of environmental concerns into EC policies', *European Environmental Law Review*, vol. 9, no. 7, pp. 207–218.

Haigh, N. (ed.) (2005) *Manual of Environmental Policy: The EU and Britain*, Institute for European Environmental Policy, Maney Publishing, Leeds.

Héritier, A. (2001) *New Modes of Governance in Europe: Policy Making Without Legislating?* Max Planck Project Group, Preprints, 2001/14, available at: www.coll.mpg.de/pdf_dat/2001_14online.pdf (accessed 5 July 2012).

Hinterberger, F. and Zacherl, R. (2003) *Ways Towards Sustainability in the European Union*, SERI Institute, Vienna.

Hix, S. (2005) *The Political System of the European Union*, 2nd edition, Palgrave, Basingstoke.

Hontelez, J. (2005) 'The impact of European NGOs on EU environmental regulation', in F. Wijen *et al.* (eds) *A Handbook of Globalization and Environmental Policy*, Edward Elgar, Cheltenham.

Jans, J. (2000) *European Environmental Law*, 2nd edition, Europa Law Publishers, Groningen.

Jordan, A.J. (2001) 'The European Union: an evolving system of multi-level governance . . . or government?', *Policy and Politics*, vol. 29, no. 2, pp.193–208.

Jordan, A.J. (2002) 'The implementation of EU environmental policy', in A. Jordan (ed.) *Environmental Policy in the EU*, Earthscan, London.

Jordan, A. and Lenschow, A. (2000) 'Greening the European Union: what can be learned from the leaders of EU environmental policy?', *European Environment*, vol. 10, no. 3, pp. 109–120.

Jordan, A.J. and Lenschow, A. (eds) (2008) *Innovation in Environmental Policy? Integrating the Environment for Sustainability*, Edward Elgar, Cheltenham.

Jordan, A.J. and Lenschow, A. (2010) 'Environmental policy integration: a state of the art review', *Environmental Policy and Governance*, vol. 20, no. 3, pp. 147–158.

Jordan, A. and Liefferink, D. (eds) (2004) *Environmental Policy in Europe: The Europeanization of National Environmental Policy*, Routledge, London.

Jordan, A. and Schout, A. (2006) *The Coordination of the European Union: Exploring the Capacities for Networked Governance*, Oxford University Press, Oxford.

Jordan, A., Wurzel, R. and Zito, A. (2005) 'The rise of "new" policy instruments in comparative perspective', *Political Studies*, vol. 53, no. 3, pp. 477–496.

Judge, D. and Earnshaw, D. (2004) *The European Parliament*, Palgrave, Basingstoke.

Kassim, H. (2003) 'The European administration', in J. Hayward and A. Menon (eds) *Governing Europe*, Oxford University Press, Oxford.

Knill, C. and Lenschow, A. (eds) (2000) *Implementing EU Environmental Policy*, Manchester University Press, Manchester.

Krämer, L. (2005) 'The dispersion of authority in the European Union and its impact on environmental legislation', in F. Wijen *et al.* (eds) *A Handbook of Globalization and Environmental Policy*, Edward Elgar, Cheltenham.

Kraemer, A. *et al.* (2001) *Results of the Cardiff Process: A Report to the Federal German Environmental Agency and the Federal Environment Ministry*, Ecologic, Berlin.

Kraemer, R., Klassing, A., Wilkinson, D. and von Homeyer, I. (2002) *EU Environmental Governance*, final report, Ecologic/IEEP, Berlin/London.

Lee, N. and Kirkpatrick, C. (2001) 'Methodologies for sustainability impact assessments of proposals for new trade agreements', *Journal of Environmental Assessment Policy and Management*, vol. 3, pp. 395–412.

Lenschow, A. (1999) 'The greening of the EU: the Common Agricultural Policy and the structural funds', *Environment and Planning C*, vol. 17, pp. 91–108.

Lenschow, A. (ed.) (2002) *Environmental Policy Integration*, Earthscan, London.

Lenschow, A. (2005) 'Environmental policy', in H. Wallace, W. Wallace and M. Pollack (eds) *Policy Making in the EU*, 5th edition, Oxford University Press, Oxford.

Macrory, R. (1999) 'The Amsterdam Treaty: an environmental perspective', in D. O'Keefe and P. Twomey (eds) *Legal Issues of the Amsterdam Treaty*, Hart Publishing, Oxford.

Metcalfe, L. (2000) 'Reforming the Commission: will organizational efficiency produce effective governance?', *Journal of Common Market Studies*, vol. 38, no. 5, pp. 817–841.

Moravcsik, A. (2005) 'The European constitutional compromise', *EUSA Review*, vol. 18, no. 2, pp. 1–7.

OECD (2001) *Sustainable Development: Critical Issues*, OECD, Paris.

OECD (2002) *Governance for Sustainable Development: Five OECD Case studies*, OECD, Paris.

Pallemaerts, M. *et al.* (2007) *Does the EU Sustainable Development Strategy Contribute to EPI?* Ecologic: EPIGOV concerted action, Berlin.

Pearce, D. (1998) 'Environmental appraisal and environmental policy in the EU', *Environmental and Resource Economics*, vol. 11, nos 3–4, pp. 489–501.

Peters, G.B. (1998) 'Managing horizontal government', *Public Administration*, vol. 76, pp. 295–311.

Peters, G.B. and Wright, V. (2001) 'The national coordination of European policy-making', in J. Richardson (ed.) *European Union: Power and Policy-Making*, Routledge, London.

Peterson, J. (1997) 'States, societies and the EU', *West European Politics*, vol. 20, no. 4, pp. 1–23.

Sbragia, A. (2000) 'The EU as coxswain', in J. Pierre (ed.) *Debating Governance*, Oxford University Press, Oxford.

Sbragia, A. (2002) *The Dilemma of Governance with Government*, Jean Monnet Working Paper 3/02, NYU School of Law, New York.

Sbragia, A. (2005) 'Institution-building from below and above', in A. Jordan (ed.) *Environmental Policy in the European Union*, 2nd edition, Earthscan, London.

Schout, A. and Jordan, A.J. (2005) 'Coordinating European governance: self organising or centrally steered?', *Public Administration*, vol. 83, no. 1, pp. 201–220.

Scott, J. and Trubek, D. (2002) 'Mind the gap: law and new approaches to governance in the European Union', *European Law Journal*, vol. 8, no. 1, pp. 1–18.

Stubb, A., Wallace, H. and Peterson, J. (2003) 'The policy making process', in E. Bomberg and A. Stubb (eds) *The European Union: How Does It Work?* Oxford University Press, Oxford.

Weale, A. *et al.* (2000) *European Environmental Governance*, Oxford University Press, Oxford.

Weale, A. and Williams, A. (1992) 'Between economy and ecology? The single market and the integration of environmental policy', *Environmental Politics*, vol. 1, no. 4, pp. 45–64.

Wilkinson, D. (1997) 'Towards sustainability in the European Union?', *Environmental Politics*, vol. 6, no. 1, pp. 153–173.

Wilkinson, D. (1998) 'Steps towards integrating the environment into other EU policy sectors', in T. O'Riordan and H. Voisey (eds) *The Transition to Sustainability*, Earthscan, London.

Wilkinson, D. (2007) *EPI at EU Level*, EPIGOV State of the Art Report, Ecologic: EPIGOV concerted action, Berlin.

Wilkinson, D., Benson, D. and Jordan, A.J. (2008) 'Green budgeting', in A. Jordan and A. Lenschow (eds) *Innovation in Environmental Policy? Integrating the Environment for Sustainability*, Edward Elgar, Cheltenham.

Wilkinson, D., Fergusson, M., Bowyer, C. *et al.* (2004) *Sustainable Development in the European Commission's Integrated Impact Assessments for 2003, Final Report*, IEEP, London.

Wilkinson, D., Skinner, I. and Ferguson, M. (2002) *The Future of the Cardiff Process*, IEEP, London.

Wilkinson D. *et al.* (2005) *For Better or Worse? The EU's 'Better Regulation' Agenda and the Environment*, IEEP, London.

Wurzel, R. (2001) 'The EU presidency and the integration principle', *European Environmental Law Review*, vol. 10, pp. 7–15.

14 Policy implementation

Andrew Jordan and Jale Tosun

Summary guide

The implementation of policy in the EU is widely regarded as being problematic. Yet, both public and academic understanding of this crucial stage of the EU policy process remains relatively limited. Indeed, for a long time, a number of factors kept the whole issue of poor implementation down or off the political agenda, but today it is much more politicized, pushed along by the campaigning activities of NGOs and pro-integration actors such as the European Parliament. A whole host of solutions to the EU's implementation problems have been offered, some of which could, if deployed, even compound the problem. But in many respects, the causes of poor (or at least imperfect) implementation reside in the very structure of the EU. Consequently, there are likely to be no panaceas.

Introduction

Implementation is very much at the 'sharp end' of the EU policy process. The success of EU policies – and with them the whole European integration project – are often judged by the impacts they have on the ground. If, however, the *acquis* is not fully implemented, EU policies risk becoming paper exercises with little tangible effect on environmental quality but serious distorting impacts on the Single Market. On the face of it, all is not well in the environmental field. At the end of 2009, 451 of the 1860 infringements (i.e. 24.3 per cent) of EU policy related to environmental legislation (CEC, 2010a: 79). Moreover (according to the Commission (CEC, 2010b: 3)), the number of petitions to the European Parliament raising issues concerning the incorrect application of environmental law were higher than in any other policy area. Speaking in 2011, the then Commissioner for the Environment, Janez Potočnik argued that improving this situation represented one of his main priorities:

I want to use the *acquis* to achieve our environmental objectives like greater resource efficiency, like restoring and saving biodiversity and fighting climate change. Better implementation is a tool – a means to an end. Non-implementation has its costs: economic, environmental, personal and social.

(Potočnik, 2011)

In fact, a recent report for the Commission estimates that the costs of not fully implementing EU environmental policy are around 50 billion euros a year (COWI *et al.*, 2011). Potočnik was of course not the first politician to identify these problems or the first to vow to address them. In fact, poor (or at least imperfect) implementation remains enduringly problematic in the EU – it has been described as 'a policy problem without a political solution' (Jordan, 1999).

In order to understand why this situation has arisen and, even more importantly, why the EU has struggled to address it, one has to appreciate the wider academic and political context in which implementation takes place. Implementation has often been the poor relation in policy analysis, only emerging as a separate focus of sustained academic study in the late 1960s (Jordan, 1997). In one of the first systematic studies, Pressman and Wildavsky (1984) explained why a politically popular federal employment programme in the United States failed to live up to prior expectations (see Box 14.1).

Box 14.1 The birth of implementation policy analysis

In 1973, Jeff Pressman and Aaron Wildavsky published one of the first systematic studies of policy implementation. The subtitle of their book paraphrases its central message: 'How great expectations in Washington are dashed in Oakland; or, why it's amazing that federal programmes work at all . . .'. They showed that successful implementation in a multi-level governance system such as the US requires countless linkages to be built between a bewilderingly large number of actors whose cooperation is needed to turn a policy promise into action on the ground (what they termed the 'complexity of joint action'). Goals, they argued, should therefore be made clearer, proper resources should be furnished to implementing officials and a chain of command put in place to control them all. As all these things are by their nature unlikely ever to appear in a perfect form, their overall policy recommendation was both gloomy and disarmingly simple: politicians should not promise what they cannot deliver; to do so will lead only to 'disillusionment and frustration' (Pressman and Wildavsky, 1984: 6). But the problem here is that politicians win elections by making promises. By contrast, few politicians win friends (or votes) by highlighting instances of policy failure or by building better functioning implementation structures. Since then the field of research on these topics has grown massively (for a good review, see Hill and Hupe, 2008).

Many of their points are very relevant to the current state of policy implementation in the EU. First, when it comes to putting the *acquis communautaire* into effect at the national level, the Commission, the body which formally oversees implementation, is on a steep upward slope, possessing neither the political resources nor the legal competence to delve substantially into what Pressman and Wildavsky termed the complexity of joint action (see Box 14.1), especially at the national level. Why, then, did the architects of the EU construct a political system with so many intricate and extended inter-linkages, and thus endowing it with an inbuilt 'pathology of non-compliance' (Mastenbroek, 2005: 1114)? Second, far from creating political disillusionment in the EU policy process, environmental policy continues to be one of the few elements of the European project that enjoys widespread public appeal. A recent opinion poll revealed that 95 per cent of EU citizens believe that protecting the environment is important and 64 per cent thought that the associated policies should be decided at a European level (CEC, 2011a: 7). Third, instead of reducing the output of new legislation (one of Pressman and Wildavsky's main suggestions) and concentrating on strengthening policy delivery structures, the tide of new environmental regulation emanating from 'Brussels' remains strong (Farmer, 2011). Indeed, if there is one thing the EU is unequivocally good at, it is the 'mass production of law' (Berglund *et al.*, 2006). The key question is this: can it become equally good at implementation?

In this chapter, we systematically address these three puzzles first by outlining the main characteristics of the implementation process. Next, we explain why and how non-implementation changed from a political non-issue in the EU to one that attracts a great deal of political attention and academic study. We then describe the extent of the implementation problems in the EU, before addressing some of their root causes. In a next step, we shed light on some of the strategies – both potential and adopted – for reducing the scale of the EU's implementation problems. Finally, we make some concluding remarks about whether implementation is still a 'policy problem without a political solution' (Jordan, 1999) and identify future challenges, both political and academic.

Summary points

- Policy implementation in multi-level governance contexts is seldom straightforward.
- The implementation of policy in the EU is widely regarded as being relatively problematic, yet there are no strong indications that it is undermining public support for EU action.
- In many respects, the reasons for poor implementation reside in the very structures of the EU; consequently, there may well be no panaceas.

Policy implementation: actors, governance procedures and analytical perspectives

In the EU, responsibility for policy implementation is shared between a number of different actors. Ultimately, the responsibility for executing Community law lies with the member states (Article 4 [3], TEU). But as the 'guardian of the treaties' (Article 17 [1], TEU), the Commission is in charge of overseeing how they transpose and ultimately apply EU law. The Commission's core instrument for ensuring this happens is the so-called infringement procedure (as set out in Article 258, TFEU). If the Commission believes that an infringement has taken place, it first establishes informal contacts with the competent national authority in the state in question, in order to discuss the problem and identify ways to overcome it (Collins and Earnshaw, 1992; Knill, 2006). Depending on the results of these informal discussions, the Commission may decide to send a formal letter (an 'Article 258 letter') to the member state, summarizing the situation and asking for further clarifications. If the infringement persists, the Commission produces a formal 'reasoned opinion' explaining why it believes that the member state in question has breached Community law. Finally, if that member state does not comply with the terms of this opinion within a given time limit, the Commission can appeal to the European Court of Justice (ECJ), which decides whether the member state has infringed a legal obligation. The member state in question is then obliged to take the necessary steps resulting from the ECJ's judgment. Together, these form the main stages of the EU's *compliance* procedure – compliance meaning conformity with a particular law or policy.

The implementation of EU law thus has three dimensions: the adoption of requested measures before a specified deadline (*notification*); conformity to the EU act in question (*transposition*); and its correct integration into the national regulatory framework (*application*). With formal transposition, the focus is on enabling the incorporation of EU laws into the national legal order. Practical application, on the other hand, refers to the degree to which EU-induced legal modifications result in corresponding adjustments in national regulatory practice (Knill and Lenschow, 2000: 9–14). Consequently, there are two main types of implementation problems in the EU: the first relating to notification and/or transposition; the second to the practical application of EU laws (see also Chapter 7).

Macrory (1992: 354) argues that the first are difficult but by no means impossible for the Commission to detect, requiring scrutiny of the relevant national legislation, whereas the latter can be extremely difficult to identify. The main reason for this is that the Commission is almost entirely dependent upon member states reporting back on what they are actually doing, or on whatever national environmental groups and private actors choose to submit via the formal complaints procedure (Wilkinson, 1994). DG Environment's direct powers of inquiry are limited to seeking comments from member states. On-site visits and other 'spot checks' by Commission officials are of limited value: they are usually extremely time-consuming, politically fraught and can easily be blocked by member states who are under no legal obligation to cooperate (Jordan, 1999). Putting all this together, one can say that the responsibility for policy implementation is dispersed among a number of actors. The complexity of joint action is high and the Commission's enforcement powers are slow and indirect.

Pressman and Wildavsky's pioneering analysis of implementation problems in the US led to the development of a 'top-down' perspective in which the focus is on the shortfall between the goals embodied in particular directives and their practical effect in member states (see Hill and Hupe, 2008: Chapter 3). Most analyses in this vein of scholarship have been designed to investigate the extent to which policy outputs conform to the objectives set out in legislation. In other words, was the necessary implementing legislation enacted? Did it incentivize street-level bureaucrats to conform? Many of the 'black-letter' accounts of implementation by lawyers fall into this category. In practice, implementation in the EU does not follow this kind of direct, top-down logic. More often than not, it involves intense political interaction between those who framed the policy in the first place and those charged with implementing it. Crucially, the Commission is strong in the policy formulation process but a great deal of the responsibility for putting policies into effect (i.e. notification, transposition and application) rests on the shoulders of member states. The member states are also heavily involved in the adoption process (see Chapter 5) and they are also responsible for implementing the resulting laws too. In a sense, then, the process is not at all top down. Indeed, the Commission knows that if certain member states are constantly pressured to implement Community laws, it might endanger political support for the wider integration process (Jordan, 1999). Indeed, when the Commission has tried to strong arm states into complying with environmental laws, it has found itself under significant political pressure to be less interventionist (Jordan, 2000).

These complex, two-way interactions between the Commission, the member states, and public and private actors, suggest that implementation is really a political bargaining process (Jordan, 1999), in which some policy goals undergo significant refinement during the implementation phase. The question then arises of precisely how much modification is acceptable from an environmental as well as a political point of view. The EU has been wrestling with this basic question since the very dawn of EU environmental policy in the 1970s (see Chapter 2).

Summary points

- The responsibility for policy implementation is shared between a number of different actors working at different levels of governance.
- The Commission is primarily responsible for overseeing implementation, but it is remote and cannot easily compel member states to fall into line. Disagreements between the two can be resolved by the ECJ, but many are informally resolved well before this formal step is reached.
- The Commission's enforcement procedures to drive compliance are slow, tortuous and relatively weak.
- In practice, therefore, implementation as a whole is less a top-down process of putting agreed policies into effect, and more an ongoing process of adjustment and bargaining.

Policy implementation in the EU: from 'unpolitics' to politics?

The 'unpolitics' of implementation

Until the early 1990s, the implementation of the environmental *acquis* was a taboo subject, rarely discussed in policy circles. Why was this? First of all, none of the main players had a strong incentive to raise its political profile, so a conspiracy of silence prevailed. For obvious reasons states preferred not to advertize their own failings and there has always been a well-established 'gentleman's agreement' not to draw attention to or become involved in the sovereign affairs of other states. It is telling that not a single court case has been brought by one state against another for poor implementation (see Chapter 7). Meanwhile, the Commission was fully engaged in the task of developing the basic framework of environmental law in the absence, it should be noted, of a firm treaty base (see Chapter 2). The last thing it wanted to do was pick fights with particular member states, and certainly not the larger and more powerful ones.

Second, policy success at this time was commonly appraised on the basis of the amount of legislation adopted rather than its long-term effectiveness. During a long tenure in the UK Environment Ministry, one minister observed that the sharing of the Presidency (see Chapter 5) created an unhealthy competition to agree as much ambitious legislation as possible (HOLSCEC, 1987: 12). Third (according to Macrory, 1992: 350), many of the first laws were adopted when directives were commonly viewed as a 'commitment of policy intention' rather than a 'genuine legal obligation'. In advance of a firm indication from the ECJ that directives were indeed legally binding in their entirety, a distinctly *de minimis* view of European law prevailed. Few states ever expected to have to fully implement them (Haigh and Lanigan, 1995: 23).

Fourth, it was not entirely clear what should happen if an infringement was suspected. Article 7(1) TEU identifies the Commission as the legal 'guardian of the treaties' with responsibility for ensuring their provisions are applied. But for a long time the treaties gave no clear guidance on how cases of non-compliance were to be processed. Consequently, the Commission developed its own informal enforcement procedure (described above), which gradually became more formalized. Nowadays, non-compliance can have legal consequences in two stages. At the first stage (Article 258, TFEU), the Commission can refer the non-compliant member state to the ECJ (see above). The second stage is defined by Article 260, TFEU. It arises only if the member state fails to comply with the ECJ's judgment. It ends with the Commission applying to the ECJ for a second time, and perhaps asking for a financial penalty to be imposed on the member state in question. The ECJ can either impose a lump sum or penalty payments. Lump sum penalties are designed to ensure that a similar infringement does not occur again. Penalty payments, in contrast, are a more coercive tool to encourage member states to comply quickly with a previous judgment (Jack, 2010: 8).

The politics of implementation

Starting in the late 1980s, this cosy state of affairs started to change and gradually non-implementation became the much more political issue that it is today. First, the single market programme (see Chapter 1) sharpened the perception, particularly within industry circles, that comparable regulatory efforts were needed in order to ensure fair competition (Weiler, 1988). The steady growth of the environmental *acquis* after the mid-1980s (see Chapters 1 and 2) was the second major development. After all, without it, there could by definition be no implementation 'problem'. The third important development concerned a series of rulings by the ECJ (see Chapter 7). According to neofunctionalist legal scholars, these adopted an increasingly maximal (or pro-integration) interpretation of EU law. Often they arose from cases of non-compliance and, crucially, many were made against the wishes of states (Alter, 1998). The fourth development related to the increasing power of other EU institutions, most importantly the European Parliament. Members of the European Parliament (MEPs) drew attention to some particularly shocking cases of non-compliance (see Chapter 8). These crises pushed the whole issue up the political agenda. They were also instrumental in forcing the Commission to develop an improved surveillance system and to publish annual reports on implementation, starting in 1983 (see Jordan, 1999). Finally, there was increasingly active campaigning by environmental groups (see Chapter 9). National NGOs soon realized that they could use EU law to gain greater leverage over their own national governments. In accordance with Article 227 TFEU, EU citizens and organizations now have the right to petition the European Parliament about the non-application of EU law (Krämer, 2009). The overall number of petitions has grown steadily and by the end of 2009, DG Environment was responsible for handling 430 petitions, which represented about a third of the total (CEC, 2011b).

At the same time, more and more academics have started to study implementation (see, for example, Jordan, 1999; Knill and Lenschow, 2000; Haverland, 2003; Börzel, 2003; Holzinger *et al.*, 2006). Whereas the first studies focused on basic institutional incompatibilities – mostly referred to as 'institutional misfits' – between European requirements and domestic conditions in the member states, more recent analyses have sought to shed greater light on how the preferences of different domestic actors explain the overall patterns of implementation (see Mastenbroek, 2005). On this basis, states have been divided up into different categories – those that routinely obey, those that obey EU laws when domestic politics allow, and those that rarely obey (Falkner and Treib, 2008: 296–298). However, fine-grained analyses that generate and test specific explanations are still limited in number. So too are empirical accounts that go beyond the stage of formal transposition. In fact, scientific knowledge of the situation regarding the practical application of Community law (i.e. the environmental effectiveness of laws) is still very limited – a point re-made in Chapter 15.

Summary points

- A number of factors helped to keep the issue of implementation off the political agenda and out of the public eye.
- Starting in the late 1980s, implementation became much more of a political issue, pushed along by the campaigning activities of NGOs and pro-integration actors such as the European Parliament.
- Yet, public and academic understanding of the implementation stage remains far more limited than the earlier policy stages.

How big and widespread are the EU's implementation problems?

This section essentially adopts a simple top-down approach to explore the extent of the EU's implementation problems. The first and most obvious question to ask is, just how big is the problem? The simple answer is that the implementation of EU environmental policy is definitely imperfect. Moreover, there seems to be notable inter-state variation, i.e. some member states routinely obey EU laws but others do so far less frequently. However, a great deal depends on the source of the implementation data used. There are, after all, a number of different ways in which the Commission monitors the application of Community law. In addition to under-taking its own studies and assessments, the Commission investigates complaints from EU citizens and organizations, and petitions and questions from MEPs. The Commission can use reports submitted by member states themselves as a means of detecting breaches of Community environment law, as well as information generated through its own investigations.

These sources are used by the Commission to assemble an empirical picture of the scale of the problem. However, as we shall see, it is far from complete. What the data shows is that at the end of 2009, there were a total of 1,860 infringements of EU legislation, of which 451 (24.3 per cent) related to EU environment legislation (CEC, 2010a: 79). The fact that about one-quarter of all infringements are found in the area of environmental policy underlines the scale of the problem. Table 14.1 shows the open infringement cases being pursued against member states. Spain had the highest number, most relating to nature and water legislation, followed by Italy and Ireland which have more than 30 open infringements each. The newer (post-2004) member states appear to fare rather better, although caseloads tend to build up slowly over time so the situation may well change in the future as their domestic publics become attuned to the possibilities created by EU law. Even so, some of the EU-12 states (e.g. the Czech Republic and Poland) are already generating caseloads approaching those of the older member states.

The other thing to remember is that the newer member states benefit from extended deadlines for transposing EU law. Table 14.2 gives an overview of the number of transitional arrangements in place. Again, there is significant variation across the EU. Thus Romania has benefited from the largest number of transitional

Table 14.1 A ranking of open infringement cases

Member states	Number	(%)	Member states	Number	(%)
Spain	40	8.9	Malta	12	2.7
Italy	35	7.8	Romania	12	2.7
Ireland	34	7.5	Hungary	11	2.4
Czech Republic	26	5.8	Lithuania	11	2.4
France	26	5.8	Estonia	10	2.2
United Kingdom	26	5.8	Sweden	10	2.2
Greece	24	5.3	Luxembourg	9	2.0
Poland	23	5.1	Germany	8	1.8
Portugal	23	5.1	Cyprus	7	1.6
Belgium	20	4.4	Finland	6	1.3
Slovakia	19	3.5	Latvia	6	1.3
Bulgaria	17	3.8	Slovenia	6	1.3
Denmark	13	2.9	the Netherlands	5	1.1
Austria	12	2.7	Total	451	100

Source: Based on CEC (2011c).

Table 14.2 Transitional arrangements relating to environmental laws

Member states	Number	Earliest date	Latest date
Romania	11	2008	2018
Poland	10	2005	2017
Bulgaria	9	2008	2014
Latvia	8	2004	2015
Malta	7	2004	2009
Slovakia	7	2006	2015
Estonia	6	2006	2015
Cyprus	4	2005	2012
Hungary	4	2005	2015
Lithuania	4	2006	2015
Czech Republic	3	2005	2010
Slovenia	3	2007	2015

Source: Based on CEC (2004).

arrangements and also the longest single extension (in relation to the directive on the treatment of urban waste water, which has been extended from 2007 until 2018). These transitional arrangements complicate the already difficult task of working out the true scale of the EU's implementation 'problem'.

Table 14.3 illustrates the number of infringements by stages as of 31 December 2009. To increase the comparability of the figures, the distribution of infringement cases by policy sectors (%) is also reported. Remarkably, environment-related infringements dominate for each stage of the infringement procedure. In this respect, it is equally important to note that non-compliance with environmental directives is very persistent, which is indicated by the share (some 40.4 per cent of the total cases under scrutiny by the ECJ in accordance with Article 260 TFEU).

Table 14.3 Stages of the infringement procedure by sector

Sectors	Formal letter		Reasoned opinion		Referral to ECJ		Art. 260 TFEU	
	N	(%)	N	(%)	N	(%)	N	(%)
Legal services	3	0.16	1	0.11	0	0.00	0	0.00
Economic and financial affairs	1	0.05	0	0.00	0	0.00	0	0.00
Enterprise and industry	150	8.09	48	5.49	14	3.97	3	3.03
Competition	7	0.38	6	0.69	1	0.28	5	5.05
Employment, social affairs and equal opportunities	141	7.60	74	8.46	16	4.53	5	5.05
Agriculture and rural development	5	0.27	4	0.46	2	0.57	1	1.01
Energy and transport	292	15.74	103	28.77	27	7.65	15	15.15
Environment	452	24.73	225	25.71	100	28.33	40	40.40
Information society and media	27	1.46	16	1.83	9	2.55	3	3.03
Maritime affairs and fisheries	11	0.59	7	0.80	4	1.13	0	0.00
Internal market and services	289	15.58	176	20.11	88	24.93	20	20.20
Regional policy	0	0.00	0	0.00	0	0.00	0	0.00
Taxation and customs union	303	16.33	129	14.74	44	12.46	2	2.02
Education and culture	7	0.38	1	0.11	1	0.28	1	1.01
Health and consumers	79	4.26	31	3.54	15	4.25	1	1.01
Justice, freedom and security	63	3.40	32	3.66	13	3.68	3	3.03
External relations	0	0.00	0	0.00	0	0.00	0	0.00
Trade	0	0.00	0	0.00	0	0.00	0	0.00
Development	0	0.00	0	0.00	0	0.00	0	0.00
Enlargement	1	0.05	1	0.11	1	0.28	0	0.00
Eurostat	0	0.00	0	0.00	0	0.00	0	0.00
Human Resources and Security	1	0.05	1	0.11	1	0.28	0	0.00
Budget	23	1.24	20	2.29	17	4.82	0	0.00
European Anti-Fraud Office	0	0.00	0	0.00	0	0.00	0	0.00
Total	1,855	100	875	30.26	353	100	99	100

Source: Based on CEC (2010c).

Summary points

- There are undoubtedly many problems associated with the implementation of EU environmental policies.
- The problems in this sector do appear to be worse than those in other sectors, as indicated by the share of cases in accordance with Article 260, TFEU.
- Nonetheless, implementation and enforcement are shaped by a great deal of political bargaining and the Commission struggles to obtain timely information.
- Consequently there is no entirely objective 'scientific' measure of the overall scale of non-implementation; reliable inter-state comparisons of performance are notoriously difficult to make.

The underlying causes of the EU's implementation problems

If the overall scale of the implementation problem is contested, what is known about the underlying causes? As noted above, a major contributory factor is the EU's institutional structure which shares out power and responsibilities among the main actors rather unevenly. This structural imbalance ensures that the EU's constituent bodies, i.e. the Commission and the ECJ, are geographically and politically dissociated from what goes on at the ground level in member states. In Pressman and Wildavsky's terms, the 'complexity of joint action' is many orders of magnitude more elaborate than that required to give effect to a national statute. However, the problem goes deeper still. Majone (1996) has argued that the EU is a *regulatory* state. Member states have in other words deliberately limited its ability to 'tax-and-spend' (see Chapter 17). Consequently, actors seeking deeper integration (such as the Commission and the European Parliament) have a powerful incentive to propose ambitious pieces of legislation which impose their primary costs on the actors charged with implementing them, namely, the member states. The need, moreover, to secure agreement among many actors in the decision-making process has, at least in the past, given the Commission little incentive to point out the full implications of its proposals (see Chapter 12).

Given these basic incentive patterns and institutional structures, it is hardly surprising that so many 'great' environmental expectations born in Brussels and Strasbourg are dashed by weak and inconsistent implementation at the national level. In fact, conflicts surrounding the speed and scope of implementation are an integral part of the political game-play between state and non-state actors in the EU (Kellow and Zito, 2002). Thus, supranational actors propose legislation which is deliberately ambitious in an attempt to deepen European integration; states then kick back when those policies fail to fit their national interests and institutional features; supranational actors then react by pushing for greater implementation. And so the game continues, perhaps leading eventually to demands for stronger implementation structures or the policy in question to be revised. In many respects, the deep and enduring tension between the intergovernmental and supranational parts of the EU is more starkly revealed in the implementation phase than in any other. Somehow, a *supranational* legal order spun by actors with maximalist beliefs has to be reconciled with a state-dominated system of policy implementation.

In this game, the Commission is heavily reliant on the national administrative apparatus of its member states. It is also disadvantaged by the preferred tool of EU environmental policy, i.e. the *directive*. Directives are binding in terms of the overall objective to be achieved, but leave states to determine the detailed arrangements for putting them into practice. Not surprisingly, member states almost always prefer directives to the main alternative – regulations – which are far more prescriptive and are directly effective (i.e. they do not need to be transposed). Even the Commission's ultimate sanction, a reference to the ECJ, is a relatively blunt weapon. Although the ECJ can rule that member states are in breach of EU environmental law, all it can do is to impose financial penalties. To date, there have only been three ECJ judgments that have done this: Commission v. Greece, Case C-387/97; Commission v. Spain, Case C-278/01; and Commission v. France, Case C-121/07 (CEC, 2011c). Furthermore, it takes many years before any case even appears before the ECJ. In these three cases, the time elapsed between Articles 258 and 260 corresponded to 93, 68 and 52 months respectively (Jack, 2010: 19–20).

Finally, it is not necessarily always the case that non-implementation is intentional. National administrative capacities matter for the effectiveness of policy implementation, but can differ hugely within and between different states (see, for example, Knill and Lenschow, 2000). Nor is 'full' implementation necessarily better than 'partial' implementation. To an extent common, harmonizing policies must always be interpreted to reflect national conditions and circumstances. The point at which reasonable adjustment shades into deliberate non-compliance is ultimately a value judgement.

Summary points

- Implementation is not a clear-cut bureaucratic activity; nowadays it is just as politicized as earlier stages of the EU policy process.
- The Commission and the ECJ are limited in what they can do to force states to comply with EU rules. Fines are in theory available but are rarely applied.
- There is seldom complete agreement on the precise level of implementation to aim for in specific cases; much depends on informal bargaining between different actors.

Responding to the situation: what has been done?

As the whole matter has become more politicized, the EU has been forced to respond. For example, since 1984, the Commission has presented an annual report to the European Parliament on the application of EU law, although, as noted above, they say more about transposition than practical implementation. Better implementation was also a cornerstone of the Fourth (1987–1992) and Fifth (1993–2000) Environmental Action Programmes (EAPs). It remains a priority in the Sixth EAP (2002–2012). Starting in the late 1980s, the Commission embarked on a confrontational approach which involved targeting large, non-implementing states such as the UK and taking them to the ECJ (Jordan and Liefferink, 2004: 213). This proved to be highly controversial and contributed to many demands from many states for the Commission to pursue a less interventionist approach (Jordan, 2000), consistent with the principle of subsidiarity.

Since then, a whole raft of measures to improve implementation have been proposed (Jordan, 1999), ranging from empowering the Commission to make on-site inspection visits (as is done in the fields of competition law and fisheries) to making it easier for non-state actors to seek redress through the EU legal system. Some have even argued that steps should be taken to prevent small groups of states from vetoing policy at the adoption stage. However, this could be a double-edged sword as far as implementation is concerned. On the one hand, it may substantially upgrade the adoption of tougher environmental legislation by ameliorating the well-known 'joint decision trap' (Jordan *et al.*, 2012). On the other hand, any improvement in the level of protection may be undone if states are forced to implement legislation they consider to be unacceptable or do not have the capacity to implement. Scharpf (2006: 857) suggests that a difficult balance has to be struck: lowering the threshold needed for a majority may well exacerbate implementation problems, which could undermine the political stability of the EU by making common rules more unpopular.

The underlying problem that Scharpf is in effect alerting us to is that the more assertive responses to the implementation problems could well be deeply at odds with the *realpolitik* of the EU which, despite all the evidence of greater supranationality (EU-level institutions, direct effective law, etc.), is still dominated by 27 member states, each with its own political culture, set of legal traditions, administrative practices and environmental circumstances. At root, it is and probably will always be a consensus-seeking organization which employs soft power resources (Jordan *et al.*, 2010: 42–43). The overriding norm of appropriate behaviour is one of *negotiated* not imposed enforcement. Thus errant states are rarely disciplined too much by EU institutions, or embarrassed politically.

The responses that the EU has adopted to its implementation problems very much reflect these well-established ways and means of governing, i.e. ones that seek to build bridges between different actors rather than seek conflict and more top-down forms of control. For example, there is now a Network for the Implementation and Enforcement of Environmental Law (IMPEL). This network, which comprises national and European regulators, was originally set up in 1992. It aims to ensure a more effective application of environmental legislation through the mode of greater networked governance – namely, awareness raising, capacity building, systems of peer review, the exchange of implementation-related information as well as the building in of enforceability issues at the policy design stage (see, for example, its 'better regulation checklist') (IMPEL, 2010). The Commission has also recognized that national judges play a key role in the implementation of EU environmental law (CEC, 2007; 2008). The EU Forum of Judges for the Environment, established in 2004, promotes the enforcement of national, European and international environmental law.

At the same time, a raft of so-called 'horizontal' directives has been adopted to support and extend these measures. Three directives are worth noting: one on standardized reporting (Directive 91/692/EEC); another on environmental liability (2004/35/EC); and a third on the protection of the environment through criminal law (2008/99/EC). The Standardized Reporting Directive (91/692/EEC) was a rather belated response to the lack of information on the real state of implementation in the member states. According to Haigh (2003, Release 24, 11.6-3), existing reporting requirements embedded in particular directives were 'inconsistently worded, often unclear, and as often disregarded by both member states and the Commission'. This effectively left the Commission, supposedly the overseer of the whole process (see above), to operate in the dark. The directive requires member states to send information on implementation to the Commission every three years in the form of a sectoral report covering other related directives. Ironically, however, the implementation of this procedure was itself slow and patchy (Farmer, 2011). The number of sectoral directives addressed by the directive is now declining as they are revised or repealed and the reporting obligations are incorporated into the texts of the new legislation. Nonetheless, timely and detailed reporting remains an enduring problem in the EU.

Directive 2004/35/EC establishes a framework based on the 'polluter-pays' principle (see Article 191 [2], TFEU). It complements the civil liability system as it deals with the 'pure ecological damage' and is therefore based on the powers and duties of public authorities (CEC, 2011d). Meanwhile Directive 2008/99/EC was a greatly delayed response to the long-held view that there was a need for some degree of harmonization of national penalties for violations of key provisions of Community environmental law, even in situations where there are no transboundary implications, in order to ensure a level playing field for regulated actors within the internal market. It seeks to ensure that member states treat a number of acts contravening Community law as criminal offences under domestic law and provide for criminal penalties whenever these acts are committed by individuals. Crucially, states are left to determine the type and level of those penalties, as this matter does not fall within the Community's sphere of competence.

Recommendation 2001/331/EC provides minimum criteria for environmental inspections in the member states. These non-binding criteria govern the planning, carrying out, following up and reporting on environmental inspections in order to strengthen compliance with EU laws. An evaluation concluded that while it had led to improvements in some member states, it had not been fully implemented in all member states (COM (2007) 707). It also suggested that the Recommendation should be amended 'in order to improve its implementation and strengthen its effectiveness'. Given this heterogeneity, differential implementation is probably to be expected.

Summary points

- A whole host of different solutions to the EU's implementation problems have been suggested.
- Some of the more assertive ones have not been taken up, given widespread fears that they could make the whole problem worse, not better.
- Instead, the EU has focused on less confrontational (i.e. more networked) forms of governance such as better reporting and more standardized forms of inspection.
- However, implementation of these measures is by no means perfect either.

Conclusion and future challenges

In 2008, the European Commission published a communication on implementing European Community environmental law (COM (2008) 773), its first major statement on the matter since 1996. In it, the Commission sought to downplay the importance of enforcement action through infringement proceedings before the ECJ and instead stressed the need for more measures aimed at preventing breaches from occurring. In practice, this means relying on the horizontal measures described in the previous section, on working with states by issuing inspection and reporting guidelines and doing more to ensure that policies are adequately designed in the first place. When this more preventative approach fails, the Commission has said it will focus its efforts on dealing with those breaches that it considers to be particularly 'fundamental' and/or 'systemic', namely those that seriously damage human health or the environment, or which concern big infrastructure projects or interventions involving EU funding or significant adverse impacts. In September 2009, the Secretariat General of the Commission set up a system to record all complaints and enquiries, and to ensure the Commission's enforcement resources are more effectively deployed. In the most serious cases, a special complaint form has been created to collect the sort of information the Commission will eventually need in order to take enforcement action (CEC, 2011e).

In many respects, the Commission seems to have arrived at pragmatic solutions to the three puzzles outlined in the very first section. First, it has adopted many measures that increase its ability to challenge persistent offenders (e.g. the levying of financial penalties), but which do not radically overturn the structural imbalance between itself (the overseer) and the main implementing bodies, namely, the member states. The second puzzle concerned the enduring public popularity of

EU environmental policy despite the many ongoing implementation problems. There, the Commission realizes all too well that a balance has to be struck here in the sense that while members of the public often support its attempts to challenge states, if this is perceived to go too far (as it did in the late 1980s and early 1990s), public support for the EU may well suffer. The Lisbon Treaty of course now permits 'citizens' initiatives' to be taken on salient topics (see Chapter 3). It will be interesting to see whether environmental interest groups use this to mobilize a broader public demand for stronger and more intrusive forms of enforcement. Finally, the EU has tried to address the third puzzle – the fact that much new legislation continues to emerge despite the implementation problems – by trying to engage in better (Radaelli, 2007) or 'smarter' forms of regulation (CEC, 2010d) (see also Chapter 12). Time will tell whether these initiatives actually produce better implemented legislation. Academics have a role to play here as much of the existing literature still fails to address what is arguably the 'real' implementation problem; that is, delivering political outcomes in the form of a better environment. Important research questions here include establishing whether polluting emissions were reduced by the required amount and calculating the corresponding impact on environmental quality. Intuitively, these seem more pertinent than asking about patterns in transposition rates or the time taken to issue ECJ rulings given that the ultimate purpose of EU policy is to protect the environment. This point is taken up in Chapter 15.

To conclude, the troublesome implementation of EU policies is but a microcosm of the wider story of integration and the conflicting forces and contradictions which have characterized the EU throughout its journey from an intergovernmental agreement to a multilevel polity. These contradictions include the maintenance of unity in diversity, the competition between national priorities and supranational imperatives, and the distribution of powers between actors at different spatial levels of government. If anything, they are more starkly revealed in the implementation phase, when the EU's policies are put to the test, than at earlier stages in the policy process where symbolic gestures and rhetorical commitments are more likely to secure political support. Poor implementation in the EU remains very much a 'safety valve' to prevent these and other conflicting political demands from building up in Europe and disrupting the entire integration process (Olsen, 2007: 246). Setting the whole issue of implementation in this wider political and historical context certainly offers a more three-dimensional alternative to the common perception that EU environmental policies are inherently 'good' and that poor implementation of them is necessarily pernicious. Rather, 'post decisional' (Puchala, 1975) politics are an integral and, we suspect, never-ending part of the wider struggle between actors at different governance levels to shape the European integration process.

Summary points

- In the past, the EU has veered between more and less interventionist approaches to address implementation problems.
- Nowadays, the Commission's preferred approach is to adopt a more pragmatic combination of the two approaches.
- Implementation is at the sharp end of the EU policy process, where sharply conflicting demands about the need for 'more' or 'less' European integration eventually have to be reconciled.
- Consequently 'poor' implementation is likely to remain a policy problem in search of a political solution.

Key questions

1 What are the main causes of the EU's implementation problems?
2 How does implementation in the EU differ from implementation in national contexts?
3 To what extent is non-implementation in the environmental sector worse than other sectors? Why might this be the case?
4 Which actors (state and non-state) interact to shape the implementation of EU policy?
5 Which factors prevented implementation problems from being openly discussed and addressed before the late 1980s?
6 How well are the new (post 2004) member states (the EU-12) complying with EU environmental policy relative to the EU-15?
7 What could, in theory, be done to reduce implementation problems in the EU and why have some of these solutions not even been trialled?

Guide to further reading

- For early attempts to study implementation in broad terms, see Hawke (2002) and Haigh (2003). For a more recent update, see Milio (2010).
- Knill and Lenschow (2000) sought to show how poor implementation fed demands for alternative instruments. Jordan and Liefferink (2004) go beyond the implementation of particular laws to study the Europeanizing effects of whole areas of EU policy.
- For a flavour of the scholarly debate about implementation and compliance patterns in the EU, see Falkner *et al.* (2005), Mastenbroek (2005) and Falkner and Treib (2008).

References

Alter, K. (1998) 'Who are the "masters of the treaty"? European governments and the ECJ', *International Organisation*, vol. 52, no. 1, pp. 121–144.

Berglund, S., Gange, I. and van Waarden, F. (2006) 'Mass production of law: routinization in the transposition of European directives: a sociological-institutionalist account', *Journal of European Public Policy*, vol. 13, no. 5, pp. 692–716.

Börzel, T.A. (2003) *Environmental Leaders and Laggards in Europe: Why There is (Not) a 'Southern Problem'*, Ashgate, Aldershot.

CEC (Commission of the European Communities) (2004) 'Chapter 22 – Environment', available at: http://ec.europa.eu/enlargement/archives/enlargement_process/future_prospects/negotiations/eu10_bulgaria_romania/chapters/chap_22_en.htm (accessed 30 June 2011).

CEC (2007) *Communication from the Commission: A Europe of Results – Applying Community Law* (COM (2007) 502 final), Commission of the European Communities, Brussels.

CEC (2008) *Communication on Implementing European Community Environmental Law* (COM (2008) 773/4), Commission of the European Communities, Brussels.

CEC (2010a) *2009 Environmental Policy Review*, (SEC (2010) 975 final), Office for Official Publications of the European Communities, Luxembourg.

CEC (2010b) *27th Annual Report on Monitoring the Application of EU Law* (COM (2010) 538), Commission of the European Communities, Brussels.

CEC (2010c) *Annexes I to III: Accompanying Document to the 27th Annual Report on Monitoring the Application of EU Law (2009)* (SEC (2010) 1144), Commission of the European Communities, Brussels.

CEC (2010d) *Communication from the Commission to the European Parliament, the Council, the European Economic and Social Committee and the Committee of the Regions: Smart Regulation in the European Union* (COM (2010) 543), Commission of the European Communities, Brussels.

CEC (2011a) *Special Eurobarometer 365: Attitudes of European Citizens towards the Environment (Provisional Summary)*, Commission of the European Communities, Brussels.

CEC (2011b) 'Legal enforcement: strategic cases', available at: http://ec.europa.eu/environment/legal/law/setting.htm (accessed 20 June 2011).

CEC (2011c) 'Legal enforcement: statistics on environmental infringements', available at: http://ec.europa.eu/environment/legal/law/statistics.htm (accessed 20 June 2011).

CEC (2011d) 'Environmental liability: introduction', available at: http://ec.europa.eu/environment/legal/liability/index.htm (accessed 20 June 2011).

CEC (2011e) 'Legal enforcement: complaints, petitions and other sources of infringement information', available at: http://ec.europa.eu/environment/legal/law/complaints.htm (accessed 29 June 2011).

Collins, K. and Earnshaw, D. (1992) 'The implementation and enforcement of EC environmental policy', *Environmental Politics*, vol. 1, no. 4, pp. 213–249.

COWI, ECORYS and Cambridge Econometrics (2011) *The Costs of Not Implementing the Environmental Acquis*, Final report ENV.G.1/FRA/2006/0073, European Commission, Brussels.

Falkner, G. and Treib, O. (2008) 'Three worlds of compliance or four? The EU-15 compared to the new member states', *Journal of Common Market Studies*, vol. 46, no. 2, pp. 293–314.

Falkner, G., Treib, O., Hartlapp, M. and Leiber, S. (2005) *Complying with Europe: EU Harmonisation and Soft Law in the Member States*, Cambridge University Press, Cambridge.

Farmer, A. (2011) *The Manual of European Environmental Policy*, Taylor & Francis, London.

Haigh, N. (2003) *Manual of Environmental Policy*, Longman, Harlow.

Haigh, N. and Lanigan, C. (1995) 'Impact of the EU on UK policy making', in T. Gray (ed.) *UK Environmental Policy in the 1990s*, Macmillan, Basingstoke.

Haverland, M. (2003) 'The impact of the European Union on environmental policies', in K. Featherstone and K. Radaelli (eds) *The Politics of Europeanization*, Oxford University Press, Oxford.

Hawke, N. (2002) *Environmental Policy: Implementation and Enforcement*, Ashgate, Aldershot.

Hill, M. and Hupe, P. (2008) *Implementing Public Policy*, Sage, Thousand Oaks, CA.

HOLSCEC (House of Lords Select Committee on the European Communities) (1987) *Fourth Environmental Action Programme: House of Lords Paper 25*, The Stationery Office, London.

Holzinger, K., Knill, C. and Schäfer, A. (2006) 'Rhetoric or reality? "New governance" in EU environmental policy', *European Law Journal*, vol. 12, no. 3, pp. 403–420.

IMPEL (2010) *Better Regulation Checklist: Checklist to Assess Practicability and Enforceability of Legislation*, IMPEL, Brussels.

Jack, B. (2010) 'Enforcing member state compliance with EU environmental law: a critical evaluation of the use of financial penalties', *Journal of Environmental Law*, vol. 23, no. 1, pp. 73–95.

Jordan, A. (1997) 'Overcoming the divide between comparative politics and international relations approaches to the EC: What role for "post-decisional politics"?', *West European Politics*, vol. 20, no. 4, pp. 43–70.

Jordan, A. (1999) 'The implementation of EU environmental policy: a problem without a political solution?', *Environment and Planning C*, vol. 17 no. 1, pp. 69–90.

Jordan, A.J. (2000) 'The politics of multilevel environmental governance: subsidiarity and environmental policy in the European Union', *Environment and Planning A*, vol. 32, no. 7, pp. 1307–1324.

Jordan, A. and Liefferink, D. (eds) (2004) *Environmental Policy in Europe: The Europeanization of National Environmental Policy*, Routledge, London.

Jordan, A.J., Huitema, D., van Asselt, D.H., Rayner, T. and Berkhout, F. (eds) (2010) *Climate Change Policy in the European Union: Confronting the Dilemmas of Mitigation and Adaptation?* Cambridge University Press, Cambridge.

Jordan, A.J., van Asselt, H., Berkhout, F., Huitema, D. and Rayner, T. (2012) 'Climate change policy in the European Union: understanding the paradoxes of multi-level governing', *Global Environmental Politics*, vol. 12, no. 2, pp. 43–66.

Kellow, A. and Zito, A.R. (2002) 'Steering through complexity: EU environmental regulation in the international context', *Political Studies*, vol. 50, no. 1, pp. 43–60.

Knill, C. (2006) 'Implementation', in J. Richardson (ed.) *European Union: Power and Policy-Making*, Routledge, London.

Knill, C. and Lenschow, A. (eds) (2000) *Implementing EU Environmental Policy: New Directions and Old Problems*, Manchester University Press, Manchester.

Krämer, L. (2009) 'The environmental complaint in EU law', *Journal for European Environmental & Planning Law*, vol. 6, no. 1, pp. 13–35.

Macrory, R. (1992) 'The enforcement of Community environmental laws: critical issues', *Common Market Law Review*, vol. 29, no. 2, pp. 347–369.

Majone, G. (1996) *Regulating Europe*, Routledge, London.

Mastenbroek, E. (2005) 'EU compliance: still a black hole?', *Journal of European Public Policy*, vol. 12, no. 6, pp. 1103–1120.

Milio, S. (2010). *From Policy to Implementation in the European Union: The Challenge of a Multi-Level Governance System*, I.B. Tauris, London.

Olsen, J. (2007) *Europe in Search of Political Order*, Oxford University Press, Oxford.

Potočnik, J. (2011) 'Achieving our objectives by effective implementation', speech given at a stakeholder conference on the Communication on Implementation Brussels, 15 June 2011, available at: http://europa.eu/rapid/pressReleasesAction.do?reference=SPEECH/11/440&format=HTML (accessed 20 June 2011).

Pressman, J. and Wildavsky, A. (1984) *Implementation*, University of California Press, Berkeley, CA.

Puchala, D. (1975) 'Domestic politics and regional harmonisation in the European Communities', *World Politics*, vol. 27, no. 4, pp. 496–520.

Radaelli, C.M. (2007) 'Whither better regulation for the Lisbon agenda?', *Journal of European Public Policy*, vol. 14, no. 2, pp. 190–207.

Scharpf, F.W. (2006) 'The joint-decision trap revisited', *Journal of Common Market Studies*, vol. 44, no. 4, pp. 845–864.

Weiler, J. (1988) 'The White Paper and the application of community law', in R. Bieber, R. Dehousse, J. Pinder and J. Weiler (eds) *1992: One European Market?* Nomos, Baden-Baden.

Wilkinson, D. (1994) *The State of Reporting by the Commission in Fulfilment of Obligations Contained in EC Environmental Legislation*, Institute of European Environmental Policy, London.

15 Policy evaluation

Per Mickwitz

Summary guide

In order to develop new environmental policies, it is important first to evaluate those that have already been adopted. However, this intuitively simple idea is difficult to apply in practice, no more so than in the complex governance context of the EU. Attributing impacts to specific policies is challenging, and making evaluations useful for political decision making is even more demanding. Five approaches for dealing with these challenges are discussed, namely: side-effect evaluation; intervention theories; triangulation; multi-criteria analysis; and participation-based evaluation. How and why these approaches are (or are not) utilized in the EU is described and explained. Recently, emphasis on retrospective evaluation has increased in the EU, and the focus has broadened from evaluating expenditure programmes to legislation and other non-spending policies. Nonetheless, more effort is needed to create a well-established culture of policy evaluation in the EU.

Introduction

'The car taxation reform has increased the popularity of low-emission cars' was the headline of an article in the largest Finnish newspaper, *Helsingin Sanomat*, on 26 January 2011. It stated that because of the tax reform, which made taxation dependent on carbon dioxide (CO_2) emissions, the average CO_2 emissions of new cars had dropped from 180 grams per kilometre in 2006 to less than 150 in 2009. Impressive! But how do we know as observers that the lower emissions were due to the tax reform and not caused by other factors? In addition to taxation, a wide set of other policy measures have been applied with the aim of reducing CO_2 emissions from cars. These include EU policies such as voluntary agreements with the car industry and a requirement to provide information to consumers about CO_2 emissions based on the Labelling Directive (1999/94/EC). In addition, many factors other than public policies affect car purchasing decisions. Over the three years 2007–2009, there was a financial crisis and large sports utility vehicle (SUVs) – at least temporarily – went out of fashion.

In order to say anything meaningful about the impact or effectiveness of a particular reform, a policy evaluation is required. Evaluation is based on the very simple idea (Vedung, 2010) that policies can and should be improved by systematic determination of their merit, worth or value (Scriven, 1991). Why should one bother and expend scarce resources on looking backwards and trying to evaluate the impacts of past policies or programmes? There are two main reasons: first, evaluations may provide crucial insights for learning and developing new policies, and, second, evaluations are important to ensure accountability. But evaluation is hard to practise, especially in the complex governing context of the EU.

This chapter is concerned with the evaluation of environmental policies in the EU, and specifically the evaluation of policies and programmes. This implies that some important evaluations, such as those of key actors, including the European Environmental Agency (EEA) (Technopolis, 2008), are beyond the scope of this chapter. Evaluation is frequently defined so that it includes both prospective (ex ante) and retrospective (interim or ex post) evaluation. In this chapter, 'evaluation' will be limited to retrospective studies (as by Vedung, 1997); prospective studies (Impact Assessment or *ex ante* evaluation) are discussed in Chapter 12. Since there are numerous links between prospective and retrospective evaluations, I will also comment on *ex ante* evaluations and then return to the relationship between the two at the end of this chapter. Although my focus is on EU policies, they may be evaluated at different levels – the whole EU, one or a few member states, one municipality or certain target groups or stakeholders – and from many different perspectives.

The social and economic systems, such as the mobility system, causing the environmental problems that policies and programmes try to affect are very complex and not fully understood. Although greater research does increase knowledge, environmental policies must always be formed and implemented in a context predominated by uncertainty and ignorance. These policies should, therefore – at all levels, from the EU to the local – be reflexive and based on continuous learning from past experiences. This implies that, while it is crucial that policies be based on careful pre-assessment (see Chapter 12), in order to develop and refine the policies and programmes before they are adopted and implemented, they should also be retrospectively evaluated much more than is currently the case.

Since the idea of policy and programme evaluation is so simple, why is evaluation practice so difficult? The reasons can be grouped into two categories: first, challenges related to producing credible evaluation results; and second, the difficulties linked to making evaluations relevant. On account of the complexities of socio-technical systems, it is extremely difficult to determine the effects of any individual policy or programme when a multitude of other factors – some of them other policies and programmes – influence the same system. There are several interlinked terms describing this challenge, which Vedung (1997) and Mickwitz (2003) call the 'impact problem'; others approach it through the concept of 'attribution' (Sanderson, 2002), whereas Ferraro (2009) discusses it from the standpoint of 'counterfactual thinking'. Undertaking evaluations that are actually used is the second and trickiest aspect of evaluation. Environmental policy decision making is always political and involves many actors and many different interests, and a lot of other information than that provided by formal evaluations is used. In such situations, the influence of particular evaluations maybe small; in practice, they may well be completely ignored.

In the EU, these two generic problems are, if anything, even more accentuated than those pertaining to national policy evaluation. Nowadays, EU environmental policies are formed and implemented in a setting that can be characterized by the notion of multi-level governance (see Chapter 1 and Box 15.2). This concept is helpful in understanding the relationships among the actors involved in commissioning, producing and using evaluations. The three processes of commissioning, producing and using evaluations are hugely dependent on each other. If an evaluation is framed and commissioned by a single EU institution and carried out in a non-participatory way, it is not very likely that it will become widely used at the national and local level or by NGOs.

This chapter has two aims: first, to discuss how contemporary evaluation has addressed the two challenges that make evaluation so hard to practise (i.e. production of credible evaluation results and usable evaluations) and, second, to discuss current features of evaluations of EU environmental policies and programmes as well as prospects for development.

Summary points

- Evaluating environmental policies is in principle important both for policy learning and for accountability.
- Evaluating environmental policies is difficult to achieve in practice, because it is hard to produce credible results and even harder to produce usable evaluations.
- The EU is a complex system of multi-level governance, which adds considerably to the practical difficulty of evaluating policies.

Contemporary evaluation approaches

This section will review five approaches to evaluation developed in areas (e.g. social policy, education and development aid) where evaluations has been traditionally undertaken. These are side-effect evaluation; intervention theory-based (or programme theory-based) evaluation; triangulation; multi-criteria evaluation; and participation-based evaluation.

Side-effect evaluation

The EU generally focuses its demands for evaluation on the effectiveness or cost-effectiveness of specific policies, with effectiveness meaning 'attaining the specific objectives set and achieving the intended results' (CEC, 2008: 40). While evaluating the effectiveness of regulations is necessary, it is seldom sufficient. It is necessary because objectives are key elements used in the policy formation process in order to have policies adopted, and, therefore, they should be followed up. It is not sufficient largely because of side-effects, but also because changes in the dynamic context of policies might make established goals irrelevant at a later stage.

Policies and programmes seldom turn out exactly as intended. This is to some extent due to poor implementation; what is provided – by member state and local-level institutions – is not exactly what was expected (see Chapter 14). It may also be because the drafting of policies was based on incorrect assumptions (Hoogerwerf, 1990). But it is also because policies, especially important ones, tend to be used in complex and changing contexts, where there are many other actors as well as external factors and the interactions between these are uncertain. The effects of policies, even when extensively planned, are therefore often unanticipated. Or, in the words of the philosopher Karl Popper (2003: 104), 'although we may learn to foresee many of the unintended consequences of our actions . . . there will always be many we did not foresee'. Popper (ibid.: 105) therefore argues that 'the main task of the social sciences . . . is the task of analysing the unintended social repercussions of intentional human actions'.

The 'side-effects evaluation' model (Vedung, 1997: 49ff) is a response to the criticism concerning the limitations of goal achievement or effectiveness evaluations. In this model, the effects of the policies being evaluated are first divided into anticipated and unanticipated effects. Then they are categorized according to whether the effects occur inside or outside the target area, and finally a qualitative categorization is made of the effects. The unanticipated effects are often only partially known before an evaluation is actually undertaken. Therefore, one important task, sometimes even *the* most important task, of an evaluation is to reveal unanticipated effects not previously known. For example, an evaluation of Finnish environmental permits established that the crucial role of temporary relaxations of permit conditions for the development and diffusion of new technologies was an unanticipated side-effect of the intended flexibility of the permit system (Hildén *et al.*, 2002).

Intervention theory-based evaluation

Programme theory, or the more generic intervention theory, has become a key concept in contemporary evaluation. An intervention theory can be seen as a model 'of the microsteps or linkages in the causal path from program [or, more generally, intervention] to ultimate outcome' (Rogers *et al.*, 2000: 10) on the basis of the detailed assumptions of how the intervention is intended to work. The word 'theory' in 'intervention theory' easily causes confusion, since it may be misinterpreted as referring to scientific theory, whereas in fact it refers to how an intervention should work, not how it actually works when implemented. Intervention theories are thus tools in the evaluation process for assessing the *actual* implementation and the effects that policies and programmes have had in practice.

Hansen and Vedung (2010) argue that a fully developed intervention theory should have three elements: situational; causal; and normative. The situational theory is about the context and the issue the intervention should address (the size of the problem, the causes of the problem, etc.). The causal theory is about how a particular intervention – directly or indirectly – would have an impact on the issue. The normative theory is about why a situation achieved through the intervention would be preferable.

Interventions are almost always based on several intervention theories, not just one, since different stakeholders often have different expectations of an intervention (Weiss, 2000). An evaluation using intervention theories should therefore reflect these different assumptions by constructing multiple intervention theories instead of just one (see Box 15.1). Constructing and comparing the intervention theories used by different parties, such as the European Commission, national ministries, regional administrations, and regulated companies or citizens, could be especially important for EU environmental policies.

Box 15.1 Evaluating integrated pollution control

When national legislation and regional implementation do not simply transpose and implement EU regulations, the target groups or addressees may actually change. Accordingly, utilizing multiple intervention theories reflecting the assumptions of different parties at different levels might be useful. For example, the directive concerning integrated pollution prevention and control (96/61/EC) and the Finnish Environment Protection Act (2000/86), through which it is transposed and implemented, have largely been based on the assumption that the main target group is large-scale industrial factories. When the new Finnish Environmental Protection Act was drafted, it was, however, decided at the national level to extend the Directive's scope – by including all activities that had earlier been required to have a permit, of any sort. This shifted the scope, but also the focus, from the large installations covered by the directive to much smaller units and other types of units than large industrial factories. An evaluation showed that in Finland the largest category of permits in the first two years was actually permits for farms (Mickwitz *et al.*, 2003). Utilizing this information to reformulate the assumptions about how the directive functions would be an important contribution to debates at EU level as well as in Finland about future permit applications.

Multi-criteria evaluation

Evaluation is by its very nature normative, so some value criteria on which to base the judgements must be utilized. When one uses more than a single criterion, whether that is effectiveness or any other, a more comprehensive debate about the policies can be facilitated through the evaluations. Criteria of different categories can be used, such as general evaluation criteria, economic criteria and criteria related to democracy. Because of the frequently discussed 'democratic deficit' of the EU (see Chapters 9 and 12), criteria such as acceptability, transparency, participatory rights and equity, which are important in any policy evaluation, have a particular salience in the evaluation of EU policies. While these criteria are important in their own right, they are also related to the other criteria, since acceptable and transparent policies might also have greater impacts and be more effective.

Triangulation

There is no unique and universal answer to how one should empirically examine the impacts of a particular policy. Often, however, approaches using several types of data and methods instead of only one are appropriate, especially in the environmental policy context. This is known as 'triangulation' (Scriven, 1991). Four types of triangulation can be distinguished: (1) multiple methods; (2) multiple data sources within one method; (3) multiple analysts; and (4) multiple theories.

One reason for using triangulation is to empirically examine links which are assumed in intervention theories, but there are other reasons as well. Triangulation is a good way to identify the unanticipated effects of policies; several evaluators applying many perspectives (theories) examining multiple types of data with a number of methods are more likely to uncover interesting and unexpected effects than a single evaluator using only one method of evaluation. Utilization of many data sources and methods is also crucial when multiple criteria are used to assess the policy. Not all data or all methods can have the same role in analysing all the criteria in any multi-criteria evaluation. Nor can they have the same role for all stages in all alternative intervention theories. Emphasizing triangulation is instead about starting out to define several rather than a few ways to address these issues, and in the process to stress the interplay between different data, methods and researchers. Using several methods simultaneously provides many benefits, but it is also challenging and often resource-intensive. Often a multi-disciplinary evaluation team is required to achieve the necessary rigour. Since all disciplines have their own terminology and styles of reasoning, communication between evaluators with a background in different fields is not always easy.

There is a particular need for triangulation in relation to the evaluation of EU policies and programmes. This is because the legitimacy, and hence use, of a particular evaluation at EU level require wide coverage, preferably including all member states. At the same time, finding the impacts of policies on complex socio-technical systems requires detailed approaches that take into account all the relevant factors – many of which often are context-specific and some of which depend on local ecological features – and that recognize the multi-level governance nature of policy formation and implementation. Triangulation is often the only way to address both these requirements.

Participation-based evaluation

The frequently observed lack of use of evaluation findings (Patton, 2008) has resulted in a wide range of efforts to promote the use of evaluations. Michael Patton states that:

> [E]valuations should be judged by their utility and actual use; therefore, evaluators should facilitate the evaluation process and design any evaluation with careful consideration of how everything that is done from beginning to end, will affect use ... the focus in utilization-focused evaluation is on *intended use by intended users*.
>
> (ibid.: 37; emphases in the original)

Key aspects of utilization-focused evaluation are therefore to determine the intended users and to facilitate use throughout the process. The main tools for achieving this are participation and cooperation.

Nowadays, promoting the use of evaluations is seen as not only necessary but even mandatory. It may, however, also be problematic to achieve, since the interactions with potential users can and should influence evaluations but not affect the integrity of the evaluators while they are undertaking their analysis. Yet the potential problems of involving intended users and stakeholders in evaluations do not imply that they should not be involved. On the contrary, evaluations without any involvement are far more problematic. Promoting the use of evaluations requires extensive transparency of the evaluation results as well as in the evaluation process and methods used.

Summary points

- Most policies have unintended side-effects; revealing them is one of the most important challenges facing policy evaluators.
- Assessing impacts and finding side-effects is best achieved by a plurality of data, methods, analysts and theories, as well as evaluation criteria.
- 'Intended use by intended users' should be an important guiding principle throughout an evaluation, not just when it has been completed.

Policy evaluation: demand and supply

Except in a few 'pioneering' countries, policy and programme evaluation is a recent phenomenon in Europe. The pioneering evaluation countries were Germany, Sweden and the United Kingdom in Europe, and outside Europe they were the United States and Canada (Furobo and Sandahl, 2002). In these countries, policy evaluation started as early as the 1960s. For many of the countries that developed policy and programme evaluation practices later, EU requirements were an important driver. The use of EU funding, the Structural Funds in particular, was coupled with requirements for evaluation, which stimulated the emergence of evaluation practices across Europe – for example, in Finland, Ireland and Spain (ibid.) and more recently in newer member states such as Poland (Stern, 2009). The diffusion of evaluation practices across Europe is important because it created an evaluation community of actors. Even more importantly, it established a culture that is essential also for the evaluation of environmental policies.

A second important feature of the diffusion of evaluation is that it has spread not only across countries but also across policy domains. Evaluation first emerged in the 1960s in connection with large-scale welfare reforms; therefore, evaluation cultures developed especially strongly in social policy and education. In the EU, evaluation concentrated largely on policies based on EU funding and has only recently expanded to encompass regulations and other policies (ibid.). When compared to many other policy domains, environmental policy and programme evaluation emerged later and is still not well institutionalized (Mickwitz, 2003).

Demands for evaluations in the EU

The demands for evaluation of EU environmental policies arise from two main sources. First, general evaluation requirements in the EU also extend to environmental policies and programmes. Second, environmental policies often include their own specific demands for evaluation. The most important general requirement for evaluation is stated in the EU's Financial Regulation (CEC, 2008) and specified in a series of communications (e.g. CEC, 2007). The importance of evaluation is also stressed in another communication, entitled *Smart Regulation in the European Union* (CEC, 2010a: 11) (see Chapter 17), with the aim to 'ensure the quality of regulation throughout the policy cycle, from the design of policy to its evaluation and revision'. Among other things, this communication (CEC, 2010a: 3) states that 'implementing existing legislation properly and amending it in the light of experience is as important as the new legislation'. The communication on evaluation (CEC, 2007: 3) recommends evaluation because: it produces 'information that is essential to evidence-based decision making for planning, designing and implementing EU policies'; it 'enhances the legitimacy of decisions and the accountability of decision-makers' in addition to 'transparency and democratic accountability'; and 'supports the Commission in better communicating the added value of the [EU] to the European citizen'.

Evaluations of environmental policies are also required by the EU environmental policies themselves. This is, however, a fairly recent phenomenon. The

Fifth Environmental Action Programme (EAP), adopted in 1993, still contained no articulated demands for policy evaluations. On the basis of the discussions about the Fifth EAP, the task of evaluating policies was clearly stated in the Sixth EAP, adopted in June 2002. Paragraph c of Article 10 (EC, 2002: 14) states that the objectives of the programme shall be pursued by 'improvement of the process of policy making through . . . *ex post* evaluation of the effectiveness of existing measures in meeting their environmental objectives'. In addition to these demands many EU regulations and directives contain requirements for evaluations. For example, the Monitoring Mechanism Decision (280/2004/EC) requests member states to report to the Commission, by 15 March 2005 and every second year after that, 'quantitative estimates of the effect of policies and measures on emissions by sources and removals by sinks of greenhouse gases between the base year and subsequent years, including 2005, 2010 and 2015, including their economic impacts to the extent feasible' (EC, 2004: 4). However, different evaluation and monitoring requirements related to EU environmental policies are not always consistent, resulting in an inefficient use of evaluation resources.

Key actors

If one takes a top-down perspective, there is no doubt that the European Commission is a key actor in EU policy evaluation. Most evaluations of EU policies are commissioned by the Commission, outsourced on the basis of standard procurement procedures, and intended to support its decision making and strategies (Stern, 2009). Other EU institutions, such as the European Parliament or the Council, are not involved and are largely ignored when intended use is planned. On its web site, DG Environment lists seven evaluations undertaken in 2010 and six in 2009.[1] All 13 of these were undertaken by consultancies, often consortia, under service contracts with the Commission (i.e. DG Environment). In some cases (e.g. the 'Study on the Implementation Effectiveness of the Environmental Liability Directive and Related Financial Issues'), the evaluation by the consultancy was followed up by a formal report by the Commission (CEC, 2010b).

The European Court of Auditors is an EU institution established by the EU treaties to audit the EU's finances. It inspects EU funds in order to ensure that they are correctly accounted for and spent in accordance with EU rules. Since the European Court of Auditors – as many national audit institutions do – also considers whether the best value is obtained for the money spent, the focus has grown from just legal audits and spending control to audits that closely resemble evaluation (Stern, 2009). Some of these evaluations resembling audits concern environmental policies.

In the late 1990s, the European Environmental Agency (EEA) became more active in policy evaluation. The EEA started the Reporting on Environmental Measures project, which in 2001 published a report, *Reporting on Environmental Measures: Are We Being Effective?*, which at that time represented the state of the art on environmental evaluation concepts and methods (EEA, 2001). In the early 2000s, the EEA organized seminars on policy evaluation, which were important for enabling environmental evaluators in Europe to network, and published several policy evaluations, on, for example, wastewater treatment and waste management (EEA, 2005). During that time, evaluation was also emphasized in the strategy of the EEA for 2004–2008. In the Foreword to the strategy (EEA, 2004: iii), Lars-Erik Liljelund referred to 'the increased emphasis that will be placed on evaluations of policy effectiveness'.

More recently, the EEA has become less visible in policy evaluation. This might be because policy evaluation is not a task of the agency under its new regulation (Regulation EC No. 401/2009), which in relation to evaluation only states the need 'to provide the Commission with the information that it needs to be able to carry out successfully its tasks of identifying, preparing and evaluating measures and legislation in the field of the environment' (EC, 2009: 14). Nonetheless, the EEA has continued to publish evaluation studies, for example, an effectiveness evaluation of waste-management policies (EEA, 2009).

The EU also funds a lot of environmental research. In, for example, the Seventh Framework Programme, the environment (including climate change) has a budget of €1.9 billion for 2008–2013. Many of the projects funded focus largely on natural sciences, but multi-disciplinary projects that include work packages focusing on policies are becoming more common. Some of these projects also undertake studies, which can be viewed as evaluations.

Summary points

- The demand for evaluations of EU policies and programmes has increased.
- Many actors are involved in commissioning, producing and using evaluations, but the role of evaluation is often quite weak.
- In the late 1990s, the EEA became more active in policy evaluation, but more recently it has became less visible in policy evaluation activities.

The main policy evaluation practices in the EU

In this section, the practical role of the five evaluation approaches that were presented above at the conceptual level is discussed.

Side-effect evaluation

Evaluation in the EU is very focused on goal achievement or effectiveness; in that sense, side-effects have had a secondary role. At the same time, many important EU policy strategies are based on the idea of side-effects. For example, the EU's better regulation strategy was largely based on the idea that regulations have undesired side-effects on competitiveness and the conditions for growth and jobs (CEC, 2005). While this may well be true for many regulations, it should, however, also be acknowledged that the side-effects of some regulations on competitiveness, growth and jobs can also be positive (Porter and van der Linde, 1995). Utilizing a side-effect evaluation perspective more fully would imply that the assumption of undesired side-effects on competitiveness should be tested, but it would also imply expanding the realm of potentially important side-effects. One policy challenge demanding a greater focus on potential side-effects is that of environmental policy integration, which was headlined in Article 6 of the 1997 Amsterdam Treaty (see Chapter 13) for details.

The Commission's *Evaluation Standards* (CEC, 2007) do not address side-effects at all. This is quite interesting, as the EU guidelines for (*ex ante*) Impact Assessment (CEC, 2009; see also Chapter 12) place great emphasis on a side-effect perspective, even more than that, they use the term 'side-effect'. The Impact Assessment guidelines stress the importance of assessing likely economic, social and environmental impacts, intended as well as unintended, and provide a checklist of 35 example impact categories, among them property rights, land use, social inclusion and the protection of particular groups. For any particular regulation, most of these impacts would clearly be side-effects.

Very frequently, (*ex post*) evaluations of environmental policies in practice ignore all side-effects, or, if any side-effects are addressed, mainly positive impacts are briefly covered. Evaluations that fully reveal unanticipated side-effects are rare or perhaps even altogether absent. For example, a recent comprehensive evaluation of the Sixth EAP (Ecologic, 2011) only deals with the goals and approaches of the programme, and its only extension is to the environmental aspects of the EU Sustainable Development Strategy and the Lisbon Strategy. Issues such as economic growth and European competitiveness are considered to be factors influencing implementation, but the side-effects of the programme on these issues are not evaluated.

Intervention theory-based evaluation

Among the contemporary approaches to evaluation discussed above, the one which is least visible in the Commission's *Evaluation Standards* (CEC, 2007) and in evaluations of environmental policies is the intervention theory approach. This is quite surprising, given the popularity of the approach among – also European – evaluation scholars and its importance in the Commission's guidelines for Impact Assessment (CEC, 2009), which include the application of causal models as an approach for identifying impacts.

Multi-criteria evaluation

The Commission has clearly adopted a multi-criteria approach, but some criteria are deemed more important than others. Already at the top of its evaluation web page,[2] the Commission stresses three criteria, stating:

An evaluation typically answers questions concerned with: relevance: do the objectives correspond to the needs and problems? effectiveness: to what extent were the set objectives attained? efficiency/cost-effectiveness: were the results achieved at a reasonable cost?

In the Commission's *Evaluation Standards* (CEC, 2007: 23), the following criteria are listed: 'effectiveness, efficiency/cost-effectiveness, relevance, coherence, sustainability, utility and/or community added value, and where relevant the contribution to broader strategic objectives'. The Standards stress that the criteria listed should be used 'whenever relevant' and that additional criteria may be added. In practice, policy evaluations of environmental policies have largely been focused on effectiveness: whether the main environmental goals of the policies have been achieved. This can be seen in the efforts by the EEA and in the evaluations commissioned by the Commission during 2009–2010.

Triangulation

The Commission's *Evaluation Standards* (CEC, 2007: 23) emphasize that 'The evaluation must be conducted in such a way that the results are supported by evidence and rigorous analysis'. It also stresses that the evaluation report must be transparent with respect to the information sources and methods used. These standards do not state which kind of data or methods should be used, but emphasize that the quality of the evaluation should be assessed on the basis of, among other things, 'appropriate methods, reliable data, [and] sound analysis'.

In practice, all evaluations of EU policies use triangulation at least to some degree. They are all conducted by teams of evaluators (multiple analysts). Most evaluations use several types of data, most frequently employing a combination of document analysis, statistics, surveys and expert consultations through interviews or workshops (multiple data sources). To some extent, several methods are used, largely due to the nature of the different data sources and the different criteria (multiple methods). At the same time, in many evaluations, neither the quantitative nor the qualitative analyses are very sophisticated; frequently only descriptive statistics and opinions of experts are reported, without any further analyses. Many evaluations lack any theoretical perspectives, whether based on social sciences or on intervention theories (multiple theories).

Participation-based evaluation

Participation is a tricky issue in the EU context (see Chapter 18) because of the large numbers and huge variety of actors affected by, as well as involved in, the implementation and preparation of policies. The communication on evaluation (CEC, 2007: 8), recognizes the need to cooperate with stakeholders in a context of multi-level governance. It states: 'Community actions are often implemented in cooperation with national governments or other organizations . . . To establish close cooperation with stakeholders involved in national-level monitoring and evaluation is therefore important to ensure relevant and useful evaluation results'. Public participation is, however, not addressed at all, only internal consultation at the Commission level. The communication of the results to stakeholders is only briefly dealt with. Although stakeholders are not considered in the Commission's Standards, they are referred to in the guide on how to assess the quality of an evaluation (CEC, 2011). Two of the criteria that should be taken into account when the soundness of an evaluation is judged are that 'the report reflects an appropriate range of stakeholders consulted' and 'inputs from important stakeholders are used in a balanced way' (CEC, 2011: 7). One can expect that stakeholders and participation will receive more emphasis in the future, taking into account the Commission's promotion of what it terms 'smart regulation' (CEC, 2010a) (see also Chapter 12).

In practice, evaluations of EU environmental policies very often involve some form of participation. Mostly participation is related to data collection (i.e. stakeholders filling in questionnaires), being interviewed or participating in workshops. Sometimes stakeholders are asked to comment on problem descriptions and later on the findings and recommendations. There is rarely participation in framing the evaluation, creating the terms for references or choosing evaluation methods or criteria.

The other side of participation is the independence of evaluators to draw conclusions and make judgements without interference, which is crucial for the reliability of evaluations. Independence is mentioned in the Commission's *Evaluation Standards* (CEC, 2007: 23) which states: 'Evaluators must be free to present their results without compromise or interference, although they should take account of the steering group's comments on evaluation quality and accuracy'. But (according to Stern, 2009: 72), 'there is a widespread perception in the evaluation community that independence is not always highly valued'. But if one adopts a less Brussels-centred approach to the evaluation of EU environmental policies, many more actors come into view (see Box 15.2).

Box 15.2 The evaluation of European climate policies

Recently, Huitema *et al.* (2011) studied 259 evaluations of climate policy, undertaken in six EU member states. About half of these evaluations were undertaken by universities and research institutes, while consultancy firms produced about one-fifth. International and national governmental agencies also produced many evaluations, while NGOs and industry groups produced only a few evaluations. Of these evaluations, the majority (58 per cent) were not commissioned; these were mainly funded by domestic or EU research projects. Of the commissioned evaluations, most were ordered by national governments (59 per cent), but also international organizations, NGOs and industry groups.

The meta-analysis of climate policy evaluations by Huitema *et al.* also gives insights into the practice of evaluation in Europe. First, it confirms the dominance of effectiveness as an evaluation criterion. Out of 259 evaluations, 213 used effectiveness as a criterion, followed by efficiency in 74 cases and cost-effectiveness in 72. Other criteria, such as fairness, coordination with other policies and legitimacy, are sometimes used, but not very frequently. Another interesting observation by Huitema *et al.* is that 201 studies used one or two criteria and only then evaluations used four or five criteria while no studies used more than that. Huitema *et al.* (ibid.: 193) also assessed to what degree 'the involvement of stakeholders went further than being an object of study'. They found that 'the overwhelming majority of the evaluations in the database do not meet the basic criterion of a participatory analysis (up to 95.8 per cent, depending on method of measurement)'. Finally, Huitema *et al.* (ibid.: 188) found that 'the use of multiple methodologies is not rare, but that more than half of the evaluations use only one methodology'.

The use of policy evaluation in the EU

To improve its evaluation functions and in response to suggestions by the Court of Auditors and an external evaluation of the use of evaluation results in the Commission, a communication was issued in 2007 entitled *Responding to Strategic Needs: Reinforcing the Use of Evaluation* (CEC, 2007). It was aimed at addressing the criticism received by improving the 'relevant coverage, focus and timing' of evaluations, by integrating evaluation into 'management, strategic planning and programming cycles' and through 'better communication of evaluation results'. These are all well justified actions addressing the problems revealed, but at the same time the improvements sought are difficult and will require resources and time to achieve.

The Court of Auditors in 2005 pointed out 'that legislation and other non-spending policies are not yet systematically evaluated' (CEC, 2007: 5). This was one of the reasons for the Commission shifting the focus of evaluations and making the evaluation of legislation and non-spending policies mandatory. This shift in focus clearly supports the use of EU environmental policy evaluations, since environmental policies are largely based on EU regulations, directives and decisions.

The Commission states that better communication of evaluation results 'requires a careful assessment of what type of information is useful to whom' (ibid.: 11). However, this is not just a requirement for better communication; such an assessment is essential for the use of evaluations but can be influential only if it is taken into account at all stages, including planning, commissioning and conducting evaluations. Unfortunately, the intended user base for EU-commissioned evaluations has been, and still is, mostly limited either to the Commission or often just the DG or unit commissioning the evaluation. The Communication empha-sizes cooperation with national stakeholders in order to enhance both the quality and use of evaluations. This aim 'can also be fostered by setting up evaluation networks with those involved at national level, as several DGs have done or plan to do' (ibid.: 8). Such a network for environmental policy and programme evaluations would be highly desirable. It would not only enhance the quality and use of evaluations commissioned by the Commission but also improve the quality and use of all evaluations that are commissioned by others (national and local authorities, NGOs and interest groups). In the United States, the Environmental Evaluators Networking Forum (EENF), with annual gatherings in Washington, DC, was established in 2006.[3] It later expanded to include Canada. If the efforts of the EENF Europe could be linked to the networking efforts emphasized in the Communication, this would be very beneficial for the future evaluation of EU environmental policies and environmental evaluation in Europe more broadly.

Summary points

- Recently, the emphasis on retrospective evaluation has increased in the EU, and the focus has broadened from expenditure programmes to legislation and other non-spending policies.
- Environmental policy evaluations largely focus on the question of effectiveness.
- Multiple analysts and multiple data sources are almost always used, while the use of multiple theories is exceptional.

The evaluation of EU environmental policies: conclusion and future challenges

In the past few years, the EU has seen increased emphasis on – the simple idea of – retrospective evaluation. In this time, the focus of EU evaluations has expanded from expenditure programmes to include legislation and other non-spending policies. The EU's environmental policies are evaluated by a varied cast of different actors. Some evaluations are broad, such as that of the Sixth EAP, while others are focused on specific policy measures. Despite these developments, EU environmental policy evaluation is still quite unsystematic and mostly ad hoc. Environmental policy evaluations largely focus on effectiveness, i.e. whether the environmental objectives of the policies adopted are being achieved. Effectiveness evaluation is essential, but it is not sufficient. The development of EU environmental policy would be better served if evaluations provided assess-ments of a variety of side-effects and use criteria other than effectiveness to a greater degree than hitherto. So far, intervention theories have been used far too seldom in evaluations of EU environmental policies. While multiple analysts and multiple data sources constitute the rule rather than the exception, there is great need for improvements in use of multiple theories. Furthermore, there is room for improvement in the methodological rigour of the quantitative as well as qualitative methods used in evaluations. Descriptive statistics of survey distributions or quotes from expert interviews are data descriptions but not analysis *per se*. Finally, there is a need to combine comprehensive EU analyses with detailed local case studies. So far, neither the scale nor the quality of the EU's evaluation efforts have really matched the difficulties of this task.

Although much can be done to produce more credible evaluation results, the biggest challenges are related to making evaluations more relevant and widely used. Reaching these goals of strengthening evaluation use would require more focus on 'intended use by intended users', a wider perception of intended users than just the Commission or DG Environment, and the promotion of unintended uses by a variety of users through greater transparency and broader dissemination.

The Commission has made significant progress in recent years in *ex ante* Impact Assessments (see Chapter 12). Hopefully a similar development can be achieved with respect to retrospective evaluation as well. Data, methods, theories and experiences are often largely the same and should be shared more. As pointed out by Hildén (2011), important environmental problems are not solved by a single policy or one programme; instead, they are addressed repeatedly, by the modification of existing policies and the adoption of new ones. In such a context, the Impact Assessments of new policies should be based on retrospective evaluations of existing ones. The most crucial thing is to build a stronger community of European environmental evaluators. For this purpose, a forum would be required where actors commissioning, using and producing environmental evaluations can come together and share insights and experiences. Such a network would, for example, provide a forum to address the very practical problem outlined at the very beginning of this chapter – how to fully evaluate the Finnish car tax reform. This effort could be informed by comparisons with similar evaluations in other countries and might also consider the implications for future EU climate policies.

Summary points

- The importance of evaluating EU environmental policies is becoming more widely recognized.
- The EU is searching for ways to link evaluations of existing policies to the Impact Assessment of new ones under the heading of 'smart regulation'.
- Improving environmental evaluations will require a stronger community of European environmental evaluators.

Key questions

1   Why is it important to evaluate EU environmental policies?
2   What are the main challenges associated with policy evaluation?
3   Which approaches to evaluation are considered to be especially relevant to environmental policy evaluation, and why?
4   Who are the key actors in EU environmental policy evaluation, and what are their roles?
5   How are the main evaluation approaches used in contemporary environmental policy evaluation in the EU?
6   How could the practices of EU environmental policy evaluation be improved?

Guide to further reading

- Crabbé and Leroy (2008) offer a more in-depth introduction to environmental policy evaluation.
- Vedung (1997) provides the seminal European book on policy evaluation.
- Binbaum and Mickwitz (2009) assemble a number of articles on key methodological challenges associated with environmental policy evaluation.
- Mickwitz (2003) offers a specific framework on how to evaluate environmental policies.

Acknowledgements

I am grateful to Dr Paula Kivimaa for comments on a draft of this chapter. It was written as part of a project funded by the Academy of Finland (Decision 127288).

Notes

1   A list of environmental policy evaluations is available at: http://ec.europa.eu/dgs/environment/evaluation_reports.htm (accessed 5 July 2012).
2   The Commission's evaluation web page is available at: http://ec.europa.eu/dgs/secretariat_general/evaluation/index_en.htm (accessed 5 July 2012).
3   Information about the Environmental Evaluators Networking Forum is available at: www.environmentalevaluators.net (accessed 5 July 2012).

References

Binbaum, M. and Mickwitz, P. (eds) (2009) 'Environmental program and policy evaluation: addressing methodological challenges', *New Directions for Evaluation*, vol. 122, Summer, Jossey-Bass, San Francisco.

CEC (2005) *Better Regulation for Growth and Jobs in the European Union*, Communication of the Commission to the European Parliament, Commission of the European Communities (COM (2005) 97), European Commission, Brussels.

CEC (2007) *Responding to Strategic Needs: Reinforcing the Use of Evaluation* (SEC (2007) 213), European Commission, Brussels.

CEC (2008) *Financial Regulation and Implementing Rules Applicable to the General Budget of the European Communities: Synoptic Presentation*, Office for Official Publications of the European Communities, Luxembourg.

CEC (2009) *Impact Assessment Guidelines* (SEC (2009) 92), European Commission, Brussels.

CEC (2010a) *Smart Regulation in the European Union* (COM (2010) 543), European Commission, Brussels.

CEC (2010b) *Report from the Commission to the Council, the European Parliament, the European Economic and Social Committee and the Committee of the Regions Under Article 14(2) of Directive 2004/35/CE on the Environmental Liability with Regard to the Prevention and Remedying of Environmental Damage* (COM (2010) 581), European Commission, Brussels.

CEC (2011) 'Quality assessment form', available at: http://ec.europa.eu/dgs/secretariat_general/evaluation/docs/quality_asses_form_en.pdf (accessed at 18 September 2011).

Crabbé, A. and Leroy, P. (2008) *The Handbook of Environmental Policy Evaluation*, Earthscan, London.

EC (2002) 'Decision No. 1600/2002/EC of the European Parliament and of the Council of 22 July 2002 laying down the Sixth Community Environment Action Programme', *Official Journal of the European Communities*, L242(45), pp. 1–15.

EC (2004) 'Decision No. 280/2004/EC of the European Parliament and of the Council of 11 February 2004 concerning a mechanism for monitoring Community greenhouse gas emissions and for implementing the Kyoto Protocol', *Official Journal of the European Communities*, L49(47), pp. 1–8.

EC (2009) 'Regulation (EC) No. 401/2009 of the European Parliament and of the Council of 23 April 2009 on the European Environment Agency and the European Environment Information and Observation Network', *Official Journal of the European Communities*, L126(52), pp. 13–22.

Ecologic (2011) 'Final report for the assessment of the 6th Environmental Action Programme', 21 February 2011, available at: http://ec.europa.eu/environment/newprg/pdf/Ecologic_6EAP_Report.pdf (accessed 9 August 2011).

EEA (European Environmental Agency) (2001) *Reporting on Environmental Measures: Are We Being Effective?*, Environmental Issue Report No. 25, European Environment Agency, Copenhagen.

EEA (2004) *EEA Strategy 2004–2008*, European Environment Agency, Copenhagen.

EEA (2005) *Policy Effectiveness Evaluation: The Effectiveness of Urban Wastewater Treatment and Packaging Waste Management Systems*, European Environment Agency, Copenhagen.

EEA (2009) *Diverting Waste from Landfill: Effectiveness of Waste-Management Policies in the European Union*, EEA Report No. 7/2009, European Environment Agency, Copenhagen.

Ferraro, P. J. (2009). 'Counterfactual thinking and impact evaluation in environmental policy', in M. Birnbaum and P. Mickwitz (eds) *Environmental Program and Policy Evaluation: New Directions for Evaluation*, vol. 122, Summer, Jossey-Bass, San Francisco, pp. 75–84.

Furubo, J.-E. and Sandahl, R. (2002) 'Introduction: A diffusion perspective on global developments in evaluation', in J.E. Furubo, R.C. Rist and Sandahl, R. (eds) *International Atlas of Evaluation*, Transaction Publishers, New Brunswick, NJ, pp. 1–23.

Hansen, M.B. and Vedung, E. (2010) 'Theory-based stakeholder evaluation', *American Journal of Evaluation*, vol. 31, no. 3, pp. 295–313.

Hildén, M. (2011) 'The evolution of climate policies: the role of learning and evaluations', *Journal of Cleaner Production*, vol. 19, no. 16, pp. 1798–1811.

Hildén, M., Lepola, J., Mickwitz, P., Mulders, A., Palosaari, M., Similä, J., Sjöblom, S. and Vedung, E. (2002) *Evaluation of Environmental Policy Instruments: A Case Study of the Finnish Pulp and Paper and Chemical Industries*, Monographs of the Boreal Environment Research, vol. 21, Helsinki.

Hoogerwerf, A. (1990) 'Reconstructing policy theory', *Evaluation and Program Planning*, vol. 13, no. 3, pp. 285–291.

Huitema, D., Jordan, A., Massey, E., Rayner, T., van Asselt, H., Haug, C., Hildingsson, R., Monni, S. and Stripple, J. (2011) 'The evaluation of climate policy: theory and emerging practice in Europe', *Policy Sciences*, vol. 44, no. 2, pp. 179–198.

Mickwitz, P. (2003) 'A framework for evaluating environmental policy instruments, context and key concepts', *Evaluation*, vol. 9, no. 4, pp. 415–436.

Mickwitz, P., Ollikka, K., Sjöblom, S. and von Troil, C. (2003) 'The decisions according to the Environmental Protection Act during the two first years', *Ympäristöjuridiikka*, vol. 24, no. 1, pp. 27–47 (in Finnish).

Patton, M.Q. (2008) *Utilization-Focused Evaluation*, 4th edition, Sage, Thousand Oaks, CA.

Popper, K. (2003) *The Open Society and Its Enemies*, Volume Two: *Hegel and Marx*, Routledge Classics, London.

Porter, M. and van der Linde, C. (1995) 'Toward a new conception of the environment competitiveness relationship', *Journal of Economic Perspectives*, vol. 9, no. 4, pp. 97–118.

Rogers, P.J., Petrosino, A., Huebner, T.A. and Hacsi, T.A. (2000) 'Program theory evaluation: practice, promise, and problems', in P.J. Rogers, T.A. Hacsi, A. Petrosino and T.A. Huebner (eds) *Program Theory in Evaluation: Challenges and Opportunities, New Directions for Evaluation*, vol. 87, Fall, Jossey-Bass, San Francisco, pp. 5–13.

Sanderson, I. (2002) 'Evaluation, policy learning and evidence-based policy making', *Public Administration*, vol. 80, no. 1, pp. 1–22.

Scriven, M. (1991) *Evaluation Thesaurus*, 4th edition, Sage, Newbury Park, CA.

Stern, E. (2009) 'Evaluation policy in the European Union and its institutions', in W.M.K. Trochim, M. M. Mark and L.J. Cooksy (eds) *Evaluation Policy and Evaluation Practice, New Directions for Evaluation*, vol. 123, Jossey-Bass, San Francisco, pp. 67–85.

Technopolis (2008) 'Effectiveness evaluation of the European Environment Agency: revised final report', available at: www.eea.europa.eu/about-us/documents/effectiveness-evaluations/2008/effectiveness-evaluation-of-the-european-environment-agency.pdf (accessed 3 August 2011).

Vedung, E. (1997) *Public Policy and Program Evaluation*, Transaction Publishers, New Brunswick, NJ.

Vedung, E. (2010) 'Four waves of evaluation diffusion', *Evaluation*, vol. 16, no. 3, pp. 263–277.

Weiss, C.H. (2000) 'Which links in which theories shall we evaluate?', in P.J. Rogers, T.A. Hacsi, A. Petrosino and T.A. Huebner (eds) *Program Theory in Evaluation: Challenges and Opportunities*, *New Directions for Evaluation*, vol. 87, Fall, Jossey-Bass, San Francisco, pp. 35–45.

16 The EU as an actor in global environmental politics

Tom Delreux

Summary guide

This chapter analyses the interactions between the EU and global environmental politics and policy making. It gives an overview of the EU's status as a partner in international environmental negotiations and as a party to multilateral environmental agreements. In order to understand how the EU functions internally in the context of international environmental negotiations, it is important to understand the internal division of competences, the external representation and the internal coordination process in the EU. This chapter also reviews the various roles the EU plays in international environmental negotiations, the impact that the EU can have on global environmental politics and the future challenges confronting the EU as it seeks to exert international leadership.

Introduction

The EU is an important – even an 'influential' (Rhinard and Kaeding, 2006: 1024) – actor in international environmental negotiations. Therefore, if one wants to understand the processes and outcomes of international environmental negotiations, one needs to be familiar with the role played by the EU. Also, developments at the international level have an influence on the EU, its policies and the extent to which it can be a global actor. Hence, European and international environmental politics and policies are constantly interacting and thus mutually constitutive.

This chapter examines this interaction and is structured as follows. The next section analyses the EU as a partner in international environmental negotiations and as a party to multilateral environmental agreements (MEAs). This is followed by three sections which explore the way the EU functions internally when it acts in international environmental negotiations. First, the legal side of the question focusing on competences and the relevant treaty provisions is examined. Second, the way the EU is represented in international environmental negotiations is discussed. Third, how a common EU position is developed on a particular issue and to which extent the EU also succeeds in remaining a unified actor during the international negotiations is explored. The following section considers the impact of the EU on international environmental politics by analysing the role the EU plays in global environmental politics and policy making. Special attention will be paid to the question of the EU's leadership in international climate change negotiations. The final section presents the conclusions.

Summary points

- The EU is an important actor in international environmental negotiations.
- Developments at the international level have an influence on the EU,
  its policies and the extent to which it is and can be a global actor.
- Hence, European and international environmental politics and policies
  are constantly interacting and mutually constitutive.

The EU and international environmental negotiations

The EU is now fully recognized as an important actor in global environmental politics and policy making. It enjoys international legal personality and so is able to become a party to MEAs. This means that the EU, just like other states, can become a subject of the rights and duties of international agreements. The EU then takes the status of a so-called 'Regional Economic Integration Organization' (REIO), which is a legal concept allowing the EU to act legally at the international level (Bretherton and Vogler, 2003). The EU is nowadays a party to about 60 MEAs (Vogler and Stephan, 2007; Parker and Karlsson, 2010), which cover a broad range of environmental domains including air, biotechnology, chemicals, climate change, biodiversity, soil, waste and water policies. Table 16.1 lists the major MEAs that have been concluded by the EU.

Not only is the EU a full party to all major MEAs; it also fully participates in international environmental negotiations. In practice, the EU – as the only non-state actor around the negotiation table – is considered like a 'normal' negotiation partner during international environmental negotiation processes (e.g. it is allowed to speak or to table proposals). Many environmental negotiations take place under a United Nations (UN) framework. This mostly means that the negotiations are conducted under the auspices of the UN Environmental Programme (UNEP). In such a UN context, the EU is formally an observer, not a full member. Legally speaking, the main difference between an observer and a full member is that an observer has no voting rights. In practice, however, this lack of voting rights does not seem to be important, since international environmental politics is characterized by a consensus logic (i.e. formal voting is very

Table 16.1 Major multilateral environmental agreements to which the EU is a party

Agreement	Year adopted	Issue
Convention on Long-range Transboundary Air Pollution	1979	air
Bonn Convention on the Conservation of Migratory Species	1979	biodiversity
Vienna Convention on the Protection of the Ozone Layer	1985	air
Montreal Protocol on the Protection of the Ozone Layer	1987	air
Basel Convention on Hazardous Waste	1989	waste
Espoo Convention on Environmental Impact Assessment	1991	governance
UN Framework Convention on Climate Change	1992	climate change
UN Convention on Biological Diversity	1992	biodiversity
UN Convention to Combat Desertification	1994	soil
UN Kyoto Protocol	1997	climate change
Aarhus Convention on public participation in environmental decision making	1998	governance
Rotterdam Convention	1998	chemicals
Cartagena Protocol on Biosafety	2000	biotechnology
Stockholm Convention	2001	chemicals

Source: European Commission (2011).

unusual). Moreover, the majority of today's international environmental negotiations are conducted in Conferences or Meetings of the Parties (COPs or MOPs) to existing MEAs. COPs and MOPs are annual or bi-annual gatherings of the parties to an existing environmental treaty, organized for follow-up discussions. The climate change negotiations are currently conducted in the COPs to the United Nations Framework Convention on Climate Change (UNFCCC). Likewise, global negotiations on biodiversity take place in COPs of the Convention on Biological Diversity (CBD). As the EU is usually a formal party to the mother treaties under which umbrella such COPs and MOPs are organized, it enjoys the same rights and status as the other parties. This means that in almost all day-to-day international environmental negotiations, the EU *de facto* acts as fully-fledged negotiation partner.

The EU has not always been fully accepted and recognized as a partner in the negotiations and as a party to MEAs, however. It has been a long struggle for the EU to secure this place in international environmental politics. This struggle ensued from a number of sources, including: the constantly evolving division of competences between the EU and the member states; the lack of precedents of an actor without the formal status of a state fully participating in global environmental politics; and the feelings of uncertainty about those issues experienced by the international negotiation partners (Sbragia, 1998).

Summary points

- The EU is a party to all major MEAs, covering a wide variety of issue areas.
- The EU is able fully to participate in international environmental negotiations, either as an observer in the UN context or as a party to the mother treaty in various COPs and MOPs.
- In the past, it was a struggle for the EU to be accepted as an actor in global environmental politics, but its recognition is nowadays uncontested.

Competences for international environmental negotiations

The EU's evolution into a major international environmental actor also relates to the growing scope of environmental competences the EU has gained. Indeed, to be an international environmental actor, the EU needs the competences to act in the external environmental domain. The scope of the external environmental competences has been growing since the 1970s in two ways. On the one hand, through various treaty changes, the member states have attributed more and more external competences to the European level. Those competences, mentioned in the treaties, are called 'express powers'. Environmental competences – and *a fortiori* external environmental competences – have only been part of the treaties since the Single European Act (see Chapter 2). Besides attributing environmental competences for internal European environmental policy, the SEA also explicitly mentioned the external dimension of environmental policy in Article 130r (currently Article 191 of the Treaty on the Functioning of the European Union (TFEU)).

As well as express powers, the EU gained external environmental competences in a more indirect way. Rulings by the European Court of Justice (ECJ) (see Chapter 7) increased the scope of the external competences of the EU, including in the environmental area. In the 1970s, a number of court cases – the most important one being the ERTA case (Case 22/70) – established the so-called 'parallelism' doctrine. This basically means that the EU has the competences to act externally in all areas where it has the competences to act internally (Verwey, 2004). In other words, the EU has the competences to conclude MEAs on all those issues on which it has internal environmental policy. In contrast to express powers, these external competences are called 'implied powers'.

Environmental competences in the EU – both internal and external ones – are shared competences. Unlike exclusive competences, where member states are no longer allowed to act, shared competences still leave some room for political action to the member states. The shared nature of environmental competences is stipulated in Article 4 TFEU. The shared nature of environmental competences is important because it implies that the external environmental policy of the EU is the responsibility not of the EU institutions alone (like exclusive competences) nor of the member states separately (like national competences). By contrast, it means that the EU's relation with international environmental politics should be a joint undertaking of actors at the European and national levels. This mainly reveals itself in the EU's representation in international fora.

Summary points

- The EU has external environmental competences that are express powers, i.e. they are explicitly mentioned in the treaties.
- The EU also has external environmental competences that are implied powers, i.e. created by the case law of the ECJ which established a parallel relationship between internal and external competences.
- Environmental competences are shared competences, meaning that both the EU and the member states are responsible for the EU's external environmental policy.

External representation in international environmental negotiations

To understand the EU's representation in international environmental negotiations, a distinction needs to be made between, on the one hand, its representation in negotiations that are intended to result in a legally binding agreement and, on the other hand, the EU's representation in negotiations that are not leading to legally binding agreements but rather to political agreements, such as COP decisions. In other words, the envisioned type of outcome of the negotiations determines to a large extent how the EU is represented around the international negotiation table, at least when the legal rules are followed.

Let us first consider how the EU negotiates international legally binding MEAs. Such treaties are usually called 'Conventions' or 'Agreements', but they can also take the form of 'Protocols' or 'Amendments'. Because environmental competences are shared competences in the EU, MEAs are so-called 'mixed agreements', i.e. international treaties to which the EU and the member states are a party (Leal-Arcas, 2001). When the EU and the member states become a party to the negotiated MEA, they all have the right to be represented around the international negotiation table, each for their own competences. As a consequence, the EU representation in negotiations leading to a legally binding MEA is a 'dual representation' (Sbragia, 1998), consisting of an EU part and a member states part. Both parts of the EU representation are organized differently.

On the one hand, the European Commission negotiates on behalf of the EU for all issues falling under the EU's exclusive competences. This is the result of the combination of Article 218 TFEU and Article 17 (Treaty on European Union) TEU, which stipulates that in such a situation the EU should be represented by a 'Union negotiator' (Article 218 of the TFEU) and that the Commission should act as this Union negotiator for EU competences (Article 17, of the TEU). In other words, these treaty provisions now bar member states from negotiating internationally on issues for which the EU has exclusive competences.

On the other hand, when the member states and the EU share competence, the member states formally have two possibilities. Either they opt to conduct the negotiations separately, i.e. without a common EU negotiator, or they decide to pool their voices and to designate a common negotiator, who is usually the rotating Presidency of the Council of Ministers (see Chapter 5). Whereas the delegation of negotiation authority to the Commission for exclusive EU competences is a legal obligation, the appointment of the Presidency requires a political choice. Taking these two dynamics together, from a legal perspective, when the EU negotiates legally binding MEAs: environmental competences are *shared competences*, making MEAs *mixed agreements*, negotiated via *dual representation by the Commission and the Council Presidency*.

This conceptual triangle came under pressure in the beginning of 2010, when the Commission adopted a maximalist interpretation of the so-called 'grey zones' (i.e. those treaty provisions that are insufficiently clear and that leave room for political interpretation) of the Lisbon Treaty (see Chapter 3) to claim more competences – and even the exclusivity of the representation rights – in the EU's external environmental relations. Against this background, the Commission considered that the underlying idea that the Lisbon Treaty should increase the coherence of the EU's external relations (Degrand-Guillaud, 2009) as an argument to claim a larger role for itself, even when shared competences are at stake. Moreover, it argued that giving more representation power to the Commission was the only way to provide what the EU was said to have missed at the December 2009 climate change conference in Copenhagen: a single voice. Hence, against the background of the Lisbon grey zones and the Copenhagen experience, tensions on who should have the power in the EU's external environmental relations arose between the Commission and the member states (see also Chapter 3). The case of the EU's representation in negotiations leading to a new international mercury treaty (see Box 16.1) illustrates that sometimes more attention tends to be paid to questions on the internal balance of power and the institutional equilibrium, than to substantive positions or strategies.

Box 16.1 Internal battles after Lisbon: the case of the mercury negotiations

In June 2010, the first International Negotiation Committee to prepare a global legally binding instrument on mercury convened in Stockholm under the auspices of UNEP. The question on the EU representation in these negotiations led to the toughest inter-institutional battle in the post-Lisbon context. The Commission recommended a full negotiation mandate to the Council. It was not so much the fact that the Commission made recommendations for a mandate that led to highly tense inter-institutional relations (because it is common practice that the Commission can negotiate for the EU part of the shared competences), but rather the scope of the mandate it recommended. The Commission recommended the Council grant it a mandate so that the Commission would be the only EU negotiator on all issues, as if it were an international negotiation touching upon exclusive (as opposed to shared) competences. Arguments about the EU's coherence and necessity to have a single voice, rooted in the Commission's maximalist political interpretation of the Lisbon Treaty, substantiated the Commission's claim. The member states completely rejected the Commission's request since they wanted to avoid the situation where the grey zones of the Lisbon Treaty would be occupied by the Commission.

The member states prepared a counter-proposal in which they made use of an innovation – and grey zone – of the Lisbon Treaty, namely the possibility to appoint a 'Union's negotiating team' (Article 218, TFEU). Building on this grey zone, the Council proposed that the Commission and the rotating Presidency would jointly form such a 'negotiating team'. A consequence of this option was that the Presidency would also be able to negotiate issues falling under EU competences. The Commission interpreted this as a loss of the powers it had won many years ago (namely to be the sole negotiator for issues falling under EU competences). This inter-institutional battle culminated in the Commission withdrawing its recommendation and leaving the EU without any negotiation mandate for the negotiation session in Stockholm. This is said to have led to embarrassing situations at the international level, where the internal division in the EU was extremely clear for its external partners and where the coherence – let alone the single voice – seemed to be further away than ever.

Only one month before the second negotiation session on the mercury treaty (in Chiba, Japan, January 2011) the member states finally granted a mandate to the Commission so that the EU's external representation for this negotiation session was guaranteed. The Commission was granted a negotiation mandate for those matters falling within the Union's competences. Hence, despite the big inter-institutional battles of 2010, the final outcome was a standard mandate, in which the Commission gained the responsibility for negotiating the EU part of the shared competences and the other part was left to the member states, represented by the Presidency.

Having now discussed the EU's representation in negotiations leading to a legally binding MEA, let us now focus on the EU's representation in negotiations that do not lead to a legally binding agreement. Here, Article 218 TFEU is not applicable because it only relates to the negotiation of 'agreements', which is – in line with the Vienna Convention on the Law of Treaties – interpreted as treaties that are legally enforceable and that contain precise obligations and rights of their parties.

This means that the EU's representation in normal COPs or MOPs is not regulated in the treaties and that the Commission has not automatically the legal rights to be the EU negotiator in such settings (unless an MEA is being negotiated in a COP or MOP, of course).

In practice, the EU is usually represented by the rotating Presidency in COPs or MOPs. Yet member states still hold the formal right to take the floor themselves. If they do so, they usually do not contradict what the Presidency has said and they do not openly deviate from the agreed European line, but they support the statement made by the Presidency. In such negotiations, the role played by the Commission is very similar to the role of a 'normal' (large) member state. It intervenes – and is often influential – in the internal coordination process (i.e. the internal decision-making process in the EU on a common position to be defended at the international level, cf. infra), for which it provides know-how and expertise.

However, in practice, the system of dual representation in negotiations leading to a legally binding agreement is not followed nearly as completely as the formal framework suggests. This is also the case for the negotiation arrangement with only the Presidency in the lead in negotiations which do not result in a legally binding agreement. By contrast, the way the EU is represented in international environmental negotiations is often through an *ad hoc* and informal negotiation arrangement. This means that the EU often opts for a representation system that is considered to be the most useful and feasible in a particular international negotiation session. The formal system, which in the case of treaty negotiations is based on the internal division of competences, is often left behind. Consequently, the exact way the EU negotiates in international environmental negotiations varies from negotiation session to negotiation session, i.e. it mainly depends on practical and pragmatic considerations. A good example is the EU representation during international climate change negotiations conducted at the level of experts and diplomats (in contrast to the negotiations at ministerial level). In such (technical) negotiations, the EU is represented by so-called 'lead negotiators', who speak from behind the Presidency's nameplate but come from another member state or even from the Commission. Since the Bali climate conference (2007), the main international climate change negotiations are conducted in two 'Ad Hoc Working Groups' (one with all the parties to the UNFCCC, the other only with the Kyoto Protocol parties). In both Ad Hoc Working Groups, the EU is represented by a lead negotiator, who negotiates on behalf of the EU for a longer period than the six-monthly rotating Presidency (Delreux and Van den Brande, 2010).

Summary points

•   Because of the shared nature of environmental competences, legally binding MEAs are mixed agreements, formally negotiated by a system of dual representation.

- In international environmental negotiations not leading to a legally binding agreement, the EU is usually represented by the rotating Presidency of the Council.
- In practice, the EU's representation in international environmental negotiations often does not follow the formal rules, but is determined by informal and pragmatic considerations.

Internal coordination in international environmental negotiations

To understand how a European position to be expressed in international environmental negotiations is developed internally and how the internal coordination process functions in the context of such negotiations, a distinction can be made between three stages: *before*, *during* and *after* the international negotiations.

Before the European negotiators leave Brussels for the international environmental conference, the internal coordination process is principally conducted in the Environment Council (see Chapter 5). However, since the Commission attends all Council meetings, it can also play a role in this stage of the coordination process, a bit like a 28th member state. The Council's centre of gravity for the EU's internal coordination is the Working Party on International Environmental Issues (WPIEI), composed of national experts from the member states (with Commission officials attending). The WPIEI convenes in various configurations, such as the WPIEI Climate Change, the WPIEI Biodiversity or the WPIEI Global (dealing with e.g. the UN Commission on Sustainable Development (CSD)). For some international environmental negotiations, the EU coordination is limited to the WPIEI, whereas for other negotiations the WPIEI only conducts the preparatory work for the Working Party on the Environment (WPE, i.e. the working party in the Council consisting of the Brussels-based 'environment attachés' to the permanent representations of the member states) and for COREPER I (*Comité des représentants permanents*, i.e. here the meeting of the 27 deputy permanent representatives of the member states) and the ministerial meeting of the Environment Council. The EU coordination for CSD is an example of the first case. Here, the EU positions are determined in EU position papers, agreed by the experts in the WPIEI and are not discussed by the ministers. By contrast, the EU positions for e.g. climate change negotiations take the form of Council Conclusions, adopted by the Environment Council, but technically they are prepared by the WPIEI (and the WPE) and politically by COREPER I.

Most EU positions are indeed determined through position papers or Council conclusions. There is, however, an important exception: when the Commission is appointed as European negotiator in case of negotiations leading to a legally binding agreement (see above), the Commission also receives a mandate (formally 'negotiating directives') from the Council. Such a mandate usually consists of two parts. On the one hand, it stipulates that the Commission is authorized to negotiate the issues falling under EU competences, that the Commission should ensure that the EU is able to become a party to the future MEA and that the Commission should cooperate with the member states in the course of the international negotiations. On the other hand, as an annex to the mandate, the Commission also gets some substantive instructions. These are, however, usually very broad. They generally stipulate that the Commission may not commit the EU to an MEA that contradicts existing European environmental legislation. When the international negotiation process evolves, the mandate is then further refined into more concrete European positions under the form of position papers or even Council conclusions.

During the course of an international negotiation, daily EU coordination meetings are organized (or in some cases even more than once a day). In practice, the member states and the Commission usually meet in the morning before the start of the international meetings. These meetings are usually attended by the same people who were present at the preparatory WPIEIs in Brussels and they resemble very much the working methods of the WPIEI. Coordination meetings have a double function (Delreux, 2011). First, the European actors discuss the common lines to follow and they develop and/or refine, if necessary, European positions. Second, these meeting also fulfil an information function: for many (smaller) member states, which have relatively few people in the international negotiations, it is quite difficult to follow all the policy developments at the international level in detail. The debriefings by the Commission, the Presidency, the lead negotiators (if applicable) and even by national officials who have an official function at the international level (e.g. chairing a contact group or being a member of the Bureau), help the other member states to keep up-to-date on the progress of the international negotiations. Moreover, pooling the available information of 27 member states and the Commission can strengthen the EU's negotiation capacity at the international level.

EU coordination meetings have, however, also a disadvantage: they are very time-consuming. The time spent in internal coordination meetings cannot be used for informal contacts with the negotiation partners, e.g. to make the necessary package deals 'in the corridors'. This not only seems to be the case in international environmental negotiations, but it is equally applicable to EU external relations in other policy domains (e.g. Elgström, 2007).

Just like the system in which lead negotiators are used to conduct the negotiations on behalf of the EU (see above), a similar system of informal division of labour among actors in the EU is used in the internal coordination process. Indeed, also here, personal capabilities, expertise and know-how from the various actors in the EU are employed, irrespective of their institutional or national affiliation. Under the formal umbrella of the Presidency, the work related to the internal development of the EU position or the external representation of the EU is informally divided among the officials participating in the EU decision-making process. The officials who take on these tasks can come from the Commission or from any member state, but it is rather their personal contribution to the EU decision-making process that matters. In the CSD, for instance, this informal division of labour has led to a system of 'lead countries', which are responsible for leading the internal development of the EU position on a particular set of issues. In many international environmental negotiations, such informal processes in which member state and Commission officials are informally put into action, has become an uncontested and informally institutionalized practice. Such a system allows the EU to divide the work, to make use of all the expertise and know-how available in the EU, to involve the member states in the negotiations and to guarantee continuity in the internal coordination process (Delreux and Van den Brande, 2010).

Coordinations '*sur place*' not only occur in EU coordination meetings, but also 'on the spot', i.e. in the room where the international negotiations are taking place. Usually, the European negotiators (the Commission, the Presidency and/or a lead negotiator) sit around the negotiation table behind the nameplate of the EU and/or the Presidency. Behind the negotiators, the officials from the other member states are normally seated. Their role is twofold. On the one hand, these member state officials control whether the EU negotiator sticks to the previously agreed EU position. In this respect, Commission, Presidency or lead negotiator officials sometimes refer to 'the mothers-in-law' sitting behind them (Delreux, 2011). On the other hand, this set-up also allows negotiators to coordinate on the spot with the member states, to verify whether a particular intervention would be appropriate, to check whether a certain standpoint is still covered by the EU position or to ask for additional arguments to be used in the negotiations. When the international negotiations reach their end game, they are often conducted in so-called 'Friend of the Chair Meetings' or other restricted settings that the member states cannot attend and where the EU is only represented by its negotiator(s).

Given these various institutional fora for internal coordination, does the EU manage to present a common position and a coherent message in international negotiations? The answer is relatively positive, although it varies from case to case. Mostly, the EU is able to speak with a single voice. For instance, in climate change negotiations, notwithstanding often difficult internal coordination among the member states, the EU is usually able to present a coherent EU position (Parker and Karlsson, 2010). This does not, however, mean that this single voice needs to be expressed by 'a single mouth', to use the wording by former Trade Commissioner Pascal Lamy (Lamy, 2002). In other words, the EU's effectiveness is not necessarily undermined when multiple people speak on behalf of the EU ('multiple mouths'), but they have to defend the same line ('single voice'). In other cases, the single voice ambition of the EU has not been realized, e.g. in the negotiations on the Aarhus Convention (Delreux, 2009) (see Chapter 18). The main determinants of the EU's ability to act coherently in international environ-mental negotiations seem to be the internal preference heterogeneity among the member states, the level of politicization of the international negotiations (e.g. climate change negotiations are more politicized than negotiations on chemicals) and the existence of internal EU legislation on the issues discussed at the international level (if something is already regulated in the EU, the likelihood that member states will agree on it is higher) (Delreux, 2011).

After a deal on a MEA has been reached at the international level, it still has to be ratified (or 'concluded' in EU jargon) by the EU, before its rights and duties become legally binding on the EU. Importantly, this ratification requirement only holds for legally binding agreements and, as a consequence, not for COP or MOP decisions. It is precisely this feature of an international environmental agreement, which makes it legally binding. In the EU, ratification is the responsibility of the Council of Ministers and the European Parliament. Since ratification is characterized by a 'take it or leave it' logic, the Council and the Parliament cannot amend the MEA further in this stage. This means that after an international negotiation session, the negotiated MEA needs to be accepted by the Council and the Parliament in order to be fully accepted by the EU. The requirement that the European Parliament, next to the Council, also ratifies MEAs is a novelty introduced by the Lisbon Treaty (see also Chapter 3). At the moment, it remains to be seen whether the additional parliamentary ratification hurdle will change the EU's ability to conclude MEAs, since no MEAs have been signed and put forward for ratification since December 2009. History teaches us that the EU (albeit then only the Council and not yet the Parliament) has always ratified the MEAs it had signed and that ratification of MEAs as such has usually not been difficult, although it mostly takes a couple of years between the MEA's signing and its ratification by the EU. Additionally, because MEAs are mixed agreements to which the EU and the member states are parties, also the member states also need to ratify the agreement at their domestic level (generally also with parliamentary approval).

Summary points

- EU positions for international environmental negotiations are determined in the Council, where the WPIEI occupies a central place.
- During the course of an international negotiation, internal coordination not only occurs in frequent EU coordination meetings, but also by coordination 'on the spot'.
- MEAs need to be ratified by the Council and the European Parliament, as well as by the member states separately.

The external role of the EU and the vexed question of leadership

The EU is usually an advocate of strong environmentally friendly measures at the international level and it occupies a position in global environmental politics that is much more in favour of strong international environmental regulation than other countries (nowadays mainly the US and the BRIC countries i.e. Brazil, Russia, India and China). Therefore, the EU is widely recognized as a leader in international environmental politics (Zito, 2005). The EU's leadership is principally observed in international climate negotiations (Schreurs and Tiberghien, 2007; Oberthür and Roche Kelly, 2008). Yet the EU is also said to be a leader in biotechnology negotiations on the Cartagena Protocol (Falkner, 2007) and chemicals negotiations under the Rotterdam and Stockholm Conventions (Vogler, 2011). The EU's environmental leadership only started at the end of the 1980s. The negotiations on ozone (the Montreal Protocol) and waste (the Basel Convention) are considered the first instances of European leadership. In the 1960s and 1970s, by contrast, it was mainly the US that was the leader in international environmental politics, but the US and the EU have been 'trading places' since the mid-1980s (Kelemen and Vogel, 2010).

How can the EU's leadership in global environmental politics be explained? In the literature, three main explanations are identified. First, being a 'multilateral microcosm of the international system itself' (Oberthür and Roche Kelly, 2008: 43), the EU has always been in favour of multilateralism and regulatory measures at the international level. This not only holds true in the environmental domain, but it is a general characteristic of the external action of the EU. The EU's attachment to multilateralism, on environmental policy but also beyond, increasingly contradicts the sovereignty approaches of mainly the US and China. Second, leading on international environmental affairs also contributes to the EU's aim to profile itself as a civilian or 'soft' power (as opposed to a military power) (Scheipers and Sicurelli, 2007). Third, the EU's leading position at the international environmental level can also be prompted by the wish of producers in the member states to maintain a competitive position at the global market. Following this reasoning, the EU aims to create a level playing field by trying to export its own (relatively stringent) environmental legislation to the international level so that not only European producers, but also their global competitors, have to meet similar standards (Kelemen, 2010). This dynamic is much the same as the leader–laggard dynamics within the EU (see Chapter 5).

As mentioned, the argument about the EU's leadership has mainly been made with regard to international climate change negotiations. However, this claim has also been qualified in the literature with some scholars arguing that the EU has not (yet) fulfilled its leadership potential (Ott, 2001), that it has only been able to attempt leadership (Schunz, 2011) or that the EU is even characterized by a 'leadership deficiency' (Sjöstedt, 1998). Confirming the leadership analysis, on the other hand, is the EU's support for the Kyoto Protocol and for a comprehensive post-2012 successor agreement that is currently being negotiated (Parker and Karlsson, 2010) (see also Box 16.2). As far as the post-2012 agreement is concerned, the EU was the first UNFCCC party proposing post-2012 emission reduction targets in 2007, which were then concretized with the adoption of the so-called '20-20-20 targets', in which the EU committed itself to a 20 per cent reduction (and 30 per cent if other countries engaged in similar efforts) of greenhouse gas emissions, to get 20 per cent of its energy consumption from renewables and to increase its energy efficiency by 20 per cent (all by 2020) (Kulovesi *et al.*, 2011).

Box 16.2   The building blocks of the EU's international climate change policy

From the negotiations on the UNFCCC in the beginning of the 1990s to the current negotiations on a new climate change agreement, the EU's approach has consisted of three building blocks. First, the EU wants to reach comprehensive climate agreements. In EU jargon, the 'environmental integrity' of the international agreements needs to be guaranteed, meaning that it has to imply sufficiently stringent measures to combat climate change (i.e. mitigation) and to counter the consequences of the occurring climate change (i.e. adaptation) in an effective way. Second, the EU's preference is to conclude a global agreement in the multilateral UN framework and in particular under the UNFCCC architecture. This not only implies that all UN member states can become a party to the agreement, but also that they are involved in an inclusive, UN-wide, negotiation process. Third, the EU has always been in favour of a legally binding instrument (i.e. a treaty), which can be legally enforced. Indeed, international law has always been a key component of the EU's external climate policies.

The question remains, however, to what extent the EU's (perceived) climate leadership is successful. The EU's débâcle at the Copenhagen Conference suggests that its leadership has already been questioned. The EU was not only 'completely sidelined' (Missiroli, 2010: 428) in the end game of the negotiations, but also the outcome of the talks (the Copenhagen Accord) did not meet the EU's expectations (Jordan *et al.*, 2010). More generally speaking, the three building blocks of the EU's external climate policy seem to be under pressure. First, the talks do not seem to lead to an outcome that is as comprehensive and as 'environmentally integral' as the EU wants. Second, the multilateral character of the negotiations under the UNFCCC umbrella is increasingly uncertain, since recent developments show that the centre of gravity is gradually moving to less multilateral fora such as the G20 or the Major Economies Forum. Finally, a legally binding and enforceable instrument is not the most likely outcome of the current negotiations, since major players like the US and China do not seem to be willing to go further than a 'pledge and review' system. Additionally, the EU's 'leading by example' approach does not always work, since the EU's internal climate policies do not seem to be as effective as they were initially presented (for instance, the EU's emissions trading scheme suffers from some weaknesses) (see Chapter 17).

The literature on the EU's leadership in international climate change negotiations usually distinguishes between *structural, directional* and *idea-based* leadership (Schreurs and Tiberghien, 2007; Oberthür and Roche Kelly, 2008; Parker and Karlsson, 2010). Structural leadership or 'power-based leadership' (Vogler, 2011) means that the EU is able to use carrots and sticks to achieve its desired outcomes. The EU's diplomacy vis-à-vis Russia to assure the entry into force of the Kyoto Protocol or the financial commitments for mitigation in developing countries in the run-up to the Copenhagen conference can be seen as examples of this kind of leadership. Directional leadership refers to the EU 'leading by example'. Here, the EU's relatively ambitious internal climate change policies, such as the 20-20-20 targets or the EU's emissions trading scheme, demonstrate the European commitment to fight climate change. Finally, idea-based leadership means that the EU has an impact on international climate change policy agendas (see Chapter 11). By supporting the scientific conclusions of the Intergovernmental Panel on Climate Change (IPCC), and, for instance, consistently referring to the 2° target in its policy documents, the EU contributes to the more general understanding that climate change should be urgently and effectively tackled.

Given the observation that the EU is an important actor in international environmental politics, able to present a high degree of bargaining power, advocating strong multilateral regulation and seeking to lead in this area, a key question nevertheless remains: does the EU actually matter? Does the EU make a difference and can it have an impact on international environmental politics? Based on an analysis of the EU's influence in a number of international environmental fora, Vogler and Stephan (2007) argue that the EU is mostly able to influence the agenda setting, but that this is much more difficult as far as the outcome of the negotiations are concerned. This is also confirmed in other negotiations, where a mismatch has been observed between, on the one hand, the EU's aspirations and demands, and, on the other, its ability to deliver (Chaban *et al.*, 2006). This tension resembles the 'capability–expectations gap' in the EU's external relations more generally (Hill, 1993). Several factors play a role here. Among these are the EU's lack of a clear overarching strategy that can be played out in the end game of important negotiations (in contrast to the EU's often fully-fledged and detailed position papers on particular issues) and the fact that the outcome of international negotiations is often limited to the lowest common denominator of what powerful laggards like the US or China will accept.

Summary points

- The EU is often observed as a leader in global environmental politics, but its leadership role can nowadays be questioned.
- The EU's international climate change policy consists of three building blocks (environmental integrity, multilateralism, and a legally binding instrument), which are under pressure in the context of the current climate change negotiations.
- As in other areas of external action, the EU's external environmental policy is often characterized by a mismatch between its ambitions and its ability to deliver in practice.

Conclusion

The EU is a key player in international environmental politics and aims to play a front runner or leadership role across many different issue areas. Nowadays, it is accepted as a key participant in global environmental politics, despite not being a sovereign state. After a long struggle in the 1970s and 1980s, its status as a key participant has been confirmed, both *de jure* and *de facto*. Developments at the international level, but also internally, have strengthened the EU as a global environmental actor. On the one hand, its environmental competences have grown due to various treaty changes which have attributed more and more environmental competences to it. These competences have been used to create a large scope of internal environmental legislation, providing the EU with probably the most stringent supranational environmental policy system in the world. This policy system gives the EU the opportunity to 'lead by example'. ECJ rulings have gradually led to more external environmental competences for the EU as well. On the other hand, the successive enlargements of the EU would themselves have enlarged the bargaining power of the EU, which can nowadays represent 27 states, more than 500 million citizens and a vast economic market.

However, since the EU's actual impact on the outcome and the results of global environmental politics is more limited, the EU's external environmental policies still face a couple of challenges. The main challenge is related to coherence and consistency. First, coherence among the member states and the other actors in the EU is a necessary – but not a sufficient – condition to be effective at the international level. Coherence allows the EU to present a unified message, not only in the formal negotiations, but also in the diplomatic corridors. Second, coherence is also needed between various international negotiations in various policy domains (such as development and climate change politics, or trade policies and product standard-related environmental policies). Third, and probably most importantly, the EU needs to adapt to a changing world which now includes several emerging powers (e.g. the BRICs), new power axes (e.g. US–China on climate change) and systems of so-called 'club governance' (e.g. the G20) that work outside the traditional UN system.

Summary points

- The EU is a key player in international environmental politics and aims to play a front runner role across many different issue areas.
- Today the EU's status as a key player has been confirmed, both *de jure* and *de facto*. But this role was not preordained: it was the result of a long internal struggle dating back to the 1970s.
- The EU's actual impact on the outcome of global environmental politics is, however, more limited; several important challenges still have to be confronted, not least the emergence of new powers and the rise of 'club governance'.

Key questions

1 How have external environmental competences been established in the EU?
2 How is the EU represented in international environmental negotiations? Make a distinction between negotiations leading to a treaty and not leading to a treaty, as well as between formal and informal dynamics.
3 Which procedures and dynamics in the internal coordination process guarantee that the member states can be involved in the external negotiation process?
4 How can the EU's leadership in global environmental politics be explained?
5 How can the EU's climate leadership be conceptualized, what does it mean in practice and why is that concept a vexed one in the current climate change negotiations?

Guide to further reading

- A discussion of the role of the EU in global environmental politics can be found in Zito (2005) and in Kelemen (2010).
- Analyses of the internal functioning of the EU in international environmental negotiations (with a particular focus on the relation between the EU negotiator and the member states) are presented in Rhinard and Kaeding (2006) and in Delreux (2011).
- The internal and external climate change policies of the EU are examined in Oberthür and Pallemaerts (2010) and Jordan *et al.* (2010). Vogler (2011) links those developments with the EU's energy policy.

References

Bretherton, C. and Vogler, J. (2003) *The European Union as a Global Actor*, Routledge, London.

Chaban, N., Elgström, O. and Holland, M. (2006) 'The European Union as others see it', *European Foreign Affairs Review*, vol. 11, no. 2, pp. 245–262.

Degrand-Guillaud, A. (2009) 'Actors and mechanisms of EU coordination at the UN', *European Foreign Affairs Review*, vol. 14, no. 3, pp. 405–430.

Delreux, T. (2009) 'The EU in environmental negotiations in UNECE: an analysis of its role in the Aarhus Convention and the SEA Protocol negotiations', *Review of European Community and International Environmental Law*, vol. 18, no. 3, pp. 328–337.

Delreux, T. (2011) *The EU as International Environmental Negotiator*, Ashgate, Farnham.

Delreux, T. and Van den Brande, K. (2010) *Taking the Lead: Informal Division of Labour in the EU's External Environmental Policy-Making*, Institute for International and European Policy, Leuven.

Elgström, O. (2007) 'Outsiders' perceptions of the European Union in international trade negotiations', *Journal of Common Market Studies*, vol. 45, no. 4, pp. 949–967.

European Commission (2011) 'Multilateral environmental agreements to which the EC is a contracting party or a signatory', available at: http://ec.europa.eu/environment/international_issues/pdf/agreements_en.pdf (accessed 5 October 2011).

Falkner, R. (2007) 'The political economy of "normative power" Europe: EU environmental leadership in international biotechnology regulation', *Journal of European Public Policy*, vol. 14, no. 4, pp. 507–526.

Hill, C. (1993) 'The capability–expectations gap, or conceptualizing Europe's international role', *Journal of Common Market Studies*, vol. 31, no. 3, pp. 305–328.

Jordan, A., Huitema, D., Van Asselt, H., Rayner, T. and Berkhout, F. (eds) (2010) *Climate Change Policy in the European Union: Confronting the Dilemmas of Mitigation and Adaptation?*, Cambridge University Press, Cambridge.

Kelemen, D. (2010) 'Globalizing European Union environmental policy', *Journal of European Public Policy*, vol. 17, no. 3, pp. 335–349.

Kelemen, D. and Vogel, D. (2010) 'Trading places: the role of the United States and the European Union in international environmental politics', *Comparative Political Studies*, vol. 43, no. 4, pp. 427–456.

Kulovesi, K., Morgera, E. and Muñoz, M. (2011) 'Environmental integration and multi-faceted international dimensions of EU law: unpacking the EU's 2009 Climate and Energy Package', *Common Market Law Review*, vol. 48, no. 3, pp. 829–891.

Lamy, P. (2002) 'Europe's role in global governance: the way ahead', speech at Humboldt University, Berlin.

Leal-Arcas, R. (2001) 'The European Community and mixed agreements', *European Foreign Affairs Review*, vol. 6, no. 4, pp. 483–513.

Missiroli, A. (2010) 'The new EU "foreign policy" system after Lisbon: a work in progress', *European Foreign Affairs Review*, vol. 15, no. 4, pp. 427–452.

Oberthür, S. and Pallemaerts, M. (eds) (2010) *The New Climate Policies of the European Union: Internal Legislation and Climate Diplomacy*, Brussels University Press, Brussels.

Oberthür, S. and Roche Kelly, C. (2008) 'EU leadership in international climate policy: achievements and challenges', *The International Spectator*, vol. 45, no. 3, pp. 35–50.

Ott, H. (2001) 'Climate change: an important foreign policy issue', *International Affairs*, vol. 77, no. 2, pp. 277–296.

Parker, C. and Karlsson, C. (2010) 'Climate change and the European Union's leadership moment: an inconvenient truth?', *Journal of Common Market Studies*, vol. 48, no. 4, pp. 923–943.

Rhinard, M. and Kaeding, M. (2006) 'The international bargaining power of the European Union in "mixed" competence negotiations: the case of the 2000 Cartagena Protocol on Biosafety', *Journal of Common Market Studies*, vol. 44, no. 5, pp. 1023–1050.

Sbragia, A. (1998) 'Institution-building from below and above: the European Community in global environmental politics', in W. Sandholz and A. Stone Sweet (eds) *European Integration and Supranational Governance*, Oxford University Press, New York.

Scheipers, S. and Sicurelli, D. (2007) 'Normative power Europe: a credible Utopia?', *Journal of Common Market Studies*, vol. 45, no. 2, pp. 435–457.

Schreurs, M. and Tiberghien, Y. (2007) 'Multi-level reinforcement: explaining European Union leadership in climate change mitigation', *Global Environmental Politics*, vol. 7, no. 4, pp. 19–46.

Schunz, S. (2011) *Beyond Leadership by Example: Toward a Flexible European Union Foreign Climate Policy*, German Institute for International and Security Affairs, Berlin.

Sjöstedt, G. (1998) 'The EU negotiates climate change: external performance and internal structural change', *Cooperation and Conflict*, vol. 33, no. 3, pp. 227–256.

Verwey, D. (2004) *The European Community, the European Union and the International Law of Treaties*, TMC Asser Press, Den Haag.

Vogler, J. (2011), 'The challenge of the environment, energy and climate change', in C. Hill and M. Smith (eds) *International Relations and the European Union*, 2nd edition, Oxford University Press, New York.

Vogler, J. and Stephan, H. (2007) 'The European Union in global environmental governance: leadership in the making?', *International Environmental Agreements*, vol. 7, no. 4, pp. 389–413.

Zito, A. (2005) 'The European Union as an environmental leader in a global environment', *Globalizations*, vol. 2, no. 3, pp. 363–375.

Part 4

Future challenges

17 Governing with multiple policy instruments?

Andrew Jordan, David Benson,
Rüdiger K. W. Wurzel and Anthony Zito

Summary guide

The EU's role in determining the overall goals of environmental policy is widely known and well understood. In contrast, its role in determining the choice and use of implementing instruments at the European level is not nearly as well understood. Despite much talk about the merits of 'new' instruments, this chapter finds that EU environmental policy is still mainly pursued via regulatory means. There have of course been circumstances in which the EU has actively explored and even adopted non-regulatory instruments, but they have only appeared very infrequently over the past 40 years. Indeed, policy makers are much more likely to 'govern by multiple instruments' at the national level than at EU level. Moreover, for various reasons, regulation seems likely to remain the instrument of choice at EU level for the foreseeable future.

Introduction

The EU's role in determining the overall goals and targets of environmental policy in Western Europe is well known and widely understood (Weale *et al.*, 2000). However, the EU's continuing inability to select, deploy and re-calibrate the full suite of instruments has not been fully accounted for. Yet for many scholars, the way in which policy systems select, calibrate and deploy policy instruments is hugely important. For Howlett (2011: 22): 'Instrument choice . . . *is* public policy making . . . and analyzing potential instrument choices . . . *is* policy design' (emphasis in original). The whole issue of instrument choice in the EU, however, is far from clear-cut. Normative political arguments in favour of using a more diverse mix of instruments in the environmental sphere are well developed. In fact, they have been employed by advocates of both more and less European integration (see Holzinger *et al.*, 2009: 50–51; Jordan *et al.*, 2003a: 12–16). Yet instrument choices at EU level in practice remain heavily biased towards regulation. While some policy innovation (for a discussion of this concept, see Benson and Jordan,

2011) – in the form of new environmental policy instruments (for example, emissions trading) – is apparent at the EU level, regulations continue to dominate, although their relative share of the total stock of policy instruments has declined in recent years (Holzinger *et al.*, 2009; Halpern, 2010). In truth, despite these normative arguments, the EU has had a mixed experience with voluntary agreements and has failed to adopt any eco-taxes.

This discussion about policy instruments, which is often conducted at a very detailed technical level, is hugely important to those seeking to influence and/or understand EU environmental policy. It is important because the choice and application of different policy instruments, tools and techniques (similar terms which are often used interchangeably in the existing literature) arguably constitute the very essence of governing (Hood, 2007: 142–143). This is because they constitute one of the main links between steering activities within states, and policy outcomes and impacts 'on the ground'. Policy goals without the enabling policy instruments of course remain somewhat of a dead letter. The way in which the EU deploys policy instruments certainly challenges some of the early assumptions made in the policy instruments literature. For example, Doern (1981) and Phidd and Doern (1992) arranged the main instrument types on a continuum from 'self-regulation' (least coercive) at one end to 'public ownership' (most coercive) at the other. Assuming that all instruments were technically substitutable, they argued that liberal democratic states would generally prefer to employ the least coercive instruments first and then 'move along the scale' as necessary to overcome societal resistance (Howlett and Ramesh, 1995: 159). However, if one thinks about the EU, it has done precisely the opposite – leapt to the coercive end of the spectrum in the face of relatively little societal resistance.

One scholar who has systematically interrogated these patterns is Majone (1994). Essentially he argued that the EU does not govern by multiple instruments for one good reason: early on, member states deliberately limited its ability to engage in distributive and re-distributive forms of governing. By forcing the EU institutions to function at one end of Doern's spectrum, they sought to make it less state-like (and hence subservient to them). Nonetheless, the EU has shown that a great deal can be done in a policy area like the environment even with one instrument, namely, regulation. Moreover, the accumulation of regulations at EU level has impacted heavily on national policy and politics, i.e. Europeanization (see Chapters 1 and 4).

Consequently, the use of policy instruments has remained a live political issue in the EU despite and, also in a way, because of the continuing reliance on regulation. It grew especially strongly after the publication of the Commission's 2001 White Paper on Governance, which enjoined the EU to govern using a much wider array of instruments. Ever since, academics and practitioners have been discussing the different forms (Börzel, 2010) and modes (e.g. Citi and Rhodes, 2006; Jordan and Schout, 2006; Treib *et al.*, 2008) that exist in the EU. If the 1990s were dominated by the academic discussion about different levels of governance in the EU (Jordan, 2001), the 2000s have been dominated about the governing activities performed at and between the levels, through the use of a variety of different tools, methods, modes and instruments (Bähr, 2010; Börzel, 2010; Schout *et al.*, 2010). The new modes of governance have proved especially attractive objects of research (Citi and Rhodes, 2006; Jordan and Schout, 2006; Treib *et al.*, 2008), that is, policy instruments which do not rely quite so heavily on the 'pure' regulatory approach. Although there is now an extensive literature on the many different modes of governing that are in theory available to the EU, it has generally focused on the newer ones (Schout *et al.*, 2010) rather than on how they subtly interrelate with regulation (for exceptions, see Héritier and Eckert, 2008 and Jordan *et al.*, 2003a; 2003b). Those 'new governance' scholars who have studied the politics and policy of instruments have tended to do so in national settings (Kassim and Le Galès, 2010).

This chapter explores the main patterns of instrument use at European level since the dawn of EU environmental policy in the late 1960s. In particular, it investigates how well the EU has escaped the strong functional pressure to regulate by learning to *govern with multiple policy instruments*. If the answer is yes, to what extent has the EU's new modes and instruments replaced regulation – or combined with it (Jordan *et al.*, 2005)? And then in that case, what does the (un)changing pattern of policy instrument use at EU level tell us about its ability to govern effectively? The next section begins by defining some key concepts, then it summarizes the development of EU environmental policy, noting the most salient trends in instrument use. The following section introduces a number of ways to think about and understand the selection of instruments, drawn from the governance and policy instruments literatures. The specific instrument choices in the area of climate change policy are then investigated in more depth. This particular sub-field of environmental policy has enjoyed a particularly strong period of growth in the past decade or so (Jordan *et al.*, 2010) (see also Chapter 16). Therefore, if there is one sub-area where one would expect to find the EU 'governing with multiple instruments', it is probably this one. Given space constraints, this section mainly addresses instrument choices rather than their performance or 'effectiveness' (but see Chapters 14 and 15). The final section reflects on what the non-use of certain (environmental) policy instruments reveals about the EU's capacity to govern effectively.

Summary points

- The choice, calibration and operation of policy instruments are really central aspects of governance in all political settings, including the EU.
- In principle, there are many instruments that could be used to govern the EU; in practice, the EU remains heavily reliant on regulation, despite much animated discussion of the alternatives.
- A thriving and dynamic academic literature on 'new modes of governance' has emerged, but it is mostly concerned with a relatively small subset of new instruments; it has not yet fully explored the interaction between older and newer instruments.

The instruments of environmental policy

Changing times and changing priorities

Policy instruments are normally thought of as the 'myriad techniques at the disposal of governments to implement their policy objectives' (Howlett, 1991: 2). They provide a 'method through which government seeks a policy objective' (Salamon, 1989: 29). The different categories of policy instruments are set out in Box 17.1.

Box 17.1 Different categories of policy instrument

In theory, instruments can be sub-divided into a fairly limited number of categories (Salamon, 1989: 14). *Regulatory instruments* constitute a prescriptive form of governing, through which targets are established (normally by states) and then implemented by public and private actors. Failure to meet them usually triggers punitive action. *Market-based instruments* 'affect [the] estimates of costs of alternative actions open to economic agents' (OECD, 1994: 17). Eco-taxes and emissions trading schemes, long advocated by economists on cost-efficiency grounds, are the most salient in the environmental field (Wurzel *et al.*, 2012). *Informational instruments* seek to provide information to social actors with the aim of changing their behaviour (Howlett and Ramesh, 1995: 91). Finally, *voluntary agreements* are agreed between public authorities and private actors who volunteer to change their behaviour (in the case of environmental policy, to reduce polluting activities).

All these instruments have their own distinct characteristics and it is difficult to judge precisely what effects each one will have on the behaviour of target groups once it has been deployed (Salamon, 1989: 21, 28, 259). More is known about the effectiveness of regulation than the other types. And in the EU, almost all the academic work has been on the implementation of regulation (see Chapter 14) rather than the other instruments. Nonetheless it is abundantly clear that none is a panacea: rather, each one has strengths but also its weaknesses (ibid.: 21). Designing policies in part depends upon matching the right tool to the right context (Howlett, 2011). But is this how instruments are selected in the EU, i.e. from an open and widely stocked toolbox? The most pertinent issue for us then is which of the basic types has the EU relied on most heavily and why? EU environmental policy – defined broadly to include goals, standards and instruments – has evolved a great deal since the 1960s (see Chapters 1 and 2). Prior to 1972, common policy measures were mainly concerned with trade and thus had a strong internal market bias (Wurzel, 2008). There was a trickle of new EU regulations – some of which contained environmental protection requirements – but their primary aim was the prevention of trade barriers. After 1972 but before 1987, policy development entered an increasingly dynamic phase that produced a much more substantial and comprehensive framework of regulatory instruments. After the ratification of the Single European Act in 1987, policy making became even more dynamic. The Single Act stipulated that qualified majority voting should be used to adopt environmental regulations with a trade dimension. The scope and stringency of EU policy continued to grow in the 1990s, but policy instrumentation basically remained regulatory in nature. Actors favouring the use of new instruments were boosted by the publication of the Fourth Action Programme which, in 1987, proposed the adoption of non-regulatory instruments. These were in part justified by the need to improve the implementation of regulations (see also Chapter 14). In this context, 'new' environmental policy instruments (NEPIs) that were not regulatory, had an obvious and potentially quite seductive political appeal: they appeared both to lower the cost of regulation on businesses and offer a means to solve the EU's mounting implementation problems, which by then had started to generate intense friction between some member states and the EU institutions (for details, see Chapter 14).

After 1992, environmental policy entered a more contentious phase, as governments became concerned about the mounting costs and intrusiveness of EU regulations. In June 1993, the French, German and British governments compiled 'hit lists', which proposed the repatriation of more than 100 EU regulations including 24 environmental ones (see Chapter 5). In this setting, new instruments could be sold on the grounds that were more 'subsidiarity friendly'. In 1992, the Commission subsequently invested a huge amount of political capital in plans for an EU-level carbon dioxide/energy tax. Yet again, however, subsequent attempts to govern by multiple instruments made very limited progress due to industry and national government resistance. In the 2000s, climate change emerged as a strong political priority, but environmental policy as a whole struggled to make headway. Having failed to adopt an EU-wide tax, the Commission gradually warmed to the idea of trading 'licences to pollute' and eventually pushed through an EU-wide emissions trading scheme, on which more below.

The EU: governing with multiple instruments?

After 40 years of development what is the overall pattern of instrument use in the EU? It is certainly not quite as mono-instrumental as Majone originally suggested; the EU *has* adopted some NEPIs. Consequently, the relative share of regulation vis-à-vis the total stock of instruments has gradually declined since the 1970s (Holzinger *et al.*, 2009; Halpern, 2010; Jordan *et al.*, 2005). Furthermore, if one moves down to the national level, it becomes clear that some states have moved their regulation in the direction of greater coerciveness whereas others have moved it in the other direction (Jordan and Liefferink, 2004). Meanwhile, an existing NEPI, the EU's eco-label scheme, has continually suffered from a low public profile. In part, this reflects the strong desire of member states (such as Germany) to protect their long-established and successful national eco-label schemes, and partly the lack of interest among European producers and retailers, many of whom have established their own bespoke labelling schemes. Similarly, the Commission's attempts to develop EU-wide voluntary agreements have mostly floundered, only really being viable in fairly coherent policy sectors (such as car manufacturing) dominated by a small number of large producers. The European Parliament remains deeply suspicious of the lack of external scrutiny, especially if they are adopted outside the Community Method (in which it has an established role).

However, if one moves down to the national level, the pattern of choices is different again (Jordan *et al.*, 2005). Eco-taxes are relatively common, voluntary agreements (at least in some states) are much more popular and eco-labels are numerous. Consequently, the existing literature suggests that the best place to look for 'governance using multiple instruments' is the policy systems of the 27 member states. This level has certainly been the focus of more recent academic work on policy instrument selection and design activities (Daugbjerg and Tingaard Svendsen, 2002; Jordan *et al.*, 2005).

Summary points

- Policy instruments are the devices employed by policy makers to put their objectives into effect.
- The literature normally differentiates between four main sub-types: regulatory instruments; market-based instruments; informational instruments; and voluntary instruments.
- Over the past 40 years, various attempts have been made to employ a wider array of instruments at EU level, yet with some obvious exceptions, regulation remains the main instrument of choice.

The governance of the EU: a policy instruments perspective

Sadly there is no single theory of policy instrument choice – let alone theory of EU policy instruments – that can be used to explain this pattern. Indeed, the policy instruments literature has tended to study instruments in rather narrow and, dare we say, quite instrumental terms. When the production of better definitions and typologies was not the overriding concern, analysts have tended to be motivated by a more normative urge to advocate particular types of instruments (a bias which is particularly apparent in the more economic accounts). What is particularly striking about Majone's analysis is that it searches for underlying explanations for the use of broad categories of instrument, rather than the selection and calibration of specific instruments. Consequently, it should be thought of as a theory of the macro-level. Commission entrepreneurship, businesses looking for a level playing field and environmental ministries seeking to secure politically popular protection measures (while passing on the costs to industry and/or lower levels of governance) were all cited by Majone as critical drivers of the use of regulation.

Many of his predictions have been borne out. For example, his claim that the growth of the regulatory state at EU level was not fully foreseen or supported by states (Majone, 1994: 98) has generally been borne out (Weale *et al.*, 2000: 20). Its reliance on regulation has also created new political foci, e.g. the emergence of specialized agencies, the courts as key governors and the growing influence of technical specialists and their associated lobby groups (see Chapters 7, 9 and 12). Majone also accurately foresaw the rise of countervailing political pressures to audit, assess and otherwise tame the rise of the regulatory state at EU level – witness the debates about 'better regulation' and Impact Assessment (see Chapter 12).

Nonetheless, flaws have been identified in Majone's account. Writers such as Scharpf (1996) have highlighted the tendency for the EU to select certain sub-types of regulation rather than others. He did so by differentiating between *product* regulation and *process* regulation – a distinction which had hitherto escaped the attention of Majone and, it should be said, an entire generation of policy instrument scholars. He argued that the number of environmental product standards grew particularly quickly in the EU because a functioning single market requires national standards (on things like car exhausts) to be harmonized (or at least approximated) as products are more widely traded across borders. In contrast, the EU has been relatively slower at adopting common standards governing production facilities and processes (Weale *et al.*, 2000: 35), which lie behind the borders. Second, Majone's is very much a theory of the macro-level; it does not so readily account for the selection and calibration of particular regulations. Finally, although Majone was at great pains to acknowledge that long-term shifts do occur in the modes and instruments of governing over time (Majone, 1996: 34–35), there remains the lurking suspicion that he thought that the EU would essentially remain 'mono-instrumental'. Is this realistic? The environmental policy sector has certainly witnessed intense debates about the role of policy instruments, and research does suggest that some non-regulatory innovations (e.g. emissions trading) have been successfully introduced (Jordan *et al.*, 2011). Moreover, these 'new' instruments are now interacting with traditional regulation in subtle and puzzling ways: sometimes co-existing; sometimes combining with them; and sometimes replacing them altogether (Jordan *et al.*, 2005).

Linder and Peters (1989) have made the most systematic attempt to map out the most salient variables affecting instrument choices at a more meso and micro-level. Their starting point was the subjective perspective of the policy makers who ultimately make instrument choices. Their choices are a function of several factors. First, there are the specific features or 'attributes' of individual instruments vis-à-vis 'the problem' to be tackled (ibid.: 45). For example, the effectiveness of voluntary agreements is, as noted above, likely to be higher in sectors dominated by a small number of large players. Second, what is the *prevailing policy style* (Richardson, 1982) – is it more or less statist – and what is the nature of the society being governed? Is it generally cohesive or fractured? (Linder and Peters, 1989: 50). Third, what is the *prevailing organizational culture* in which those making instrument choices operate? It used to be said that the European Commission's services were dominated by lawyers and generalists, whereas economists (who might have been expected to advocate economic instruments such as taxes) were under-represented (Page, 1997). Finally, what is the prevailing *problem framing*? Regulation is, for example, an obvious way to govern the cross-border trade in products (Holzinger *et al.*, 2009), particularly those that are highly damaging (in which case an outright ban is probably the most functionally appropriate).

More recently, scholars have tried to incorporate all these variables (be they macro, meso or micro) into broader theories of the policy process, namely those focusing on the importance of ideas ('ideational'), institutions ('institutional') and the chaotic interplay of many different elements ('episodic'). *Ideational* approaches regard ideas as the main driver of instrument choices: it is often said that policy making is mostly characterized by learning about the performance of particular instruments (Howlett and Ramesh, 1993: 15). In these situations, what Linder and Peters (1989) termed the 'attributes of instruments' assume much greater importance. However, sometimes policy failures and/or crises open a given area to substantial changes in thinking (see Chapter 11), and with it the possibility of using new instruments. The crucial question is as follows: under precisely which circumstances are we likely to encounter significant shifts in instrument choices (Hall, 1993; Sabatier, 1998)?

By contrast, more *institutional* approaches argue that the political context in which instruments choices are made is more important. Institutions contain standard operating procedures and norms that facilitate the choice of particular kinds of instruments. Linder and Peters (1989) were very aware of the role of institutionalized cultures in particular organizations and policy systems which may constrain instrument choices. Moreover, instruments generate path dependencies, as actors alter their preferences to fit older instruments and new problems are visualized through the prism of existing instrument choices. Consequently, instrument choices need to be studied over longer periods of time (i.e. their 'careers' – Lascoumes and Le Galès, 2007: 7), rather than via a series of static snapshots.

Finally, the more *episodic* theories view the policy process as being inherently unstable: preferences are unclear; actors operate under conditions of uncertainty; and organizations lack the time to do comprehensive assessments of every instrument's effectiveness. According to these approaches, the policy process resembles less a rational-linear process of choosing between the available instruments to find the best one and more an unpredictable jumble of ideas, problems, solutions and decision-making priorities jockeying for attention (Kingdon, 1984; Baumgartner and Jones, 1993). Because of the chaotic way in which these different elements interact, success at defining the agenda (similar to Linder and Peters' (1989) notion of problem framing), depends on luck as well as power resources. Thus instruments may be chosen in a more random way, as and when political and institutional opportunities permit. The next section employs these three approaches to interpret and decode instrument selection choices in the area of EU climate policy.

Summary points

- There is no single theory of policy instruments that can be employed to explain the entire pattern of instrument use at EU level.
- Majone's theory of the regulatory state goes a long way to explaining the causes and implications of the EU's heavy reliance upon regulation.
- However, other theories which operate at meso and/or micro levels are needed to explain the complex instrument mixes that can now be observed in the environmental sector.

The instruments of EU climate policy

Table 17.1 summarizes the main climate policy instruments found at EU level, grouped according to the four main sub-types outlined above.

The Commission – and particularly DGs Environment and Climate Action – have long advocated the idea of using eco-taxes to pursue sustainability. As noted above, the Commission's most concerted effort came in the early 1990s. However, its proposal for a carbon tax was thwarted by a powerful coalition of industrialists who feared it would impose a competitive disadvantage on them in world markets.

Table 17.1 EU climate change policy: major policy instruments, 1992–2010

Type of instrument	Major policy instrument	
Regulatory instruments	1992	Monitoring CO_2 emissions
	2001	Electricity from renewable energy
	2003	Energy performance of buildings
	2003	Biofuels
	2004	Promotion of combined heat and power
	2009	Climate change and energy package of instruments (covering CO_2 emissions; carbon capture and storage; renewable energy; revision of emissions trading; 'Effort sharing' agreement)
	2009	CO_2 emissions from light duty vehicles
	2009	Monitoring guidelines for emissions from aircraft
Market-based instruments	2004	Upper and lower limit for national fuel taxes
	2003	Emissions trading (functioning from 2005)
	2008	Directive to include aviation in the emissions trading scheme
Informational instruments	1992	Energy labelling
	1992	Eco-labelling
	1993	Eco-management and Audit Scheme (EMAS)
	1999	Consumer information on fuel economy of and CO_2 emissions from passenger cars
Voluntary instruments	1999/2000	Car emissions (supplanted by 2009 EU Regulation)

Source: Updated from Jordan *et al.* (2011).

This coalition was aided and abetted by some member states who were opposed to giving the EU new powers. The need for Council unanimity on all such matters allowed the most sceptical states (the UK – principally on sovereignty grounds; Spain on economic ones), to veto the proposal, even though there was a growing number of companies (mostly specializing in renewable and energy-efficient technologies) that stood to benefit from higher carbon/energy prices. Thereafter, political support gradually drained away and the EU was eventually only able to adopt a directive (in 2003), which established a broad framework for harmonizing national taxes on energy products including electricity. However, it was hedged in with so many derogations and transition periods, that it could hardly be described as a textbook market-based instrument.

This case demonstrates that *ideational* approaches can help to understand the growing political attractiveness of 'ecologically modern' ideas favouring eco-taxes. *Episodic* approaches, by contrast, try to explain the Commission's attempted seizure of an opportunity (which was provided by the international climate change negotiations at Rio). A sufficiently strong advocacy coalition in favour of the proposal to secure the adoption of the EU's first market-based fiscal policy instrument could not be secured. The actual instrument selection strongly therefore reflects *institutional* constraints (i.e. the unanimity requirement) and national interest politics (i.e. sovereignty issues).

The development of the EU's *emissions trading system* (or ETS) was, in stark contrast, breathtakingly fast (Jordan *et al.*, 2010). The Commission issued a proposal in 2001, which was adopted by member states just two years later. The EU's scheme, which became operational in 2005, is the world's first and so far only transnational carbon trading scheme. There were three main reasons why it was adopted so quickly. First, several states (particularly the UK and Denmark as well as the Netherlands and Sweden) acted as pioneers. Having already adopted (or planned to establish) their own national schemes, they saw EU-level action as a means to reduce competitive disadvantages. Second, it offered a policy solution to the immediate political 'problem' of how the EU would actually deliver on the reduction commitments it had entered into at Kyoto (Jordan *et al.*, 2010: 65–66). *Episodic* theories point to the unexpected policy window created by Kyoto which was actively championed by most member states. In other words, the Commission itself created the policy window even though at the time it and most of its member states were opposed to the use of emissions trading. Third, emission trading was unencumbered by the unanimity requirement regarding agreement on taxes in the Council. Here institutional factors had an enabling as opposed to a constraining effect (for the initially quite inchoate emissions trading advocacy coalition); not being a tax, it could be adopted under qualified majority voting rules. Fourth, the system itself was designed in such a way that some of the most serious objections by member states were taken into consideration. For example, the Commission had originally proposed the auctioning of all emissions allowances (i.e. the approach advocated by economists' textbooks), but member states insisted on their right to distribute (for free) the emission allowances in the first few phases.

The rapid and unforeseen inter-linkage of problems, solutions and politics does seem to fit the predictions of *episodic* theories; the idea of the Commission acting as some kind of policy instrument entrepreneur also fits nicely. In fact, the first phase (2005–2007) was officially described as one of 'learning by doing'. Nonetheless, some critical choice-related issues remained open, not least the ability of states to affect the scope and the calibration of the instrument. Some brutally exploited this freedom to protect their high energy users. But during the second phase (2008–2012), the Commission secured support from the majority of states for a tougher stance. In the third phase (2013–2020), there will be one single cap set at EU level (as opposed to 27 separate caps) and over time the proportion of allowances that are auctioned will rise to 50 per cent. There is, therefore, evidence that lessons learned in earlier phases have shaped the design of subsequent phases, although institutional path dependencies have constrained the performance of this particular instrument: numerous derogations and extensions having been created for particular industries and/or energy-producing companies.

The most salient *informational* instruments in EU environmental policy are the aforementioned eco-label and EMAS (the EU's eco-management and audit scheme). Both instruments have struggled against better established national standards (in the case of eco-labelling) and the International Standard Organization's (ISO) less demanding eco-audit ISO 14000 standards. The EU's energy label arguably has enjoyed more success. It was adopted in 1992 as part of the EU's (climate change) strategy to provide consumers with more information so that they can make better informed purchase decisions on energy-consuming products. The EU energy label rates the energy consumption of traded products (such as light bulbs and refrigerators). However, attempts to make it more stringent have become mired in a deep controversy, splitting member states and EU institutions. Of the three theories identified above, the *institutional* approach seems better able to explain the pattern of choices despite the fact that the more lenient ISO 14000 Standard has unexpectedly turned out to be more popular with many European firms than EMAS.

The most high-profile *voluntary agreement* was that concluded between the association representing European automobile manufacturers and the Commission. Established in 1999, its aim was to reduce CO_2 emissions from passenger cars, which are an important source of greenhouse gas emissions in the EU. The Commission initially proposed to regulate, but European car manufacturers, backed by the industry Commissioner, fought hard for what they perceived to be an administratively less burdensome instrument, namely a voluntary agreement. The functional appropriateness of agreements to mature sectors such as car manufacturing was noted in the third section. The manufacturers won that particular battle and a voluntary agreement was duly adopted, which was quickly followed by similar agreements between the EU and their Japanese and Korean counterparts.

At first, the producers achieved some emission reductions, but gradually progress faltered as consumers bought more of the heavier cars such as sports utility vehicles. In 2004, the Commission warned that unless emissions were reduced, it would have no choice but to regulate. Because the situation did not improve, the Commission proposed a new regulation, which was eventually adopted in 2008. Interestingly, the new regulation is possibly *more*, not less, hierarchical than the one originally proposed by the Commission in the 1990s, and this at a time when the EU as a whole was seeking to adopt softer and less intrusive modes of governing consistent with the Lisbon Agenda. For example, it enables the Commission to levy fines on car manufacturers (i.e. *not* states) that exceed their targets. Again, the *institutional* approach outlined above does seem better able to explain this pattern of choices, but still has to account for the decision to trial voluntary agreements in the first place, given the EU's strongly regulatory past.

Finally, Table 17.1 clearly illustrates the EU's continuing reliance on *regulation* in this otherwise dynamic and, at least in some respects, quite uncertain policy sub-field. Many of these regulations address products, the free trade in which is an integral part of the EU's single market, or monitoring requirements. As the EU's desire for international climate leadership has grown, its climate policy instruments have, if anything, become *more*, not less, regulatory (both in quantitative and stringency terms). For example the EU's 2009 climate-energy package of measures contained no less than six separate items of legislation (Jordan *et al.*, 2010: 74–76). Again, while there is evidence of learning and, as noted above, some slightly quixotic instrument choices (the sudden appearance of emissions trading, for example), on the whole, instrument choices do appear to have been heavily constrained by *institutional* factors.

Summary points

- There are no EU-level eco-taxes and the only actors who seem genuinely capable of choosing them are the member states.
- Voluntary agreements have been tried but found wanting and the most insignificant innovation to date has been the ETS.
- The most common instrument of climate policy (at least in terms of the number of measures adopted) is still regulation.

Conclusion

Building on the broad claim that an instrument-focused approach offers a different but crucial perspective on the processes of governing, this chapter began by asserting that any credible attempt to fully understand the EU's ability to govern must consider how it selects policy instruments. It reveals that policy instrument choices are anything but incidental; they are both an outcome of intense political struggles to govern the EU and also an important generator of new forms of politics and policy at EU and national levels. The sudden emergence of the EU emissions trading system or the ongoing debate about EU-wide (eco-)taxes, powerfully underlines the relevance of this point. Moreover, if policy instruments are not adequately designed and implemented by policy states, policy problems will not be tackled, and environmental quality (and social welfare) will suffer. In the case of climate change, the risks associated with policy failure are not simply grave but possibly even catastrophic.

Among academics, interest in instruments seems to be experiencing a resurgence (Schout *et al.*, 2010). However, it still remains unclear whether the newest modes and instruments really deserve the analytical attention that they have received. We could, with some justification, question whether they have genuinely usurped regulation as the EU's instrument of choice in this sector. Has the EU really escaped the functional pressure to regulate (and only regulate) by learning to govern using *multiple policy instruments*? Even in the politically highly dynamic sub-area of climate change, the EU remains almost as deeply wedded to regulation as it did when environmental policy making started in the late 1960s. For sure, the EU has successfully 'imported' instruments first used outside Europe (emission trading was originally pioneered in the US and will eventually govern a significant percentage of EU emissions) and built on pre-existing instrument choices made at the member state level (witness, for example, the various attempts to use voluntary agreements and informational devices), but essentially it remains a *regulatory state* – hinting at limitations on policy instrument selection and use not fully accounted for in the more ideational and episodic theoretical approaches.

In summary, different combinations of preferences and institutional limits have meant that the EU uses few voluntary agreements in environmental policy (and, it should be noted, with limited success), struggles to use eco-labelling schemes and has been unable to agree EU-wide eco-taxes. Policy instrument 'innovation' (Benson and Jordan, 2011), is only really discernible with respect to emissions trading. So whereas the responsibility for governing environmental policy targets, goals and timetables does seem to be steadily accumulating at EU level, the power to choose and fine tune policy instruments is not. There have been conditions in which the EU has actively explored and even adopted non-regulatory instruments, but they seem to occur relatively episodically. Voluntary agreements seem to be easier to adopt when the problem to be tackled encompasses a small number of relatively large actors (e.g. car producers vs. farmers). The adoption of some other types of instrument (e.g. taxation) is barely even on the agenda for discussion in most states. Moreover, the EU's ability to steer environmental objectives through financial incentives, or 'green budgeting', remains constrained by its limited (re)distributive capabilities (Wilkinson *et al.*, 2008). If one is looking for evidence of governors 'governing by multiple instruments', the best place to look is not the EU, but the 27 member states (Jordan *et al.*, 2005).

Clearly, therefore, the EU is not mono-instrumental, but regulation seems very likely to remain the instrument of choice for EU environmental policy in general and EU climate policy in particular. The EU ETS is one, admittedly significant, exception. In this case, one actor (the Commission) was able to behave entrepreneurially because of help received from other actors (principally those member states and influential business groups as well as the Parliament) and a permissive set of institutional conditions (not least the availability of qualified majority voting). Finally, this chapter has focused on instrument choices. It is conceivable that fewer instruments overall will be adopted as a result of better regulation type initiatives, and that their overall ambition level will be less than in earlier phases of EU environmental policy. One of the most active areas in EU environmental policy in the future may be the reformulation and possibly dismantling of existing instruments and policies (see Chapter 20).

The environment is often held up to be an area of regulatory policy making (Lowi, 1972), yet the patterns of instrument selection described above are surprisingly similar to the modes and forms of governance found in other policy areas. According to Börzel (2010) and Héritier and Rhodes (2011), a great deal of governance in the EU remains hierarchical – the basic decision-making system allows binding laws to be adopted without the consent of each and every member state; regulation is the instrument of choice in many areas. In the 'shadow of hierarchy' (Börzel, 2010) other, more market- and network-based forms of governance are to be found, but they are dominated by private not public actors, and seem to rely on the presence of the state for their legitimacy and effectiveness. Forms of (re)distributive governance remain under-utilized. In effect, scholars are confirming the general pattern first observed by Majone, but in ways that raise new puzzles and questions about how the EU governs.

Summary points

- An instrument-focused approach offers a different but very revealing perspective on the processes of governing.
- Policy instrument choices are anything but incidental and bureaucratic – they are both an outcome of political struggles and an important generator of new forms of politics and policy at EU and national levels.
- The EU essentially remains a *regulatory state* but a range of different theories is needed to explain what types of regulation are adopted, their precise focus and stringency.
- Policy instrument innovation at EU level is only really discernible with respect to emissions trading.
- The EU is not mono-instrumental, but regulation seems likely to remain the main instrument of choice among EU environmental policy makers.

Key questions

1 What are the main types of policy instrument and what are their relative strengths and weaknesses?

2   How has the pattern of instrument choices in EU environmental policy changed over the past 40 years?
3   To what extent and why do the patterns of instrument selection at EU level differ to those found at the national level?
4   Regulatory instruments are widely employed but have been poorly implemented. Could the same be said about non-regulatory instruments?
5   Does climate policy exhibit the same or a different pattern of instrument use as other areas of environmental policy?

Guide to further reading

- For good reviews of the policy instruments literature, see Linder and Peters (1989), Eliadis *et al.* (2007), Schneider and Ingram (1990) and Howlett (2011).
- A number of attempts have been made to describe and explain patterns of instrument use at EU level, such as Jordan *et al.* (2005), Holzinger *et al.* (2009) and Wurzel *et al.* (2012).
- For an introduction to the wider but related literature on different modes of governance across the EU, see Treib *et al.* (2008), Citi and Rhodes (2006) and Héritier and Rhodes (2011).

References

Bähr, H. (2010) *The Politics of Means and Ends: Policy Instruments in the EU*, Ashgate, Farnham.

Baumgartner, F. and Jones, B. (1993) *Agendas and Instability in American Politics*, University of Chicago Press, Chicago.

Benson, D. and Jordan, A. (2011) 'What have we learnt from policy transfer research? Dolowitz and Marsh revisited', *Political Studies Review*, vol. 9, no. 3, pp. 366–378.

Börzel, T. (2010) 'European governance: negotiation and competition in the shadow of hierarchy', *Journal of Common Market Studies*, vol. 48, no. 2, pp. 191–229.

Citi, M. and Rhodes, M. (2006) 'New modes of governance in the EU: a critical survey and analysis', in J.E. Jorgensen *et al.* (eds) *Handbook of European Politics*, Sage, London, pp. 463–482.

Daugbjerg, C. and Tingaard Svendsen, G. (2002) *Green Taxation in Question*, Palgrave, Basingstoke.

Doern, B. (1981) *The Nature of Scientific and Technological Controversy in Federal Policy Formulation*, Science Council of Canada, Ottawa.

Eliadis, P., Hill, M. and Howlett, M. (2007) 'Introduction', in P. Eliadis, M. Hill and M. Howlett (eds) *Designing Government: From Instruments to Governance*, McGill Queens University Press, Montreal, pp. 3–20.

Hall, P. (1993) 'Policy paradigms, social learning and the state', *Comparative Politics*, vol. 25, no. 3, pp. 275–296.

Halpern, C. (2010) 'Governing despite its instruments? Instrumentation in EU environmental policy', *West European Politics*, vol. 33, no. 1, pp. 59–70.

Héritier, A. and Eckert, S. (2008) 'New modes of governance in the shadow of hierarchy: self-regulation by industry in Europe', *Journal of Public Policy*, vol. 28, pp. 113–138.

Héritier, A. and Rhodes, M. (eds) (2011) *New Modes of Governance in Europe*, Palgrave, Basingstoke.

Holzinger, K. *et al.* (2009) 'Governance in EU environmental policy', in I. Tömmel and A. Verdun (eds) *Innovative Governance in the EU*, Lynne Rienner, Boulder, CO, pp. 45–62.

Hood, C. (2007) 'Intellectual obsolescence and intellectual makeovers: reflections on the tools of government after two decades', *Governance*, vol. 20, no. 1, pp. 127–144.

Howlett, M. (1991) 'Policy instruments, policy styles and policy implementation', *Policy Studies Journal*, vol. 19, no. 2, pp. 1–21.

Howlett, M. (2011) *Designing Public Policies: Principles and Instruments*, Routledge, London.

Howlett, M. and Ramesh, M. (1993) 'Patterns of policy instrument choice', *Policy Studies Review*, vol. 12, nos 1–2, pp. 3–24.

Howlett, M. and Ramesh, M. (1995) *Studying Public Policy*, Oxford University Press, Oxford.

Jordan, A.J. (2001) 'The European Union: an evolving system of multi-level governance . . . or government?', *Policy and Politics*, vol. 29, no. 2, pp. 193–208.

Jordan, A.J. and Liefferink, D. (eds) (2004) *Environmental Policy in Europe*, Routledge, London.

Jordan, A.J. and Schout, A. (2006) *The Coordination of the European Union: Exploring the Capacities for Networked Governance*, Oxford University Press, Oxford.

Jordan, A.J., Benson, D., Wurzel, R. and Zito, A.R. (2011) 'Policy instruments in practice', in J.S. Dryzek, R.B. Norgaard, and D. Schlosberg (eds) *Oxford Handbook of Climate Change and Society*, Oxford University Press, Oxford, pp. 536–549.

Jordan, A.J., Huitema, D. *et al.* (eds) (2010) *Climate Policy in the European Union*, Cambridge University Press, Cambridge.

Jordan, A., Wurzel, R.K.W. and Zito, A.R. (eds) (2003a) *New Instruments of Environmental Governance*, Frank Cass, London.

Jordan, A., Wurzel, R.K.W. and Zito, A.R. (2005) 'The rise of "new" policy instruments in comparative perspective: has governance eclipsed government?', *Political Studies*, vol. 53, no. 3, pp. 477–496.

Jordan, A., Wurzel, R.K.W., Zito, A.R. and Brueckner, L. (2003b) 'European governance and the transfer of "new" environmental policy instruments', *Public Administration*, vol. 81, no. 3, pp. 555–574.

Kassim, H. and Le Galès, P. (2010) 'Exploring governance in a multi-level polity: a policy instruments approach', *West European Politics*, vol. 33, no. 1, pp. 1–22.

Kingdon, W. (1984) *Agendas, Alternatives and Public Policies*, HarperCollins, New York.

Lascoumes, P. and Le Galès, P. (2007) 'Introduction: understanding public policy through its instruments', *Governance*, vol. 20, no. 1, pp. 1–22.

Linder, S. and Peters, B.G. (1989) 'Instruments of government', *Journal of Public Policy*, vol. 9, no. 1, pp. 35–58.

Lowi, T. (1972) 'Four systems of policy, politics and choice', *Public Administration Review*, vol. 32, no. 4, pp. 298–310.

Majone, G. (1994) 'The rise of the regulatory state', *West European Politics*, vol. 17, no. 3, pp. 77–101.

Majone, G. (1996) *Regulating Europe*, Routledge, London.

OECD (Organisation for Economic Cooperation and Development) (1994) *Managing the Environment: The Role of Economic Instruments*, OECD, Paris.

Page, E. (1997) *The People Who Run Europe*, Oxford University Press, Oxford.

Phidd, R. and Doern, B. (1992) *Canadian Public Policy*, Methuen, Toronto.

Richardson, J. (ed.) (1982) *Policy Styles in Western Europe*, George Allen & Unwin, London.

Sabatier, P. (1998) 'The advocacy coalition framework', *Journal of European Public Policy*, vol. 5, pp. 98–130.

Salamon, L. (1989) *Beyond Privatisation: The Tools of Government*, Urban Institute Press, Washington, DC.

Scharpf, F.J. (1996). 'Negative and positive integration in the political economy of European welfare states', in G. Marks *et al.* (eds) *Governance in the European Union*, Sage, London, pp. 15–39.

Schneider, A. and Ingram, H. (1990) 'Behavioural assumptions of policy tools', *Journal of Politics*, vol. 52, no. 2, pp. 510–529.

Schout, A., Jordan, A.J. and Twena, M. (2010) 'From old to new governance in the European Union: explaining a diagnostic deficit', *West European Politics*, vol. 33, no. 1, pp. 154–170.

Treib, O. *et al.* (2008) 'Modes of governance: towards a conceptual clarification', *Journal of European Public Policy*, vol. 14, no. 1, pp. 1–20.

Weale, A. *et al.* (2000) *Environmental Governance in Europe*, Oxford University Press, Oxford.

Wilkinson, D., Benson, D. and Jordan, A. (2008) 'Green budgeting', in A. Jordan and A. Lenschow (eds) *Innovation in Environmental Policy?* Edward Elgar, Cheltenham.

Wurzel, R.K.W. (2008) 'Environmental policy', in J. Hayward (ed.) *Leaderless Europe*, Oxford University Press, Oxford.

Wurzel, R.K.W., Zito, A.R. and Jordan, A.J. (2012) *Environmental Governance in Europe: A Comparative Analysis of 'New' Policy Instruments*, Edward Elgar, Cheltenham.

18 Involving the public?

Irina Tanasescu

Summary guide

Public participation is a crucial element in any democracy, be it at national or EU level, but the involvement of the public in EU-level decision making remains especially problematic. Other than occasional petitions and protests, 'the public' only really participates via voting in elections for the European Parliament; most day-to-day decision making is dominated by organized groups. This chapter explores the concept of public participation and discusses the EU's alleged democratic deficit before moving on to assess the direct involvement of stakeholders in its policy processes. It concludes that while the practical arrangements are in place to secure a more effective participation of interest groups across different stages of the policy-making cycle, this does not, *per se*, address the deeper problem of how to move the EU closer to its citizens.

Introduction

It is a truism that the public should participate in decision making to ensure that it is democratically legitimate. Public participation is an important element in the making and implementation of all EU policies, even more so for environmental ones which are often said to be of particular interest to its citizens (European Commission, 2011a). In fact, given that most environmental measures adopted at national level originate at the EU level, it is of utmost importance to understand who does or does not have a voice in EU environmental policy making.

The scope of this chapter is limited to what happens in Brussels, that is to say the interaction between the public (be it citizens or organized groups) and the EU institutions. Many items of EU environmental legislation contain provisions for public participation. The Water Framework Directive, for instance, provides for the inclusion of all stakeholders in the discussions leading to the formulation of the River Basin Management Plans. However, this belongs to the implementation phase, i.e. by and in the member states, and therefore lies outside the scope of this chapter.

In order to explore the challenges of public participation at EU level, this chapter proceeds as follows. It starts with a general discussion of participation in the context of EU policy making in order to clarify who participates. It is argued that it is not 'the public' (understood as ordinary citizens) *per se* who participate in day-to-day policy making, but rather organized groups (NGOs, business associations, etc.). The following section moves on to discuss the institutional opportunities for participation at EU level, in an attempt to shed light on how the EU institutions view and in turn structure participation. In the following section a policy cycle approach is used to investigate the two most crucial stages as regards public participation in the field of environment policy, namely, policy preparation and implementation. Finally, conclusions are drawn on the achievements so far and challenges ahead for public participation at EU level.

Summary points

- Public participation is a crucial element in any democracy, be it at national or EU level.
- Nevertheless, the involvement of the public in EU-level decision making remains problematic.
- Given that the majority of national environmental measures originate in provisions adopted at the EU level, it is important to understand what impact 'the public' has on the decision-making process in Brussels.

Public participation and the democratic deficit

While there are ways for 'the public' to participate in EU policy making (e.g. by voting in European Parliament elections), they are considered by many to be insufficient (e.g. Quittkat, 2011). The EU's alleged 'democratic deficit' has attracted a lot of attention since the early 1990s and the 'no' vote on the ratification of the Maastricht Treaty in Denmark in 1992. This event was then repeated on a number of occasions: when the Irish voters rejected the Nice Treaty in 2001: when the French and Dutch voters rejected the EU Constitution in 2005: and when the Irish voters again voted no to the ratification of the Lisbon Treaty in 2008. These negative votes indicated a growing gap between 'the public' and the EU; a gap that many attributed to the lack of a true European public sphere and to the ineffective communication between Brussels and national level (Bee and Bozzini, 2010). It also triggered a shift in the academic discussions on democracy at the EU level from an institution-centred perspective to a more civil society one. According to an institution-centred perspective, the main problem was the limited involvement of the European Parliament – the only institution directly elected by the citizens – in decision making. Public opinion and public participation (or the lack thereof) were not considered to be an issue (authors often referred to the 'permissive consensus' surrounding the EU integration project until the 1990s) (Chryssochoou, 2010). Successive treaty revisions have addressed this problem and the Parliament is now on an equal footing with the Council in the vast majority of issue areas (with the notable exception of foreign policy and defence) (see Chapter 8). According to a more civil society-oriented perspective, however, the EU has a democratic deficit due, among other things, to the basic inability of citizens to *directly* influence and participate in the work of the EU institutions.

'Public participation' refers to the direct involvement of citizens in policy making. It can be achieved through a variety of different routes. However, at EU level, the means for the public to directly influence policy decisions are narrower than in national contexts. EU citizens can vote in the elections for the European Parliament, but in practice turn-out is poor – only about 43 per cent of EU voters actually voted in the 2009 elections (European Parliament, 2009). The citizens can also send petitions to the European Parliament and appeal to the European Ombudsman and, since the ratification of the Lisbon Treaty, invite the Commission to consider specific measures under the new European Citizen Initiative (see Chapter 3). In addition, citizens can join protests targeted at the European institutions (the biggest example to date being the protests triggered by the Commission's 2005 proposal for a Services Directive), or take part in an on-line consultation organized by the Commission.

There is no standard definition of the democratic deficit and some authors (most notably Moravcsik, 2002) even question whether such a deficit exists. Follesdal and Hix (2005) summarize the debate in the literature by constructing a list of five common themes, each of which serves both as a diagnosis and a possible treatment of the democratic deficit. These are:

1   the increase in executive power at the centre (EU institutions) and the weak control of national parliaments over EU-level decision making;
2   the weakness of the European Parliament;
3   the lack of truly 'European' elections;
4   the distance between the EU and voters/the public;
5   the occurrence of 'policy drift', meaning the distance between the outcome of EU policies and voter preferences.

While the first elements point to an institution-centred understanding of the democratic deficit, to which institutional solutions have been brought via treaty changes (notably via the increase in powers of the European Parliament and the involvement of national parliaments), the final point is directly linked to the question of public participation. If policies diverge from public preferences, it is not only because national governments push for EU-level measures that they would not be able to defend at home. In addition, due to the lack of truly European electoral debates, it is organized interests that make their voices heard in the policy-making process (with an over-representation of business interests over diffuse interests) (see Chapter 9 for further details).

A possible remedy to the democratic deficit can be found in democratic theories that no longer have the nation state as their main reference point, namely, theories of deliberative democracy. By insulating decision making from concepts of national identity and traditional views of representative democracy, alternative understandings of legitimate decision making come to the fore; ones which are directly relevant to a post-national and multi-levelled governance system such as the EU.

Following Hoskyns (2000: 3):

> Deliberative democracy is relevant in this context because it goes beyond these aspects of democracy (i.e. representation) to address more centrally the issue of participation, and to suggest how, if participation is broadened, different perspectives and points of view can be accommodated. In doing so, it both assumes and helps to create a public space for debate and action – features most notably lacking in the EU as at present constituted.

Indeed, several authors (see Cohen and Sabel, 1997; Eriksen, 1999; Neyer, 2006, Tanasescu, 2009) have used the idea of deliberative democracy either to study existing patterns of interaction at the EU level, or to offer a normative vision of what the EU could look like. These visions show that deliberation at the EU level, unlike deliberation at local level, is never between ordinary citizens. Individuals deliberating at the EU level are in most cases experts (such as member state experts in comitology committees) or representatives of interest groups. Interest groups, in turn, are often incapable of serving as intermediaries between the EU institutions and the citizens, due to their elite nature (Warleigh, 2001) (see also Chapter 9).

Summary points

- Public participation at EU level is seen widely as a key part of tackling the perceived democratic deficit (understood, among others, as a lack of impact of the citizens on the final outcome of EU policies).
- Nevertheless, 'public' participation is limited to EU elections and occasional petitions and protests; most day-to-day participation is monopolized by organized interests.
- EU-level interest groups cannot, alone, be the answer to the democratic deficit.

The institutional opportunities for participation: the Commission

Given the complexity of decision making at the EU level, the opportunities for participation are, by their nature, spread across a range of institutional actors. Indeed, most EU institutions not only welcome contributions from citizens and organized groups, but also have well-established and structured patterns of consultation. Given the relatively closed nature of the Council (see Chapter 9), this section will concentrate on how the Commission and the European Parliament organize their consultation processes.

Given its privileged role as a legislative initiator, the Commission is a privileged interlocutor for organized interests (see Chapter 6). Chapter 9 discusses why lobby groups target the Commission, but one obvious question to ask in this chapter is, why might the Commission even want to listen to third parties? Laffan (2002: 130) argues, on the one hand:

> given the paucity of Commission staff, the spatial scope of EU regulation, Europe's deep diversity and the technical nature of EU regulation, the Commission has developed an interdependent relationship with interest groups. It needs their expertise and support if it is to successfully frame 'yesable' packages.

On the other hand, involving citizens and organized interests in the preparation of proposals is a way for the Commission to address criticisms that it is remote and opaque. Public participation in the policy preparation stages brings an input legitimacy that the Commission, as an unelected body, would otherwise struggle to deliver (see Box 18.1).

Box 18.1 Input, output and throughput legitimacy

In the EU literature, a distinction is often made between two different sources of legitimacy. *Input legitimacy* refers to the principles of representation and accountability. This means that, in order to be legitimate, a system must ensure the direct representation of the people in decision making. Put differently, it is 'government *by* the people'. *Output legitimacy*, on the other hand, refers to how far the public is satisfied with policy outcomes. It is 'government *for* the people', in which decisions are legitimate because they are effective. Both input and output legitimacy are needed in a stable democracy. However, the EU is sometimes said to suffer from weak input legitimacy due to limited public participation in the EU policy-making process.

A third category has recently been added to the debate, namely *throughput legitimacy*. This focuses on the quality of the governance processes (Schmidt, 2010: 4) and emphasizes the role of participation in EU policy making. In other words, government *with* the people. The legitimacy of the EU is thus seen to depend on a combination of all three sources, in an interdependent and mutually reinforcing relationship.

Last but not least, it is a legal obligation: Article 11 of the Treaty on European Union (TEU) stresses that 'the Commission shall carry out broad consultations with parties concerned in order to ensure that the Union's actions are coherent and transparent'. In addition, this Article mentions the maintenance of an open, transparent and regular dialogue between the European institutions and civil society.

This general provision is often deemed to be too vague to effectively safeguard the participation of third parties. Nevertheless, additional legal obligations to consult arise both from international agreements and particular legislative acts. The Aarhus Convention of the UN (signed by all EU member states and transposed by Directive 2003/35/EC) provides for public participation and access to information in specific environmental decisions (see Box 18.2). Institutionalized frameworks of consultation have been also established via secondary law (legislation). For example, a Commission Decision (97/150/EC) created the European Consultative Forum on the Environment and Sustainable Development that, between 1997 and 2001, brought together 26 members from across the spectrum of interests (ranging from businesses to local authorities, consumer and environmental groups). Similarly, an EU Eco-labelling Board was established by Regulation (EC) No 66/2010.

Box 18.2 The EU and the Aarhus Convention

The Convention on Access to Information, Public Participation in Decision Making and Access to Justice in Environmental Matters (commonly known as the Aarhus Convention) was signed by the EU in 2001. It establishes a series of rights in relation to the environment, namely access to: information; decision making; and justice should the first two principles not be satisfied. Since the EU is a party to the Convention, a set of measures have been adopted at the EU level to implement it:

- The first pillar is implemented through Directive 2003/4/EC on public access to environmental information.
- The second pillar is implemented through Directive 2003/35/EC which provided for public participation in respect of the drawing up of certain plans and programmes relating to the environment.
- The third pillar is implemented through Regulation (EC) No 1367/2006 on the application of the provisions of the Aarhus Convention to Community institutions and bodies.

Provisions for public participation in environmental decision making are also to be found in a number of other environmental directives, such as Directive 2001/42/EC on the environmental assessment of certain plans and programmes and the Water Framework Directive (2000/60/EC).

(European Commission, 2011b)

Consultation principles

Several documents produced by the Commission throughout the 1990s gradually established a framework governing its interaction with third parties. A seminal document was the 2001 White Paper on governance, which established 'participation' as a principle of good governance both in relation to EU-level and national policy making. Moreover, in order to optimize participation at the EU level, the Commission also proposed to introduce a code of conduct, comprised of minimum standards that would make clear when, whom, how and on what issues to consult (European Commission, 2002). This spelt out a set of principles that should govern the Commission's attitude towards third parties, namely: participation; openness; accountability; effectiveness; and coherence. It also established a set of minimum standards that should be met by the institution when consulting (see Box 18.3).

Box 18.3 The Commission's minimum standards for consultation

In 2002, the Commission established a set of minimum standards that should be met when consulting, namely that:

- The content of the consultation is clear.
- Relevant parties have an opportunity to express their opinions.
- The Commission publishes consultations widely in order to meet all target audiences, in particular via the web portal 'Your Voice in Europe'.
- Participants are given sufficient time for responses, namely 8 weeks for public consultations and 20 working days notice for meetings.
- Acknowledgement and adequate feedback are provided.

(European Commission, 2002)

Nevertheless, many have challenged the Commission's vision of 'participation'. According to Magnette (2003: 148): 'the concrete reforms suggested by the White Paper focus on a limited conception of participation: it will probably remain the monopoly of already organized groups, while ordinary citizens will not be encouraged to become more active'.

Moreover, the White Paper revealed that the Commission understood participation to mean a process initiated by the EU institutions, limited to non-decision and targeted at organized actors (ibid.: 150). Moreover, its minimum standards of consultation only apply to selected consultations in the policy formulation phase (see Chapter 12). In addition, they are not legally binding because, as the Commission explains:

> a situation must be avoided in which a Commission proposal could be challenged in Court on the grounds of alleged lack of consultation of

interested parties. Such an over-legalistic approach would be incompatible with the need for timely delivery of policy, and with the expectations of the citizens that the European Institutions should deliver on substance rather than concentrating on procedures.

(European Commission, 2002: 10)

The legal status of the standards has, therefore, been the subject of contention, with some voices arguing, on the one hand, that they should be legally binding, and the Commission, on the other hand, saying that they will be followed despite their non-binding status. That said, these principles and guidelines are applicable to all DGs and Commission Services (each of which also have their own traditions and practices of consultation).

Following the 2006 Green Paper on the Transparency Initiative, a 'Register of Interest Representatives' was set up, linked to a code of conduct (see Chapter 9). While registration on the register was not compulsory for lobbyists, incentives were given to organizations to register (such as automatic consultation alerts). Many questioned the effectiveness of a voluntary register and code of conduct and pushed for a compulsory solution, but the Commission resisted. A small step towards increased formalization, however, occurred when the Commission and the European Parliament created a Joint Register in 2011 (see also Chapter 9).

Consultation instruments

The Commission interacts with third parties on the basis of different participatory tools. These tools give body to the consultation requirements and are the concrete tools allowing it to reach out to the stakeholder community. The list is not exhaustive, as new instruments can always be created and others lose their relevance, but it nonetheless illustrates the range and variety of tools used:

- *Consultation documents*: Green Papers and White Papers are the classic Commission approach to consultations. They are both consultation documents (non-legally binding), targeted at the outside world and meant to shape the Commission interaction with stakeholders and streamline the feedback to the consultation process. They are meant to provide stakeholders with a basis for comments, prior to a legislative proposal being drafted.
- *Expert groups*: comprise national and/or private sector experts. They are set up by the Commission to provide it with expert advice, particularly in the preparation of legislative proposals and policy initiatives. In addition, expert groups also provide advice for the Commission in its tasks of monitoring and coordinating or cooperation with the member states' (European Commission, 2011a). Expert groups can be consulted by the Commission at any stage of the policy cycle and their role is limited to providing advice. This means that, unlike comitology committees (which are also made up of experts, but representing exclusively member state administrations (see Chapter 6)), they have no formal decision powers. According to the minimum standards of

consultation, when the Commission creates an expert group, it needs to make sure that all the interests in the particular sector are represented and, if it is not the case, compensate for the lack of input of specific interests via other consultation tools.

- *Other tools*: among the other tools used, it is worth mentioning the European Business Test Panel, the on-line questionnaires conducted through the 'Your Voice in Europe' website, structured dialogues, conferences, seminars, various ad-hoc meetings, and so on.

In most cases, a mix of tools – each with its own set of advantages and dis-advantages – is used for a particular consultation exercise (see Box 18.4). For instance, while on-line questionnaires allow the institution to gather the input of numerous organizations and individuals, expert groups allow in-depth discussions, among selected participants to take place.

Box 18.4 The mix of consultation instruments: some practical examples

- For the 2003 Communication on Integrated Product Policy, the Commission consulted stakeholders on the basis of a Green Paper, organized a general workshop, a conference and seven thematic work-shops.
- For the 2007 Review of the Community Strategy to reduce CO_2 emissions from passenger cars and light commercial vehicles, the Commission organized an on-line public consultation and a public hearing.
- For the 2008 Communication on the EU Strategy on Better Ship Dismantling, the Commission launched a consultation on the basis of a Green Paper and organized four stakeholder workshops.

Conclusion

To summarize, the Commission seems to favour an open and inclusive approach. This is matched by a self-regulatory approach towards third parties, rendered slightly more formal with the advent of the Joint Register. Several authors argue that this open and inclusive approach to consultation is the way to avoid asymmetric information as it ensures that all the voices that have a stake in a decision can be heard (i.e. input legitimacy). The large number of voices the Commission listens to also helps strengthen its power base in inter-institutional negotiations, thus helping to consolidate and expand its powers.

Nevertheless, the minimum standards of consultation only cover a narrow set of consultations. In addition, the Lisbon Treaty also covers particular consultation formats (notably the social dialogue), and the Aarhus Convention deals with specific environmental policy areas. Finally, there has been a pronounced lack of legalization in the area of public participation: all the documents dealing with it are non-legally biding texts (i.e. White Paper, Communications). A conscious attempt has been made to avoid the emergence of case law in this area.

The institutional opportunities for participation: the European Parliament

The European Parliament is, *par excellence*, the institution representing the people of the EU. Citizens directly elect Members of the European Parliament (MEPs) who are supposed to nurture strong connections with their constituencies back home. Increases in the Parliament's powers in the past few decades have turned it into an institution with a strong say in the decision-making process (see Chapter 8 for details). Accordingly, increased attention is being paid by lobbyist community to their relationship with the Parliament (see Chapter 9).

However, the relationship between the European Parliament and organized groups is difficult to grasp. The Parliament has historically been the only EU body that created a system of accreditation for stakeholder representatives, made up of both a register and a code of conduct (see Chapter 9). As it traditionally stood, this system was limited to the collection of a minimum amount of information from the lobbyists in exchange for a pass to enter the Parliament buildings. The holders of the access rights to the European Parliament had to abide by a set of principles listed in the Parliament's Rules of Procedure, mainly stating their interest and refraining from fraudulent acquisition and use of information. Any breach could lead to the withdrawal of the pass. It is important to note that these rules 'remain informal and are not legally enforceable by a third party judicial body' (Bouwen, 2007: 270). Since the creation of the Joint Register of interest representatives in June 2011, the conditions for the award of the pass are the ones listed in the Code of Conduct linked to the Register. Within the Parliament, there are different consultation practices across different parliamentary committees and, despite some attempts to codify and standardize relations with civil society, considerable differences remain.

Following the publication of the 2001 White Paper on governance, a struggle took place between the Parliament and the Commission over third party consultations. Faced with the willingness of the Commission to broaden existing consultation practices and to widen the range of consulted organizations, the Parliament was quick to remind the Commission that

> consultation of interested parties . . . can only ever supplement and never replace the procedures and decisions of legislative bodies which possess democratic legitimacy; only the Council and the Parliament, as co-legislators, can take responsible decisions in the context of legislative procedures.
>
> (quoted in ibid.: 275)

As a follow-up, the Commission took 'a defensive tone' (ibid.: 276) in the 2002 Communication that followed the White Paper. The Commission started by recalling the role of the Parliament and of the advisory bodies in the consultative process. It then moved on to defend its right of engaging in direct consultations with civil society, but left out the idea of partnership or accreditation. Bouwen's assessment of the conflict between the two institutions in this instance is that the Parliament's reaction can be attributed to its fear of seeing the powers of the Commission increased by its strengthened relationship with civil society (that would lead to increased informational advantages and legitimacy). Stakeholder consultations are, therefore, much more than an information-gathering exercise. They become an important lever in inter-institutional negotiations.

Several studies have looked into the question of who the European Parliament consults with. Beate Kohler-Koch (1997: 6) argues that:

> The parliamentarians act as individual members. Due to the weak leading structures within the Political Groups their independence is rather high. At the same time, they are under severe time pressure. They have to travel between Strasbourg, Brussels and their home countries. They have to keep in contact with their political base at home, attend plenary sessions and meetings with the Political Groups and Committees. The Parliamentarians are not well staffed, they have to rely on other sources of information. Furthermore, they cannot always assess which proposals of the Commission will have implications for their constituency. As a consequence, they have to be open to lobbying.

While all sorts of organized interests target MEPs, they seem to attract interest groups from issue areas such as the environment or consumer protection. There is also a strong business lobby targeting the European Parliament. Nevertheless, the Parliament is also receptive to civil society groups, and is rewarded by the constant support of NGOs for its institutional powers within the EU.

To summarize, the image of the relationship between the European Parliament and interest groups is a complex one. On the one hand, the European Parliament is the only EU institution to have put in place a system of accreditation for lobbyists. On the other hand, its interactions with groups are still far from clear. The European Parliament has been reluctant to accept the European Commission's position as the main interlocutor for stakeholders and has become increasingly receptive to interest group positions. This in turn has propelled the issue of transparency and lobbying high onto the Parliament agenda (in particular to make MEPs reveal the names of all the people they have consulted in the drafting of their reports). However, the issue has yet to be resolved and it will be interesting to see whether the promises of increased transparency in the relationship between MEPs and lobby groups will materialize.

Summary points

- There is no unitary approach to stakeholder consultations common to all the EU institutions.
- Given its role in the policy-making process and its monopoly right of legislative initiative, the Commission remains the privileged inter-locutor for third parties.
- The European Parliament is an increasingly attractive lobbying target for those representing organized interests.

Participation dynamics in practice: the Energy Using Products Directive

In order to illustrate the dynamics and challenges of participation in EU-level policy making, it is worth investigating how the different interests were involved in a particular case, namely, the preparation and implementation of the Energy Using Products Directive (EuP) (2005/32/EC). The EuP Directive is a framework directive which aims at creating a coherent legislative framework for eco-design requirements covering the totality of energy-using products, ranging from home appliances to industrial products. Being a framework directive, it does not, as such, impose any obligations on manufacturers; it rather limits itself to defining the rules and conditions for the Commission to do so at the implementation stage, either via implementing measures or via self-regulation by the industry.

Policy preparation

The Directive was adopted via co-decision in 2005. The initial proposal, submitted by the Commission in August 2003, was the result of the merger of two previous proposals, Electrical and Electronic Equipment (EEE) draft Directive and Energy Efficiency Requirement for End-use Equipment (EER) draft Directive.[1] The consultation process during the preparation of the proposal is presented by the Commission itself in the explanatory memorandum accompanying the text. Formal consultations on the EEE draft directive started in September 2000 with bilateral meetings with EU industry associations, including both large individual companies and small and medium-sized enterprises associations. At the same time, bilateral discussions also took place with environmental NGOs and with the standardization body CENELEC on the topic of a 'new approach' to standardization and its possible use within the framework of the directive. A first attempt at bringing together stakeholders across the spectrum was made in November 2000, when the Commission organized a meeting of around 70 people representing manufacturers, suppliers, waste management facilities, NGOs and member states. According to the Commission: 'The meeting focused on the principles lying behind the proposal with the aim of stimulating interest and creating a basic level of understanding among all stakeholders' (European Commission, 2003: 13). In March 2001, a new multilateral meeting took place, during which the Commission presented a new draft of the directive that received mixed comments. Discussions on the text continued via bilateral meetings in 2001 and with a technical workshop on implementation issues in February 2002. The debates in the workshop were preceded by a working document published by the Commission which attracted a set of written stakeholder comments.

As far as the draft EER directive is concerned, stakeholders were consulted on the basis of a working document and then during a workshop in April 2002. According to the European Commission:

> The minutes of the workshop were circulated together with the comments made by the stakeholders. There was a broad acceptance of the proposed approach. However, representatives from the industry asked the Commission services to avoid possible overlapping and/or contradictions with the EEE initiative.
>
> (ibid.: 14)

No further specific consultations were organized for the EER proposal; the EEE consultations were also supposed to gather views on the EER proposal itself and a possible merge of the two directives (Tanasescu, 2009).

Some time in mid-2002, the decision to merge the two proposals was taken and a first draft of the combined (EuP) Directive was presented in November 2002 at a stakeholder meeting. Environmental NGOs were critical of the text and some even suggested abandoning the idea of merging the EEE and EER proposals. In contrast, industry and consumer representatives seemed happy with the merger. Industry wanted to maximize the role of self-regulation, while consumer and environmental NGOs were glad about being able to follow up on the preparation of specific implementing measures. Following the meeting, the minutes and the comments received were circulated and a new set of written contributions was called for. While there was a seemingly broad acceptance of the main building blocks of the directive (i.e. legal basis, framework Directive and implementing measures), questions were raised concerning several aspects and in particular especially the involvement of stakeholders in the drafting of implementing measures. Following this written round of stakeholder comments, the Commission modified the draft and then focused on getting the proposal through its internal decision-making system (see Chapter 12). No further systematic contacts with stakeholders occurred between December 2002 and August 2003, when the proposal for a directive was adopted by the Commission.

This brief overview of the stakeholder involvement in the genesis of the EuP proposal reveals several things. First, stakeholders were involved from the outset and their participation continued throughout the drafting process. Multiple meetings, workshops and written consultations were organized, thus allowing the Commission to gather information and stakeholders to make their voice heard. This overview does not of course cover the substance of the discussions and points of contention, but does allow one to see that consultation can be more than a rigid, one-way exercise. Second, stakeholders are keen to secure, at the policy preparation stage, their place in the implementation of the directive. Discussions about the best policy instruments and the ability of NGOs to follow the work demonstrate this to have been the case.

Policy implementation

Following the adoption of the proposal by the Commission, it was then discussed in co-decision by the European Parliament and the Council. In the final text, as adopted in 2005, several formats for stakeholder involvement in the policy implementation stage can be identified, all gravitating towards a specially created body, the Consultation Forum. Initially, the Consultation Forum was added during co-decision due to pressure from the European Parliament. The Parliament's position was due both to lobbying and to its own desire to secure maximum involvement for stakeholders in the implementation of the directive in exchange for its own loss of control at the implementation stage. The main tasks of the Forum are

> to contribute in particular to the definition and review of the implementing measures, to monitoring the efficiency of the established market surveillance mechanisms and to the assessment of voluntary agreements and other self-regulatory measures taken in the context of the Directive. The Forum is also consulted by the Commission during the periodic modification of the working plan.
>
> (European Commission, 2011c)

It was first put together following a call for applications for organizations interested to take part and it currently comprises around 60 members (the EU member states and acceding countries, plus interest groups from across the spectrum). Its activities are well documented on the Commission website; its agendas and documentation are publicly available.

Participation requirements are embedded in the instruments chosen for the implementation of the directive. Two main instruments are foreseen: implementing measures adopted via comitology (delegated acts after Lisbon) and voluntary commitments from industry. Stakeholders have a role in both formats, mostly via the involvement of the Consultative Forum, but also via format-specific instruments.

Comitology has long been highlighted as an opaque and bureaucratic way of taking decisions (see Chapters 12 and 6). The increase of the power of the European Parliament over comitology and the attempts of the Commission to render the works of the committees more transparent (notably via the Comitology Register) have slowly paved the way for the opening up of the committees to outside interests. In this case, the Commission decided to allow interest groups to have a say on the draft implementing measures by first having them scrutinized by the Consultative Forum. What we get, therefore, is an 'open comitology' in which the formal decisions are taken in the traditional way (i.e. comitology) but that also third parties are given a say in the process (albeit without giving them a formal vote in comitology). Following the alignment of the EuP directive with the Lisbon Treaty, implementing measures are now adopted by the means of 'delegated acts' (see Chapter 12). According to Article 290 of the TFEU, the Commission no longer needs to consult a comitology committee prior to the adoption of such an act, therefore the Commission now consults the Consultation Forum only, thus putting on an equal footing the formal voices of member state experts and stakeholders. It is also worth mentioning that the Commission's work on the implementing measures is informed by studies (commissioned to third parties) and that stakeholders can comment during their elaboration. One can of course question the ability of interest groups (with a general vocation) to critically assess very technical documents, but the fact that the underlying scientific base of political decisions is also put to stakeholder scrutiny is worth mentioning.

As far as voluntary agreements are concerned, the Consultation Forum discussed the draft guidelines proposed by the Commission for the evaluation of self-regulatory initiatives. Interestingly, the guidelines provide for the involvement of civil society at large in the monitoring of such initiatives:

> The self-regulatory initiative must be publicised, including through the use of Internet and other electronic means of disseminating information. The same must apply to interim and final monitoring reports. Interested stakeholders, including NGOs and consumer organisations, must be invited to comment on a self-regulatory initiative and have access to the relevant information (e.g. annual reports, meetings of the monitoring/steering body).
>
> (ECEEE, 2011)

At the time of writing, no such agreements had been concluded within the framework of the directive, but two were actively under discussion.

Reviews of the ability of voluntary environmental agreements to deliver have been mixed, however (e.g. see Jordan *et al.*, 2005; Tanasescu, 2009). In addition, the lack of stakeholder involvement in their monitoring and the absence of the European Parliament in their scrutiny, have been pinpointed as especially problematic aspects. For now, in the framework of EuP, stakeholder participation is theoretically secured, but it remains to be seen how such agreements will be monitored in practice.

Summary points

- Participation is not a one-off exercise; some stakeholders remain active throughout the policy cycle and their role is just as important during the policy-making and comitology stages.

- This has implications both for interest groups and EU institutions: the former need to spread their resources across all the policy-making stages, while the latter need to think about the most appropriate formats and tools for consultation.
- In the choice of policy instruments, NGOs generally prefer the legal certainty of traditional, legislative instruments, while industry tends to favour voluntary agreements.

Conclusions and future challenges

Stakeholder participation at the EU level is complex and contested. Interest groups have multiple institutional interlocutors in Brussels, each with their own interests and preferred approaches to consultation. Moreover, there is no unitary approach per interlocutor, with the European Commission, for instance, having a narrow set of horizontal principles and guidelines and multiple DG-specific approaches. Stakeholder consultation requirements, albeit not based on strong horizontal legal requirements, are often embedded in individual pieces of legislation. On the one hand, this is a significant development as it gives stakeholder involvement a strong legal grounding. On the other hand, it contributes to the fragmentation of the consultation landscape, with instrument-specific formats and practices. Therefore, one of the main challenges is how to secure the involvement of third parties in the decision-making process *across* the policy cycle in a consistent way, based on legal requirements.

Given the Commission's unwillingness to make the minimum standards and practical guidelines legally binding, as well as the increasing tendency to embed such requirements into individual pieces of legislation, a possible way forward could be the harmonization of such requirements across legal acts. Increased consultation is welcome, but the question then arises of the capacity of stakeholders to follow policy developments in a meaningful way. Indeed, there have been cases of extensive consultation in the field of environmental policy that led to consultation fatigue (the case of Integrated Product Policy is discussed in Tanasescu, 2009). A major challenge is, therefore, for EU institutions to consult extensively but also meaningfully, making sure stakeholders have a chance to share their views without incurring excessive costs.

This chapter has revealed that public participation in EU policy making is mostly dominated by interest groups rather than individual citizens. While instruments for gathering popular input exist (such as the Commission's on-line consultation), in practice, the voice of individual citizens is not really heard in the consultation process (but see Chapter 3 for details of the new European citizen initiative). A major challenge in EU environmental policy is, therefore, to reflect on how concerned individuals can be better involved. But who is the best institutional interlocutor? The European Parliament is a natural candidate but, as the analysis above shows, in practice, it is the European Commission that is the centre of gravity for interest representation.

In their exploration of ways to increase public participation in EU decision making, Nanz and Dalferth suggest a constitutional framework that secures public participation by creating an interface between the citizens and decision makers. They argue:

> It would . . . specify the procedural requirements for legitimate decision making in terms of transparency, equal access to public participation, inclusion of all affected citizens and responsiveness to the input from the participatory processes. Using this framework, all actors involved, and most importantly political decision-makers, would be held accountable.
>
> (2010: 9)

This legal framework would be complemented by a methodology to use the adequate formats for gathering citizen input, mostly along the lines of the deliberative methods used at local and national levels (such as deliberative polls, consensus conferences, etc.). These suggestions point to the core of the complexity of participation, as it currently stands: given the lack of a clear and consistent legal framework enabling the participation of groups and individual citizens, the practice of favouring aggregated positions and special interests will continue. If the consultation of organized groups cannot remedy the democratic deficit, due to the organizational structure and the lack of political socialization inside the groups, then the solution can only really lie in ensuring that citizens are meaningfully involved in day-to-day decision making. How this can be achieved in practice is a matter requiring further reflection, but the deliberative experiments that have been flourishing in other contexts over the past years provide interesting examples of what is possible (see, for instance, the Danish Board of Technology, 2011). The opening up of previously closed formats, such as comitology, to interest groups is already a first step towards increasing participation. The next step would be securing the participation of citizens. If this were possible, it would do a lot to address the democratic deficit in the EU.

Summary points

- Organized interests dominate the participatory arena at the EU level.
- One of the main challenges ahead lies in opening up participation to individual citizens, through deliberative polls and consensus conferences.
- These would need to address the fragmented nature of current consultation practices, by securing strong legal groundings for consultation and striking the right balance between frequency, technical difficulty and the need to include all interested voices.

Key questions

1 What is the EU's 'democratic deficit' and how in theory could it be tackled?
2 What is actually being done by different parts of the EU to address the 'democratic deficit' and why?
3 Select a particular item of EU environmental policy, and using published documentary sources see if you can identify which actors participated in the policy process, when and on what matters.
4 What kinds of roles do interest groups play in EU policy making, and how do they interface with 'the public'?
5 What challenges have to be overcome to increase the public's participation in EU environmental policy making?

Guide to further reading

• For a more detailed discussion of civil society and its role in EU policy making, see Kohler-Koch *et al.* (2008).
• For an assessment of on-line instruments for gathering public input, see Quittkat (2011).
• A deeper analysis of the Commission's consultation practices can be found in Tanasescu (2009).

Note

1 The draft proposal on the impact on the environment of electrical and electronic equipment (the EEE draft directive) was originally prepared by DG Enterprise and the draft proposal on energy efficiency requirements for end-use equipment (the EER draft directive) was originally prepared by DG Energy and Transport.

References

Bee, C. and Bozzini, E. (eds) (2010) *Mapping the European Public Sphere: Institutions, Media and Civil Society*, Ashgate, Farnham.
Bouwen, P. (2007) 'Competing for consultation: European civil society and conflict between the European Commission and the European Parliament', *West European Politics*, vol. 30, no. 2, pp. 265–284.
Chryssochoou, D. (2010) 'Europe's contested democracy', in M. Cini and N. Pérez-Solórzano Borragán (eds) *European Union Politics*, Oxford University Press, Oxford.
Cohen, J. and Sabel, C. (1997) 'Directly-deliberative polyarchy', *European Law Journal*, vol. 3, no. 4, pp. 313–342.

Danish Board of Technology (2011) 'The consensus conference', available at: www.tekno.
dk/subpage.php3?article=468&toppic=kategori12&language=uk (accessed 10 September
2011).

ECEEE (European Council for an Energy Efficient Economy) (2011) 'Voluntary
agreements under the eco-design Directive', available at: www.eceee.org/Eco_design/
process/Voluntary_Agreements/ (accessed 10 August 2011).

Eriksen, E.O. (1999) 'The question of deliberative supranationalism in the EU', *ARENA
Working Papers*, 99/4.

European Commission (2002) *Towards a Reinforced Culture of Consultation and
Dialogue: General Principles and Minimum Standards for Consultation of Interested
Parties by the Commission* (COM (2002) 704), European Commission, Brussels.

European Commission (2003) *Proposal for a Directive of the European Parliament and of
the Council on Establishing a Framework for the Setting of Eco-design Requirements for
Energy-Using Products and Amending Council Directive 92/42/EEC* (COM (2003)
453), European Commission, Brussels.

European Commission (2011a) 'Transparency Register', available at: http://ec.europa.eu/
transparency/regexpert/faq/faq.cfm?aide=2 (accessed 10 August 2011).

European Commission (2011b) 'Aarhus Convention', available at: http://ec.europa.eu/
environment/aarhus/legislation.htm (accessed 10 October 2011).

European Commission (2011c) 'Eco-design consultation forum', available at: http://ec.
europa.eu/energy/efficiency/ecodesign/forum_en.htm (accessed 10 August 2011).

European Parliament (2009) *Post-electoral Survey First Results: Focus on the Vote by Age
Group, Public Opinion Monitoring Unit, Report EB71.3 16/12/09*, European Parliament,
Brussels.

Follesdal, A. and Hix, S. (2005) 'Why there is a democratic deficit in the EU: a response to
Majone and Moravcsik', *European Governance Papers*, no. C-05-02.

Hoskyns, C. (2000) 'Deliberative democracy and the European Union', paper presented at
the Political Studies Association, UK, 50th Annual Conference, 10–13 April, London.

Jordan, A. *et al.* (2005) 'The rise of "new" policy instruments in comparative perspective:
has governance eclipsed government?', *Political Studies*, vol. 53, pp. 477–496.

Kohler-Koch, B. (1997) 'Organized interests in the EC and the European Parliament',
European Integration on-line Papers (EIoP), vol. 1, no. 9.

Kohler-Koch, B., De Bièvre, D. and Maloney, W. (eds) (2008) 'Opening EU governance to
civil society: gains and challenges', *CONNEX Report Series* No. 5, Mannheim.

Laffan, B. (2002) 'The European Commission: promoting EU governance', in J.R. Grote
and B. Gbikpi (eds) *Participatory Governance: Practical and Societal Implications*,
Leske and Budrich, Opladen.

Magnette, P. (2003) 'European governance and civic participation: beyond elitist
citizenship?', *Political Studies*, vol. 51, pp. 1–17.

Moravcsik, A. (2002) 'In defence of the "democratic deficit": reassessing legitimacy in the
European Union', *Journal of Common Market Studies*, vol. 40, no. 4, pp. 603–634.

Nanz, P. and Dalferth, S. (2010) 'Making citizens' voices heard – and listened to: thoughts
on public participation in Europe', available at: www.participationinstitute.org/
wp-content/uploads/2010/12/Making_their_voice_heard_FINAL_2010.pdf (accessed
13 October 2011).

Neyer, J. (2006) 'The deliberative turn in integration theory', *Journal of European Public
Policy*, vol. 3, no. 5, pp. 779–791.

Quittkat, C. (2011) 'The European Commission's online consultations: a success story?',
Journal of Common Market Studies, vol. 43, no. 3, pp. 653–674.

Schmidt, V. (2010) 'Democracy and legitimacy in the European Union revisited: input, output, and "throughput"', paper prepared for delivery to the European Union Studies Association's biannual meetings, 3–6 March, Boston, MA.

Tanasescu, I. (2009) *The European Commission and Interest Groups: Towards a Deliberative Interpretation of Stakeholder Involvement in EU Policy-Making*, VUB Press, Brussels.

Warleigh, A. (2001) '"Europeanizing" civil society: NGOs as agents of political socialization', *Journal of Common Market Studies*, vol. 39, no. 4, pp. 619–639.

19 Developing more sustainably?

Marc Pallemaerts

Summary guide

This chapter provides a critical account of the development of EU policies in the field of sustainable development. These policies evolved as a result of the interaction between internal political drivers and the EU's response to a number of key UN conferences. The EU's commitment to sustainable development has been formalized in successive revisions of the treaties and is now one of its fundamental goals. However, the development and implementation of the EU's policies in this area have been disappointing. The EU's Sustainable Development Strategy has been heavily affected by its ambiguous relationship to the Lisbon Strategy for growth and jobs, which has received far higher political priority. The future of the EU's sustainable development policies is uncertain and it is possible that the EU will return once again to a narrower focus on environmental policy.

Introduction

When the European Economic Community (EEC) was established in 1957, environmental protection, let alone the broader concept of sustainable development, was not perceived as an important issue of public policy at the national and European level. However, the emergence of the environmental movement in the 1960s and 1970s forced governments to start addressing environmental issues (see Chapter 2). Though the early focus was on local and national environmental issues, the international dimensions of the ecological crisis emerged on the agenda of a range of international organizations including the United Nations (UN) and the European Commission.

The first UN Conference on the Human Environment, held in Stockholm in 1972, gave an important boost to the launch of EEC environmental policy and the elaboration of a First Environmental Action Plan (EAP) was endorsed shortly after. Contrary to what is often erroneously assumed, this conference not only addressed the environmental concerns of the industrialized world, but also the development concerns of the Third World (United Nations, 1972; Pallemaerts, 1992; 2002). It did not yet, however, use the term 'sustainable development': this term was only propelled into wide use a decade and a half later by the Brundtland Report, *Our Common Future*, published in 1987 (see Box 19.1).

Box 19.1 When is development sustainable?

The Brundtland Report was produced by the World Commission on Environment and Development and named after its Chair, Gro Harlem Brundtland. It famously defined sustainable development as 'development that meets the needs of the present without compromising the ability of future generations to meet their own needs' (WCED, 1987: 43). The report went on to explain that sustainable development contains within it two key concepts:

1   the concept of 'needs', in particular the essential needs of the world's poor, to which overriding priority should be given; and
2   the idea of limitations imposed by the state of technology and social organization on the environment's ability to meet present and future needs.

Sustainable development was thus presented as a way to progressively transform society, where the welfare of the disadvantaged in the present generation (in both the North and the South) should be prioritized, while maintaining the ecological systems upon which everyone depends. Therefore, Brundtland took a deliberately anthropocentric stance by placing sustainable development firmly within the economic and political context of international human development.

The EEC participated in the Stockholm Conference as an observer, represented by the then European Commission President, Sicco Mansholt. In his address to the conference, Mansholt highlighted the fundamentally different nature of environmental problems in the North and the South. He denounced the inequitable character of the excessive use of energy and natural resources in the rich countries of the North, which, he argued: 'involves stealing what should be preserved for those now living in wretched poverty and for future generations to whom we should bequeath a liveable world' (Mansholt, 1972: 6–7). Even after 40 years of EU environmental and sustainable development policy, this statement still stands out as being rather visionary.

This chapter provides a historical account of the development of EU policies in the field of sustainable development. These policies evolved as a result of inter-action between internal political drivers and the EU's response to international debates on environmental protection and sustainable development matters. While the concept of sustainable development policy *per se* first appeared almost two decades after the development of EU environmental policy, some nascent aspects were already evident far earlier. For example, the integration of environmental concerns into other EU policies (see Chapter 13) was promoted by the First EAP and also found its way into the Single European Act (Article 130r[2]) (see Table 19.1). The next section of this chapter, however, starts with the first explicit

Table 19.1 Key events in the EU's pursuit of sustainable development

Date	Event	Comment
1972	First United Nations Conference on the Human Environment held in Stockholm (June)	Addressed the environmental concerns of the industrialized world, and the development concerns of the South
1987	Brundtland Report published	Popularizes the term 'sustainable development'
1992	UN Rio 'Earth Summit' (June)	The main outputs include Agenda 21 and the Rio Declaration
1992	Maastricht Treaty (signed)	A reference to 'sustainable growth' is added, the existing commitment to environmental policy integration is strengthened
1997	Amsterdam Treaty (signed)	Established sustainable development as one of the overriding objectives of the EU and linked it to environmental policy integration
1997	Rio +5 UN Conference (June)	All UN members agree to draw up sustainable development strategies
1998	Cardiff European Council (June)	Start of the Cardiff Process of environmental policy integration
2000	Lisbon European Council (March)	Lisbon Strategy for 'economic and social renewal' adopted
2001	Göteborg European Council (June)	First EU Sustainable Development Strategy adopted
2002	World Summit on Sustainable Development (September)	This Rio+10 Summit emphasizes global poverty issues
2005	European Council (March)	Re-launch of the Lisbon Strategy for 'growth and jobs'
2006	Renewed Sustainable Development Strategy adopted (June)	A 'renewed' strategy was adopted by the European Council
2007	Lisbon Treaty (signed)	This completed the EU's legal formalization of sustainable development
2010	European Council (June)	A new 'Europe 2020' strategy replaced the Lisbon Strategy

references to sustainable development in discussions in the European Council, i.e. when it actually became an item on the EU political agenda. This is followed by a critical account of the genesis of the EU's first Sustainable Development Strategy (SDS). Tensions between this strategy and a parallel high-level economic and social strategy – the Lisbon Strategy – are then discussed, followed by an account of the 'renewal' of the SDS in 2006. The following section then explains how the Lisbon Treaty has completed the legal formalization of sustainable development. How the political reaction to the post-2008 economic crisis is affecting the anticipated, but now delayed, revision of the EU's SDS is subsequently explored. This chapter concludes with some reflections on the future prospects for sustainable development policy in the EU.

Summary points

- When the EEC was established, environmental protection, let alone the broader concept of sustainable development, was not perceived as an important policy issue.
- The first UN Conference on the Human Environment, held in Stockholm in 1972, not only addressed the environmental concerns of the industrialized countries in the North, but also, the development concerns of countries in the South.
- The concept of sustainable development contains environmental, social and economic dimensions; finding practical ways to balance the three is widely regarded as a key challenge.

The emergence of sustainable development in EU political and legal discourse

Sustainable development was only mentioned in European Council Conclusions for the first time in 1988. The Rhodes European Council in December 1988 stated that solutions to environmental problems must be found 'in the interests of *sustained growth* and a better quality of life' (European Council, 1988: Annex I; emphasis added). But the next paragraph introduces 'sustainable development' in conjunction with the principle of integration:

> Within the Community, it is essential to increase efforts to protect the environment directly and also to ensure that such protection becomes an integral component of other policies. *Sustainable development must be one of the overriding objectives of all Community policies.*
>
> (ibid.: Annex I; emphasis added)

Even at this early stage, this wavering of political discourse between 'sustained growth' and 'sustainable development' reveals a certain ambivalence towards the new concept.

The Dublin European Council in June 1990 was less hesitant in embracing the concept of sustainable development. Referring to the completion of the internal market in 1992 and the resulting growth in the economy, it states: 'There must be a corresponding acceleration of effort to ensure that this development is sustainable and environmentally sound' (European Council, 1990: Annex II). It calls, in particular, for better integration of environmental considerations into sectoral policies.

The Treaty of Maastricht was concluded in 1992, the very year in which the international debate on sustainable development culminated in another UN Conference on Environment and Development (UNCED) in Rio de Janeiro. The new treaty provided an opportunity to translate the European Council's newfound political commitment to sustainable development into treaty language. However, in the end, no direct reference to sustainable development as an objective of the EU was included. It merely referred to 'economic and social *progress* which is balanced and *sustainable*' (TEU, Article B; emphasis added) and '*sustainable* and non-inflationary *growth* respecting the environment' (TEU, Article 2; emphasis added).

It is highly revealing that the only part of the EC Treaty (TEC), as amended at Maastricht, which referred to sustainable *development* was that related to development cooperation (Title XVII). In Article 130u TEC, the objective of the Community's policy in this sphere is described as to 'foster the sustainable economic and social development of the developing countries'. In 1992, the EU was not yet prepared to practise what it preached, apparently considering sustainable development to be an appropriate objective for developing countries but not its own internal policies.

Though sustainable development failed to gain full legal recognition in the treaties in 1992, the concept nevertheless continued to make headway in the political discourse of the EU, most notably in the Fifth EAP, which was prominently entitled *Towards Sustainability* (European Commission, 1992). This identified sustainable development as a long-term objective for the EU's internal policies. Externally, the programme was ostensibly designed as an important contribution to the preparatory process for the UNCED, with a view to positioning the Community in the global vanguard of the advocates of sustainable development.

In retrospect, the Fifth EAP not only constituted, as the Commission later observed, 'the Community's first commitment to sustainable development' (European Commission, 1999: 5), but it was also its first strategy for sustainable development in all but name. When it approved the 'general approach and strategy' of the Fifth EAP, the Council in fact referred to it as 'a strategic approach to sustainable development' (EU Council, 1993). The fifth programme already addressed most of the key themes (environmental integration into key sectors, climate change, energy, transport, agriculture, biodiversity, cost internalization, etc.) that would later feature in the EU's first proper SDS.

Although generally decried as a failure, the 'Rio+5' summit, held in June 1997 in New York, did result in an agreement for all countries to draw up a national strategy for sustainable development by 2002 (United Nations, 1998: 14). This political commitment later proved instrumental in initiating the policy process which would lead to the adoption, in June 2001, of the EU SDS. More immediately, 'Rio+5' helped put the objective of sustainable development back on the internal political agenda of the EU in a year in which it was involved in yet another process of treaty reform.

Indeed, it was the 1997 Treaty of Amsterdam which eventually ensured the legal recognition of sustainable development as an objective under the treaties. According to the TEU, as amended by the Treaty of Amsterdam, the Union 'shall set itself the following objectives: . . . to promote economic and social progress . . . and . . . to achieve balanced and *sustainable* development' (Article 2, TEU; emphasis added). Article 2 of the TEC was again amended to set the Community the task, *inter alia*, 'to promote . . . a harmonious, balanced and *sustainable* development of economic activities' (Article 2, TEC; emphasis added). It should be noted, however, that this new objective did not replace the notion of 'sustainable and non-inflationary growth', introduced by the Treaty of Maastricht, which continues to appear in Article 2 of the TEC as a separate objective, without the proviso of 'respecting the environment'. While 'sustainable growth' was thus reduced to its purely economic dimension, environmental protection gained recognition as an objective in its own right in the new version of Article 2 TEC, which henceforth also included the distinct objective of 'a high level of protection and improvement of the quality of the environment'.

The strongest reference to sustainable development was to be found in the new Article 6 TEC (now Article 11, TFEU), which set out the obligation to integrate environmental protection requirements into the definition and implementation of other Community policies and activities, 'in particular with a view to promoting sustainable development'. While the integration principle already appeared in the former Article 130r(2) TEC as amended by the SEA (see Chapter 13), it was given far greater prominence by virtue of being directly linked to the promotion of sustainable development. According to Article 6 TEC, environmental integration is the main means of promoting sustainable development. This provision puts considerable emphasis on the environmental dimension of sustainable development, by stressing that other policies must take into account ecological constraints. But the reference to the promotion of sustainable development might also, conceivably, be interpreted as implying constraints on environmental integration resulting from the other two 'pillars' of sustainability – namely, economic and social development.

Responding to this new Article 6, in June 1998, the Cardiff European Council 'invite[d] all relevant formations of the Council to establish their own strategies for giving effect to environmental integration and sustainable development within their respective policy areas' (European Council, 1998: 13). An interesting semantic shift should be noted in passing: whereas Article 6 of the treaty and the Commission's Communication referred to integrating *environmental* requirements into Community policies *with a view to promoting sustainable development*, the European Council, for its part, referred to giving effect to environmental integration and *sustainable development* in policies, thereby implying that sustainable development is a broader objective that cannot be achieved through environmental integration alone.

The so-called Cardiff Process gradually withered away in the years following its launch, despite some well-intentioned efforts on the part of DG Environment and a few individual Council presidencies to keep it alive (see Chapter 13 for details). In the meantime, the European Council had launched a second 'strategic' process under the banner of sustainable development. In doing so, it shifted political attention away from the implementation of Article 6 TEC, looking for other ways to promote sustainable development. In 1999, the Helsinki European Council invited the Commission to present 'a proposal for a long-term strategy *dovetailing policies for economically, socially and ecologically sustainable development*'(European Council, 1999: paragraph 50; emphasis added). This proved to be the start of a new era of policy making which became known as the EU SDS.

Summary points

- Sustainable development was only mentioned in European Council Conclusions for the first time in 1988.
- Wavering political support for 'sustained growth' and/or 'sustainable development' continued for some years and reveals just how ambivalent attitudes were to the concept.
- The 1997 Treaty of Amsterdam eventually ensured the formal recognition of sustainable development as a legal objective under the treaties.

The 2001 Sustainable Development Strategy

In 2000, the first preoccupation of the EU was not with sustainable development, but with more immediate concerns, namely the long-term competitiveness of the European economy and the growing gap in economic performance between the EU and its main trading partners. This concern led to the adoption of the so-called Lisbon Agenda aimed at boosting economic growth and employment (see below). However, a number of external events drew the EU's focus back to sustainable development. First, the decision of the UN General Assembly, in December 2000, to convene a World Summit on Sustainable Development (WSSD) in Johannesburg in 2002 gave a new sense of urgency to the existing commitment made by the EU and its member states at 'Rio+5' to elaborate sustainable development strategies. Second, the intention of the Swedish Presidency to make sustainable development one of the main agenda items of the Göteborg European Council in June 2001 further increased the pressure on the Commission. In addition, the rise of the anti-globalization movement, which had culminated in the political débâcle of the World Trade Organization conference in Seattle in November 1999, also convinced EU political leaders of the need to respond to growing public concern about the negative consequences of globalization. Finally, the failure of the UN climate change conference in The Hague in December 2000, followed by the US government's rejection of the Kyoto Protocol a few months later, had laid bare the widening transatlantic rift on global environmental policy and it galvanized European politicians to demonstrate leadership in this area.

In 2001, the Commission published a Communication on a *European Union Strategy for Sustainable Development* (European Commission, 2001a), barely one month prior to the date of the Göteborg European Council. This effectively left no time for preparation of the high-level decision making through normal institutional processes and, as a result, the outcome of the decision making at Göteborg was highly ambiguous.

The Commission's proposal effectively narrowed down the scope of the SDS to environmental issues. Two social issues (i.e. poverty and ageing) identified in the preceding stakeholder consultation were excluded on the grounds that relevant objectives and measures had already been agreed as part of the Lisbon Process. In the end, the Commission formulated a number of cross-cutting policy proposals (relating to policy coherence and decision making) and a set of headline objectives and specific measures in four priority areas: climate change; transport; public health; and natural resources.

The 2009 Göteborg European Council did not adopt the Commission's proposed strategy as such; it merely agreed upon '*a* strategy for sustainable development which completes the Union's political commitment to economic and social renewal and adds a third, environmental dimension to the Lisbon strategy' (European Council, 2001a: paragraph 20; emphasis added). The actual content of this strategy is outlined only in the most general terms in a section of the Presidency Conclusions.

While the Commission's proposal had limited itself to formulating proposals with respect to the internal aspects of sustainable development, the Göteborg European Council asked the Commission 'to present a communication . . . on how the Union is contributing and should further contribute to *global* sustainable development', as part of the EU's preparations for the WSSD (European Council, 2001a: paragraph 26). The Commission therefore prepared another Communication, entitled *Towards a Global Partnership for Sustainable Development* (European Commission, 2002), which was designed to serve two quite different, though interrelated purposes: first, to complement the SDS with measures addressing the sustainable development dimension of the EU's external policies; and, second, to 'identify strategic components' of the EU's negotiating position for the WSSD (ibid.: 3).

This second Commission communication on the SDS was not formally submitted to, let alone endorsed by, the European Council. It was therefore never an integral part of the SDS, notwithstanding the Commission's claim that it should be viewed as such (ibid.: 19). In Johannesburg, the EU, by now a self-proclaimed global leader on green issues (see Chapter 16), suffered from a credibility problem, because of the gap between its sustainable development rhetoric and its unwillingness to address the negative impacts of some of its own trade and agricultural policies (Moosa, 2002). The rather disappointing outcomes of the Johannesburg conference (Pallemaerts, 2003) made it difficult to maintain public and political attention on the sustainable development agenda in the EU after 2002.

When it adopted the SDS at Göteborg, the European Council also undertook to review its implementation (European Council, 2001a: paragraph 25). Indeed, the development of the SDS was envisaged as an iterative process, whereby objectives would be periodically re-evaluated and further developed as implementation progressed and conditions evolved.

But this review process never materialized. After 2001, the Council did not undertake a more detailed examination of the proposals contained in the original Communication and the General Affairs Council did not effectively exercise the coordinating role assigned to it. As a result, the bulk of the Commission's SDS Communication was left in a limbo. The governance arrangements for the SDS did, however, include a monitoring and review procedure which was tied to the Spring European Council meetings. However, in practice, the annual monitoring and review procedure was transformed into a *pro forma* exercise, which did not result in any further development of the strategy.

Summary points

- In 1997, the EU committed itself to draw up a 'national' strategy for sustainable development by 2002.
- The Commission published a Communication on a *European Union Strategy for Sustainable Development* in 2001 which was discussed at the Göteborg European Council.
- This strategy suffered from several weaknesses which inhibited its implementation.

The Sustainable Development Strategy versus the Lisbon Agenda

The adoption, in 2000, of the Lisbon Strategy by the European Council had a significant pre-emptive impact on the terms of the subsequent policy debate: from the outset, it meant that the parallel policy process on sustainable development was doomed to be little more than a sideshow. In March 2000, the Lisbon European Council had launched a set of structural reforms designed to promote research and development, innovation and competitiveness, complete the internal market and 'modernize' the labour market and national social security systems. The resulting Lisbon Strategy was oriented towards what it termed a 'new strategic goal' for the EU, which was to have been achieved by 2010, namely, 'to become the most competitive and dynamic knowledge-based economy in the world, capable of sustainable economic growth with more and better jobs and greater social cohesion' (European Council, 2000: paragraph 5). To many policy makers, the ambiguous goal of sustainable development was just a distraction.

To achieve its objectives, the Lisbon Strategy provides for a combination of measures at EU level and the coordination of the member states' national economic policies through a new method, described as the 'open method of coordination' (OMC) (see Chapter 12). The European Council was to set general goals and guidelines combined with timetables and indicators of progress at EU level, while the member states were expected to 'translat[e] these European guidelines into national and regional policies by setting specific targets and adopting measures' (ibid.: paragraph 37). Thus, the convergence of national and regional policies was to be encouraged through a process of regular monitoring and peer review, based on indicators and benchmarks. This process was to be led by the European Council itself, which pledged to hold an annual meeting every spring to review progress (European Council, 2000: paragraph 36).

The Lisbon Strategy, as originally conceived and adopted in 2000, focused exclusively on economic and social objectives. There was only a muted reference to sustainability, in line with the wording in Article 2 TEC. As the 2001 Stockholm European Council put it prior to Göteborg:

> *Lisbon has successfully integrated economic and social matters.* The sustainable development strategy, including the environmental dimension, to be adopted at the Göteborg European Council in June will *complete and build on* the political commitment under the Lisbon strategy.
>
> (European Council, 2001b: paragraph 50; emphasis added)

The Commission never intended to address issues of economic policy in the SDS, but initially contemplated a strategy encompassing both environmental and social objectives. Eventually, however, this intention was abandoned in the Commission's Communication of May 2001, as has already been mentioned above. The Commission did not propose objectives and measures in the social field, on the grounds that these had already been fixed in the Lisbon Strategy. Its Communication did, however, refer to the social objectives and measures of the Lisbon Strategy, which it listed in an annex, as 'an integral part of the EU Strategy for Sustainable Development' (European Commission, 2001b: 10). The 2001 Göteborg European Council, for its part, took a somewhat different approach by stating that the SDS 'adds a third, environmental dimension to the Lisbon Strategy' (European Council, 2001a: paragraph 20).

So, what exactly was the relationship between these two strategies? Was the social pillar of the Lisbon Strategy part of the SDS, as the Commission proposed? Or was the SDS effectively the 'third pillar' of the Lisbon Strategy, complementing its pre-established economic and social objectives with an environmental dimension? Or was the SDS an independent strategy, separate from the Lisbon Strategy but complementary to it, as the Stockholm European Council seemed to suggest? These questions were never clearly answered by the EU institutions, which seemed to hesitate between the latter two options, shifting their view from one to the other depending on the context and circumstances.

The way in which the annual review process at the Spring meetings of the European Council was organized from 2002 to 2006 seemed to imply that Lisbon and Göteborg were to be treated together as a single, integrated strategic process. The European Council itself routinely described these meetings as 'annual meetings on the economic, social and environmental situation in the Union', whereas the Commission, at least in some documents, referred to the 'Lisbon strategy of economic, social and environmental renewal' (e.g. European Commission, 2003), implying that the SDS had effectively been subsumed under the Lisbon Strategy. The same could be inferred from European Council Presidency Conclusions (e.g. European Council, 2004: paragraph 9). However, the 'strategic goal' of the Lisbon Strategy was never reformulated to encompass all three pillars of sustainable development in a balanced manner, continuing instead to focus exclusively on economic and social aims.

Instead, the medium-term review of the SDS process was treated by the European Council as a mere formality, and was overshadowed by the 'relaunch' of the Lisbon Strategy in 2005. In its synthesis report to the 2005 Spring European Council meeting, the Commission described the Lisbon Strategy as 'an essential component of the overarching objective of sustainable development'. At the same time, the Commission argued that the Lisbon and the SDS were different but 'mutually reinforcing' strategies aimed at the same goal, but 'producing their results in different time frames' (European Commission, 2005: 6). In order not to distract attention from the 'immediate target' of growth and jobs, the review of the SDS was simply postponed.

The mid-term review and 'relaunching' of the Lisbon Strategy in 2005 could, theoretically, have provided an opportunity for a re-examination of its 'strategic goal' in order to properly integrate the objective of sustainable development into it. However, the Commission and the European Council chose to dissociate the sustainable development dimension from the core objectives of the Lisbon Strategy, and thus treated Lisbon and the SDS as separate but complementary instruments (European Commission, 2005). By prioritizing the re-launch of the Lisbon Strategy and leaving the review of the SDS (originally planned for 2004) to be dealt with later in a different process, the question of the compatibility of the Lisbon objectives with sustainable development was again conveniently avoided.

If sustainable development had truly been regarded as 'the overarching objective', this would have implied a hierarchical relationship between this objective and other policy objectives. From such a perspective, it would have been more logical to further clarify the 'overarching' economic, social and environmental objectives of the SDS in a comprehensive manner before setting short-term operational economic and social policy objectives focusing on economic growth and employment only and giving political priority to achieving these goals. The review of the Lisbon Strategy in 2005 tended to narrow its primary focus even further, rather than broadening its sustainability perspective. Despite the fact that they were both adopted by the European Council, in practice, the Lisbon and

Göteborg strategies were clearly not accorded equal political importance (EESC, 2009). The SDS was presented as an integral part of the Lisbon Strategy whenever this helped to strengthen the latter's legitimacy.

Summary points

- Adopted just prior to the launch of the EU SDS, the Lisbon Strategy for growth and jobs had a pre-emptive impact on the subsequent policy debate on sustainable development.
- The relationship between these two strategies has never been satisfactorily explained (were they supposed to be mutually reinforcing or separate?).
- The Lisbon Strategy has, in practice, received far more political backing; indeed, its relaunch in 2005 served only to narrow its focus on economic matters even further.

The 'renewal' of the EU Sustainable Development Strategy

The SDS might well have been altogether abandoned, if the EU had not suddenly been faced with a major institutional and political crisis as a result of the rejection of the Constitutional Treaty by voters in France and the Netherlands in May 2005 (see Chapter 3). In this new political context, highlighting the environmental and social dimension of the European project became an attractive strategy for European leaders in search of a narrative to re-legitimize the EU. Reviving the SDS was one of the initiatives that conveniently served this purpose.

The first step in this process was the adoption by the June 2005 European Council of a three-page *Declaration on the Guiding Principles for Sustainable Development*, setting out a series of 'key objectives' and 'policy guiding principles' for the renewed SDS (European Council, 2005: 28–30). This declaration, the result of an initiative of the Luxembourg Presidency, passed almost entirely unnoticed, and remarkably little political debate or amendments preceded its adoption.

This sudden, newfound high-level political consensus could only be explained by the special political circumstances in which EU leaders found themselves in 2005. The same European Council meeting announced that a 'renewed' SDS would 'if possible' be adopted before the end of the year (European Council, 2005: paragraph 8), but, as the Commission had barely managed to issue its proposals for the review beforehand, this next step had to be postponed until June 2006. The Commission engaged in the review exercise very reluctantly and refrained from formulating ambitious proposals. Yet under the political impetus of the Austrian Presidency, the Council took the leadership and negotiated a completely new text of a 'renewed' SDS (EU Council, 2006: Annex), which was formally adopted by the June 2006 European Council (European Council, 2006) (see Box 19.2).

Box 19.2 The 'renewed' Sustainable Development Strategy

A renewed Sustainable Development Strategy was launched in 2006. It contained the following elements.

Key objectives

- Environmental protection.
- Social equity and cohesion.
- Economic prosperity.
- Meeting international commitments.

Policy guiding principles

- Promotion and protection of fundamental rights.
- Solidarity within and between generations.
- Open and democratic society.
- Involvement of citizens.
- Involvement of businesses and social partners.
- Policy coherence and governance.
- Policy integration.
- Use best available knowledge.
- Precautionary principle.
- Make polluters pay.

Key challenges to be addressed

- Climate change and clean energy.
- Sustainable transport.
- Sustainable consumption and production.
- Conservation and management of natural resources.
- Public health.
- Social inclusion, demography and migration.
- Global poverty and sustainable development.

(Based on European Council, 2006).

The renewed version of the SDS was formulated as a single, coherent document, elaborating on the 2001 version of the strategy, and incorporating – in full – the declaration of guiding principles adopted one year earlier under the Luxembourg Presidency. Though largely a compilation of previously agreed policies, the 'renewed' SDS was clearly structured around a set of overall objectives leading on to operational targets and specific actions. The four priority areas identified in

2001 were confirmed but two more were added: social cohesion and the EU's role in promoting sustainable development at the global level.

The renewed strategy also contained more detailed arrangements for implementation, monitoring and follow-up and specified what would be expected not only of other EU institutions, but also, significantly, of member states. The Commission was to draw up a progress report on the implementation of the SDS, covering both the EU level and the member states, every other year. The SDS review process was formally disconnected from the Lisbon Strategy review process: the bi-annual reports were to be submitted to the December European Council, which was to review progress and strategic direction (European Council, 2006) while the annual Spring Council would continue to focus on the Lisbon Agenda.

The 2006 SDS devoted a separate section to clarifying the relationship between the SDS and the Lisbon Strategy. This focused on 'synergies' and 'complementarity' while carefully fudging the controversial issue of hierarchy. However, the real order of precedence between both strategies was made clear in a part of the text, concerning the SDS review process, in which it was explicitly stated that the European Council would 'provide general orientations on policies, strategies and instruments for sustainable development, *taking account of the priorities under the Lisbon Strategy for growth and jobs*' (European Council, 2006: paragraph 38; emphasis added).

Finally, the renewed SDS concluded with a call for EU institutions to 'improve internal policy coordination between different sectors'. The General Affairs Council's mandate to ensure 'horizontal coordination', initially given by the Göteborg European Council, was confirmed, but other Council configurations were also given responsibility to oversee implementation in their respective sectors (European Council, 2006: paragraph 44).

Summary points

- The political and institutional crisis that faced the EU in 2005 after the rejection of the EU Constitution pushed the SDS back up the political agenda.
- A 'renewed' SDS was subsequently adopted by the EU Council in 2006.
- The renewed strategy contained more detailed arrangements for implementation, monitoring and follow-up.

Sustainable development in the Lisbon Treaty

The process of legal formalization – or 'juridification' – of the EU's commitment to sustainable development as a policy objective was completed by the Lisbon Treaty (see Chapter 3). Since the entry into force of the Treaty of Lisbon in 2009, sustainable development features prominently in the new Article 3 TEU. This article is now the key treaty provision laying down the basic objectives of the Union. It is mentioned twice, as an objective to be pursued both *internally* and *externally*. Not only shall the EU 'work for the sustainable development of Europe' (Article 3[3], TEU), but it shall also, 'in its relations with the wider world', 'contribute to peace, security, *the sustainable development of the Earth*, solidarity and mutual respect among peoples, free and fair trade, eradication of poverty and the protection of human rights' (Article 3[5], TEU; emphasis added). These external objectives are further echoed in specific new provisions on the external action of the Union, whose aims include, *inter alia*, 'foster[ing] the *sustainable economic, social and environmental development* of developing countries, with the primary aim of eradicating poverty' (Article 21[2](d), TEU; emphasis added) and 'help[ing] develop international measures to preserve and improve the quality of the environment and the sustainable management of global natural resources, *in order to ensure sustainable development*' (Article 21[2](f), TEU; emphasis added).

Detailed provisions spelling out the objectives and principles of the EU's different internal and external policies are to be found in the TFEU (i.e. the revamped TEC) (see Chapter 3). The TFEU contains a section on principles common to all policies and activities of the EU, including the integration principle (Article 11, TFEU), as well as specific provisions governing each of the EU's sectoral policies in the economic, social and environmental fields.

Summary points

- The legal formalization of the EU's commitment to sustainable development as a policy objective was completed by the Lisbon Treaty.
- Sustainable development is now repeatedly mentioned in the treaties: as a basic objective of the EU in the new Article 3 TEU; in Article 21 TEU, concerning the external action of the Union; and in Article 11 TFEU, setting out the integration principle.
- The EU is now legally committed to pursuing sustainable development both internally and externally (i.e. in its relations with 'the wider world').

'Europe 2020' and the decline of the SDS

Soon after the adoption of the Lisbon Treaty, Europe was struck by the worst economic and financial crisis since the start of the process of European integration. One of the consequences of this post-2008 crisis was a marked decline in high-level policy attention to long-term policy objectives such as sustainable development. It had also become obvious that the Lisbon Strategy had run out of steam and should be replaced by a new political narrative. A process aiming towards 'an ambitious and revamped new strategy', and a new time horizon for its achievement – of 2020 – was put in place by the European Council (European Council, 2009: paragraph 17). A set of specific issues to be addressed by this new strategy included 'ageing populations, increasing inequalities and climate change' as well as 'the benefits offered by a greener economy' and the need to ensure 'economic, social and territorial cohesion' within the Union (European Council, 2009: paragraphs 17–18).

The debate on the future of the Lisbon Strategy happened to coincide with a scheduled review of the SDS three years after its 'renewal' in 2006. The Commission (European Commission, 2009) and the Swedish Presidency (EU Council, 2009) conducted this exercise in a rather cursory manner and the SDS was soon seen as 'a strategy in crisis' (EESC, 2009). However, the future status of the SDS in this new political landscape remained vague. According to the European Council, the SDS 'will continue to provide a long-term vision and constitute the overarching policy framework for all Union policies and strategies' (European Council, 2009: paragraph 21). But, more significantly, EU leaders failed to act on a number of specific recommendations formulated in the Presidency's review report that were designed to strengthen the governance mechanisms of the SDS. Instead, the December 2009 European Council merely stated that governance 'should be reinforced' (without specifying when and how) and suggested 'clearer links to the future EU 2020 strategy and other cross-cutting strategies' (without clarifying the nature of such links) (ibid.: paragraph 22). Thus, EU leaders rather seemed to be setting the stage for a silent demise of the SDS in the wake of the development of the new high-profile medium-term strategic framework for 2020. The Commission had also given only lukewarm support to the continuation of the SDS process in its own review report (European Commission, 2009: 15).

In the subsequent 'Europe 2020' policy-making process, the broader, overarching policy objectives of sustainable development were once again entirely marginalized and narrowed down to a subset of short- and medium-term economic policy objectives with a rather light touch of ecological modernization and social cohesion discourse. In the EU's new grand strategy, the environmental dimension of sustainability has effectively been reduced to energy and resource efficiency. What is most symptomatic of this trend is that the very words 'sustainable development' are not mentioned once in the text of the main 'Europe 2020' policy document, which was nonetheless entitled 'A strategy for smart, sustainable and inclusive growth' (European Commission, 2010). This document was submitted to the European Council in March 2010 and endorsed by EU leaders in June of that year.

It was ironic that at the very moment of its elevation to an overriding objective of the EU in the Lisbon Treaty, sustainable development was fading from high-level political discourse to be replaced once again by the reductionist notions of 'sustainable growth' and a 'green economy' – the political buzzwords in the run-up to the next big UN conference, Rio+20. It seems that the SDS has virtually been 'mainstreamed' into oblivion.

Formally, the future of the SDS remains to be decided by the European Council. The renewed SDS provided that EU leaders 'will decide *when* a comprehensive review of the EU SDS needs to be launched' no later than 2011 (EU Council, 2006: paragraph 45). But, interestingly, the Commission's 2009 review report referred to a 'future decision on *whether* to launch a comprehensive review of the EU SDS, as originally anticipated in 2006', suggesting that the continuation of the strategy was not a foregone conclusion (European Commission, 2010: 15; emphasis added). The Swedish Presidency's report recalls the 2011 deadline but it is apparent from its account of the discussions that took place in a 'Friends of the Presidency' group that there is little real consensus as to the 'possible future orientation of the SDS' and its place in the new European policy environment (European Council, 2009: 6).

Summary points

- The post-2008 economic crisis led to a marked decline in high-level policy interest in long-term policy objectives such as sustainable development.
- A new 'Europe 2020' strategy replaced the Lisbon Strategy in 2010; it reduced the environmental dimension to energy and resource efficiency. The words 'sustainable development' were not even mentioned.
- After 2010, the future of the EU SDS started to look very uncertain.

Conclusion

Over the past 40 years, the process of European integration has shown a remarkable ability to respond to new political challenges and societal concerns, such as environmental issues and, subsequently, the broader sustainable development agenda. Gradually, increasing attention has been devoted to sustainable development as an overarching objective of the EU encompassing not only an environmental, but also a social and an economic dimension. As a result, the EU's political commitment to sustainable development has become a key element of its legal objectives and very identity.

These commitments were strongly encouraged by international developments and especially the succession of UN conferences. Such a reactive position stands in contrast to the more usual leadership role that the EU takes in international environmental governance (see Chapter 16); it will be interesting to see how the EU responds after the Rio+20 conference. Internal political drivers have also been important in the development of EU sustainable development policy. A historical perspective reveals that sustainable development has not only progressed in the EU when particular Presidencies have pushed it up the agenda (for example, the Swedish Presidency in 2001), but also when the discourse of sustainable development has served to advance European integration (for example, in the wake of the rejection of the EU Constitution in 2005).

Despite the political rhetoric, however, and new treaty provisions on sustainable development in the founding treaties, the ongoing debate on the strategic orientations of EU policy and the uneasy relationship between the SDS and the Lisbon Strategy show that the member states and the EU institutions still regard 'sustainable development' as a new label for environmental policy rather than a truly overarching cross-sectoral policy paradigm integrating economic, social and environmental objectives. The most recent evolution of political discourse in the wake of the post-2008 economic and financial crisis and the launch of 'Europe 2020' reveals a tendency to narrow still further the EU leaders' vision of sustainability, i.e. towards a rather one-dimensional concept of eco-efficiency. Therefore, despite several decades of pursuing sustainable development in the EU, its place in EU governance and policy making is still far from secure.

Summary points

- European integration has shown a remarkable ability to respond to new political challenges and societal concerns, including sustainable development.
- As a result, the EU's political commitment to sustainable development has become a key element of the Union's objectives and legal identity.
- However, high-level political actors have continued to regard sustainable development as mainly an environmental add-on to existing policies, rather than an overarching policy goal.
- The future of the EU's sustainable development policy looks (highly) uncertain and tends towards a further narrowing to the one-dimensional concept of eco-efficiency.

Key questions

1 How did international events help to shape the EU's interpretation and pursuit of sustainable development?
2 How has the EU's commitment to sustainable development evolved in the EU treaties?
3 What were the main weaknesses of the EU's original SDS adopted in 2001?
4 How did the Lisbon Strategy affect the implementation and development of the SDS?
5 What are the current prospects for the SDS and why?

Guide to further reading

- For a succinct introduction to the idea of sustainable development, see Baker (2006).
- For a more detailed analysis of the debate at the Rio and Johannesburg UN summits, see Pallemaerts (1992; 2003).
- A more expansive overview of EU sustainable developmental policy can be found in Pallemaerts and Azmanova (2006), and Baker *et al.* (1997; 2007).
- Jordan *et al.* (2012a; 2012b) offer a more political perspective on the governance of sustainable development in the EU.

References

Baker, S. (2006) *Sustainable Development*, Routledge, London.

Baker, S. (2007) 'Sustainable development as symbolic commitment: declaratory politics and the seductive appeal of ecological modernisation in the European Union', *Environmental Politics*, vol. 16, no. 2, pp. 297–317.

Baker, S., Kousis, M., Richardson, D. and Young, S. (1997) *The Politics of Sustainable Development: Theory, Policy and Practice within the EU*, Routledge, London.

EESC (2009) 'Opinion of the EESC on the outlook for the sustainable development strategy', NAT/440, 5 November 2009.

EU Council (1993) 'Resolution of the Council and the Representatives of the Governments of the Member States, meeting within the Council of 1 February 1993 on a Community programme of policy and action in relation to the environment and sustainable development', *OJ* 1993, C 138/1.

EU Council (2006) 'Renewed EU Sustainable Development Strategy', EU Council Doc. 10917/06, Annex, EU Council, Brussels.

EU Council (2009) '2009 Review of the EU Sustainable Development Strategy: Presidency Report,' EU Council Doc. 16818/09, EU Council, Brussels.

European Commission (1992) *Towards Sustainability: A European Community Programme of Policy and Action in Relation to the Environment and Sustainable Development* (COM (92) 23), Vol. 2, European Commission, Brussels.

European Commission (1999) *Europe's Environment: What Directions for the Future? The Global Assessment of the European Community Programme of Policy and Action in Relation to the Environment and Sustainable Development* (COM (1999) 543), European Commission, Brussels.

European Commission (2001a) *Consultation Paper for the Preparation of a European Union Strategy for Sustainable Development* (SEC (2001) 517), European Commission, Brussels.

European Commission (2001b) *A Sustainable Europe for a Better World: A European Union Strategy for Sustainable Development* (COM (2001) 264), European Commission, Brussels.

European Commission (2002) *Towards a World Partnership for Sustainable Development* (COM (2002) 82), European Commission, Brussels.

European Commission (2003) *Report to the Spring European Council, 21 March 2003 on the Lisbon Strategy of Economic, Social and Environmental Renewal* (COM (2003) 5), European Commission, Brussels.

European Commission (2005) *Working Together for Growth and Jobs: A New Start for the Lisbon Strategy* (COM (2005) 24), European Commission, Brussels.

European Commission (2009) *Mainstreaming Sustainable Development into EU Policies: 2009 Review of the European Union Strategy for Sustainable Development*, (COM (2009) 400), European Commission, Brussels.

European Commission (2010) *Europe 2020: A Strategy for Smart Sustainable and Inclusive Growth* (COM (2010) 2020), European Commission, Brussels.

European Council (1988) 'Presidency Conclusions', Rhodes European Council, 2–3 December, European Council, Brussels.

European Council (1990) 'Presidency Conclusions', Dublin European Council, 25–26 June, European Council, Brussels.

European Council (1998) 'Presidency Conclusions', Cardiff European Council, 15–16 June, European Council, Brussels.

European Council (1999) 'Presidency Conclusions', Helsinki European Council, 10–11 December, European Council, Brussels.

European Council (2000) 'Presidency Conclusions', Lisbon European Council, 23–24 March, European Council, Brussels.

European Council (2001a) 'Presidency Conclusions', Göteborg European Council, 15–16 June, European Council, Brussels.

European Council (2001b) 'Presidency Conclusions', Stockholm European Council, 23–24 March, European Council, Brussels.

European Council (2004) 'Presidency Conclusions', Brussels European Council, 25–26 March, European Council, Brussels.

European Council (2005) 'Presidency Conclusions', Brussels European Council, 16–17 June, Annex I, European Council, Brussels.

European Council (2006) 'Presidency Conclusions', Brussels European Council, 15–16 June, European Council, Brussels.

European Council (2009) 'Presidency Conclusions', Brussels European Council, 10–11 December, European Council, Brussels.

Jordan, A.J. Benson, D. and Rayner, T. (2012a) 'The governance of sustainable development in the EU: synthesis and analysis', in R. Cörvers, P. Glasbergen and I. Niestroy (eds) *European Union, Governance and Sustainability*, Open University in the Netherlands, Heerlen.

Jordan, A.J., Benson, D. and Rayner, T. (2012b) 'The governance of sustainable development in the EU: looking to the future', in R. Cörvers, P. Glasbergen and I. Niestroy (eds) *European Union, Governance and Sustainability*, Open University in the Netherlands, Heerlen.

Mansholt, S. (1972) 'Statement of the President of the Commission of the European Communities to the United Nations Conference on the Human Environment', Stockholm, 8 June, Doc. CAB/I/36/72-E.

Moosa, V. (2002) 'Battle for the WSSD: Valli Moosa, Minister of Environment, talks to Ben Turok, 20 September 2002', *New Agenda*, 4th quarter, pp. 13–31.

Pallemaerts, M. (1992) 'International environmental law from Stockholm to Rio: back to the future?', *Review of European Community and International Environmental Law*, vol. 1, no. 3, pp. 254–266.

Pallemaerts, M. (2002) 'Stockholm Declaration', in A.S. Goudie (ed.), *Encyclopedia of Global Change: Environmental Change and Human Society*, Oxford University Press, Oxford/New York, vol. 2, pp. 392–393.

Pallemaerts, M. (2003) 'Is multilateralism the future? Sustainable development or globalisation as "A comprehensive vision of the future of humanity"', *Environment, Development and Sustainability*, vol. 5, no. 1–2, pp. 275–295.

Pallemaerts, M. and Azmanova, A. (eds) (2006) *The European Union and Sustainable Development: Internal and External Dimensions*, VUB Press, Brussels.

United Nations (1972) 'Stockholm Declaration on the Human Environment', UN Doc. A/CONF.48/14 (1972), United Nations, New York.

United Nations (1998) 'Earth Summit + 5: programme for the further implementation of Agenda 21', United Nations Department of Public Information, New York.

World Commission on Environment and Development (1987) *Our Common Future*, Oxford University Press, Oxford.

Part 5

Conclusion

20 EU environmental policy at 40

Retrospect and prospect

Andrew Jordan and Camilla Adelle

Summary guide

This chapter summarizes the main characteristics of EU environmental policy, specifically those which most clearly distinguish it from international and national policies. Second, it reflects on the challenges that the advocates of EU action have had to overcome to build an EU role in this area. It analyses how and why the focus of policy making has shifted from securing the EU's authority to act, to much more process-centred priorities such as ensuring that policy is evidence-based, fully implemented and insightfully evaluated. Finally, it looks forward and identifies some of the most salient factors that may challenge EU environmental policy makers in the coming decades.

Economic expansion is not an end in itself. Its first aim should be to enable disparities in living conditions to be reduced. It must take place with the participation of all the social partners. It should result in an improvement in the quality of life as well as in standards of living. As befits the genius of Europe, particular attention will be given to intangible values and to protecting the environment, so that progress may really be put at the service of mankind.

(Statement from the Paris Summit, 19–21 October 1972)
(Bulletin of the European Communities, October 1972, No. 10)

Introduction

With this bold statement, agreed in Paris in October 1972, the heads of the then 12 member states of the EU formally instigated a process of developing a common environmental policy. Although some minor items of environmental policy were already on the statute book in 1972, most of them had been developed by states in their own unique, national settings. While extensive and wide-ranging, these policies did not fully address the increasingly transboundary nature of many environmental problems. The Paris meeting sought to break decisively with this pattern of independent action and marked the formal beginning of EU environmental policy as we now know it. Shortly afterwards, the Commission began to draft an environmental action programme to steer the rest of the EU towards the European Council's vision of a more sustainable Europe – one that still seems remarkably visionary today.

In 1972, other supranational bodies such as the OECD and UN were also embarking on similar journeys. But since then, the EU has moved much further and faster than they have towards a pattern of deep and enduring policy coordination. Today, environmental policy is a front-ranking objective of the EU. It is also a relatively mature area of EU activity, which is 'broad in scope, extensive in detail and often stringent in effect' (Weale *et al.*, 2000: 1). In many areas of policy, which touch upon all levels of governance from the international right down to the street level, the EU is an advocate of high environmental standards.

The chapters of this book have charted the EU's journey from the late 1960s to the present day, pinpointing the key stages and the most important impacts of its environmental policy. These impacts are codified in the structures, policies and operating instruments of the EU, namely DG Environment, the Environment Committee of the European Parliament, the European Environment Agency (EEA), as well as several hundred items of law and policy. This chapter has three main purposes. First of all, it summarizes the main characteristics of EU environmental policy, especially those which most strongly distinguish it from international and national policy. Second, it reflects on the challenges that the advocates of common policies have overcome in the past 40 years to build an EU role in this area. It analyses how and why the focus of policy making has shifted from securing the EU's political and legal authority to act, to more process-centred priorities such as ensuring that policy is evidence-based, fully implemented and regularly evaluated. Third, it looks forward and identifies some of the most salient challenges that may emerge in the coming decades.

Summary points

- EU environmental policy formally commenced at a meeting of heads of state in 1972.
- Over the following 40 years, the EU has made much more progress in developing coordinated policies than other, broadly comparable environmentally-focused organizations such as the OECD and the UN.
- This chapter summarizes the main characteristics of EU environmental policy, outlines the issues that had to be overcome to develop the EU's role in this area, and looks forward to identify the challenges that may emerge in the coming decades.

The main characteristics of EU policy

As it has developed and matured, EU environmental policy has assumed certain defining characteristics. Importantly, these characteristics differentiate EU policy from policy developed at the national and international levels. Without wishing to be exhaustive or to over-state the uniqueness of the EU, we can conclude that EU policy is:

- *Relatively broad in its focus:* it ranges from much older sectoral concerns such as waste, air and water pollution, through to more modern ones that criss-cross many sectors such as genetic modification, biofuels, carbon capture and storage, and access to environmental information. With a set of mixed foci like this, EU environmental policy is little different from most national policies in the industrialized world.
- *Actively informed by (and in turn has been engineered to give effect to) a set of guiding principles:* these principles have been steadily enshrined in the founding treaties (Benson and Jordan, 2012) and further developed in the Commission's six action programmes. Some of these principles – 'the polluter shall pay' and 'damage should be rectified at source' – are fairly typical of most national environmental policies. But others are strongly associated with the EU. These include 'precaution', 'subsidiarity', 'sustainability' and 'environmental policy integration'. In a sense, these four principles in particular have come to define the EU's own philosophy of environmental protection, which in general terms seeks to reconcile economic development with a high quality of environmental protection.
- *Relatively ad hoc in nature*: EU policy is the product of 'political action but not of political design' (Weale *et al.*, 2000: 488). It is an intricate patchwork (Héritier, 2002) comprising many different elements of national policy, and is not the product of some overarching master plan drawn up in Brussels in 1972. Lacking a secure legal basis – on which more below – the Commission consciously eschewed grandiose plans. Instead, it focused on the more technical matter of how to harmonize standards in an emerging single market. Where problems spanned political borders or involved a clear trade dimension, the 'value added' of EU involvement was more obvious to all concerned and common policies were adopted relatively quickly (to this day, the EU is much more active in relation to the governance of traded products than production processes). But many issues which are now actively governed by the EU, do not exhibit a strong trade dimension: zoos, bathing and drinking water quality, waste water treatment, bird habitats and renewable energy supplies, to name just a few. The vast majority of international organizations do not involve themselves in 'local' matters such as these, but the EU does. And, crucially, there are still some areas where the EU's role is not completely accepted – and hence the Council operates on the basis of unanimous voting in the Council, just like a conventional international organization. These include land use planning, water resources and the selection of energy

supplies. To sum up, the EU is more active than an international organization in some policy areas, but less active than a state in others.

- *Mainly regulatory in nature*: despite much talk about new instruments and significant learning interactions between states, regulation remains the EU's main instrument of choice. Unlike many national governments, the EU mainly operates as a 'regulatory state' in the environmental sphere. The lack of a sound legal base in the treaties for fiscal measures has certainly played a part in retarding the use of environmental taxes, as has political resistance from vested interests. Meanwhile, voluntary agreements have been trialled but not extensively employed at EU level. Yet the EU still has many more policy instruments in its toolbox than other international organizations. It is inconceivable that any UN body would ever be granted the same power to regulate that the EU has, for example.

- *Ambitious with respect to both its scope and its effect*: one of the most fundamental weaknesses of international policy is that it struggles to rise above the lowest common denominator of state preferences. But history teaches us that EU environmental policies have consistently gone well above the lowest common denominator of state preferences (see Chapter 4). The precise reasons for this have varied from issue to issue, but include the entrepreneurial activities of EU-level actors such as the Commission and the Parliament, expansive rulings by the ECJ, and the campaign activities of NGOs and other lobby groups. EU policies have, in turn, imposed significant costs on powerful actors such as business (Chapter 10). But some of these actors – the water and waste industries to name just two – have grown massively since 1972 on the back of EU requirements, and now actively support clear and decisive EU action.

- *A powerful determinant of national policy and politics*: a very significant proportion of national policy (the figure that is often quoted is around 80 per cent) is now decided in or involves the EU. No international organization reaches as deeply into the daily affairs of sovereign states as the EU. It is impossible therefore to understand the environmental policy of any of the member states without understanding EU policy (Haigh, 2000: xi), as the two have become inextricably intertwined. Europeanization is the process through which EU-level policies affect and transform domestic policy and political systems. In the past 10 years, analysts have shown that every member state has been deeply Europeanized by the EU, even those so-called environmental leader states (Chapter 5) that strongly encouraged the EU to adopt high standards. In states with less well developed environmental policies, the combined EU effect since 1972 has been significantly greater (Jordan and Liefferink, 2004). Crucially, EU policy creates a set of minimum standards which member states of all levels of ambition and internal capacity find difficult to abandon when political and economic conditions change.

- *Flexible enough to allow differences in national approach*: while some core aspects of national policy have become much more similar through their interaction with EU policy and there are basic minimum requirements, there has been no long-term convergence towards a standard 'EU-inspired' model of policy. The 27 member states still process environmental policy in a noticeably different way, leading to different approaches and standards in some sub-areas (see above). Despite what some Eurosceptics may think, 'Brussels' is therefore not all powerful – there is a basic and fundamental 'diversity in unity' (see Chapter 4), which is facilitated by the widespread use of directives, which dictate the ends rather than the means of policy. This approach to governing means that more multi-levelled environmental governance in the EU has not (yet) produced a completely uniform approach (Weale *et al.*, 2000: 468).

- *Affected by (and in turn directly impacts) standards in other parts of the world*: the EU is an international actor in its own right (see Chapter 16), which actively seeks to export its preferred standards to the rest of the world. It does so directly via its trading and aid-giving relationships, but also indirectly via processes of international treaty making (see Chapter 16). Within Europe, the EU has used its enlargement and neighbourhood policies to influence the policies of its near neighbours. Well beyond Europe, the EU's 'soft power' influence manifested itself in the US government's opposition to plans to include the international aviation industry in the EU ETS. It was also at work in Canada's concerted efforts to influence the EU's policies on tar sands (see Chapter 9). However, the flow of influence runs both ways (Chapter 11). For example, Chapter 19 noted that the conclusions of the 1972 Paris summit – which are quoted in the epigram of this chapter – were a direct response to the world's first international environmental conference held in Stockholm in June 1972. Similarly, the EU Emissions Trading Scheme (EU ETS) would not have been formed had the EU not previously signed up to an international (Kyoto) protocol in 1997 (Chapter 17).

- *Relatively popular with EU citizens*: unlike some other policy areas in which the EU is active, the basic rationale for EU involvement is widely understood and appreciated by the public. Eurobarometer polls regularly attest to the relatively high levels of support across the EU 27 for EU-level action (Eurobarometer, 2011). Although this support is not unconditional – on which more below – it nonetheless represents a significant, and some might say quite surprising, achievement given the rather weak democratic pedigree of much EU action in this area.

Summary points

- As it developed and matured, EU environmental policy assumed a number of unique characteristics, which differentiate it from international and state policy.

- These characteristics include policy that is: broad in focus; informed by guiding principles; relatively ad hoc; mainly regulatory; ambitious in scope and effect; and relatively popular with its citizens.
- EU environmental policy is a powerful determinant of national policy and politics, but flexible enough to allow differences in national approach. It also affects, and is affected by, international standards.

Environmental policy at 40: a stocktake

The EU as a system of multi-level governance

Having summarized the main characteristics of EU environmental policy, what can be said about the wider political system in which it is embedded? As the discussion above has revealed, the EU does not fit easily into the conventional categories used by policy analysts, being neither a sovereign state nor a relatively toothless international organization. There are of course still the same basic levels of governance that existed in 1972 (i.e. international, national and sub-national), but the EU now represents a distinct level of governance in its own right. Moreover, at this new level, there are many more environmental actors – and a correspondingly greater environmental bureaucracy – than ever existed in 1972, greatly exceeding what one would normally expect to find in an international organization. It may not mean a great deal to those living outside the Brussels 'beltway', but it is politically very significant that the environment has its own designated ministerial forum – the Environment Council (see Chapter 5). The European Parliament too has its own committee dealing with environmental affairs, and the EU has an agency – the EEA – based in Copenhagen, whose main task it is to collect and disseminate environmental information. It is immensely important in politics to have strong institutional anchor points like this, when policy agendas are, as they are in the EU, in constant flux.

In addition to these entities, there are also many other actors who, while being attentive to EU-level activities, principally operate at a national level (e.g. national ministries and agencies, national parliaments, political parties and some lobby groups). Finally, the chapters of this book have identified yet another sub-set of actors that moves seamlessly between all these levels (environmental lobby groups and national civil servants, for example, as well as internationally-oriented businesses and lobbyists).

If the EU is not a state or an international organization, what kind of political system is it? The term that is used to describe such a complex and heavily populated system is 'multi-level governance'. Given this, we might say that over the course of the past 40 years, the EU has constructed a *multi-level system of environmental governance* which is utterly unique in the world. Green political theorists have long debated what form a state should adopt in order to be environmentally successful (Dobson, 2000). Many believe that conventional states are too big and ponderous to deal with local matters, but too small and puny to deal with problems that span borders. In the EU, some think they have found the best of both forms; it being the 'closest real-world approximation' that we have to a genuinely 'green state' (Eckersley, 2004: 251).

Whether or not the EU manages to fulfil these theoretical expectations is a compelling question that we shall return to in the final section. What should be clear, however, is *why* EU environmental policy continues to puzzle academics, be they experts in European integration, comparative public policy or political parties. It is the blend of dynamism, uniqueness and complexity. Given the scale and reach of its regulatory power, the EU also motivates many practitioners (from interest groups (Chapter 9) to business associations (Chapter 10)) to become involved in its policy process. Regardless of their own deeply held views about the value of greater environmental protection or, for that matter, European integration, it is clear that many different types of people have been driven to engage with and learn more about the EU. This is because regardless of whether one desires more or less of either, the EU is now a fact of life.

The process of evolution: challenges overcome

One point which emerges from the chapters in Part 1 is that environmental policy has developed 'against the odds' (Chapter 2). Its current structure and policy activities simply could not have been foreseen by those working in the late 1960s. Three aspects in particular worked against the pursuit of strong environmental measures. First of all, EU environmental policy lacked an uncontested basis in the Treaty of Rome (Chapter 2). Although that changed in the 1980s, environmental protection still does not have the same quasi-constitutional status in the treaties as that of free trade (Chapter 7). When the two have conflicted, the latter has generally been treated as the overriding priority. EU policies which restrict trade are 'always very carefully defined and bounded' (Sbragia, 2000: 223).

Second, the EU has always had, and in all probability will continue to have, a strongly economic focus (see Chapters 11 and 13). EU policy has expanded further and faster when actors have successfully exploited the synergies of environmental protection and the pursuit of economic growth – principally via the ideological framing of ecological modernization (Chapter 10).

Third, there has never really been a strong, EU-wide party political coalition pushing for stronger environmental policies (Chapter 4). The Greens have been the most consistent champions. They have enjoyed some electoral success in the Northern states and of course in the Parliament itself (Chapter 8), but even today they have very little presence in the southern and the eastern parts of the EU (at the time of this writing, there are no Green Members of the European Parliament (MEPs) in the 12 newest states – the 'EU 12'). Those seeking stronger environmental policies have therefore had to secure political support from alternative sources – from businesses, lobby groups and national environment ministries. The wider implications of this weak political anchoring are explored in the final section.

Over time, the EU has found ways to deal with, but not fully overcome, these unfavourable starting conditions. The production of new environmental legislation has grown steadily over time. In the period since the publication of the second edition of this book (2005), one dominated by economic crises and significant social tensions, the EU has still managed to adopt a number of significant new policies, for example:

- a new regime covering the 'registration, evaluation, authorization, production and restriction of chemicals' (REACH) (Regulation (EC) No. 1907/2006);
- new policies to adapt the EU to the impacts of climate change (including a Directive on Floods (2007/60/EC) and a White Paper (COM (2009) 147);
- a range of new climate and energy policies covering (among other things) vehicle emissions (Regulation (EC) No 715/2007), renewable sources of energy (2009/28/EC) and carbon capture and storage (2009/31/EC);
- a directive on energy use in buildings (2010/31/EU).

There is, though, a powerful sense in which the EU has now attained a kind of political and institutional equilibrium, which rather befits a middle-aged organization. If the first three phases of EU environmental policy making (described in Chapter 2) were dominated by the youthful urge to build institutions, colonize new policy niches and establish a legal toehold, the current phase is concerned with issues of a more procedural nature. The next section explores these issues in a little more detail.

A governance system in equilibrium?

After 40 years of development, actors in the EU have found new things to disagree about. They certainly continue to compete to expand their own powers. Think of the Commission's determination to expand the scope of the EU's international environmental powers (specifically in the area of mercury policy), for example (see Chapter 3). The Parliament's new powers in the area of international environmental policy (namely, its power to veto new international agreements) are also still being tested. Yet far weightier matters – whether or not the EU should have legal power in this area or whether the Commission should be involved at all in international diplomacy – have more or less been settled. The fact that successive treaties have had progressively less of an impact on the EU's basic legal–administrative 'constitution', and that each one has taken far longer to adopt than its predecessor (Chapter 3), tells us that the focus of conflict has shifted from high principles and legal competence, to the sorts of practical matters that have long concerned national policy makers: things like openness, transparency, policy coordination, policy implementation and *ex post* evaluation, etc.

For example, more and more effort is being devoted to reforming and fine-tuning existing policies, as opposed to developing entirely new ones. One need only inspect the EU's current legislative agenda to see the full extent to which policy making in the EU is now dominated by the need to update what is already on the statute book (see Chapter 11). EU environmental policy has, to quote Wildavsky (1996), increasingly 'become its own cause' (i.e. more or less self-perpetuating). Thinking only about the period specifically since 2005, the EU has significantly overhauled a great deal of existing legislation in areas such as waste (a new Waste Framework Directive (2006/12/EC)), air quality (the Air Quality Framework Directive (2008/50/EC)), industrial emissions (the Industrial Emissions Directive (2010/75/EU)) and of course chemicals (REACH (1907/2006)).

With greater maturity have also come more responsibilities. The EU has certainly come under pressure to change the way it processes policy. For example, the Impact Assessment system has been established to ensure that new proposals are more evidence-based and better coordinated across different policy areas. Member states have been particularly active in pushing the Commission to change its *modi operandi* (Chapter 6). This has served to make policy making more predictable and far less 'stealthy' than when environmental policy was in its infancy. The political challenges associated with improving implementation (Chapter 14) and expanding post-adoption evaluation (Chapter 15) have also become more salient, and the Commission is no longer quite so anxious to legislate at each and every opportunity. In a way, it does not have to: its basic competence to act is more or less accepted. Whether or not its interventions are deemed to be fully legitimate is another matter entirely (see below)

What most defines the current phase is that the most salient political issues are no longer about whether or not the EU should act, but are more to do with *how* it should act, with whom and for what purpose (see Chapter 11). This shift certainly does not imply an end to environmental politics in the EU, but it does usher in a different *kind* of politics. The next and final section of this chapter examines what kinds of opportunities and constraints are likely to emerge in this new political era. It starts with the most immediate and most obvious question of all (how will the EU do what it wants to do?), then moves to examine those of a more existential nature (e.g. the EU's relationship with its citizens and, ultimately, its ultimate purpose in life).

Summary points

- EU environmental policy has grown steadily since 1972 despite unfavourable starting conditions.
- Over the course of the past 40 years, the EU has managed to construct a multi-level led system of governance, encompassing its own environmental bureaucracy and a wide array of practitioners.
- Policies in this area have a relatively strong institutional anchoring at EU level, but a somewhat weaker political anchoring in national political systems.

- In the 2000s, EU environmental policy attained a sort of political and institutional equilibrium; policy making is now concerned with procedural issues (e.g. fine-tuning existing policies) rather than developing completely new policies.

Looking to the future: emergent challenges and opportunities

EU environmental policy has already addressed many significant challenges. Two in particular deserve to be mentioned. First of all, it has coped with many of the pressures arising from successive enlargements. The EU has expanded massively in the past 40 years, from just six states in 1957 to 27 in 2007, mostly, it should be noted, for 'non-environmental' reasons. Each new wave of entrants has increased the economic, social and administrative diversity of the EU. Many of the chapters in this book reveal that the effects of enlargement have worked both ways. Thus, at the same time as the new states have struggled to adapt to the rhythms and procedures of the EU, the EU has had to adapt itself to their needs and circumstances. Whether or not the EU can continue to absorb more states is a very salient question, however. The determination shown by the EU 12 states to water down the EU's climate energy package in 2008, for example, may be a portent of things to come (Chapter 5). The scale of the EU's implementation problem also raises doubts about whether it has genuinely 'coped' with the problem of enlargement, or just displaced it from the policy making to the policy implementation phase.

Second, and related to this, it has managed to find new ways to manufacture agreement among a growing cast list of actors, which originally just included states and the EU institutions, but now includes myriad lobby groups that operate in and around Brussels as well as other civil society groups such as local authorities. In order to avoid total policy gridlock, the Council has, for example, adopted complex voting arrangements and extended them to more and more sub-areas (see Chapter 5). Meanwhile the Commission has developed a variety of approaches to achieve agreement, such as differentiated compliance deadlines and complex burden-sharing agreements. It also employs a variety of consultative mechanisms, road mapping and other soft strategy development exercises to ensure its proposals secure political buy-in. And finally the Parliament has successfully developed and employed informal means to achieve early agreement with other actors (see Chapter 8). The EU's success at coping with more actors can be measured, first and foremost, in terms of new policies adopted (see above). It is not the old Monnet Method of integration by stealth, but nor is it the standard form of intergovernmental bargaining that one finds in international organizations.

What challenges are likely to dominate environmental policy making in the future? The first and most immediate relates to the *instruments of policy*. By now, the EU's role in determining the overall goals of environmental policy should be obvious to you, the reader. In contrast, its ability to determine its choice of implementing instruments is still restricted, not least by states. Despite much talk about the merits of 'new' instruments such as eco-taxes or emissions trading, EU policy is still mainly pursued via regulatory means. There have of course been circumstances in which the EU has successfully adopted non-regulatory instruments (the EU ETS being an obvious case in point), but they have tended to appear very infrequently and have not always out-performed regulation (the voluntary agreement on car emissions, for example, see Chapter 17). The EU has also adopted new instruments to change policy-making processes (Impact Assessment, for example) and/or govern in situations where its competence is contested (e.g. the use of the Open Method of Coordination in the area of climate change adaptation).

The EU's capacity to adapt itself to new circumstances by adapting its *modus operandi* (through processes such as comitology) should also not be underestimated. Yet, it is debatable whether the EU will be able to achieve all its ambitions (namely coordinated, inclusive, cost-effective, subsidiarity-friendly policy that protects the environment) with such a relatively restricted toolbox. Much more 'wicked' policy challenges such as unsustainable development or resource inefficiency typically involve very many actors operating in different sectors and across many different levels of governance. These require a more multifaceted, 'bigger picture' perspective that goes well beyond the actor coalitions that have usually been targeted by EU policy interventions. Take sustainable consumption and production for example. Large retailers such as supermarkets are uniquely placed to drive improvements in resource efficiency by cutting down on unnecessary packaging and withdrawing multi-buy discounts which encourage consumers to over-consume. But they have not really been exposed to EU policy action before. The Commission's 2008 action plan on sustainable consumption and production sought to establish a constructive relationship with them. The Commission noted that some retailers do make a difference by voluntarily adopting environmentally friendly business practices, but that there are still numerous obstacles to sustainability in this area (ENDS Europe, 2011). It established a forum to share best practices, but only a minority of retailers have joined and/or been actively involved. Regulation is probably going to have to play a part in more effective policy responses, but it has limitations (which are well known and difficult to overcome) and, as yet, there is no clear agreement on which it should focus on. Other instruments could be adopted, such as voluntary agreements and eco-labelling, but finding the right combination of different tools and instruments is proving to be a real challenge.

Fritz Scharpf would presumably view this as an example of a much wider set of limitations which bear upon the EU's problem-solving capacity. That is to say, as the EU's influence spreads and deepens, the best available EU-level solutions (such as green taxes or voluntary agreements) seem to be progressively denied by the diversity of actor preferences, at the same time as the kinds of national policy approaches which used to be available to states which wanted to act (border taxes, for example, or export subsidies), are increasingly denied by the rules and procedures of European integration. In other words, in practice, the EU may not represent the 'best of both worlds' as green political theorists thought. The big question is whether the EU can ensure that its problem-solving capacities keep pace with its evolving policy ambitions. If they do not, policy failures will stack up, the environment will fail to be protected, and this will further undermine the EU's already battered political image.

The second challenge is therefore to ensure that policies continue to *drive environmental progress*. In the first 40 years, the EU devoted more of its energies to creating a suite of policies, and issues of policy implementation and *ex post* evaluation took a back seat. That is changing as more and more actors question the achievements of EU integration. In the period since 1957, GDP in the EU has grown steadily, and this has facilitated massive developments in transport, health and educational infrastructure (Eurostat, 2009: 8–9), particularly in the states that joined after 1972. But these socio-economic gains have come with significant social and environmental costs attached. In the transport sector, the benefit of increased mobility in the EU has been tempered by growing air pollution, traffic accidents and noise. Negative effects are also visible in the agricultural sector, where the EU-supported intensification of production has come at the price of *inter alia* biodiversity decline and water pollution. The EU's target, set in 2000, to halt biodiversity loss by 2010, was missed by a long way. Despite common fisheries policy, fish stocks in the EU have been depleted well below sustainable levels of exploitation (Eurostat, 2009: 10). And finally, although recycling rates have increased across the EU, per capita waste generation remains relatively high despite a raft of policy interventions. In summary, we can conclude that the most acute forms of pollution are now well on the way to being addressed in the EU (EEA, 1995). However, 'only in a few cases has there been significant decoupling of economic growth from the associated environmental pressures' (EEA, 2003: 7). 'More efforts are necessary ... to get [the EU] on the pathway to sustainable development' (Eurostat, 2009: 27), or what the Paris Summit originally termed 'the quality of life'.

The third challenge is how to secure these additional efforts in an *era of acute economic austerity*. In the past, EU environmental policy has been relatively immune to the vicissitudes of the economic cycle. But in the 2000s, European leaders started to invest more of their energy in improving the economic competiveness of the EU and boosting its fairly anaemic levels of growth in a concerted effort to keep pace with the rising economic powers of Brazil, India and, most of all, China. Great hopes were invested in the Lisbon Process of economic renewal (2000–2010), which was driven by a much more pro-economic Commission, headed by José Manuel Barroso. Those promoting the Lisbon Agenda argued that without economic re-structuring, austerity in the EU will become 'the new normal' rather just a passing phase. As the debt crisis deepened in late 2011, member states eventually agreed to Germany's demands for the Eurozone to move towards a much deeper form of economic union, in which EU institutions would be vested with stronger powers to oversee state taxation and spending.

These economic challenges have undoubtedly affected environmental policy. For example, in the 2000s, the Commission started to retreat from some of its ambitious promises to pursue environmental policy integration and deliver more sustainable forms of development. After the Copenhagen Climate Summit in 2009, it lost enthusiasm for more ambitious emission reductions (namely a 30 per cent reduction target by 2020) (Jordan *et al.*, 2010), fearing that they could lead to large industries relocating to states with lower standards ('carbon leakage'). New money for new environmental purposes such as CCS could well become harder to find. And urgent bailouts to keep countries like Greece afloat could, if environmental groups' fears are fully realized, support dirty sources of energy and unsustainable patterns of transport (WWF, 2012). Meanwhile, for the very first time, the Commission started to openly question the need for another environmental action programme (the seventh) (COM (2011) 531 final). Environmental pressure groups like action programmes because they are comprehensive and, while not legally binding on the EU, are 'politically binding'. But critics feel they have served their purpose and are unnecessary. Meanwhile, the Commission may find itself under even greater political pressure to engage in 'Better Regulation' to drive environmental progress without increasing the regulatory burden on business. As noted above, working out what this means in a specific area like unsustainable consumption can be very difficult indeed. Finally, a less obvious but potentially very significant threat could arise in the medium term if moves towards a two-speed Europe centred on the Eurozone (see the Preface for details) start to disrupt the single market. EU environmental policy first emerged in the slipstream of the internal market programme. If a two-speed Europe eventually begins to produce a two-speed single market, environmentalists may have to confront the prospect of a two-speed environmental policy.

Then, again, the politics of continuing austerity will doubtless also generate opportunities for those willing and able to show that their activities have an economic value. It was notable that DG Environment (2011) produced a consultancy report in 2011 that sought to calculate the social costs of *not* implementing current EU environmental rules. The total – some €50 billion per annum – was dominated by health-related impacts due to excess air pollution exposure. Areas of environmental policy such as air pollution, waste and water pollution, as well as climate change and energy security, may well find it easier to adjust to the rapidly emerging political discourse of 'Green Growth' (Bina and La Camera, 2011; Bowen and Fankhauser, 2011), or what some environmentalists fear might be plain old economic growth with some environmental trimmings. But others, such as biodiversity, where the connections to human health are not as direct, may find it harder to make a political case for continuing protection, hence the emerging debate about ecosystem services. Paradoxically, deeper European integration may also open up new opportunities to develop common fiscal policies, principally eco-taxation, which in the past has always failed to overcome the need for unanimity requirement in the Council. Such taxes could be levied on internal sales to generate new sources of revenue, or they could be levied on imports from jurisdictions with lower environmental standards. There may also be opportunities to coordinate value added taxes in ways that encourage the sale of energy-saving devices such as insulation and less energy-using products.

Fourth, there is the ongoing challenge of ensuring that *the EU remains democratically legitimate*. No system of governance – let alone a young, multi-levelled one with relatively insecure democratic foundations – can possibly hope to endure unless it is seen as legitimate by its citizens. As described in Chapters 2 and 4, the EU began life as 'an elitist project', supported by an implicit and often quite passive acceptance among the public that deeper European integration was an inherently 'good thing'. Environmental policy has benefited greatly from the Monnet Method of integrating 'by stealth'. In many ways, 'it can be regarded as a textbook illustration of the Monnet method at work' (Weale *et al.*, 2000: 488).

There is plenty of evidence to suggest that Europeans have become disillusioned with this way of working. The turn-out at European parliamentary elections has been in decline for a long time, anti-EU political parties are on the rise and the ability to secure support for further treaties via popular referenda can no longer be relied upon. The Euroscepticism which first flared in the early 1990s has proved to be far deeper and longer-lasting than anyone initially thought. The passive consensus in favour of 'more Europe' seems to have waned, replaced by a 'constraining dissensus' (Hooghe and Marks, 2008). Indeed, so serious is this constraint perceived to be, that politicians cannot even be sure that they will secure popular approval for the economic reforms they need to put in place to stabilize the Eurozone, and thus ensure the continuing existence of the EU.

So what is to be done about it? One option might be to concentrate on producing more of the policy outputs that citizens do care about. This is what political theorists term 'output legitimacy' and it is what EU environmental policy makers have arguably spent the past 40 years working on. If what matters is what is valued by the public, then their efforts have achieved some quiet successes. As noted above, Eurobarometer polls regularly cite the environment as one of the most popular of all the EU's policies. However, it is an open question whether green arguments can be used to secure something far, far greater: a more secure relationship with the EU's citizens. In the case of very salient issues such as climate change, for example, 'better opportunities for output legitimacy are hard to imagine' (Warleigh, 2010: 308). The problem is that not all areas of environmental policy are as high profile as climate change. In fact, a lot of environmental policy is concerned with very dry technical details, even though their repercussion may have popular appeal. Moreover, the EU lacks a deep and dynamic public sphere at EU level; at any one point in time, some issues are high up the political agenda in some states but low down in others (Chapter 11). Working out what is politically popular for the EU as a whole could prove to be very tricky indeed. And what is politically popular today may not necessarily be good for the environment or satisfy the interests of those who are not yet born (inter-generational equity – a fundamental axiom of sustainable development).

Finally, it should be remembered that the interests of citizens are not something which the EU has been used to engaging with directly before. The EU institutions are relatively isolated from everyday political discourse at the national level; much of their time is devoted to dealing with special interest groups that mobilize at EU level to secure selective benefits (Hix, 2005: 407). It is they that shape and dominate political agendas at EU level, not citizens, national parliaments or, for that matter, national political leaders (see Chapter 11).

In practice, legitimacy has at least two faces or sides (Scharpf, 1999). Another way to enhance the legitimacy of the EU might therefore be to focus more on the input side, for example, by involving citizens directly in the EU's decision-making process. Hix (2008) is of the opinion that the EU can and should do more to legitimize itself by undertaking modest institutional reforms which help to politicize salient issues that do affect the lives of citizens (Warleigh, 2010: 297), and thus draw more and more of them into its orbit. In theory, this idea sounds very appealing. The Treaty of Lisbon went some way towards addressing the input side by further empowering the European Parliament in EU-level decision making and allowing citizens to directly petition the Commission to legislate in new areas (the European Citizen Initiative, see Chapter 3). Steps have also been taken to make EU activities more open and transparent. In practice, though, Chapter 18 made it quite clear that the EU is struggling to act coherently on this matter; it is not even clear which EU institution should take the lead. Theorists such as Habermas (2009) and Hooghe and Marks (2008) warn that this is a secondary matter because the EU cannot be expected to legitimize itself; other actors will have to play a part too (Schmidt, 2006). Yet, states have become extremely adept at playing blame games with the EU: they quickly claim the credit for EU policies that do deliver, but blame them when things do not go as well. Environmental lobby groups do not engage in nearly so many of these credit claiming and blame avoidance games, but nor do they always fully explain the role or importance of the EU to their supporters. Consequently when the EU does things well, many of its citizens do not get to know about it.

At present, EU environmental policy appears to be scoring relatively well in terms of output legitimacy, but is evidently finding it difficult to shake off the habits of the past. Its automatic reflex is, when challenged, to act stealthily to achieve the consensus it perceives is needed to adopt new policies. In the Environment Council, for example, a very high percentage of policy dossiers (85–90 per cent) are agreed without any open discussion among ministers (Chapter 5). Even when there is open discussion, it is often completely hidden from the public because all its meetings are held behind closed doors. When votes are taken they involve such complicated rules that a calculator is needed to work out who has won (Chapter 5). Even the Parliament – the EU's only directly elected institution – is not averse to behaving stealthily when it feels it has to: Chapter 8 reports on how it has made greater use of informal trialogues with the Commission and the Council to avoid policy dossiers becoming stuck in long and drawn-out conciliation negotiations. The role of the plenary is then restricted to rubber stamping what has been agreed behind closed doors, rather than opening up the issue to public debate and contestation.

The fifth and final challenge is probably the most existential of all: to decide what is to be the *main purpose and hence direction of European integration*. From its inception in the 1950s, the EU has been an elite project, introduced without a political vote, its popularity sustained by economic growth. As growth and competitiveness have dipped, more and more people have started to question its purpose, in much the same way as heads of state did in Paris 40 years ago. It is clear that the Commission's Lisbon Strategy to boost growth, jobs and competition, and its successor, Europe 2020, have failed to excite public interest. The environmental sector has sought to promote an alternative vision – sustainable development – around which the EU could unite (see above). Although this has successfully functioned as a long-term vision for the EU, it has not yet won sufficient political backing to really determine its day-to-day operations. More often than not, the 'development' part of sustainable development trumps the 'sustainability' part (Warleigh, 2010: 301). Chapter 19 investigated how far the EU has fulfilled its commitment to implement the principle of sustainable development, both internally and in its interactions with other parts of the world. It found that it has been 'mainstreamed into oblivion' and now risks becoming little more than a new label for environmental policy.

To conclude, after 40 years of more or less continuous development, environmental policy is now a front-ranking objective of the EU, enshrined in the founding treaties, supported by a powerful network of environmental committees, ministries and agencies, as well as pressure groups and political parties. Given the rather unfavourable starting conditions that pertained in 1972, this is no mean achievement. Policy making has achieved a sort of equilibrium in the EU, but policy development activities continue and the whole question of environmental protection looks set to remain a live political issue for the foreseeable future. So it is an equilibrium, but of a dynamic kind. This is because the long-standing tension between the pursuit of economic growth and environmental protection will keep resurfacing at EU level, not least because environmental policy has a well-developed and deeply entrenched set of supporters that will fight their corner when threatened. In the EU, the past has always been a poor guide to the future, so one can only guess at what kinds of political and policy issue will emerge in the next 40 years. One thing is clear though: what eventually emerges from the EU's efforts to develop policy in this area will have wide-ranging and long-lasting impacts on those who live within and well outside its borders.

Summary points

- One of the challenges facing environmental policy lies in the best choice of implementing instruments: the EU's heavy reliance on regulation may limit its capacity to solve 'wicked' policy problems such as unsustainable consumption which demand a mixed approach.
- Another challenge is how best to adjust to the rapidly unfolding politics of austerity, which may generate negative consequences but also some new opportunities for environmental policy makers.

- While some very salient areas of environmental policy could provide the EU with much needed 'output legitimacy', other areas are less high profile and may be less able to address its democratic deficit.
- Environmental policy has attained a dynamic equilibrium, but we are unlikely to witness an end to environmental politics, given the long-standing and deep-rooted tensions between the pursuit of economic growth and environmental protection.

Key questions

1   What are the main characteristics of EU environmental policy?
2   In what ways is EU environmental policy similar to conventional state policies? In what ways is it different, and why?
3   How does the current phase of environmental policy differ from earlier phases?
4   Which challenges – both big and small – are likely to emerge in the next 40 years or so and how likely are they to be overcome by environmental policy makers?
5   Which do you think is likely to be the most difficult challenge of all and why?

References

Benson, D. and Jordan, A.J. (2012) 'Environmental policy', in M. Cini and N. Pérez-Solórzano Borragán (eds) *European Union Politics*, 4th edition, Oxford University Press, Oxford.

Bina, O. and La Camera, F. (2011) 'Promise and shortcomings of a green turn in recent policy responses?', *Ecological Economics*, vol. 70, no. 1, pp. 2308–2316.

Bowen, A. and Fankhauser, S. (2011) 'The green growth narrative: paradigm shift or just spin?', *Global Environmental Change*, vol. 21, pp. 1157–1159.

DG Environment (2011) *The Costs of Not Implementing the Environmental Acquis*, Final report ENV.G.1/FRA/2006/0073, COWI-ECORYS and Cambridge Econometrics, DG Environment, Brussels.

Dobson, A. (2000) *Green Political Thought*, 3rd edition, Routledge, London.

Eckersley, R. (2004) *The Green State*, MIT Press, Cambridge, MA.

EEA (European Environment Agency) (1995) *Europe's Environment: The Dobris Assessment*, EEA, Copenhagen.

EEA (European Environment Agency) (2003) *Europe's Environment: The Third Assessment*, EEA: Copenhagen.

ENDS Europe (2011) 'Finding a common approach on SCP', *ENDS Europe*, 23 May.

Eurobarometer (2011) *Special Eurobarometer 365: Attitudes of European Citizens Towards the Environment: Provisional Summary*, June, Eurobarometer, Brussels.

Eurostat (2009) *Sustainable Development in the European Union*, European Commission, Brussels.

Habermas, J. (2009) *The EU: The Faltering Project*, Polity, Cambridge.

Haigh, N. (2000) *Manual of Environmental Policy: The EU and Britain*, London, Elsevier.

Héritier, A. (2002) 'The accommodation of diversity in European policy making and its outcomes', in A. Jordan (ed.) *Environmental Policy in the EU*, Earthscan, London.

Hix, S. (2005) *The Political System of the EU*, Basingstoke, Palgrave.

Hix, S. (2008) *What's Wrong with the European Union and How to Fix It*, Polity Press, Cambridge.

Hooghe, L. and Marks, G. (2008) 'A postfunctionalist theory of European integration', *British Journal of Political Science*, vol. 39, pp. 1–23.

Jordan, A., Huitema, D., van Asselt, H., Rayner, T. and Berkhout, F. (eds) (2010) *Climate Change Policy in the European Union*, Cambridge University Press, Cambridge.

Jordan, A.J. and Liefferink, D. (eds) (2004) *Environmental Policy in Europe*, Routledge, London.

Sbragia, A. (2000). 'The European Union as coxswain', in J. Pierre (ed.) *Debating Governance*, Oxford, Oxford University Press, pp. 219–240.

Scharpf, F. (1999) *Governing in Europe*, Oxford University Press, Oxford.

Schmidt, V. (2006) *Democracy in Europe*, Oxford University Press, Oxford.

Warleigh, A. (2010) 'Greening the European Union for legitimacy? A cautionary reading of Europe 2020', *Innovation: The European Journal of Social Science Research*, vol. 23, no. 4, pp. 297–311.

Weale, A., Pridham, G., Cini, M., Konstadakopulos, D. Porter, M. and Flynn, B. (2000) *Environmental Governance in the EU*, Oxford University Press, Oxford.

Wildavsky, A. (1996) *Speaking Truth to Power*, Transaction Publishing, New Brunswick, NJ.

WWF (Worldwide Fund for Nature) (2012) 'Environment jeopardised by economic bail-out plans, warns WWF', WWF press release, 10 January, available at: http://mediterranean.panda.org/?203071/Environment-jeopardised-by-economic-bail-out-plans-warns-WWF (accessed 12 January 2012).

Index

Printed in the USA/Agawam, MA
January 3, 2013

571615.046